3-7-01

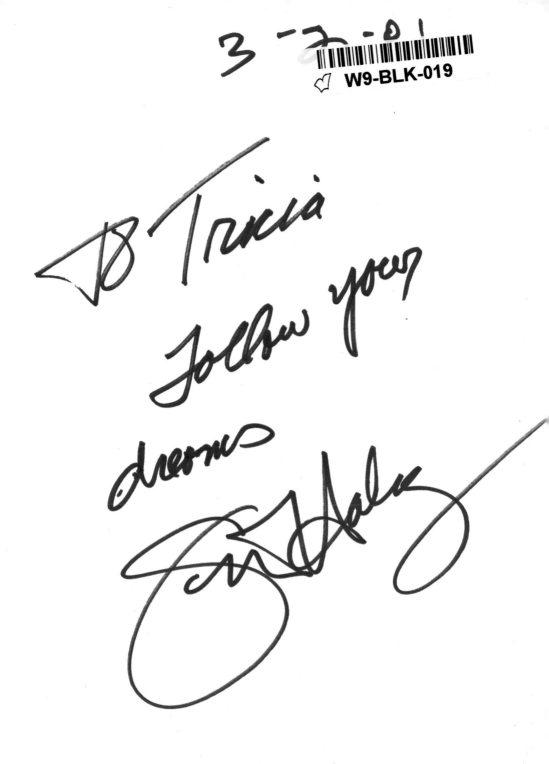

To Tricia

Follow your

dreams

HOW TO MAKE IT IN THE MUSIC BUSINESS

Jim Halsey

with John Wooley

HAWK Publishing

HALSEY BOOKS

Published in the United States by HAWK Publishing Group and Halsey Books.

HAWK and colophon are trademarks belonging to the HAWK Publishing Group.

Printed in the United States of America.

Library of Congress Cataloging in Publication Data
Halsey, Jim, 1930—
How to Make It in the Music Business/Jim Halsey—HAWK Publishing ed.
p. cm.
ISBN 1-930709-20-X (Soft cover)
ISBN 0-9673131-5-5 (Hard cover)
1.Music
2. Reference
I. Title
[PS3563.I42145R4 1999]
813'.54 80-52413
CIP

HAWK Publishing web address: www.hawkpub.com
Halsey Books web address: www.halseybooks.com

H987654321

Graphics Credit:
1. Book design by Carl Brune
2. Cover and back in part by Bob McConnell
3. Additional graphics by Ryan Gardenhire

Dedication

To my wife of 20 plus wonderful years, Minisa Crumbo—a teacher, a spiritual guide, a mentor, an inspiration, a cheer leader, a healer, a great artist, and my best friend.

To my family, my loved ones—

To my son Sherman, a creative, imaginative thinker and visionary with great eyes, ears, ideas, and a load of talent.

To my daughter Gina, the healer, physician, and conscience for the world.

To my daughter Cris, the skier, the positive thinker, and mom.

To my son Woody, the airline pilot, musician, and family man.

To my mentors who have consulted, inspired, and taught:

> *Elon Robley*
>
> *Simon Kalis*
>
> *Leo Zabelin*
>
> *Norman Weiser*
>
> *Glenn Hybarger*
>
> *Hank Thompson*
>
> *Mack Sanders*
>
> *Harry "Hap" Peebles*
>
> *E.O. Stacy*
>
> *Woody Herman*
>
> *Lee Zhito*
>
> *Larry Jones*
>
> *Dr. Jerry Walker*
>
> *Joseph Rael*
>
> *Marcellus Williams*
>
> *Wayne Creasy*

To my Cherokee and English Ancestors.

To Dick Howard and John Hitt.

To the many people who were a part of The Jim Halsey Company . . . and to our customers, artists, and clients. It was always our goal to "make them satisfied."

Table of Contents

PART THREE
Secrets of The Jim Halsey Company

PART FOUR
Now It's Your Turn

APPENDICES

Preface

In 1990, my company, The Jim Halsey Company, Inc., was the No. 1 country music agency in the world, representing 41 top country and pop acts. We had agents all over the globe. Every day, spotlights shone on our stars, as they entertained audiences from Birmingham to Bulgaria. After more than 40 years in the entertainment business, The Jim Halsey Company was at the very peak of its power and influence.

And that's when I decided to sell it.

A few weeks earlier, I'd begun holding music business classes in the agency's conference room in Nashville. Young people trying to get into the business would come in, and my agents and I, along with other industry professionals, would take turns teaching them what we knew.

We held classes twice weekly, and the whole session only lasted a month. But at the end of that month, those kids had found out that, most of the time, they were wasting their time doing what they'd been doing, and they'd rearranged their whole lives to reflect what they'd learned. They'd found out what to do and whom to call on, and they'd found out what was simply a waste of time.

As I saw the impact these classes were having, I began to realize that the time was right for me to sell The Jim Halsey Company. People, of course, thought I was nuts. "Why are you doing this?" they asked me. "Are you going to retire?"

I told them no. "I'm going to be doing something else," I said. "What I want to do now is tell young people about this business—share my experiences, my formulas, my methods, so that maybe they can go out and become successful as well. "

I started writing this book in the last year that I had The Jim Halsey Company—which I ultimately sold to the giant William Morris Agency, making *it* the world's largest country music agency—and I've continued adding sections based on my experiences and observations ever since. After holding dozens of music business seminars all over the country in the first part of the '90s, I created the music and entertainment business program at Oklahoma City University, which became the first college in the world to offer a bachelor's degree in the business of entertainment, and I created, with Lee Zhito, the *Billboard* Song Contest, held annually under the auspices of the famed music-industry magazine, which offers aspiring songwriters a chance for their work to be heard by professionals. And I also continue to work with country music stars, managing both the veteran supergroup The Oak Ridge Boys, who have been with me for more than 25 years, working with my son Sherman with his up-and-coming group, The Clark Family Experience, who I think are destined for big things. These two acts join such stellar names as Roy Clark, Waylon Jennings, The Judds, Hank Thompson, Merle Haggard, Reba McEntire, Wanda Jackson, Freddy Fender, Roy Orbison, Tammy Wynette, Rick Nelson, Clint Black, Dwight Yoakam, Minnie Pearl, the Kentucky Head-Hunters, Lee Greenwood, Ronnie Milsap and Mel Tillis, all of whom were guided—and in many cases discovered—by The Jim Halsey Company.

You've probably seen performances by several of these entertainers, either live or on television. And you've probably been impressed by their power of performance.

Have you ever stopped to consider that, onstage or off, we *all* have a performance to give? That *you* have your own unique **Power of Performance**? And that if you discover the ways to give the best performance possible, discover the ways of tapping the power within you, you can be a success in whatever you choose to pursue?

As you go through this book, you'll see a lot about the **Power of Performance.** In many ways, it's the whole key to what I'm writing about. *Jim Halsey's How to Make It in the Music Business* also gives you the behind-the-scenes facts about how the music industry works, covering all the varied components of the business and stripping away their mystery, showing you how they all work together— and guiding you in choosing the part you want to play.

This is a book about success, and how to achieve it. And this is a book about life, and how to live it. The plans, methods, and formulas you'll find in these pages all come from a life of trying and testing, of finding what works and what doesn't, of succeeding and failing, of embracing the hard-won positives and tossing away the misguided negatives. Here are the principles—and the secrets—that have guided me in my more than 50 years as an artist manager, agent, and impresario. They continue to work for me in my life. They will work for you in yours.

— Jim Halsey
Tulsa, Oklahoma
June 2000

An Introduction

by

Joseph S. Bonsall

Godfather – *def.* First appeared in the 12th century as, "One having a relation to someone or something analogous to that of a male sponsor to his godchild: and as one that founds, supports or inspires that child."

– from Compton's Dictionary

I am a firm believer in what I call the crossroads theory. In essence, I believe that there are many times in your life that you consciously or even unconsciously arrive at a meaningful crossroad where an event takes place that tends to mold, shape, and influence the rest of your life on earth. Sometimes it is merely a simple decision that we make in our hearts and minds to take the right road instead of the left. Or to choose the right thing to do instead of the wrong. Many of these decisions that we make are simple and very self-directed. Most, however, are divine interventions where God in His infinite wisdom has a definite plan in mind. But you must possess an open mind and an open heart to be aware of what it is that God is trying to tell you. So many missed opportunities exist because we just weren't listening.

I believe in my heart that at the most meaningful crossroads, God places a human being right there on the fork of the road at the appropriate time. A special human being whose influence changes our hearts and our very direction forever.

The Oak Ridge Boys, as a group and to a man, found ourselves at one such crossroad in July of 1975. We were a struggling and starving bunch of boys who were not really sure of our talent or worth, and we were just about to give it all up and go home. All of a sudden, there he was, standing right smack in the middle of the road, smiling and pointing out the right way to go. That man was Jim Halsey and for 25 years now we have respectfully referred to him as our Godfather

On this night in July of 1975 Jim Halsey heard us sing for the first time. He told us that he believed that we were the most entertaining and energetic act that he had ever seen and that we were just "Three minutes away" from being the biggest act in Country Music. Of course, he meant that we needed a hit record. After all these years, Jim's famous

"Three minutes away" speech has become a part of music business folklore.

Under his leadership and management, The Oak Ridge Boys did indeed become a household name, with a wall full of gold and platinum albums that are chock full of "three minute" miracles, for which we are all so very thankful.

We remain a hard working and popular act today because of the foundation that Jim helped us to build.

Jim Halsey has spent most of his life on the cutting edge of the music business. His booking agency, The Jim Halsey Company, Inc., out of Tulsa, Oklahoma once booked over half of the major acts in country music. I know that you are about to read a lot more about the Oaks and Jim in the pages that follow, but let me just provide for you, the reader, a slight recollection of milestones, a small collage of accomplishments that were simply unheard of B.H. (Before Halsey!):

1. Country music on "The Tonight Show" when Country wasn't as mainstream as today. The Oaks alone have been on the show twenty seven times.

2. Country music acts on variety shows from every major television network.

3. Country music acts under Jim's influence headlining all the major hotels on the Las Vegas Strip. (We still do it today!)

4. Roy Clark and The Oaks touring The Soviet Union.

5. Playing international festivals from Sweden to Switzerland and from Amsterdam to the Acropolis in Nice, France.

6. Headlining venues including Radio City Music Hall to Carnegie Hall and garnering major press for each performance.

7. Playing with big symphonies in major cities.

8. Shooting videos back when there was NO CABLE TV!!

9. Appearing at the famous Jim Halsey ranch parties in Tulsa where literally every fair buyer and concert hall booker in the world attended.

10. TV shows, concert halls, fairs, theaters. Jim could book us in all of them and make a huge, bigger-than-life event out of each and every one.

11. No idea too big. No problem that cannot be solved, no mountain that cannot be climbed.

This is Jim Halsey and, believe me, there is no one quite like him. But allow me just a few more words.

Jim Halsey is the most positive thinking man that I have ever known in my life. He is not only a man of knowledge and know how, but he is a man of God who puts his Family first.

He has always possessed in his soul certain ideals and values that come from years of studying the American Indian Way of Life, which teaches us to respect all of God's Creatures and to possess a child-like love for this great land in which we live.

So you see, Jim Halsey is so much more than our manager. He is a spiritual advisor, a healer, a peacemaker, a leader and a teacher.

I have seen him dance on top of a record company president's desk and I have seen him raise a family. I have seen him fight for what is fair and right and I have watched him light up and shine like an angel when he teaches his class.

Jim has never said, "Have a nice day." He always says, "This is a great day." It is always an "incredible week," and you had better believe, that "this year is going to be the best year yet!!", even "better than last year."

What a joy to have this man as a friend and what an opportunity for a young student of the music business to read this book and to learn from the very best.

I am honored to have been asked to write a few words here about our Godfather and Impresario, Jim Halsey.

Readers, look real hard at the road ahead. I guarantee there will be a crossroad around the next bend. Listen. Pay attention. Through the words of this book you will find Jim Halsey standing there ready to point the way down the right road. Listen to him. Learn from him. He is the best of us.

– Joseph S. Bonsall, The Oak Ridge Boys
March 2, 2000

Joseph S. Bonsall is a twenty-seven year member of The Oak Ridge Boys and author of the Molly The Cat Book series published by Ideals Children's Books.

PART ONE

Success
and the
Power of
Performance

Your Foundation for Success

What is success, and how do you achieve it?

First of all, you must determine what the word "success" means to you. It's easy to be confused or heavily influenced by other people's criteria for success, or to be misled by public opinion about what constitutes a successful life. For instance, far too many people believe that material wealth equals success, an equation reinforced by movies, television and the ads you read in newspapers and magazines. It's easy to be influenced by that image of success—but it doesn't necessarily have to be *your* image. Stop and think for yourself. Ask yourself what it would take to make you feel successful. Establish your own goals based on what you really want out of life, not what others want or think you should want.

As you'll read later, I formulated my early goals after absorbing the story of Sol Hurok, told in the book *Impresario*. But even before that, I was influenced heavily by those great old musicals featuring high-school kids, the kind MGM made with Mickey Rooney and Judy Garland. Although the stars were still in high school—at least for the purposes of the movie—they were doing musical plays, they had bands and producers, and it seemed as though the manager was always the person who called all the shots and the one who maybe got the most respect. So I started out wanting to become a manager.

Then, after I read the Sol Hurok book, I became entranced with the image of the impresario. He seemed to be the grandest—the one attending all the openings, carrying his ornate walking cane, his cape flung over his shoulder. That's when I decided that, instead of getting a real job, I'd promote shows.

After you have determined what you want out of life, ask for it. That's right, ask for it! You have the right. Whom do you ask? Start by asking the Creator, and you'll begin to get your answers.

Next, make a list for your life, just like you would make a shopping list. Write down your needs and your goals. Get them down on paper, in black and white, and then put them somewhere—on your desk, the refrigerator door, the bathroom mirror—where you'll often see them. That helps make them real to you.

When I am setting goals, I get a pad of legal paper and start writing down everything I can think of that will be needed for that particular project. I start at the top of the page, enumerating everything needed to make the project successful, including money, objects, people, talent, location, and time. Don't forget to add "luck."

You'll hear this from me time and again throughout this book: *Write it down!* This practice has been of great value to me, and it will be of great value to you. Write down your goals. Put the list where you can see it every day. This brings it into the present, into the real world, and that fact in itself helps you achieve what you've written down.

The list you come up with is really a recipe for achieving your goal, whether a specific, one-time project or a lifelong plan for your life. Once you've finished it, all you have to do is follow it to its conclusion.

That's not as easy as it sounds. Sometimes, we get thrown off the path because we get confused by what other people want from their *own* lists. Many times, for instance, we're guided by what our parents think we should become. That may not be compatable with what *you* want to become. True success must be fueled from within. The goals you strive toward must satisfy your own needs mentally, physically, emotionally, and spiritually. *You must follow your own list, your own recipe for success.*

Fortunately, I had parents who supported what I did, even if they didn't understand it and weren't even sure it was a real business. But they knew I was into it, and wanted to do it, and so they supported me. Of course, I always gave them free tickets to my shows.

If material gain is your measuring stick for success, that's fine. Recognize that it's not that way for everyone, though. If you write your list, set your goal, and follow the steps you've set for yourself, you will have your success. In certain professions, the monetary rewards are greater than others. Sometimes, when you achieve success in your projects, your reward will be both material gain and internal fulfillment. Believe me: the internal fulfillment is the most satisfying thing of all, and it should be what you seek above all else.

In building my career as an artist manager, booking agent, impresario, and businessman, I have measured my success in terms of the success of my projects and events. Some of them have benefited me materially, and some have not. My goal was always to maximize my creative process and to make a success of whatever project I took on. I didn't measure my success in material terms. Later on, you'll read about a couple of projects I did, The Oak Ridge Boys and The Judds at Radio City Music Hall and Roy Clark's Soviet tours, that were not financially rewarding but were richly successful on many other levels.

To be a success, you must *focus on your goal*. Surely, you've heard this phrase before, at a graduation speech or other motivational lectures. Somebody successful always seems to be standing at a podium saying, "Establish your goal and focus upon it."

There's no better piece of advice in the world than that. But let me add something important to it, and that is: *have a purpose for your goal*. When establishing the goals you hope to achieve, determine what their purpose is and what you hope to accomplish when you succeed.

A dog chases a car. Its goal is to catch the car. But what's the dog going to do when it catches the car? In other words, what's the purpose? So many of us are going through life chasing cars, putting a lot of work and energy into trying to catch something that's ultimately meaningless. If you know the purpose of your goals, if you can say why you pursue them, you'll dodge the empty pursuits that consume so many others.

The entertainment business is no different than any other kind of business. It may be a little more creatively stimulating than most, but the formulas for success are the same. It doesn't matter whether you're looking for financial, emotional, spiritual, or creative rewards, or a combination. *You must have a goal and a purpose*. When you determine your goal, identify the purpose. You can then plan how to achieve that goal.

From the beginning, I have always been interested in building projects and artists within this framework. I have always believed in making a project an event—in making *life* an event. Each one of my projects has had a specific goal, and each one has had a specific plan and a method of achieving success. And they all had a purpose!

♪ ♪ ♪ ♪

I started my career as a promoter. It was through my early associations that I eventually became an artist manager and a booking agent. Learning to be a promoter, however, gave me an opportunity to understand all aspects of the music business: advertising, sales, marketing, promotion, artist relations, management, touring, agenting, the rodeo and fair business, television, and radio. I learned about record companies and music publishing companies and their importance to an artist's career. I learned, most importantly, about the power of teams and how their working together brought success. I learned about the **Power of Performance** each team member possessed.

I learned that by being a promoter of shows and music, I was also an important member of an essential structure, a player on the team. I learned to access my **Power of Performance**. I had the best of practical educations, with lots of planning and lots of trial and error combined with lots of failures. I worked with so many different artists that I was able to get a keen insight into how careers were being developed. I got to see a lot of the weaknesses of bad management and how disastrous it can be to an artist. I came to understand the differences between a good and a bad booking agent. As a working and learning observer, I could see when the synergy of the team members was missing—when the **Power of Performance** was lost, when all of its elements were not in working harmony. I found out in my early learning process that building a good team and harnessing every member's **Power of Performance** would bring success. Not doing so would bring failure.

While still a teenage promoter, I made up my mind that if I ever got the chance to manage an artist and exercise my **Power of Performance**, I would build a good team.

From the beginning of my show-business career, I actively sought knowledge about how to improve myself, including how to do a job better than somebody else was doing it. As a result, my on-the-job training had an early payoff.

I had been working as a promoter for Hank Thompson, an important recording artist, when he called me to be his manager. I'd been promoting Hank and his band, The Brazos Valley Boys, in various towns throughout Kansas, Missouri, Oklahoma, and Arkansas. Sometimes, I would take a string of eight to ten dates and promote a small tour. Hank told me his manager, John Hitt, was leaving for a position with Music Corporation of America (MCA), which was at that time a very large booking agency. Hank had liked my "performances," my thoroughness in promoting his dates, and he wanted to know if I would like to do it full time. In addition, he wanted me to be in charge of everything else he did professionally—his bookings, all of his business arrangements, his record and television deals, corporate sponsorship, fairs and rodeos, the works. He asked me to be both his manager and his agent.

At this time, manager-agent was not an unusual position, especially in the country field. Although Hank's western-swing style was a mixture of country, R&B, and big-band, he was considered a country act, and most of the big agencies knew very little about country music. Managers of many country acts were also expected to book dates.

It was December of 1951. I had just turned 21 and was still in college, but it didn't take me long to recognize this was my opportunity to put all of my dreams into action.

I had not really traveled outside of my four-state home area of Kansas, Oklahoma, Missouri, and Arkansas. Now Hank Thompson and his Brazos Valley Boys were asking me to book them nationally.

Before, Hank had been primarily a regional touring artist. His records had sold nationally, but he had confined his personal appearances mainly to the southwest and West Coast, with an occasional appearance in the East.

One of our first goals was to tour Hank in, at that time, all 48 states. It was important to establish my relationship with Capitol Records, Hank's recording company, and to work with them in trying to build him into a national artist. Being a promoter, I was a constant reader of the trade publications: *Billboard, Cashbox, Variety,* and *Downbeat.* Using record-sale information gleaned from those magazines, I bought a large map and systematically plotted the areas, states, and cities I wanted to cover during my first year as Hank's manager and agent.

Take it from one who knows: timing is everything.

Just as Hank and I began our relationship, he released what turned out to be one of the giant country records of all time, "The Wild Side of Life." It sold well over a million copies and spawned many sequels and parodies. I was in the right place at the right time!

Hank already had some good team members in place: the record company, Capitol Records; his record producer, Ken Nelson; a prominent music attorney, Harold Ornstein; and his music publisher, Hill and Range Songs. I was now an important member of the team, functioning both as manager and booking agent. It would be my job to coordinate the collective efforts of the team. For this, I had to access the very best of my own **Power of Performance.**

We came up with a five-year plan for Hank's career—a list of goals just like the list we talked about earlier. Our goals included expanding Hank's territory and his itinerary; getting more radio play nationwide; and creating a regional or national TV show with Hank at the center. He and I were firm believers in the power of television as a means of reaching masses of people. I went over the map, listened to the record company executives, took direction from Hank, booked the dates, went on the tour, met each promoter personally, and collected the money after every job. It was the important process of "learning the territory." It was on-the-job training!

We accomplished a lot the first year with Hank. I put all of my selling skills to work, designed a plan, established goals (with multiple purposes), and filled Hank's itinerary. Booking 225 dates in 40 states, I showed up at most of the venues with Hank. As a promoter, I had learned how an artist's personal appearances could be greatly enhanced if the team members' planning efforts were coordinated. The five-year plan was working, my methods were working, and they continued to work.

I have to confess that there were some dates included in Hank's itinerary that were more personal and meaningful to me than to anyone else. As I was getting my geography lesson firsthand, I booked some dates in areas I just wanted to see—places I had read about as a kid, but had never been able to visit. Now, I had an opportunity to see them as part of my job. Shows in places like Jackson Hole, Wyoming, the Grand Canyon, and the Cheyenne Frontier Days celebration in Cheyenne, Wyoming, were not only good dates for Hank, as we expanded his territory, but added to the color and flavor of what we were doing.

Hank Thompson is one of the most important people in my life. He is my mentor, business partner, teacher, and best of all, my friend. Because of my early relationship with Hank, I have been able to live my choice of lives. I recognized the opportunity. I accepted the challenge and used my **Power of Performance**. I asked, and I received, and I will always be grateful to God for answering my prayers and to Hank for a relationship that has lasted nearly half a century.

My long association with Hank Thompson illustrates two important things. One, *you must be able to recognize opportunities*. Two, *you must be able to take action when the opportunities arise!*

Much of my early training and most of my personal philosophy was developed while I was constantly traveling with Hank in those early years. When I took over management of this great artist, I formulated my first five-year plan, something I've done innumerable times since. I learned, early on, to follow my dreams. I agreed with the old truism, "If you don't follow your dreams, you are going to stop having them."

I had plenty of dreams and visions. I would write them down, along with my goals and their purpose. Once I had all of this down where I could see it and think about it, I'd discuss it all with Hank. I learned how to focus. All of this propelled me toward a performance that achieved the goals I'd set for myself.

So please, *don't be afraid to follow your dreams!*

Now is the time for you to begin. You have the right to ask for what you want. List your goals and their purpose, your dreams and visions, on a piece of paper. Put it in a conspicuous place, where you can't miss seeing it often. It is your plan for the future, your road map for your own personal journey. It's great to have more than one goal. Naturally, some are more important than others; you'll follow a lot of branches in the road to get to your ultimate destination.

Just as you have to pass through many cities and towns on a journey, you have to achieve some goals before going on to others. It helps to identify each goal and put it in order of importance to your overall plan. Once you've written them down, you'll be surprised how easy it is to focus on each one.

We talked about focus earlier. This is very important. You *must* be able to focus, and you must be able to *stay* focused—on your goals, and on your plan for achieving them.

Can you identify your goals, the ones you really want to achieve? Are they the product of your dreams? If they are, that's great! You are beginning to recognize the potential of your dreams. Now, you can begin turning those dreams into reality!

Accepting the Challenge

In the music and entertainment business—as in all other businesses—the difference between excellence and mediocrity can be measured in degrees. Achieving excellence and not settling for mediocrity can be as simple as an extra boost of effort or a fraction more determination. The formula for consistent excellence is relatively simple, but that doesn't mean it's easy.

What must you do to seriously pursue excellence in a music and entertainment career?

You must commit yourself to attempting what most people will dismiss as impossible. You must be determined to stretch yourself to the limits of your ability. You must take on more than you believe is possible to achieve, and you must ask your spiritual and physical helpers for the strength and guidance to achieve it.

Go to the limit. Have a goal. Have a purpose. Access your **Power of Performance**, whether you're on stage or off.

Accepting the challenge to be consistently excellent is an important part of being successful. You must be able to recognize every challenge as an opportunity that triggers your **Power of Performance**.

In the music and entertainment business, challenges sometimes arrive unexpectedly or prematurely, at times when you seem to be least ready for them. Remember: every challenge is a test. Each challenge gives you a chance to excel, to pull past mediocrity and drive to the top.

When a new challenge comes along, ask yourself these questions:

- *Am I ready for it?*
- *Is there a purpose for my taking it?*
- *Am I qualified to take it?*
- *Do I have the mental and physical stamina for it?*

- *Can I do it?*
- *Will it allow me to perform?*

You'll notice that I repeat several principles and ideas throughout this book. Here's an important one: *I never equate success with money, only with performance.*

Material wealth can be a measure of success, but it's only one of many. Real success brings fulfillment and contentment. And performance, good *or* bad, determines everyone's level of success in the music and entertainment business.

Accessing your **Power of Performance** gives you the ability to excel, to achieve success and, ultimately, contentment. No matter what your field, it's all about performance.

And that's especially true in the fascinating, fabulous, frenetic, and occasionally frustrating business of music—*my* business.

The Power of Performance

Already, you've seen the term **Power of Performance** several times in this book. You're going to see it a lot more. That's because I firmly believe it is the single most important factor in anyone's success.

Learning about this power, and finding the best ways to unleash it, is really what this book is all about. So, before we go any further, let's define it.

Power of Performance is doing your job, performing your task, accepting your mission in life, all to the best of your ability. It is giving your best performance, whether you're on stage or off. It is going for excellence, with the understanding that you're capable of achieving it. It is, simply, accessing, perfecting, and projecting your abilities and talents to make yourself the best you can possibly be—mentally, physically, emotionally, and spiritually.

Every day, you give a performance. You may be on a stage, or you may be on a telephone. You may be behind a counter, across the table from a business acquaintance, in the home of someone close to you. By accessing your **Power of Performance**, you can shape your own life and influence others by expressing your abilities in an expressive and dynamic way. It is a sure path to success.

Whatever your skills are, perfect them beyond all insecurity or doubt of ability. Know everything about your job, your craft, your artistic talents. Go the extra mile, put in the overtime hours, push your talent and energy to the limit, and then go a little farther.

Every successful person has the **Power of Performance**. Artists and musicians have it, and the ones who have perfected their **Power of Performance** are usually big stars. I discovered the **Power of Performance** as a teenager, seeing how great artists connected with their audiences. I saw that these gifted people could conduct an audience through a range of emotions, from melancholia and sadness to exhilarating joy, just like a conductor changing mood and music with the wave of a baton.

I knew, however, I could never be one of these people. Playing saxophone in the school band and with a dance combo on weekends convinced me that my real talent lay elsewhere than the stage, despite the fact that I was in love with music.

Then, a high school book-report assignment changed my life.

The book I chose was a biography called *Impresario: A Memoir of Sol Hurok* (Random House, 1946). Once I began reading it, I couldn't put it down. During his many years in show business, Sol Hurok presented nearly every type of stage attraction, specializing in bringing talent from the Soviet Union and other parts of Eastern Europe to the United States. His life had been full of glamour, talented artists, events that required creative sales and marketing, and even a certain amount of risk. What could be better for me? All through school I had been selling something. So why not sell music and entertainment?

So, although my talent—and Sol Hurok's—didn't lie in performance on a stage, I made a decision to get into the music business and become, like my inspiration, an impresario. And once I made that decision, I began turning my energies in that direction, using my **Power of Performance** in a single-minded effort to become the impresario of southeastern Kansas!

♪ ♪ ♪ ♪

It started when I booked the great western swing figure Leon McAuliffe and his band into my hometown of Independence, Kansas. It happened in October of 1949, the month I turned 19. Several months earlier, I'd begun thinking, "Well, maybe I'll get a band to put in the auditorium." I knew what to do: find a good night, put the posters out, put the handbills out, buy the ads in the paper, get on the radio stations. So finally, I decided to take the plunge, and access my mostly untried **Power of Performance** as a music promoter.

I was a big fan of western-swing pioneer Bob Wills, who had given Leon his start (as well as his trademark phrase, "Take it away, Leon"), and I'd followed Leon since his days as steel guitarist for Bob Wills' Texas Playboys. After World War II, Leon had put together his own popular Tulsa-based band, which was touring on a regional basis.

I wrote to Leon, and I got a letter back from C.M. Cooksey, his manager, saying they had a date in October that was available. They gave it to me on a straight percentage basis. While I was still at risk for the hall and everything that went along with it, as well as the advertising costs and the help, it was a minimal risk because Mr. Cooksey hadn't asked for a big guarantee.

The show night was a Thursday night, the night of the week that stores stayed open late in Independence. It was a beautiful evening, and before the show I walked the streets, wondering how everything was going to turn out. As I wandered, I noticed an unusual number of people in town, and cars with tags from Missouri, Oklahoma, and other states. I thought, "Something's going on, and maybe, just *maybe*, it's my dance."

It was. When I arrived at the auditorium to open the box office, there was already a line—an hour before Leon and his band were to begin. And when that dance kicked off with the words "Take it away, Leon," the place was full. It was jam-packed.

That was my entry into show business. I loved the music. I loved the excitement of seeing a promotion work. I loved the happiness on people's faces when they left, saying "Good dance, Jim," or "Good music, Jim," or "What a good time, Jim." That night, I knew I was in show business to stay. And even though I couldn't put it into words yet, I was learning the important idea of the **Power of Performance**.

After that, I branched out and started sending letters to other agencies and bands. I knew who to contact because I read *Billboard* and the other trade magazines that gave you performers' itineraries and told you who handled them. None of these people knew I was 19.

Neither did Mr. Cooksey, Leon McAuliffe's manager. When he came up to Independence, he was surprised to find a 19-year-old kid promoting the show. But I did a good job, and so we established a relationship that led to my playing Leon and his band about once a month in Independence and surrounding areas. By the time the mid-'50s rolled around, I was his agent, and we were busy expanding him beyond the Oklahoma, Kansas and Texas area, making him into the national figure that he and I both wanted him to be. He was a complement to Hank Thompson and Wanda Jackson, whom I was also handling, because I could call one promoter and make three sales. The efficiency and economy of having three national acts was better than having just one.

I took Leon all over the West Coast and through the Northwest. I represented him for four or five years. We remained friends forever.

♪ ♪ ♪ ♪

There must have been something about Independence—as there is with my other hometown, Tulsa—that fostered and foreshadowed the development of my **Power of Performance**. Certainly, the town has been home to others who've accessed their own **Power of Performance** in lasting ways. They range from the brilliant American playwright William Inge, creator of such powerful works as *Bus Stop, Picnic, The Dark at the Top of the Stairs*, and *Come Back, Little Sheba*, to Harry Sinclair, the famed oil baron.

Supposedly, Harry Sinclair, in his early struggling days, shot off one of his toes to collect the insurance money, which he then used to drill his first well. True or not, that story went around Independence for many years. William Inge heard it, and he put a line in *The Dark at the Top of the Stairs* about how a man shot his toe off to get into the oil business.

Flash forward to the middle 1960s. I was promoting a touring stage production (known in the business as a bus and truck show) of *The Dark at the Top of the Stairs*, starring the veteran actress Joan Blondell. It came to Independence, and when the audience heard the line about shooting off a toe, it broke into uproarious laughter and cheers. Ms. Blondell and the rest of the cast were baffled. They'd been on tour for six weeks, and that was the first time the line had ever gotten a laugh. So as the play went on, they threw the line in three or four more times, just to see what response they'd get. It brought the house down every time.

When the play was over, Joan Blondell sought me out. "What is this deal about shooting your toe off and collecting insurance money?" she asked. I told them all the Harry Sinclair story.

If there's a moral to this story, maybe it's that, on rare occasions, your performance can take on a power that even leaves *you* baffled!

Ten Keys to Power of Performance

Over the years, I have developed a 10-key method for achieving success. It is simple and effective and it will always work, no matter what your profession. It is a formula for success in life.

The better you understand and employ each of these keys, the more likely your **Power of Performance** will lead you to success. If your interest lies in becoming a manager, agent, or even a star, these 10 keys are essential. But they work in every profession, in every walk of life, and there is not a single one of them that you can't keep on developing every day of your life.

1. Talent

We all have talent. The lucky ones are born with it, but most of us have to develop it. I'm not talking just about artistic talent. I'm also talking about the talent that can help make you a successful artist manager, booking agent, record producer, executive and business person. Examine the talent you have, and see what you need to develop in order to advance toward your goal.

2. Training and Education

How do you develop your talent? Training and education is one good way. If you are a singer, songwriter, musician, or band member, for instance, you will always benefit from lessons, instructions, on-the-job training with other musicians and bands, working on the road, taking advice from other players, listening to tapes and CDs, watching television, reading, and attending concerts, conferences, and workshops. You didn't know this was training and education? It's the best type of education, and it's available to everyone.

Always work toward refining your skills. If you're interested in the business aspects of the music industry, you can follow the same rules, but make a continuous study about how things are being done. Get as much education as possible, taking courses that will benefit you in your chosen profession.

Many people start in the booking or management business by taking jobs as apprentices or assistants with large agencies or management companies. These entry-level positions—file clerk, driver, etc.—may not seem important, but, believe me, they are. Everything you do for the company is part of your education, and the more education you have, the better your chances of getting off to a good start. So pay attention!

The same thing holds for careers in the record business, music publishing, and other music industry management positions. Watching how things are done, identifying the players, listening while negotiations are in progress, and finding out how to deal with artists, managers, booking agents, and record companies all adds to your overall knowledge. This is called apprenticeship, and it's the way a lot of people get started in the music and entertainment business.

You can increase your overall understanding of the music and entertainment business by reading the trade publications, called the "trades." These are magazines and newspapers dealing with various aspects of the business. They publish stories about what's happening in the music and entertainment business, review new products and artists, chart the popularity of records in current release, make forecasts, and give information on touring groups, among other things.

Some trades—*Guitar Player*, *Bass Player*, and *Keyboard*, for instance—are specialized, targeting a very specific music industry audience. Then there are general-interest trades, like *Billboard* magazine. The true bible of the industry, *Billboard* is a weekly that covers different aspects of music, television, video, personal appearances—and now, even computers.

Some colleges and universities also offer specialized training. A lot of schools have courses dealing with the performing arts, and some even offer songwriting courses. However, fewer than 50 schools deal with the practical aspects of the music business. This has always seemed strange to me, as a lot of graduates jump right in, thinking their business degree is all they need, and find out they know nothing about the basic elements of the *music* business—such as the functions of the manager, the agent, the unions and guilds, music publishers, copyrights, record companies, publicists, music and entertainment attorneys, and the sales and marketing of artists, records and events.

Not long ago, I completed my contract as the head of the music and entertainment business program at Oklahoma City University, and I thank OCU president Dr. Jerald Walker, who shared my vision about what that program should be. My main focus now is on the Halsey Institute in Tulsa, Oklahoma. The Halsey Institute provides accelerated learning for individuals interested in entering the music entertainment business.

If you don't have access to a program like this, a good part of your education will have to be learned by experience, often in the "school of hard knocks." You can find books and tapes that will help, and sometimes there are organizations in your area that offer seminars on the music business. Take advantage of these opportunities. Remember, it is a continual process of learning. The more knowledge you have, the better equipped you are to access your own personal **Power of Performance.**

3. Personality

Sometimes it seems as though personality is like talent; some people are simply born with it. This isn't so. There are people who have the ability to present themselves better than others, but they usually can do this only after training and lots of experience. And in making a good presentation of yourself, you develop your personality.

How do you develop your presentation? Well, if you don't have confidence in yourself, and if you tend to be unfocused and rambling when you speak before others, the best things you can do is write down *exactly* what you want to say, stand before a mirror, and say it over and over and over. Pretty soon you'll be able to go in and speak, and no distraction will bother you, because if you have to, you can go to your memory and say it just as you memorized it. When you're comfortable, you can ad-lib and free-flow. Becoming good at speaking gives you self-confidence, and that bolsters your personality.

I don't care if you are a singer, a band member, an agent, a manager, or filling one of the hundreds of other positions in the music business—you can develop a direct and positive approach to others. You can develop a good personality. It's an important part of your **Power of Performance,** your method for success.

There is a good course on how to present yourself, the famous Dale

Carnegie course, available nationwide and usually offered in night sessions. I always encouraged the associates in my agency to improve their communication skills by taking the Carnegie course, and I still highly recommend it. The Carnegie course, and others like it, are immensely effective in sharpening your skills in dealing with people, whether on stage or off. In the music and entertainment business, you are constantly working with a dizzying number of people; to increase your **Power of Performance** to the maximum, your communication skills and your personality must be as effective as you can make them.

4. Attitude

This book is full of attitude; I bring it up again and again in these pages. That's because attitude is important for any accomplishment in life, and part of my method for success is developing a positive attitude and continuously maintaining it.

If your attitude is bad, nothing is going to work for you. If it's good, your attitude will enhance your dealings with others and make your performance better. If you're a performer, your good attitude will radiate out from the stage and engage the audience. If you're a musician in a band, a good attitude on the road will get you through many a trying time of bad schedules, long journeys, inadequate sound, and lousy hotel rooms. Keeping your attitude positive is only one of the important keys to making my method work, but without a good attitude, none of the others will be effective.

You have to understand that maintaining a positive attitude is, simply, an important aspect in the pursuit of a quality life. I am an eternal optimist. My attitude has always been positive. Having a good attitude doesn't mean I don't encounter problems or that difficulties don't arise. Life is a process of constant change, and with these changes often come problems, but these problems and changes bring growth. Sometimes, that's a hard fact to realize while working through one of life's difficulties, but maintaining a positive attitude always helps you get through.

When I think of attitude, I think of Leo Zabelin. Leo was, for more than 20 years, The Jim Halsey Company's in-house director of press and public relations; I had known him since the very early days of my career. Over the years, Leo had been involved with major publications and major motion picture studios. He was one of the great geniuses in the area of public relations, and Leo Zabelin knew everybody.

Because Leo was an early riser, he always arrived at our office before anyone else. While many of his colleagues were still in bed, Leo would be reading the trade magazines and the vast array of newspapers to which we subscribed. Normally, before I arrived, Leo would also go through all the telephone calls on the overnight telephone sheet, the overnight mail, and the numerous faxes or telexes that had arrived during the night. Every morning, I would enter the office full of ideas, new dreams, or just the excitement of starting a new day. And every morning, Leo would greet me with, "Hello. Well, we've got a problem today."

It was the same greeting each morning, and each morning there usually *was* a problem—often, more than one. Today, I cannot think of one which was not solvable. Some were more complex than others, but solving those is what makes us grow and learn. They are all just part of the territory.

I am a great believer in positive thoughts and positive energy and in doing everything I can to keep those energies free and flowing. This is what makes a positive performance. Since I try to be positive all the time, Leo's daily greeting didn't really bother me.

But finally, after several years, I sat down and tried to explain my approach to Leo. I told him that I saw problems as opportunities to learn. I stressed the fact that while "problem" situations were always going to be with us every day, we did not have to be negative. Maintaining a positive attitude, I said, was the key to solving all of these problems. Finally, I told him that I would prefer he not greet me every morning with "we've got a problem."

Leo understood my point and seemed to agree. He was a close friend; still, I wondered whether saying the kind of things I had to say to him had hurt his feelings and created some negative energy. I had so much respect for Leo and his knowledge that I felt he wouldn't be offended. I certainly *hoped* that was the case.

I was right. The morning after Leo and I had our talk, he met me at the door as usual—but for the first time, he had changed his salutation. "Good morning, Jim," he said. Then he hesitated. "This morning," he continued after a moment, "we've got a situation."

I complimented him on not starting the day with a problem. "It makes a positive change in our attitude when starting the day," I told him.

Then, I asked about the "situation."

"There's a fire," he said.

"Okay."

"A big fire!" Leo continued.

"All right, all right. Where's the big fire, Leo?"

"The MGM Hotel in Las Vegas," he replied. "It's burning down—and

The Oak Ridge Boys open there Thursday."

"Now Leo," I said, "that is a *problem!*"

We spent the rest of the morning ascertaining the extent of the damage. It was a very serious fire. A number of people had lost their lives and the MGM Hotel would be closed for some time. Now was the time to show ourselves, and our clients, our **Power of Performance.** Our performance wasn't on stage; we performed for The Oak Ridge Boys behind the scenes, on telephones, making useful and productive time of the weeks we suddenly had open on The Oak Ridge Boys' performing schedule.

Because a few of our other stars had taken ill on the road—a not-uncommon occurrence with touring acts—we'd had to cancel some shows around the country. Now, we could use The Oak Ridge Boys to fill the dates those acts couldn't do. The rest of the time, The Oak Ridge Boys were able to do some press and public relations, guest-star in a couple of television shows, and prepare for their next album.

Taking care of "situations" is built into the day-to-day routine of simply doing business, and accepting the challenge of everyday life with a positive attitude is an important part of being successful. We have to recognize our challenges as opportunities and then act within our **Power of Performance**. Sometimes a challenge comes unexpectedly, such as the MGM Hotel fire. Sometimes, at least in our own minds, challenges come prematurely, before we're ready for them. But remember: You are being tested with every challenge. Are you ready for it? Are you qualified for it? Do you have the mental and physical stamina for it? Can you do it?

In the case of the MGM crisis and many other challenges that went along with the booking-agency business, we did it. And we did it by accepting the challenge.

Accept the challenge. Don't be afraid to fail. If you're always afraid to fail, then you'll never accept the first assignment. And so what if you *do* fail? Isn't that the best way of learning how not to fail with the next challenge that comes your way?

Sure, it takes a little courage to set off into the unknown. But remember: You have established your goals, and you have written them down. *Now* is the time to get started.

Challenges come in many forms, and they don't always look like opportunities. Often, they do not even seem to fit in your scheme of things. Having the proper attitude when faced with these things helps you achieve success.

Examine each challenge and opportunity to determine if it will be a learning experience. Will it help make you better as a person? Will it open up new opportunities down the road? Will it bring you satisfaction and happiness? Will you grow through the challenge? Does it fit into the overall plan for achieving your goals? Can you salvage the misfortune that happens, as The Jim Halsey Company did in the MGM crisis? Have you learned to access your power?

- *If it fits, go for it!*
- *Get excited about it!*
- *Get enthused about it!*
- *Give it all you can!*

5. Enthusiasm

Get enthused! Get excited about your life, your talent, your job, your career, and the selling of yourself or your product.

Another important part of my method, an essential key, is to deal always with every aspect of the business with enthusiasm. After all, more sales are made because of a salesperson's enthusiasm than for any other reason.

Our life is comprised of selling. If you are a player, you sell from the stage, but no matter what part of the music business you're in, genuine enthusiasm will produce results and sales beyond your expectations. Sometimes things won't go as planned. The breaks may not come. But if you have prepared yourself, you'll know you have what it takes to persevere and to triumph.

Stay focused and stay enthused! Enthusiasm is one of your best sources of energy. Always greet the day with it, realizing it is an important key to your success.

By the way, I'm enthused about passing this knowledge on to you, so you can put your **Power of Performance** to work!

6. Desire

You have to have *desire*. It fuels your enthusiasm and helps you overcome a lot of disappointment and rejection. If you have the desire to make it, in spite of all adversities, you will make it.

When I think about the power of desire, I often think of Lee Greenwood, whose "God Bless the USA" is the best known of his many country music chart-toppers. For years, Lee dealt blackjack in the Las Vegas casinos by day and worked the lounges at night, determined to get out of there and get his songs heard and become a recognized international performer. He did, and I'm happy to say that The Jim Halsey Company helped him achieve his goals.

Lee Greenwood and his subsequent stardom is an impressive example of how much desire is involved in accessing your personal **Power of Performance**.

7. Persistence

My method stresses persistence: not wavering from your path, not losing focus on your goal. Stick your foot in the door of success and do not take it out until you have wedged the door open far enough for you to get through it. Do not get discouraged and give up.

Persistence keeps you on the road to success—persistence in the quality of your performance, persistence in the dedication to the work you've chosen. Realize, please, that persistence is all-important. Without it, my method won't work.

8. Self-Confidence

Self-confidence is something you develop for yourself. It comes with learning your craft. The more you do any task, the more comfortable you are with it. It is this repetition in perfecting your skills, your own **Power of Performance**, that develops self-confidence. The more you train, study, and work with your music-business skills, the more you will develop self-confidence. The more you work, the more you perform, the more comfortable you will be with the knowledge that you can do it. This is self-confidence, and it is attainable by anyone!

9. Recognize Opportunities

If you are going to be successful, you not only have to be able to recognize opportunities, you have to act when an opportunity comes your way. So many times, people pass over an opportunity because they're afraid to take action. Acting might mean changes in their lives—they could face risk and uncertainties, and they lack the self-confidence to face all of that.

If you're really going for success, you have to be able to make decisions and take risks. Examine every opportunity that comes your way. Does it offer an advancement in the areas you're interested in? What are the risks? What are the rewards? What are the sacrifices you will need to make? Write all of the risks and rewards, listing potentially positive things on one side, potentially negative things on the other. When you are through, look at it objectively. It will help you decide how to act. And remember: Even inaction is an action.

10. Commitment

This one tells the story. Commitment is different from desire. It is your promise to yourself to focus on your goal and do what is necessary to achieve it. Can you be a success at anything if you do not have a commitment to your family, your job, your friends, your ideas, your country; to God, life, and yourself? If you are committed to yourself, then you'll know what you have to do to make your life a success. The challenges you face will come more easily because you will understand how to make the necessary commitment.

Make a goal, develop a plan, and follow it through. Have a purpose. Be committed. As you become more and more involved with people, as you continue to develop your **Power of Performance**, a personal commitment will be indispensable for making your relationships grow and prosper. Do not be afraid to make a commitment and stick to it. When you do, it brings forth commitment from others.

Here's a simple equation: **Power of Performance** is a commitment, and commitment is **Power of Performance.**

In my business as artist manager and agent for a number of stars, I was constantly renewing my commitment to myself, my company, and the people we represented. We established game plans for our artists' careers—and for our own careers as well. Each year, usually, we would put down in writing what we hoped to achieve, where we wanted to go, and then we would make a commitment, or a recommitment, to the artist and the plan.

Do not be afraid to speak about your commitment or to put it in writing. People like to know where you stand. This is part of your **Power of Performance**. Even if others are sure of your ability and loyalty, when you say—as we did—"I am committing myself and the resources of my company to your career," it seems to assure success.

It is positive. It is commitment. It is **Power of Performance.**

If you are not willing to commit, how can you expect others to commit to you? How can you access your **Power of Performance** if you are not committed? After all, aren't you going for success? Aren't you willing to give all that you can?

It all goes back to that commitment to yourself. That's your first commitment and your most important one. Access your power and get your performance going for you through commitment. Do not waste your time or anyone else's if you are not ready to make a commitment.

Once you understand the importance of commitment, your life will change. It will become more interesting, because what you do with it will be solid and meaningful. Commit and be glad you did; it will reshape your life more and sooner than you can imagine.

♪ ♪ ♪ ♪

Each one of these keys is important to your **Power of Performance**; taken together, they will be of immense help in establishing your own personal discipline, learning, and work habits. Include all ten of these keys in your life. Read them and reread them. Understand them and put them into action.

And then, be ready for the trickster that can throw a wrench into even the best-laid plans: REJECTION!

The lesson of rejection, as painful as it is, must be learned by all of us. If you're lucky it will come early in your career, and you'll be able to deal with it and learn from it. Unfortunately, you probably won't see it coming.

I sure didn't, when Roy Clark and I got schooled in rejection by one of Hollywood's real heavyweights, Jack Webb.

It happened in the early 1960s, when Roy and I were getting started together. Even then, I knew that Roy Clark was, quite simply, the single most talented person I had ever met. I knew it. He knew it. Our job was getting the rest of the world to know it.

Roy was recording then for Capitol Records. He hadn't yet scored a big hit, but that didn't bother Capitol or Roy's producer, Ken Nelson, who saw the same potential in him that I did.

The movie *No Time For Sergeants*, starring Andy Griffith, had been a boxoffice blockbuster, and Warner Bros. was planning a television series based on the picture. Because of the efforts of some Capitol Records executives, Roy's name had been pitched as a possible star of the series, and he was subsequently invited to audition for the role originated by Griffith. We were told that if his reading went well, he'd have a screen test and then, if all went right, the lead in the series.

What a break for us! It was the kind of break that launches a career, and to say we were excited about the opportunity is an incredible understatement. We were ecstatic about the possibility of Roy becoming an instant television star.

I was confident, of course, that he would get the role. Things were starting to happen for us. We were on a roll, and this just felt right.

Spurred by excitement and optimism, Roy and I climbed into my car and headed across the country to California, scarcely stopping for anything. I drove. He studied his script and went over his lines as I listened and made suggestions. After three days of this, we were in Southern California and Roy, I felt, was a shoo-in for the part.

Our meeting was at Warner Bros. Studios with the series producer, Jack Webb. For years, both of us had been fans of Webb, who'd soared to fame as the laconic, no-nonsense Joe Friday on the famed TV series *Dragnet*. I have to admit that we were a little intimidated by the to-the-point character we'd seen on TV. But we weren't really worried. Roy had been over and over the script, and he was ready for his reading.

Then, we saw Webb's office. I have seen a lot of executive offices in my time, but never one as huge as this was.

We were early for our appointment, and a rather stiff and unfriendly secretary ushered us into Webb's cavernous quarters. It was really more of a palace. Dark walls rose up to impossibly high ceilings and down to marble floors full of massive oak furniture. Even all these years later, I can still see the place. It was immense—so big that every little sound echoed like thunder.

Left alone, Roy and I glanced around at the intimidating opulence and awaited the arrival of the powerful Jack Webb, this palace's king. Finally, an assistant arrived to do what pages have been doing for kings for hundreds of years: he announced to all within earshot that Mr. Webb would arrive shortly. Then we heard the echoes of leather heels snapping on the shiny marble floor. The King had arrived.

One look at Jack Webb and I knew what getting the role could do for Roy's career. I can't speak for Roy's feelings at the time, but my heart was in my throat.

By now, Webb and another associate were standing in front of us. We rose out of our chairs, ready to shake hands. Webb's assistant—the page—said, "This is Mr. Halsey, and this is Roy Clark."

And there, floating motionless in the great expanse of the king's throne room, our extended hands remained. They were not accepted by either Jack Webb or his associate.

The King looked at both of us.

I waited for him to speak.

Jack Webb didn't say "Hello."

Jack Webb didn't say "How do you do?"

In fact, he only said two words: "Too fat."

And with that he did a military about-face and left the room, his leather heels clicking on the shiny marble floor.

He might as well have said, "Off with their heads." In that instant, our dreams of Roy becoming that instant television star vanished. We were speechless. We looked at each other, open-mouthed, the weeks of anticipation and preparation, the days of driving, the dreams of TV stardom, all flashing through our minds, all dashed to pieces.

We could've reacted in several different ways to the sentence of the King. We could've given up, become angry, lost faith. For us, though, there was only one thing to do. Maybe we remembered the old adage about how you might as well laugh as cry, or perhaps it was simply spontaneous. Whatever the reason, we both broke out laughing. Our laughter filled the cavernous space of Jack Webb's office, and the echoes must have been heard throughout the whole castle.

And so, we put a humorous spin on our rejection, overshadowing our disappointment at our treatment by the King. Jack Webb had certainly exercised his **Power of Performance**; in fact, he'd done it with just two words. And we'd reacted with laughter instead of tears or anger.

There is a lesson here on rejection. Ours was direct, to-the-point, brutal, and personal. We had to accept it and make it a part of learning, a part of growing. At some point in your own career, perhaps at many points, *you* will have to accept it, too. Accepting and working with rejection is one of the most important elements of your growth, and you must learn to use it. If you can turn it around and make it a positive part of your process, you'll be well on your way to success.

♪ ♪ ♪ ♪

Everyone in the music business has an ego. Artists are usually thought to have the biggest egos, but ego is one of the things that makes you a success, no matter what part of the business you're in. Ego is your drive, your desire for acceptance and recognition. It must be acknowledged, and a certain amount of it is beneficial.

All of us, I guess, have been put in our places many times, and our egos have been bruised and bent. If you can accept reality, if you can understand what the real truth is in your life, then you can be at peace with yourself.

Part of accepting reality is striving to understand why people make the decisions they do. As I said earlier, I'm grateful to have two hometowns that I feel comfortable in and love, Independence, Kansas, and Tulsa, Oklahoma. I grew up in Independence, and sometimes, by Independence standards, my ideas may have been a little too extreme for the town, or not as important to others as they were to me. And, of course, having your ideas go unaccepted or unappreciated is a form of rejection.

In my early days with Hank Thompson, booking a lot of package tours, I became involved with two more great country stars, Tex Ritter and Merle Travis. They not only became good friends, but I bought and promoted a lot of dates with them. The three of them—Hank, Tex, and Merle—went out together on a number of package shows, and we'd all travel in the same car.

During one of these trips in the early '60s, I was telling them about Tom Mix, whom I admired a great deal, and how he'd been a city marshal in Independence before making the jump to silent-movie stardom. And Merle Travis said, " Well, you know, a friend of mine has got all of Tom Mix's memorabilia stored in a garage, out in the San Fernando Valley or someplace. You think you'd be interested in that?"

Sure, I told him. With that material, maybe we could start a Tom Mix museum in Independence.

"If you wanted it to start a museum, I think he'd give it to you," Merle said.

So I went to the Independence city fathers, and I said, "There's a possibility that we could get all this Tom Mix memorabilia—his medicine chest, his silver saddles, his pictures, his ropes, his trophies, everything. It's in storage, and some friends of mine think there's a possibility we could get it for no cost at all."

So they mulled it over, and they came back to me in a couple of weeks and said, "No, we don't think we're interested. We already have one museum in Independence."

It was only a couple of years after that, Dewey, Oklahoma, purchased the same collection for $50,000, and started what I think is a really interesting and wonderful museum. Now, of course, one of those silver saddles is worth what the town paid for the collection.

I thought that Independence should pay attention to Tom Mix, because he's a part of town history. But I guess the city fathers at the time just didn't think the idea was very good.

Many years later, in 1994, I came up with the idea of celebrating an event that happened in 1926. It was the first coast-to-coast network radio broadcast, and Independence was a big part of it. General Sarnoff, the head of NBC, rounded up all the big stars of the day, people like John

Philip Sousa and Paul Whiteman, to participate in the broadcast, and he knew he had to have Will Rogers on the roster. But Rogers was appearing live in Independence that night, and he told General Sarnoff, "If you want me, you're going to have to come to Independence, Kansas."

You can imagine the kind of electronic equipment it took in those days to make a remote broadcast. But General Sarnoff got NBC hooked up to Independence and broadcast 15 or 20 minutes of Rogers' show coast to coast.

I thought it would be a good idea to commemorate the anniversary of that broadcast in Independence each year with a banquet and the presentation of a Will Rogers Commemorative Award to a celebrity. We could even broadcast it nationally. A lot of the townspeople also thought the notion had merit, and we got underway, selling tickets to the banquet.

It was a big success. Some 250 people saw Roy Clark and Hank Thompson receive the award, and the Great Empire Broadcasting chain picked it up for broadcast on their stations. Johnny Western, the singer and air personality on Great Empire's KFDI in Wichita, told me we reached an audience of five million that evening—more people, probably, than General Sarnoff reached with his broadcast 75 years earlier.

But after that first success—the banquet, the celebrities, the national broadcast, stories and press all over America—the event was never repeated.

Sometimes, you get excited and enthused about something, and then you find that no one picks up on your excitement and enthusiasm. Although a little bit more subtle, this is a form of rejection that you may well find yourself dealing with, as I did.

♪ ♪ ♪ ♪

Accepting reality is the most important factor in a harmonious life. Accepting rejection and even giving thanks for it is a good learning experience, because rejection teaches you something. It teaches you that everybody does not think the same as you do. It gives you tolerance for other thoughts, opinions, and ideas. It's easy to get so caught up in your own ideas and opinions that you begin to think you're the only person who's important, the only one who matters.

You have to listen to other people. You have to hear their ideas and take them into consideration. When you are representing an artist, for instance, you have to listen to that artist. There will be times when you do not agree, but if you have the privilege of expressing your thoughts, you can get your own point across.

Sometimes, for instance, you'll disagree on the way something's going to be promoted, or an artist will have a certain idea about the way he or she is presented in a show. In most cases, you try to make your compromises.

A good example of this is album titles. An artist may come up with a title for their disc that they think suits their image perfectly, but their suggestion may sound anachronistic and dated. They may like what the title says to them, but to the record-buying public, it might sound totally out of date. So, delicately, you have to tell them, "You know, I think it'd be more contemporary sounding if we did this." You can't just say, "This won't work." You have to say why and make another suggestion. And in most cases, they can still tell you "no."

As I've said before, the music business is a sales business, and in the sales business, you're going to be told "no" many times. It is your averages that will take care of you. If you present one show and it is a dismal failure, it does not necessarily mean that *you* are a failure. It only means that this one particular show was not right. But if you go out and do ten shows, the law of averages will level things out. You will learn from the mistakes and grow with each show. Most likely, the majority of those shows will be successes. Learn from the failures, make adjustments and corrections, and remain flexible in your resolve to work for success.

Are you ready for some hard work? Nobody said it would be easy. But it will be rewarding.

Are you willing to sacrifice? Are you willing to apply yourself to achieving? Do you believe you have the talent? Will you train and educate yourself? Can you develop your personality? Will you maintain your positive attitude? Can you get enthused? Do you have a burning desire? Will you be persistent in achieving your goal? Will you continue building your self-confidence? Are you learning to recognize opportunities when they appear?

If you can honestly answer "yes" to these questions, then all that's left is commitment. Establish your goal with a purpose. Strive to activate your **Power of Performance**, and you'll be on your way to success.

What's next? When I began my own career, I quickly learned that the music business was many related businesses working together as a team—many teams, working as one, to support the artist. As I promoted shows, I met managers, booking agents, publicists, entertainment attorneys, record company executives, record producers, music publishers, and members of sound, lighting, and production crews. As a promoter, I was becoming a part of the team.

In Part Two of this book, I'll identify the team members and their duties. Use it to find and focus on the music-business position that *you* want!

Twenty Helpful Suggestions

Here are 20 good suggestions for cultivating habits that will help you develop your **Power of Performance**. Remember: Success is your ultimate goal, and success comes with accessing your **Power of Performance**. These suggestions will help.

1. **Always maintain a positive attitude.**

2. **Establish goals with a purpose.**

3. **Follow the Boy Scout motto: Be Prepared.**

4. **Be sincere.**

5. **Look professional.**

6. **Hand out business cards.**

7. **Shake hands firmly.**

8. **Look people in the eye.**

9. **Believe in yourself.**

10. **Believe in your employer.**

11. **Work as part of the team.**

12. Know your product.

13. Know your customer.

14. Treat your customers with respect.

15. Give your customers what they need.

16. Have answers to objections.

17. Ask for the sale (or the job).

18. Develop your memory.

19. Follow the rules.

20. Enjoy what you do!

Make these 20 guidelines a part of your life, your day-to-day routine. When you follow them, you are building your self-confidence—and self-confidence is what **Power of Performance** is all about.

Early Ethics Lessons

It's time now to talk about honesty and ethics, how important they are, and how fundamental they are to your **Power of Performance**. They are, in fact, essential to your success.

Where do you learn about honesty and ethics? Ideally in your home, as you grow up. You can also acquire a good sense of ethics from your early associations with adults in your community and from businesses, churches, temples, mosques, clubs, organizations, and schools. I acquired my own basics from my family. They were merchants in Independence, Kansas, owning and operating the Halsey Brothers Department Store, and they included my grandfather H.E., my great uncle Will, my aunt Helen, and my father Ed.

From the time I was 6 or 7 years old, I was hanging around the store. Everything about it fascinated me, from the elevator to the zippy way that cash and sales slips shot from the clerk's station to the mezzanine cashier's office.

These were still the days of the traveling salesman. And when one came to town to pitch his wares to the Halsey Brothers Department Store, I was always an interested audience. The salesmen would bring in new dresses, the latest in women's coats, woolen and cotton goods, cosmetics, notions. Especially enjoyable was the theatrical flair with which a skilled salesman would unfurl a bolt of English worsted or Scottish glen plaid. Many of these men were from New York, Chicago, or St. Louis; Grandfather would often bring them home to have dinner with us, and their tales of traveling, of seeing other merchants in other, faraway cities were spellbinding.

But even at this early age, I was most interested in listening to the negotiations, keeping in mind my grandfather's dictum: "It's only a good deal when it's a good deal for all parties." As I watched and listened, I was learning by osmosis the art of sales and negotiation, as well as getting a good lesson in business ethics—just by being there. I also learned about how the store staged events: a fall opening, a spring opening, a special sales promotion. I learned the language of the retail business: 50% off, 10% down, layaway, two of the same item for a better price than if the same items were bought individually. There were always sales, always promotions. And every so often, there were special events. I was fascinated with how things were marketed.

It was during this time that I learned the concept of the "satisfied customer." In our home, that was the key phrase that described our family's success. My grandfather and father both drilled into me that a satisfied customer is the main element in any sales transaction. The Halsey Brothers Department Store was built upon that principle, and I would later build my own entertainment business around it.

When I was 10 years old, I started selling on my own. After answering an ad on the back of a comic book, I set out to sell flower seeds door to door, first covering the immediate neighborhood and then branching out over town. By instinct, I made a presentation and politely asked for the sale, and I was very successful. My success wouldn't be measured in money, but in the prize I could claim based on the number of seed packets I sold.

I remember to this day the excitement that welled up in me as I finally achieved enough sales to get the item I wanted most . . . a telescope! It looked fantastic in the beautiful catalog the company had sent with the seeds. For the first time in my young life, I joyfully anticipated a big reward for doing something fun—selling. It sure beat all of the sweat and toil of mowing lawns. Intensely, I anticipated the arrival of the telescope, my big payoff for selling umpteen packages of flower seeds.

The package finally arrived. It was so small. How could it contain a telescope that looked from the catalog picture as though it might take up my whole backyard?

To this day, I have never been as disappointed as when I opened that package and saw the two cardboard tubes, one inside the other, with window glass at either end. This was not a telescope! The boy pictured in the catalog could hardly hold it, it was so big. I had been taken. It was a fraud! I was mad! Having worked every day after school and on Saturdays for a month to sell enough seeds for my prize, I didn't know what to do.

Actually, there was nothing I *could* do. My dad explained to me how certain unscrupulous people in business take advantage of their customers by cheating them, not giving them what they think they've bought and charging an unfair price for what they *do* get. It was not the way the Halsey Brothers Department Store operated. There, everyone worked hard to please customers, finding good merchandise and giving value at a fair price. By doing this, the Halsey Brothers assured that their clientele would continue to be not only customers, but satisfied customers! That sense of honesty and ethics is what kept the store open and fed our family for three generations.

My father taught me to accept my disappointment about the telescope, and to use it as a lesson. With a positive attitude, I accepted it, learned from it, and grew from it. It had taught me that I not only could sell, but that I enjoyed it. It also taught my 10-year-old self to go for cash next time, not prizes.

So, I found the perfect item and set out again. This time, I was selling a metal pot scrubber called Dolly Dozit, a small tool full of metal strips coiled tighter than Little Orphan Annie's hair. After some experimentation in the Halsey kitchen, I knew they worked, so I ventured out confidently, offering them to prospective customers for 10 cents each—and knowing that I would make a penny on each sale. If I sold a hundred, I told myself, I would make a dollar, and that was better than mowing lawns. After all, a dollar would buy 20 movie admissions at the local theater, or 20 nickel ice cream sodas at the Garden, a combination soda shop and beer joint. And I knew I could make a lot more than a dollar!

The term "marketing" had yet to be invented, so I didn't know anything about that, but I did know about selling and satisfying customers. My dad's sales events had taught me that it was better to offer a more attractive price if the customer bought two of something rather than just one. I applied that to my Dolly Dozits campaign. After taking part of a Saturday to mark off streets and blocks within the streets, and then to check the list I had kept of all my flower-seed customers, I was off. Filled with enthusiasm and eager to sell door-to-door in my hometown, I offered my potential customers a deal: one Dolly Dozit, the best pot-scrubber ever made and unavailable in any local store, for 10 cents—or, as a special incentive, two for a quarter.

I couldn't sell them fast enough. Everybody bought two. I don't remember exactly how many I sold that day, but it was at least two or three hundred. I sold out and made it home before dark, flushed with success.

Now comes the big lesson in ethics.

You've probably already figured it out. The price shouldn't have been two for a quarter, because that made the individual price 12 1/2 cents, not 10 cents. I had been more interested in finding a catchy sales price than doing my math, and I had failed to add things up properly.

It hit me that I had charged nearly every customer extra for buying two of something instead of one. With each transaction, I had unintentionally cheated each customer out of five cents. I felt terrible. I felt like an idiot. I was embarrassed.

Worrying all night, I realized some folks might think I had cheated them intentionally. That was hardly something that made for satisfied customers. If I were to continue selling Dolly Dozits—or anything else— I was going to have to rely on the same customers for repeat business. What was to be done? Somehow I had to rectify my mistake.

Deciding to retrace my steps, I explained to each customer that I had inadvertently made a mistake in my arithmetic, and that I would refund five cents for every two Dolly Dozits he or she had purchased. But an interesting thing happened. Because of my mistake, I inadvertently learned the concept of "up sale." Up sale is a term used a lot by the makers of today's infomercials, who try to get their call-in customers to buy another, higher-priced item than the one being advertised. What happened was that I hit upon the idea of offering a third Dolly Dozit to those customers who had already bought two.

First I apologized, telling them of my mistake and advising them they were entitled to a five-cent refund. Then I told them they could add another five cents instead, and receive another Dolly Dozit. Believe it or not, *everyone* brought out another nickel. They increased the number of Dolly Dozits in their house by one; I increased my gross revenues by 20%.

This lesson in honesty and ethics was a good one. It encompassed lessons about offering good products for good value and the then-unknown idea of up sale.

Years later, when I got into the business of promoting shows and managing and booking artists, the principle of the satisfied customer kept my company in business for a long time.

Remember, then, that *ethics are the cornerstone of any sale*. As a 10-year-old, I didn't understand that principle—at least in those terms—but I put it into practice as I began to develop my own **Power of Performance**.

PART TWO

FINDING YOUR PLACE ON THE TEAM

The Power of Teams

As I told you in Chapter 4, I learned very early that the music business is in fact many businesses, all working together. And, like any other good team, a music-business team working harmoniously provides a power far greater than any of its individual parts. Here are five important things that a team can provide:

1. A group of specialists working together as one.

2. A collective exchange of ideas.

3. Enhanced and expanded performance.

4. Extended support and multiple skills.

5. Collective problem-solving.

Building any kind of business always requires planning; it involves many other elements besides yourself. The success of my career as a talent manager, booking agent, and impresario has not been my success alone. It has been the result of careful planning and the assembling of other specialists into a team.

The "team method," with related specialists and businesses working together, is a major part of my formula for success. Even within our own company, The Jim Halsey Company, we had internal teams. You must understand this team-method principle and know that it's important for the team members to function to the best of their ability, each utilizing his or her own **Power of Performance.**

Now, let's talk about the basic members of any music-business team. There are nine essential team elements necessary to begin building an artist's career. We'll call these nine the Star Team. No matter what style of music you're doing, the Star Team will determine the level of your success.

Envision an old-time wagon wheel, with the spokes extending from the center out to the rim. The center of the wheel, the hub that supports all the spokes—or team members—is *talent*. Talent is the primary member of the team, the No. 1 component. All the spokes extend from the center, because without talent we wouldn't have a music business.

Here, then, are the nine essential members of the Star Team:

1. *TALENT*
2. *Artist manager*
3. *Record company*
4. *Record producer*
5. *Booking agent*
6. *Music / entertainment attorney*
7. *Music publisher*
8. *Press and public relations person*
9. *Promoter*

These are the essential members of any music-business team. As an artist's career grows, other important components get plugged into the extended team, such as radio, television, video, performing-rights organizations, touring companies, road managers, crew, set designers, arrangers, musicians, and sound and light technicians. These are *extended* team members that come along later.

Miraculous performance can be expected and unbelievable energy can be harnessed when every team member is performing together in sync. Understand the Star Team method, and you are on your way to success. Now all that remains is for you to decide which part of the team *you* want to be!

8

The Talent

How do you become a star in the music business? It's simple. Since this business starts with a song, all you have to do is write a hit song, sing a hit song, and get discovered!

The Jim Halsey Company represented many great talents, including The Oak Ridge Boys, Roy Clark, Tammy Wynette, Hank Thompson, Clint Black, The Judds, James Brown, Leon Russell, Ronnie Milsap, Woody Herman, Roy Orbison, Pam and Mel Tillis, Reba McEntire, Dwight Yoakam, the Kentucky Headhunters, Waylon Jennings, and Merle Haggard. All of these star acts had one thing in common: They were exceptional songwriters. In today's music business, most of the artists who break out of the pack are the ones who can create their own material.

That's what the record companies are looking for, even if much of a star's recorded material ends up being written by someone else. Check out any of the *Billboard* magazine charts and look who's on top. It's people like Garth Brooks, Tim McGraw, Steve Wariner, Michael W. Smith, Bruce Springsteen, Mariah Carey, Phil Collins, and Dwight Yoakam—acts who are great songwriters as well as great singers.

A hit song is one that becomes popular with great masses of people. Maybe it's the melody, the lyric, the subject matter, or a combination of all three, but somehow it strikes a chord within the public that resonates for a good long time, translating into sales and stardom for its creator.

What makes a hit song? One thing is for sure: Every hit has a hook, a memorable phrase, word, or melodic line that immediately identifies the song. Good songwriters—and good singers—know about the hook and how to use it.

Let's take the late Tammy Wynette, one of my favorite clients. There is no doubt that her songs were written and delivered so you would remember both the hook and her. Who doesn't know the hook of her signature song, "Stand By Your Man," which she and her producer Billy Sherrill wrote in a few minutes to finish out a recording session? Think of that phrase, that hook, and you'll hear Tammy's soaring vocal in your mind, a perfect blend of words and melody.

And talk about a hook! How about The Oak Ridge Boys multi-platinum seller "Elvira," with Richard Sterban's resonant "oom papa, oom papa, oom papa mau mau" bass line? After managing The Oak Ridge Boys for more than 25 years, watching hundreds of their shows, and listening to hour after hour of their albums, I *still* enjoy hearing them do that song—as well as their other great hits.

Another of my clients was James Brown, "The Godfather of Soul," who crossed all barriers with "It's a Man's World," "Please, Please, Please," "Papa's Got a Brand New Bag" and many more huge hits. His unique material, distinctive style, unusual arrangements, and great performances have earned him another well-deserved nickname, "The Hardest-Working Man in Show Business." I have never worked with anybody who had more focus than James Brown. He knew exactly where he wanted to go, and he had a plan for getting there. I learned a lot from him; he is an inspiration to me still.

Leon Russell's distinctive style, both vocally and instrumentally, has made him one of the great singer-songwriters of all time. He's had several hits with his own material and hundreds of other artists around the world have also recorded his compositions. A unique pianist, composer, singer, song craftsman, and showman, Leon combined his skills to create such evergreens as "Masquerade," a song that will be around forever. We were pleased to represent him.

It was my great honor to be the agent for a man I consider truly the master of singing writing and performing: Roy Orbison. Roy's great genius was in his ability to put an enchanting melody with a haunting and beautiful lyric, as he did in "Only the Lonely," "Blue Bayou," "Crying," and many others. Because he presented his masterpieces in such a unique vocal style, his records were instantly recognizable. To me, Orbison was the perfect example of a songwriter-singer whose talents work together to make both a hit song and a star.

One of the greatest artists of all time was Woody Herman. Best known as a bandleader, he also was a composer—his best-known composition, "Woodchopper's Ball," is still around today. Instrumentally, this piece has a great hook—no words, but a memorable rhythmic melody that people found easy to hum or whistle.

Another of Woody's trademark hooks was a driving, crescendo-building arrangement, bringing a musical piece to a climax that would leave the audience exhausted, only to be lifted to even greater heights by the next number. His sound was unique, with five trumpets, arrangements built around three tenor saxophones, a baritone sax and, of course, the famous Herman rhythm. A lot of Woody's style wasn't based so much on his own clarinet or alto sax solos, or his singing, but his personification of the teamwork and discipline within the whole band, working like a well-oiled machine. Woody Herman inspired respect from his players, but he also forged a discipline that pushed them to play beyond the limits of any band I've ever heard. As a leader, he produced results greater than anyone else could have. That whole band was fed by Woody's driving energy.

There's a lesson here. Like Woody Herman, always strive to be better. Always push beyond your limits.

Another of our clients, and a favorite one, was Merle Haggard. He is a good one for budding songwriters to study—and you'll notice I say "study," not "copy." Study the best, but be your own person, your own talent, even as you learn from the masters. Merle Haggard is one of these masters. He knows about hooks, and he also knows about song structure and composition. His songs about the working man are brilliant, to the point, and every hook is in place. Think of lyrical hooks like "Now I've got swingin' doors/A jukebox/And a barstool," "I turned 21 in prison/Doin' life without parole," or even "I'm proud to be an Okie from Muskogee/A place where even squares can have a ball." Add to that a distinctive vocal style that can always be recognized in the first few bars of anything he sings, and you'll see that Merle Haggard is one of the world's great song stylists.

All of these artists are not only good songwriters, but great performers as well. Each used his or her personal **Power of Performance** as a key to achieving success.

What can we learn from them?

For one thing, to succeed as a singer-songwriter, you need to come up with great hooks, both lyrically and musically. As a beginning songwriter, make your own examination of different styles, different stylists and songwriters. Use analysis, listen to the words, the music, the structure, and the vocal interpretation. Find the hooks. Don't copy. By listening to others, you can learn how to improve your own style.

Also, learn to use your own gifts. Many songwriters are inspired and creatively blessed. It's important to learn your craft so you can most effectively use what gifts you have. A great songwriter must be inspired, but anyone can learn to be a good songwriter. In fact, I have a theory that everybody is a songwriter, because all people have a song in their hearts.

There is a difference, however, between being simply a songwriter and being a good, professional songwriter. Just as someone who dashes off a poem one day isn't a professional poet, someone who writes a song or two isn't really a songwriter. As is the case with any other craft, becoming a professional takes commitment and work.

How can you become a good songwriter? First of all, find out all you can about the craft of songwriting. Some colleges and universities offer songwriting courses as part of their community-outreach or continuing education programs. Almost every large city has a songwriters' group that meets regularly, with members offering information, critiques, and support to one another. Nashville, for instance, has the Nashville Songwriters Association International, which you can check out on the Internet at www.songs.org/nsai. These groups, as well as the college classes, are also excellent places to find collaborators, people who bring in fresh perspective and synergistic energy to your efforts.

If neither of these options are available in your area, investigate some of the many books available on the subject. *Billboard* magazine, the leading weekly music publication, has a big book division, with many songwriting titles available. Check your local bookstore for *Billboard* book titles like *This Business of Music* and Mollyanne Lincoln's *How to Make a Good Song a Hit Song*. The Cincinnati-based Writers Digest Books offer several good, informative books on songwriting, too, with their *Songwriters Market* leading the way. Updated annually, *Songwriters Market* gives you a complete how-to and where-to market your songs. Writers Digest also publishes what I think is one of the best: *The Craft and Business of Songwriting* by John Braheney. Be sure to seek out and read *Everything you Always Wanted to Know About Songwriting* (Showdown Enterprises), written by the late country music star and songwriter, Cliffie Stone.

A big part of becoming a songwriter is self-taught, so it's essential to absorb all the information you can. If you happen to live in or near a city that has a lot of music activities, it will be a lot easier. You'll have activities available for songwriters, as well as regular meetings where your own songs can be played and critiqued. Some cities have clubs that feature an open-mike night for singer-songwriters. You may get the opportunity to attend seminars and workshops on writing sponsored by local organizations. Music stores and churches are also good places to find songwriting colleagues.

The more you study, the more you observe, and the more you write, the better you will become. Get all the information and help you can. If contemporary music is your interest, know what's being played on the radio in your musical genre. Keep up with music by reading *Billboard* magazine; it covers all areas of music on a weekly basis, from rock to classical. The more you understand the music business, the better equipped you'll be to proceed with your business of songwriting. Take advantage of whatever is available. When it comes to writing and performing your songs, there's no such thing as too much information.

Then, once you get your songs written and you're confident about them, what do you do? After you get past the local options of peer critique and public performance, where can you go next? Who will listen? How will you be discovered?

First, you must get someone to listen who can do something for you. And the way to begin this process is to put your songs on a demonstration tape, commonly referred to as a "demo." Your demo will be your calling card, the first way the music business will know of you and your work. It is the first and best way to be discovered.

Unfortunately, badly produced or poorly presented demos can drastically reduce your chances. While music-industry people don't have time to listen to every demo that comes across their desks, they don't want to miss out on finding someone with real talent. One of the ways they can simplify the demo-listening process is by giving only cursory attention—or no attention at all—to unprofessional demos.

How, then, can you create a demo that appeals to the eyes and ears of someone who can help you? Here are nine important tips:

1. Your demo must be on a quality cassette. You would not believe the number of demos I've received over the years that were on cassette tapes with bleed-through, distortion, break-up, or were just plain worn out by the time the music was laid onto it. Let's get real! If you're trying to sell an automobile, would you show it to a prospective buyer when it was covered with dirt, or had a flat tire? Of course not! You would have it in the best possible condition.

2. Do not put more than three songs on a cassette. Because of limited time, a music publisher or other industry figure will be more likely to listen to three songs than a whole string of them. If your songs show promise, believe me, your listener will ask for more.

3. Have lyrics typed out for easy reading. This is very important. I have received cassettes that have no lyric sheets included; if your lyrics can't be understood, the person you're trying to impress can become rapidly disinterested. I have also had lyric sheets sent to me that were totally unreadable because they were marked on and through. Make them neat and professional looking!

4. *Put your best song in the first position on the tape.* I've had people disagree with me about this. Some have said that putting your best song last builds more interest. The problem is that you can't be sure your listener will hear all three songs! I speak from experience. If you do not put your best song first, the listening party may not even get to the second or third song. You must command interest right away.

5. *Put your hook in the first thirty seconds of your song.* Use that hook, that memorable part of the lyric or melody, to put your song in the listener's mind forever.

6. *Have someone competent sing your song.* If you are not a good singer, find someone who is. A poorly performed song will turn a listener off and take attention away from lyrics and melody. This is simply human nature.

7. *Type your name, address, and telephone number on both cassette and cassette package.* This way, your demo will not get lost in the shuffle. Many times, producers and publishers have desks covered with cassettes. They are not always careful about putting each tape back into its package. You do not want them to discover you and then not be able to find out who you are.

8. *Always get permission to send your tape.* Make the necessary phone calls, write a letter, or go to the offices in person to ask for that permission. Do not send the tape until you get the green light.

9. *Be prepared for rejection.* As a songwriter, you must prepare to be the recipient of much rejection in your professional life. People, for one reason or another, may not like your masterpiece. Maybe it's just not for them, their companies, or the artists they represent. Do not despair. A lot of songs have gone around, getting turned down by everybody—and then suddenly, someone has heard something in it, and a song that was a big loser has been recorded and become a giant hit. Remember not to take rejection personally. People are rejecting the content of a song—they are not rejecting you. It is part of the growing process in the business to get rejection and then move on.

Over the years, I have heard thousands of demos. There was a time when I tried to listen to them all, but it finally became impossible. There was just too much material and too little time. I always felt badly about sending these songs back to the writer unopened, knowing I was driving a coffin nail into their dreams and hopes. There had to be a solution.

That solution came during lunch a few years ago with my close friend, the late Lee Zhito of *Billboard* magazine. Our conversation that day laid the groundwork for the Billboard Song Contest, a way for any amateur songwriter to be heard by music-industry professionals. The Billboard Song Contest accepts original songs in seven categories of music—pop, rock, country, gospel, Latin, jazz, and R&B—and uses music figures as judges at every level of competition, offering substantial prizes to those songs deemed the best in their categories.

It is getting tougher and tougher to get publishers, artists, and record companies to listen to new material. It can be done, however, and those who stick with it and do not get discouraged will eventually get through to the right people. If you are really serious about your songs, and you're not getting any response to your written requests, take your vacation time and travel to the leading recording centers: Nashville, New York, Austin, Seattle, Toronto, Vancouver, and Los Angeles. Try making personal appeals at the various offices of the music publishers, record companies, and artists. Try to get your foot in the door long enough to get a meeting. Find out what's happening in the music business community in those cities. Become involved. Search out the songwriting organizations and the open-mike nights. Check with the offices of the performing-rights organizations—BMI, ASCAP, SESAC—about their artist-development programs. Maybe two weeks of vacation is not long enough to do all of this, but it's enough for you to begin to find out for yourself how the system works. Learn all you can in the time you have.

When you become an established songwriter, it doesn't matter where you live. But when you're getting started, it's tough to do it long-distance, which is why many dedicated songwriters move to Nashville, New York, L.A., or another music city. They want to be in the middle of it all, meeting people and networking.

Incidentally, the more songs you write, the better songwriter you will become. When aspiring songwriters tell me they've written two or three songs, I know the likelihood of any of these tunes being good is pretty slim. But if they tell me they have written 25 or 30 songs, I figure they probably have one or two good ones in the bunch.

Songwriting is a craft that can be developed with work, discipline, and time. If you are serious about being a songwriter, you need to write something every day. It doesn't have to be a complete song. Daily, you can develop ideas, work on melody and lyrics. If you make the commitment and apply the discipline to work a certain amount of time every day on your music, you will be surprised at how much you'll get done and how much easier inspiration will come.

I'm sure you've heard the stories about Willie Nelson writing a hit song on the back of an envelope, sitting in a taxi on his way to the airport. Those moments of inspiration happen to all gifted songwriters. They have done their homework. They have already learned their craft, the basics of songwriting. They have achieved a certain discipline, so that when that lightning bolt of inspiration hits them, they are well-equipped to turn it into a hit song. This is where the art and the craft of songwriting meet. It's another example of the **Power of Performance.**

As a songwriter, you must accept the fact that selling is part of your business too. The more songs you offer and the more people you offer them to, the better your chances of getting them accepted. Just be prepared for the rejection we talked about and overcome it by making more calls. We've said before that self-confidence is an important part of your **Power of Performance**, and no other professional in the world has a bigger need for self-confidence than a songwriter. You must believe in your own work before anyone else will. You gain self-confidence by doing what you do best, over and over, and becoming completely at ease with your skills. Even when you do get a "no," a rejection, you can get past it by knowing it has nothing to do with your ability.

This, of course, doesn't just apply to songwriters. It applies to any talented person who strives for stardom. Being a star is an art. Recognize that it is also a business. The more you understand the business aspects, such as knowing who the players are and how everything functions together, the more you know how to deal with rejection and the more successful you'll be.

I'm not suggesting that an artist should handle his or her own business affairs—that would be counterproductive. The artist's energy should be focused totally on the stage and the studio, with managers, agents, and attorneys handling the business. What I *am* saying is that artists must know enough about the business to recognize whether their associates are doing the right kind of job.

An artist, like any other businessperson, must be honest and honorable. It is the artist who signs the contract with the promoter, the booking agency, the record company, the music publisher, and the artist manager. Some artists do not honor their work or their commitments. Their signature on a contract means nothing. These people may be few and far between, but they are often the ones you read about. Just as the **Power of Performance** lasts a long time after the artist has left the stage, so will an honorable reputation last a lifetime, long after the stardom and hit records are over.

Talent is not enough to make a star. You must go farther. In classroom discussions, many of my students have said that an artist's honesty and sincerity are more important than talent. Credibility ranks high. Charisma and stage presence are essential. To be viable artists, performers must be able to project their music and themselves. They must be able to connect and to have rapport with the audience.

For the performer/songwriter in today's market, individual style is important. Each must master his or her own technique and strive for quality of performance. This takes confidence, which comes with practice and dedication. An artist must have a willingness to learn, a love of music and entertainment, and an ability to handle rejection. An artist must recognize the importance of being a team member. There are many more things involved than talent.

An artist must be able to *deliver*. An artist must be *unique*, with that something special that sets him or her apart from all the others and makes him or her unforgettable. There is already a Reba McEntire, a Clint Black, a Shania Twain, an Oak Ridge Boys. Do not try to sound or look like one of them, or any other popular performer. Develop your own style, your own brand of uniqueness, because that's what will work for you.

All of the good players are not from Los Angeles, New York, or Nashville. They don't all live in big cities. Stars can come from anywhere, but they must be discovered.

Here are two stories, both offering important lessons about talent, discovery, and stardom.

♪ ♪ ♪ ♪

All of us in the entertainment business have, at one time or another, claimed to "discover" a talent. In reality, however, the discovery is almost always a team effort, the combined result of people working together.

Here's an example. In the early '70s, The Jim Halsey Company packaged and promoted shows for the Howard Hughes-owned hotels in Las Vegas. Our big hit at one of those hotels, the Landmark, was a continuously running revue called "Country Music USA." This revue usually played to full houses, changing headliners every two or three weeks. Since we used our own talent in the show, we were able to rotate new acts in as we added them to the Halsey Company roster.

The contract with Hughes was an important one. It brought cash flow to our company and to the artists who played the hotels. It allowed us to keep our stars steadily employed for long periods in one place, which saved them travel time, road expenses, and wear and tear on their touring vehicles. It also gave them more time for rehearsal.

There were other pluses. Because our acts were playing hotels, rooms and food were included in the contract, which cut their costs. And because they were in high-visibility Las Vegas venues, we could get higher prices for their other appearances. And because Vegas was so close to Los Angeles, we were able to bring big-time entertainment buyers in to see our artists perform under very favorable circumstances.

During one of our successful Vegas runs, I got a call from my close friend, Jim Foglesong, the president of Dot Records. Jim had just "discovered" and signed a new artist, who had first been "discovered" by a record producer in Houston named Huey P. Meaux. Meaux's own label, in fact, had released a regional hit by the artist.

"I think you'll like this artist," Jim told me. "We've just released his record on Dot, and I'm sure it's going to go to No. 1 in two or three weeks."

I told him he had contacted me at just the right time. I had an opening in "Country Music USA" for a headliner. "But," I asked him, "who's ever heard of this guy, Freddy Fender, and this song of his, `Before the Next Teardrop Falls'?"

"They'll hear of him," Jim returned. "Believe me, they will. This record is on radio stations all over the country as we're talking. Next week, it will be in heavy rotation on every radio station in America."

I told him that I'd never put anybody into a show that I hadn't seen, and I'd never signed an act for my agency who had not turned me on with his talent and a knockout performance.

"Well," Jim said, "time is of the essence."

So I took a chance. I told Jim okay. I would put Freddy Fender into an already-running hit show, and I would do it as soon as he arrived. I explained to Walter Kane, Howard Hughes' entertainment director and my friend, that I had not seen Freddy Fender, but that he came with the strongest of recommendations from Mr. Foglesong. Walter, being the impresario that he was, agreed to take a chance.

The next day during rehearsals, I asked Leo Zabelin to go to the airport and pick up our new "headliner." Not long afterwards, I had a call. It was Leo, phoning from the airport.

"You won't believe this," he said, "but all this guy has is his guitar and the shirt on his back! You're going to headline him *tonight*?"

I said, "Look, Leo. Take him into town and get him whatever he needs. Tonight, we're going to make Mr. Fender a star!"

While Leo and Freddy were in town, we changed the Landmark's marquee, spelling out F-R-E-D-D-Y F-E-N-D-E-R in letters 12 feet high. That night, with very little rehearsal, Freddy went on and displayed amazing charisma, establishing immediate rapport with the audience. He captivated them. He was a natural talent who knew how to access his **Power of Performance**.

Freddy Fender came off that stage a star. By the time his Landmark engagement closed, there were lines around the block to see him. We represented Freddy for the next dozen years, and he grew to be one of country music's biggest acts, cutting lots of hit records and playing major venues all over the world. Freddy Fender had been "discovered" by Jim Halsey . . . and Jim Foglesong . . . and Walter Kane . . . and Huey Meaux . . . and the audiences who came to see "Country Music USA" at the Landmark. His discovery had been a collective one, shared by many.

As Freddy's story shows, timing is important in this business. When Jim Foglesong called about Freddy, I just happened to have a show going with a spot that Jim's new artist could fill.

Equally as important as timing is desire. In fact, desire has to outweigh all other interests for someone to succeed. It's easy to lose your **Power of Performance** to other priorities and obligations.

I have a friend in my hometown named Jerry Webb. The Webb family has had a funeral home in Independence for several generations, and Jerry is a dedicated mortician. However, he's always had a flair for show business. A natural comedian, he's in constant demand in southeast Kansas, with all kinds of groups and organizations after him to be master of ceremonies for their events. Jerry has both the talent and the timing it takes to do comedy right—even with borrowed material, he's as funny as any big-name comedian.

Thirty years ago, the Buena Vista Club in Safford, Arizona, ran two shows a night, six nights a week. All of my artists played there at one time or another, and Earl Perrin, the owner, paid well. Plus, anytime I got stuck for a date for Roy Clark, Wanda Jackson, Mary Taylor, or Hank Thompson, Earl could always be counted on for a short-notice booking.

Then one day Earl called me. He'd booked a standup comedian for a two-week run, and the guy had suddenly canceled. Who did I have who could come in and take the date?

I told him about my friend, the undertaker, and Earl agreed to try him. He made Jerry his first real show-business offer to play for two weeks in Safford—good pay, accommodations and food, as well as billing on the club's marquee. Webb thought about it for a long time. Finally, though, he declined.

Three decades later, during a telephone conversation, I asked him why he hadn't seized that opportunity.

"It's funny," he said with a laugh. "I was just telling them at the coffee shop this morning that I should've taken that job. But I'd never heard of the place, and I would've had to leave my ambulance business for two weeks, so I decided I'd better stick around."

Who knows? Maybe Jerry would have been discovered in Safford, Arizona, by some big network television producer or an important talent scout. If he'd taken the job, he might be hosting a late-night television show or headlining in Las Vegas today.

(Although Jerry remained in Independence and didn't pursue a national career as a performer, he was instrumental in getting a couple of excellent celebrity golf tournaments into the town. Held in 1980 and 1981 and patterned after the Roy Clark Celebrity Golf Tournaments we were doing in Tulsa, the Independence tournaments attracted such high-caliber stars as Ernest Borgnine, David Huddleston, Fred MacMurray, and Roy—who, like me, remains friends with Jerry Webb.)

♪ ♪ ♪ ♪

I tell these two stories to illustrate an important point: *you have to be able to recognize opportunity when it knocks.* Maybe it will knock while you're playing a club. Maybe it will knock when someone in the industry hears your demo tape. Maybe, if you can finagle an audition before someone who can help your career, it will knock then. Several years ago, I was in my office in Nashville when two young ladies came in. They told our office staff that they were singer-songwriters, they wanted to get into the music business, and they were looking for an agent. Our staff advised them to submit a demo for consideration.

"What's a demo?" one of them asked.

Someone in our office explained that "demo" was music-biz lingo for a demonstration tape, adding, "You put your songs on a demonstration tape, and we'll listen to them."

Well, they didn't need that, they said. They had their guitars in the car. And before we knew it, they'd retrieved their instruments and were giving us an impromptu concert right there in the office.

It didn't take us long to realize that both their songs and their singing were very good. And once we found out they were mother and daughter, we felt that they had something unique to offer the country music market.

They were, of course, Naomi and Wynonna, The Judds, and they had been making the Music City rounds, knocking on the doors of managers, booking agents, record companies, music publishers—anyone who might help them break into the business.

They found their managers, Ken Stilts and Woody Bowles, the same way they found us, via a live audition. The managers got them their record company deal. After their audition for the Halsey Company, we began booking them all over the country. It was, like all music-business success stories, a team effort.

Remember Chapter 4, and the ten keys to the **Power of Performance**? The Judds walked into our office holding all those keys. Their attitude was geared for success. They had the enthusiasm and the desire. Through their persistence, they had made themselves known within the music community in Nashville. Certainly, they had self-confidence; it radiated from them. They also had the dedication to their music. They had talent—loads of it! They had personality for sure, along with enough training to get them started in the big time.

♪ ♪ ♪ ♪

Another of our soon-to-be big stars started in a different way. He was a Las Vegas lounge performer, brought to my attention by Larry McFaden.

Larry was a musician in Mel Tillis' band, the Statesiders. I had Mel headlining at the Frontier Hotel in Las Vegas, and Larry kept telling me about an entertainer who was appearing in the lounge at the Tropicana Hotel. Sure I would be interested, Larry persisted in trying to get me to see this act. Frankly, I was lukewarm, feeling that anyone who had been working in a Vegas lounge for a long time had already had his opportunities and, for whatever reason, stardom had passed him by.

Was I ever wrong. As it turned out, this lounge artist had all of the attributes necessary to make it. He was a great singer and entertainer just waiting to happen nationally. We became his agent, Larry McFaden became his manager, and that's how Lee Greenwood became a star.

Lee's success story reinforces that big secret to success: *you have to be seen and heard by someone who can help you*. As a Vegas lounge act, Lee had been seen and heard by thousands. Finally, one person—Larry McFaden—saw him and believed in him as much as Lee believed in himself. Larry brought Lee to the attention of The Jim Halsey Company, and the team that would launch Lee's stellar career began to come together.

♪ ♪ ♪ ♪

There's another way to try to get the attention of the music industry. It's called *showcasing*, and it's one very practical way of introducing your talent to a large number of potential team members.

How do you showcase? It's simple. You rent a venue and invite prospective managers, booking agents, record-company representatives, music publishers, and press people. Once you get them there, you try to impress them all with a dynamite show, so that at least some will express an interest in helping you get your career off the ground by offering you management, booking, or a potential record deal.

There are a number of music conferences across the country that also offer opportunity to be discovered. These events offer lectures, seminars, and workshops along with showcases designed to present bands and performers to conference attendees. Because the showcasing acts perform before an audience of industry professionals, a lot of deals get made at these conferences.

I have been a guest speaker at many, including South by Southwest in Austin, Texas; the New Music West Conference in Vancouver, British Columbia; and the Mississippi River Festival in St. Louis, Missouri. Other good ones include the Canadian Music Week in Toronto, Canada; North by Northeast in Toronto, Canada; and North by Northwest in Portland, Oregon; and MIDEM in Cannes, France.

Training and education, you'll remember, make up one of my keys to the **Power of Performance**, and attending conferences is one vital way of achieving this key. At least part of your success in the music and entertainment business will come from the people you know within the business. So you should always make it a point to meet as many people as you can, not just those on the business side, but other songwriters and musicians as well. If you're attending a conference or other industry function, be prepared! Have a good-quality demo tape, some professional pictures of yourself, a biographical sheet, etc. Certainly have an adequate supply of business cards.

Remember also that getting a manager or a record deal is only the beginning. You still must have a team to get to the top.

When The Kentucky Headhunters made their first record deal, with Harold Shedd at Polygram, they already had their manager, Mitchell Fox, on board. Before their first record hit the shelves, The HeadHunters did a showcase at a Nashville club, sponsored by Polygram, in an effort to find a booking agency and other team members for the band. One of my associates, Terry Cline, had already seen the band and was singing its praises to the rest of our company. When the Polygram showcase happened, our agency turned out en masse, as did the other agencies in Nashville. I was knocked out by The HeadHunters' music, but as much as anything else I liked their aura, their collective personality. I liked each one of them individually as well. Making a deal to represent them as their booking agency, we became another member of the team.

We've talked about cutting demos, playing places where people can see you, attending music conferences, and showcasing your talents. What are some other ways a beginning act can be seen or heard?

In the past several years, a lot of corporate entities—from beer and cigarette companies to hardware stores and sausage manufacturers—have begun sponsoring national talent searches, usually co-sponsored by local radio stations. Audition for these shows. Try to get into the contests. These have led to the discovery of several artists and lots of record deals.

Try in every way to build your act locally or regionally and try to enlist the help of the local media. Many times, a hometown radio personality or newspaper writer can bring you to the attention of record companies, managers, or agents.

Above all, be persistent. Getting discovered is not easy, but it is done every day. Remember, too, that when you hear about some new "overnight sensation" being discovered, it's likely to be an act that's been trying for years to break out of a limited scene into national prominence.

The Oak Ridge Boys and I discovered each other back in 1974 at a Nashville showcase put on by CBS Records. I forget what act I had gone to see. All I remember was that my attention was captured, and I was thoroughly entertained that night by a terrific gospel group, The Oak Ridge Boys. What a show! They had energy, excitement, beautiful harmonizing, good looks, lots of movement on stage—everything they needed for superstardom.

The Oak Ridge Boys were in gospel music, which was, at that time, enjoyed by a limited and very specific audience. And even though I love gospel music, I saw their potential to go past that niche audience into country, country-pop, or pop, where they could reach many, many more people.

Going backstage after the performance, I introduced myself to the four Oaks—Duane Allen, Joe Bonsall, Richard Sterban, and William Lee Golden—explained my excitement for their broader potential, and gave them my card. I came away not only deeply impressed with the excitement they created on stage, but by their enthusiasm for the business and their desire for success. They had dedication and commitment. They knew about the **Power of Performance.** They had everything but a manager and a good team working for them. I wanted to be that manager and to help them put together their own star team.

It took them awhile to make their decision. Trying to expand their audience base would mean jeopardizing their position as the No. 1 gospel group in America. They liked country music but were not exactly sure if country fans would accept them.

We decided to work together on a trial basis, and I hired them to open shows with Mel Tillis and Roy Clark, two of my biggest stars. The first date was in Buster Bonif's Theater in Warwick, Rhode Island, opening for Mel. Opening night, I made the date, anxious to see the audiences' reaction and wanting to make sure that Mel, a very important client to us, was satisfied.

I wasn't the only one blown away by The Oak Ridge Boys' opening set. That night, they received standing ovations for their show!

I remember so vividly talking with the four guys after the show that night. Standing out in the theater's parking lot, I reassured them they could entertain any audience, anywhere. I wanted to be their manager. I wanted to start building their team. I gave them an old music-biz axiom: they were only three minutes away from being superstars. That three minutes, of course, represents the playing time of a hit record.

The Oak Ridge Boys saw an opportunity. They recognized it. They went for it. They got it. Our collective **Power of Performance** would create one of the biggest country music success stories ever—and we haven't yet written its final chapter.

First, I had to let the world outside of gospel music know how great The Oak Ridge Boys were. I worked to get them in front of buyers for fairs, rodeos and special events. And I wanted the buyers for the Las Vegas showrooms to see them, too. I thought The Oak Ridge Boys could be very successful playing Vegas.

At the time, my company's three big headliners were Roy Clark, Mel Tillis, and Hank Thompson. All three agreed to use The Oak Ridge Boys to open their shows, and our relationships with other stars enabled us to put The Oak Ridge Boys in front of many other acts as well. In the risky transition from gospel to country, I needed to cover a lot of territory in the shortest amount of time possible. I had to make sure that people, including the loyal gospel fans, understood the group's new focus and where we were going with it. We needed to be on sure footing without much down time.

The Jim Halsey Company made the commitment to The Oak Ridge Boys, and that meant we would make it work! We were sure we could. But, truth to tell, we were just a little nervous, too.

As all of this was happening, I was producing the "Country Music USA" shows for Howard Hughes' Landmark Hotel, which you'll remember from the Freddy Fender story. At this time, I was constantly in Las Vegas, and Walter Kane—Hughes' entertainment director—and I had become very close friends. You'll recall that we changed the "Country Music USA" headliners every two or three weeks. Walter wasn't always familiar with the headliner names I suggested, but he had learned to trust my judgment.

With that in mind, I made my pitch for The Oak Ridge Boys.

I told Walter I knew they would be great. As an opening act, they had been wowing the country audiences who had come to see Roy Clark and Mel Tillis. And because I always leveled with Walter, I told him The Oak Ridge Boys were a gospel act, making the transition into country, with a repertoire that was 70 percent country and 30 percent gospel. Then I asked Walter if he felt there would be any objections to their doing religious music in a Las Vegas showroom.

His answer to me was very positive. "Our showrooms have Christians in them, too," he said.

I knew that the "Country Music USA" production would be a great place to showcase the talents of The Oak Ridge Boys. Although they were relatively unknown outside the gospel music world, I was able to give them 100% headline billing, good sound and lights, a good audience, and their name 12 feet high on the marquee. I brought in talent buyers, concert promoters, and a lot of television producers and talent coordinators to see this new group of ours. I wanted John Hitt, head of the Halsey Company's fair department, to see them. I also wanted my colleague Dick Howard in the audience. Dick's main responsibility was securing television bookings for our company's artists, but he also was one of my main sources for creative thinking. I knew he would have some good marketing ideas. He did, and both John and Dick became an important part of the team that built The Oak Ridge Boys.

There was another reason I pushed for The Oak Ridge Boys to headline "Country Music USA." I can laugh about it now, but then it was deadly serious. Very simply, I needed that three-week date to meet the payroll—and the hotel rooms and food that came in the package were very important parts of the contract. Believe it or not, things were running that close in the beginning.

Over the next year or so, we were able to make The Oak Ridge Boys into one of the most popular acts in Las Vegas. We finally graduated to the Frontier Hotel, and later made deals for them to appear on a regular basis at Caesar's Palace and The MGM Grand. Over more than a quarter-century, they have continued to be a popular attraction in Las Vegas, working several weeks each year at Bally's (formerly the MGM Grand). I know of no other act in show business that understands the **Power of Performance** better than The Oak Ridge Boys.

♪ ♪ ♪ ♪

You see that being discovered takes many different forms. Once you're discovered, you have to examine, every now and then, your quest for your goals. You must keep asking yourself about your dedication and commitment to those goals. In other words, you must do what The Oak Ridge Boys continually do: keep affirming that you are fully dedicated and fully committed.

You must say to yourself, "I am determined to be a success. I have goals. I have purpose. I know I have access to my own **Power of Performance.** And I know how to deal with rejection and turn it into a positive force." The artists I've represented over the years can say this. I can say this as well.

I always stress how important it is not to give up, because the ones who give up won't make it. It takes a special dedication and unwillingness to throw in the towel to make it big in the music business. A lot of people say they want it, but when it comes down to the hardships, long hours, hard work, and personal and professional rejection, a lot of people fall by the wayside. Eventually you get to a very important crossroads, and it's there that you answer the question, "Do I really want this?"

What I am constantly looking for is the next superstar. And when I ask him or her that question, I want to hear this answer: "Yes, I really want it. No matter what. I *have* to have it!" That's when I'll know that I really have something to work with.

Talent is not enough. You have to *get* the *commitment*! You have to *make* the *commitment*!

The Artist Manager

Talent—whether singer, singer-songwriter, or band—is the essential component, the hub of the music-business wheel. But, you remember, that hub must have spokes radiating from it, spokes that work together to support the center and form the wheel that moves everything forward.

Each of these spokes is a member of the Star Team. And the first spoke, the first team member to join up with the talent, is usually responsible for putting the rest of the group together—for making sure all the spokes are in the wheel, and in the right places. Like a well-built wagonwheel, a good Star Team can be counted on to hold up in any situation. Assembled and functioning correctly, a team shows that there is strength in cooperation and power in unity. Every member of a Star Team has an opportunity—and a responsibility—to tap into his or her individual **Power of Performance**.

Sometimes, the artist signs a recording contract very early in his career, making the *record company* his first team member. Other times, a *booking agent* is the first to "discover" an act. More often than not, however, it's the *artist manager* who becomes the first member of a budding performer's Star Team, the first spoke in the wheel.

The manager is the one who catches the artist's dreams. It is his business to e-x-p-a-n-d on the artist's vision and help discover, access, and perfect the artist's **Power of Performance**. Perhaps most important, the artist manager develops *a plan!* It's true that everything starts with a dream—but nothing will happen without a plan.

Why then, is a manager important?

- *The manager gets the team in motion.*

- *The manager plans the career.*

- *The manager chooses the projects.*

- *The manager helps build the organization.*
- *The manager provides motivation.*

During my first few years as a promoter of concerts and shows, I gradually became more interested in becoming an artist manager. There were a couple of reasons for this. First, I wanted to be able to focus my creative talents on one artist. Second, I wanted to help develop and build a career for that artist and reap the long-term rewards that would come with managing a successful performer.

Artist management is one of the most delicate areas of the entertainment business. By nature, musical artists are sensitive people—it's this sensitivity that helps them create their art. One of the reasons they're great artists is that they feel things deeply. Working as an artist manager, you have to be sensitive to their emotional sides. I think it all boils down to respect, which I talk about throughout this book. If you can respect someone's art and respect the artist as a person, then you can deal with him or her on sensitive issues in a comfortable and friendly manner.

When you look at the big stars appearing on television, hear their records on the radio, read of their gold and platinum record sales and big-figure incomes, you probably wonder how they got where they are. It's really no secret. Most of them started the same way, with talent and desire. Then they found someone who would help them formulate a plan to reach their goals, someone who believed in them, someone who helped them develop their **Power of Performance**. They found, in other words, a good manager.

What do you need to be an artist manager? You need good ears. You need good eyes. You need intuition, and you need the instinct it takes to discover artists with the special quality that puts them above the pack. You need to be able to set goals and develop a plan to achieve them. You need to be a salesperson, marketing expert, business planner, dreamer, psychiatrist, and good friend all wrapped into one. And you need even more. You need to learn the true meaning of two important words: *respect* and *heart*.

Respect is essential in dealing with any creative person. If you don't have real respect for artists and their art, you're not going to be effective in dealing with them. If you don't give respect, you won't get it. If you want respect from both artists and the music industry, you must respect them and it.

You also need to have heart, something that's very important when dealing with sensitive, creative people. Artists, after all, are about heart, and you must understand that if you want to be a good manager. A lot of people can make decisions based on cold, hard facts, but when you are dealing with talent and creativity, you must deal with the aspect of heart. While the best interests of your artist's career are always essential elements in effective management, being sensitive to the needs of the artist's heart should come first. Plus, on a personal level, having heart is going to make your life a lot better, more interesting, more fulfilling, and much more worthwhile

Talent is only one element—albeit an essential one—in creating a star. It must be complemented by many other elements, many of which are the responsibility of the manager. The manager, working with the artist, must set goals with a purpose and determine how those goals can be achieved. The manager must put together the rest of the spokes in the wheel to create the Star Team that will work toward those goals together.

Of course, it helps to be in the right place at the right time and to have a little bit of luck and timing. But knowing how to orchestrate plans and goals will help create the timing and the luck.

Let's get down to nuts and bolts. As an artist manager, just what can you do to create a star?

Again, we start with the essential element: the artist, the hub of the wheel, around whom all the team members revolve. Where can the artist manager find an artist, and where can an artist find the artist manager?

Everywhere!

There are fine singers, songwriters, musicians, and bands all over the world. The key is *finding someone special,* using good eyes and good ears to discover an act with something different, something unique. Then, the real work begins.

How do you find this special performer, the one you want to spend time and energy with? As a manager myself, as well as an agent, I've found acts by listening to demos and going to showcases, among other things. I've even had artists I'm already managing help me discover another act. That's what happened with my first-ever management client, the great Hank Thompson.

We were doing a live television show with Hank every Saturday afternoon on Oklahoma City's WKY-TV. From time to time, Hank would feature a young singer from the area, a high school senior named Wanda Jackson. Wanda couldn't wait to get into the music business full-time and, after she graduated, Hank helped to get her first recording contract with Decca Records. It wasn't long before her first hit single, "You Can't Have My Love," a duet with Billy Gray, was burning up the charts.

At that time, I was finishing up a two-year hitch in the Army. Luckily, I'd been able to maintain my management agreement and booking arrangement with Hank, and following my discharge, I met with Wanda and made a deal to become her representative. Now I had two important artists under exclusive representation: Hank Thompson and Wanda Jackson.

Because of her Decca Records action, Wanda was able to get a deal with Capitol Records—Hank's label—and their becoming labelmates was an important step for both of them, as well as for me.

Wanda had all of the requirements for stardom. She had an original vocal style—one that you only had to hear once to remember. She developed a good show. She was an excellent performer with a good show and a wonderful rapport with the audience. Plus, she was a good songwriter, contributing to many of her hit records. She had the desire. She had the dedication. She was unique.

She had the **Power of Performance**.

Wanda went on to score many country and rockabilly hits, becoming a successful star in a very short time. Because of pop-crossover songs like "Right or Wrong" and "In the Middle of a Heartache," she was able to play many venues not normally available to country artists. In demand as co-headliner for many artists of the day, she also opened several shows for Elvis! Dick Clark used her many times on his *American Bandstand*, the long-lived music-and-dance TV show that influenced teenagers and pop music for decades.

I tell Wanda's story to illustrate how, from the very beginning of my career, I understood the magic of the **Power of Performance**. I found out quickly how connecting and networking make things happen, and how being in the right place at the right time can give a career a needed boost.

The lessons here for you? When you plan with a purpose, set your goals, and follow your dreams, success will come.

Hank Thompson introduced Wanda to the world, and after Wanda made it, she helped usher in another new star, one who would become one of my biggest stars and dearest friends.

I had just completed a contract for Wanda to appear at the Golden Nugget in Las Vegas. It was a long-term arrangement calling for her to play through the year of 1960. Before that string of dates started, Wanda informed me she was hiring a guitar player she'd found working in a Washington, D.C., nightclub. Envisioning him as the front man for her band, Wanda described him as a multi-talented musician, singer, and showman.

When I saw him play his first concert with her, I saw that she'd been conservative in her description. He turned out to be all she'd said he was—and a whole lot more. To this day, I have not seen a greater talent.

His name? Roy Clark.

Even in 1959, fronting someone else's band, Roy had "superstardom" written all over his performance. He connected with an audience like nobody I had ever seen. I immediately recognized in Roy his magical ability to entertain anybody, anywhere, and after that show we began a relationship that has lasted for 40 years. There was no doubt then, and there is no doubt now, that Roy Clark has that "something special," a uniqueness that sets him apart from every other performer. Wherever he appears, from the finest Las Vegas casino showrooms to huge international music festivals, Roy Clark is a talent the world recognizes and enjoys as a superstar.

In the beginning, we recognized each other as having the two main ingredients of the Star Team. He had the unique talent, and I had the skills to be his manager, as well as his agent—his impresario. We soon established a friendship and rapport.

Early in an artist's career, it's important to get them onto a stage where they can be seen and heard by people who can do them some good. In the first year of my association with Roy, Wanda Jackson provided that stage. I would bring in various concert promoters and buyers to see her perform, and of course they would also have the chance to see her front man, Roy Clark.

Wanda's popularity opened a lot of doors for Roy. Her producer at Capitol Records, Ken Nelson, was the first major record-company executive to see Roy perform, and Roy piqued his interest. Eventually, Nelson and Capitol Records decided to give Roy a shot at his own recordings. We were now beginning to get the key players in place. First, as always, it was the artist. Then the manager-agent. And now a very important player, the record company.

As Wanda and her band traveled the country, Roy Clark's performances were connecting with the various critics, reviewers, and promoters for whom we were playing. They liked him! We made sure they would notice Roy, writing personal letters to everyone we could think of at each tour stop about this fantastic singer, comedian, and guitar player with Wanda's band, advising them to take notice. Roy was becoming known within the industry, and the public was enjoying him, too. He was not just hot with one segment, but with both!

It's a great situation to be hot within the industry and hot with the public at the same time, because that's something that usually doesn't happen.

Most of the time, an artist gets hot within the industry before he or she becomes popular with the fans. If you read the trades, you'll see articles predicting that an artist is "going to happen." An artist manager should keep an eye on those acts. Many times they don't have management, or the relationship with their current management is almost over. Find the opportunity; use your **Power of Performance** to make it happen.

And once you find them, remember the two most important things you can do for new acts: *get them exposure*, and *be in the right place at the right time*. Help your artist connect with both the fans and the industry. As a manager, I realized I must get exposure for my artists in many ways, including television, radio, personal appearances, press and promotion, and of course, records. Hopefully, hit records!

Some artists and managers come together with a rare chemistry that makes success inevitable. Roy and I had that chemistry, but we had a lot of work to do, too. With a common purpose, we established our goals early in our relationship. We determined our plan and we set to work exercising our **Power of Performance**—his on stage, mine in developing his career. Part of our plan was building a good team, which was my job as manager. We did, and the rest is history!

Roy and I would spend the next 30 years together blazing new trails, setting new records, and achieving what might have seemed impossible to a lot of people. We made 1+1=100! That's the kind of payoff you can get when you fully access your **Power of Performance**.

♪ ♪ ♪ ♪

An artist like Roy Clark doesn't come along every day, of course. A manager is lucky to get one superstar like that in a lifetime. But all successful acts are, to a greater or lesser extent, unique, and finding this uniqueness in an unknown performer is an important part of the artist manager's job. Listen for a particular tonal quality, an unusual style or phrasing, a curious glitch in the voice. You want someone so distinctive and unique that people will be able to recognize the voice after only a few records come out. You want people to turn on the radio, hear a few bars of a song, and know it's your artist.

Being a good, unique singer is a fine start. In today's marketplace, however, you also need someone who creates his or her own material. Look for this whole package of talent by listening to demo tapes, watching acts perform before an audience, and imagining how an artist will look on television. In a live situation, observe the audience's reactions and listen for comments.

Suppose you, as artist manager, find the artist you believe in. What comes next?

First of all, you should find out where the artist really wants to go, his or her dreams, his or her desires. Then, you should set your goals together. Is it television, records, personal appearances, performing at top venues? A combination of all of these things? Whatever the objective, plan how to get there. As manager, it's your job to get the artist seen and heard by the other members of the industry, including music publishers, record company executives, talent buyers, and other leaders. As manager, you can start putting the Star Team together by providing showcases and inviting industry representatives, some of whom will have influence with established artists. If these representatives like your act, they can help get him or her on the front half of shows, exposing your performer to a wider audience. (This usually happens after you've gotten a record deal.)

Artist manager: do you understand the job description?

A manager is a person who manages and guides the careers of artists by generating creative suggestions and discussions aimed toward proper career-building. Don't get this confused with the job of the *booking agent*. A booking agent books dates and events, arranges tours, television shows, and generally creates cash flow. We'll talk about the booking agent in Chapter 12; he's not quite ready to be plugged into our scenario.

I bring up the booking agent because there's a lot of confusion regarding the jobs of manager and agent. Maybe it's because the same person sometimes has to do both jobs, as I did with Hank Thompson early in my career. After starting in the business as a promoter, I became a combined manager-agent because someone had to do the whole job; in country music at that time, the big agencies were not equipped to handle booking for country music artists. They didn't know about country music, and they weren't really all that interested in it.

As a manager, remember that many times artists aren't really sure what they want. They know that they want to have hit records, or that they want to be stars. You must design and set in motion the plans to achieve their goals, and to make their dreams more focused. It is up to you to develop their careers.

How do you start? First, put in writing where you and the artist want to go. Lay out your plan in increments of 12, 24, and 36 months. Develop the plan and write it down in detail. I have written a plan for every artist with whom I have ever been involved. Even if the act has already achieved superstardom, you can still develop him or her in a multitude of other areas and expand the career to be bigger, better, and even more rewarding.

Another of the manager's jobs is to make certain that the artist's creative needs are fulfilled. Creativity is an important part of any artist's being; sometimes it's more important than financial needs.

For example, there's the show that Merle Haggard and the Strangers put on at the Cain's Ballroom in 1984. Larry Shaeffer, the Tulsa entrepreneur and impresario, had Hank Williams Jr. on a nationwide tour at the time, and Merle was on that tour. According to Larry, they were having coffee after one of the shows, and he happened to mention that he owned Tulsa's Cain's Ballroom, the venue that launched Bob Wills and the Texas Playboys. Merle Haggard just got all beside himself with admiration for Bob Wills, and he ended up telling Larry, "I want to go back there and play one of those noontime shows like Bob used to play every day, live over KVOO radio. I want to come in and do the whole thing."

We were Merle's agents at the time, and we arranged things with Larry at the Cain's. I even called Mr. O.W. Mayo, who'd been Bob's financial manager and announcer, and asked him to come down and do the announcing. He did, KVOO radio broadcast it, and Merle and his band did an entire program of Bob Wills songs, playing to a packed house.

It was exciting for me, because it took me back to my roots. Growing up in Independence, I listened religiously to Bob Wills over KVOO every day, with Leon McAuliffe playing steel guitar. And it was exciting for Merle Haggard. I'm sure Larry had expenses and Merle had expenses, but that was a free deal. They didn't charge any admission. To compensate financially, we had Merle booked somewhere else that night. But this show was a labor of love for him. He wanted to do it. For that period of time, he was Bob Wills. And that was more important to him than drawing a big check.

♪ ♪ ♪ ♪

A good manager must be able to tie the Star Team together and then creatively work with each member. For example, let's assume that you are down the line a bit, and you've already gotten your artist a record deal. The next thing you're talking about is touring, so you hook up with the booking agent. The booking agent creates the cash flow, the revenue, but the career direction is given by the manager, working in conjunction with the artist. Usually, in a situation like this, the manager, the booking agent, a record-company executive, and the artist all meet to coordinate plans and determine direction.

If you have a major artist, it's pointless to tour if there isn't any record product in the marketplace, since touring helps sell records. Sometimes, of course, you have to tour an act just to keep the cash coming in. Once an artist is big enough, you can usually maintain cash flow with a once-a-year tour—timed to coincide with the release of a new disc. That's when the record company wants your act out in the marketplace.

As the manager of a recording act, you must determine three things: *why* to tour, *when* to tour, and *where* to tour.

First of all, why? Is it for cash flow, record promotion, or just to maintain your presence in the marketplace? Answering that question will help provide the when and where.

For example, let's say that you as manager, along with the record company and the booking agent, decide to put an artist on tour. The company has just put out a new disc by that artist. So working together, you find a specific territory where the record is hot. Concentrate on booking your act there, excite the interest of prospective buyers with things like well-timed letters, promotional flyers, and telephone calls, and a successful series of dates is all but assured.

Although a tour is really the booking agent's responsibility, it's your job as manager to feed information to the agent so he'll know what to do and when to do it.

You, with creative planning, must develop the advertising campaign, direct-mail promotion, and other marketing plans for your artist. Many times, however, this marketing campaign will be worked in conjunction with the booking agent who's planning to take the artist on tour and the record company that's planning a release. All of these entities should work hand in hand, guided by an overall plan, enhancing the artist's **Power of Performance**. In fact, when they perform in tandem with one another, I call them *power enhancers*, individual components that make the whole effort more meaningful and important than it would be if they didn't contribute.

Are you getting the point? It's a simple one. Combined energies create **Power of Performance**, and an artist manager must be able to coordinate efforts among many entities, including the record company, the press, public relations, and the booking agency. It is all about *marketing*.

Basically, a really good manager designs a plan, makes the connections, and markets an act. The energy put into marketing ties into an artist's whole career, not just one specific area. It's far more complex and important than just getting your act booked. Working with the rest of the Star Team, a manager can choreograph the **Power of Performance** as beautifully as a fine ballet.

♪ ♪ ♪ ♪

Opportunities come every day. One of the keys to success is learning to recognize opportunities when you see them—even when they come in the form of people. Every achievement in life relies on your ability to learn from people, and putting a Star Team together is partially about learning to deal with others. As you become more sophisticated through learning to recognize opportunities and achieving your goals, you'll expand your relationships and your team.

Start today to develop the ability to recognize opportunities as they are presented to you. They come no matter what walk of life you're in. If you're an artist manger, you'll have many business-related opportunities, as well as opportunities with your artists and others.

Everyone has dreams and visions. Maybe as a child you even lived in a dream world part of the time. You know that there is nothing you cannot achieve in your dreams and visions. Don't question those dreams and visions. *Test* them. I know that if you stop believing in and following your dreams, they'll stop coming. Dreams are especially important in a creative business like ours; in fact, dreams are what show business is all about. So pay attention to them.

It is the artist manager who helps bring dreams into reality, using the elements of sales and marketing. Success comes when you put everything together, utilizing not only your own **Power of Performance**, but that of the other Star Team members. Are you beginning to see how it works?

We're talking about being an artist manager, but this teamwork principle also applies to the artist and all the other members of the Star Team. And it applies throughout an act's career. Even when he's got a big-name artist, the manager has to continue to stay on top of the career, making plans and projections and setting new goals. This is all part of it. One of the most important things in dealing with an artist is the need to constantly make things happen. If an artist has been around for a long time and is still successful, his or her career surely has been nurtured well, and there's usually been a good artist manager there in the background, still exercising a collective **Power of Performance**.

Keep this in mind: *The artist manager has to make an artist happen. And to do that takes total dedication.*

Whether an artist is just getting started in the business, or whether he or she has been around a long time, the manager's total commitment is required. A total focus on the artist and the art he or she produces is indispensable. The first time a manager stops thinking or working with dedication, someone else will pull out in front.

As a manager, you must be dedicated. You must give attention to detail. And you must be willing to follow dreams. When dealing with an artist's career, expand your thoughts even beyond your hopes for that career. Don't be afraid to dream. If an idea seems ridiculous at the time, you can always bring it back into focus and find ways to make it practical. To understand your ideas better, always *write them down*. Remember how important writing things down is to our formula for success!

When you are thinking about doing one thing with your artist—one concert or one tour, for example—explore every avenue imaginable. Work on publicity through the press and radio stations, through fan organizations, through websites, through advertising. Try to get corporate sponsorship, and go to the most powerful and influential corporations first. Work from the national to the local; local sponsorship is important as well, whether in the form of actual money or in services— a rental-car company providing transportation for the artist, a hotel giving rooms in exchange for a sponsorship mention. Expand your thoughts, and you can expand your plan. Concentrate on details. You cannot just put an artist out there and hope things will happen. As a manager, you are responsible for *making* things happen! And you can't make things happen without a plan!

When you sit down to make a plan, ask yourself questions like these:

- *Where am I starting from?*
- *Where am I going?*
- *Where do I want to be at the end of my plan?*
- *What is my goal?*
- *What is the purpose?*
- *What will be the final results?*

Once you have outlined your plan, start building a staff to help you implement the plan. These people may include Star Team members like booking agents, publicists, and promoters as well as specialists in production, lighting, and sound. You need them all to help build a show around your artist, who cannot be thrown out there on stage without some kind of presentation. It is up to you, as the artist manager, to make sure you have the best people to help make that happen. If you aren't qualified to stage the show yourself, find someone who is. A concert must be designed, paced, and most importantly, delivered in a way that connects with the audience. There's a lot of competition in the world today. If you do not have good, well-planned shows, you are going to be passed by.

As you progress, there may be literally hundreds of people involved in helping a show or tour work. Like you and your artist, they all have a performance to give. It take a lot of people to make any project happen, whether it's a show, a tour, an album, or a personal appearance. And if everyone from artist to stagehand utilizes his or her **Power of Performance** to the utmost, the result will be those two key words dear to the heart of every agent, artist, publicist, and booking agent: *repeat business*.

If there's one thing above all else that's important in selling and marketing, it's making sure the customer is satisfied. And in the music business, it's an artist's performance that's being marketed to customers. It's marketed to a record company, to a promoter, and finally, to ticket buyers. Remember those ticket-buying customers. They've paid good money to see the show, and maybe they've hired a baby sitter, driven a good distance, eaten dinner out, and paid for other things along the way. Your performer has an obligation to give them the best show possible.

Make sure your artist knows that his or her **Power of Performance** should be perfected before he or she ever sets foot on stage. Feeling good or bad has nothing to do with it. Performers are obligated to give their customers, the ticket buyers, the very best they have to offer. If they do, your customers becomes satisfied customers! Satisfied customers will buy a ticket to see your act again, buy your artist's CDs, tapes, videos and other merchandise. Best of all, they will tell other potential customers about your act, helping to build a fan base.

The worst thing that can happen is for your performer to acquire unhappy customers. Not only will they not spend another dime on your act for the rest of his or her career, they will tell everybody else about what they considered a bad performance. This trickle-up effect will touch everybody and impact everything from record sales to future bookings.

It takes a long time to build an act. A moment or two of some stupid performance, either on stage or off, can seriously damage or even destroy a career.

The manager and artist cannot always expect new places, new buildings, new promoters. If you are going to build your success, you have to establish good venues and good promoters and continue to work with them. With proper planning and promotion, you must work to make each date successful, so your artist can go back to a venue next season, and the season after that. In a perfect world, the talent always takes care of the buyer, and the buyer always takes care of the talent. But our world isn't perfect. As long as an artist has hot records, things are great! But as a manager, you must plan for the 99% of the time when your act will not be hot. There is only a certain period of time, a window, in which to take full advantage, and that's when your act is at the top of the charts. You may think hit records and hot acts last forever. They never do.

I am sure you have seen cases when artists who've been very hot become very cold. A few lucky and talented ones are cool for years and then surge back with another hot record, and their careers start all over again. As artist manager, it's up to you to establish your act's name, and the time to do that is when the artist gets his or her first hot records. Get the name recognition, the image, and the stage show established during this time, because the hot period will sooner or later come to an end. If the manager and the artist have done their jobs, they are going to be established forever.

♪ ♪ ♪ ♪

All that's necessary to accomplish all of this is to deliver, to perform! Get it? It's not just the artist's **Power of Performance**; it's the manager's as well!

Remember, satisfied customers create repeat business. And it's not just the ticket buyers. You also want satisfied promoters, which leads to repeat business. Take care of the promoters who've helped establish your artist. See that they make money on your act. Help them if they don't. There are times when, because of one circumstance or another, the show doesn't turn out financially the way you want it to. In that case, remember two adages you'll find again and again in this book: *It's only a good deal if it's a good deal for everyone involved*, and *the only good customer is a satisfied customer.*

The great Woody Herman, one of my earliest clients, had a philosophy that revolved around always keeping the promoter in business. And I know of literally hundreds of times that The Oak Ridge Boys gave money back to a promoter when something happened—a flood, disastrous weather—that wasn't the fault of either the promoter or The Oak Ridge Boys.

A few years ago, Roy Clark played the Colorado State Fair, and his contract had a very big guarantee. Once he got out there, he found out they'd been experiencing a serious drought in the area, and a lot of the farmers hadn't been able to make it on their crops that year or the year before. During his show, Roy made the announcement that he just couldn't come out there and take their money, so he was donating his performance to the Colorado State Fair.

♪ ♪ ♪ ♪

It doesn't hurt to repeat successful plans and promotions. Usually, all you have to do is change an aspect or two of the plan or promotion, and it'll work successfully over and over again, just like the movie themes that come back every year in new pictures. Later, you'll read about the promotions The Jim Halsey Company did during the annual fair buyers' convention in Las Vegas, where we reworked our sales and marketing approaches each time, building on an established base.

As we've noted before, artists are very creative people, and creative people are sensitive by nature. A lot of artists also have delicate egos. Their ideas are creative and imaginative, and their thought processes are not always as logical as those of the business person who directs and guides their careers. As a person with a business background, I have also tried to be sensitive to my artist's needs, both personal and creative. When they receive this kind of respect, they will flourish.

There are a lot of words that describe my own philosophy of living. As I told you earlier, *respect* is one of these words. I deal with people with respect. I offer respect, and I expect to get respect in return. If I cannot respect an artist with whom I am involved, it is impossible for me to do a good job. Not only do I have to respect artists as people; I also have to respect their art and their creative ability. I have been brought up to appreciate and respect anything that is done creatively and well. I'm in the country music business, but that doesn't mean I only like country music. I like jazz and classical. In fact, I like every type of music, and have albums of all kinds in my own library. I am certainly in agreement with Duke Ellington's famous statement about how there are only two kinds of music: good and bad. Good music broadens the scope of my being.

If an artist, no matter what his musical style, feels respect from you and feels that you understand what he is doing creatively, your relationship is going to be richer. You will be able to accomplish more together, because you are both working on the same plan.

Finally, then, as an artist manager, it's of paramount importance to be sensitive to your artists and their needs—it is the foundation of a successful relationship! Do not forget, perfecting your own **Power of Performance** is in your best interest, as well as in the best interest of your artists and the other members of the Star Team.

10

The Record Company

We've talked about talent, the hub of the Star Team wheel. We've talked about artist management, usually the first important spoke in that wheel. Now it's time to add another essential spoke: *the record company*.

Once a record company has been plugged into the Star Team, a whole new set of circumstances comes into play. Discs are important to a career for a number of reasons. They preserve an artists' work for all eternity. They give an artist new status with family and friends. Most important, if radio plays songs from a disc and a demand is created, they reward the performer financially. If the discs yield hits, and enough of them, a star is born.

When Thomas A. Edison invented the cylinder disc in 1877, I'm sure he never anticipated what worldwide commerce his invention would spawn. Viewed largely as a novelty, Edison's phonograph was seen as a possible way of preserving historic talks, special events, and music for posterity.

Now, recordings are a multi-billion dollar business, and one of America's principal exports. And a record company—whose **Power of Performance** lies in producing, promoting, marketing, and distribution— plays a definite and integral part in any artist's development.

Most record labels have great resources at their disposal, along with a worldwide network of people power. The creative workforce at most record companies is a great resource for the artist and artist manager, with individual departments that deal with production, artists and repertoire, press and public relations, distribution, and video promotion. The heads of these departments should all be a part of your extended planning team.

A label's promotional facilities are extensive, with the ability to get your records to radio stations worldwide, as well as in retail stores. They will finance and place your videos on music-video programs and in clubs, and they can help you get proper reviews and press. A lot of times, the artist-development department can even help in booking dates or arranging guest appearances on radio and television. A record company can help set tours and finance any shortfall—the difference between what a performer actually needs in order to do a performance properly and the amount of money he or she gets paid to do it—on an important tour, or book one of its acts into an opening slot on some major artist's tour. Many times, usually in conjunction with a manager, they'll bring other professionals onto the tour to help with staging and costuming.

The record company is a major part of the Star Team. An artist and artist manager's good working relationship with a record company not only helps shake loose advertising and promotion dollars, but also helps assure that the label's network of sales and marketing people, press-relations department, and systems of distribution are all engaged in helping build and sustain a career.

It sounds great and so easy, doesn't it? But how do you find a record company willing to be a part of your Star Team? Frankly, a lot of times even a good artist with a good manager finds it hard to get a record deal—and if the music isn't there, forget about it.

Whether artist or artist manager, you can increase your chances of landing a label by starting with good demos and a professional-looking presentation packet that includes good photos. Remember, your photo will be the very first thing anybody sees upon opening your package.

Spend a little money. Have some professional photos taken. Get a good photographer. I have had people send me presentations with pictures of themselves taken in front of Christmas trees, or in a group with a circle drawn around their face with a "this is me" scrawled across the picture. It'd be funny if it weren't so sad. Crummy amateur photos like these not only turn me off, they also influence the rest of my thinking about the artists who sent them. It may not be fair, but it's true, and it's not just true for me, but for any music-industry professional.

A good demo is an act's best sales tool. Put it with a good photo, a brief resume, any press clippings you might have, and you've got a presentation. Put it in a nice cardboard folder, one that you can buy at any department or office-supply store, and you have a professional presentation to submit to a record company.

See how simple it is? When it comes across somebody's desk, it won't be thrown out because it looks too sloppy or unprofessional. Putting together a good presentation package is generally the job of a manager; the artist can make it easier by giving the manager something to work with.

Again, it's important to emphasize that if the music isn't there, the greatest demo and the best presentation in the world won't make any difference.

Once you've got your package together, it's time to start knocking on doors. As either artist or manager, you may know someone at a record company. If you do, get permission to send your package. If you don't, it's time for some creative thinking and planning. Somehow, you must figure out a way to make contact with someone in a record company. Maybe you can get a label's attention in ways I've mentioned earlier—by showcasing your talent or attending a music industry conference. If you are properly prepared—and make sure you are—for one of these conferences, it can give you a shortcut to the music business profession. A first-class conference will cost you some money in admission fees, but it will be well worth it.

♪ ♪ ♪ ♪

It may surprise you to know that over 3,000 record labels are licensed in the United States. Many thousands more are active in other countries. So how do you know which and what kind of label you want to pitch your material to?

Here are five classifications to help you sort things out:

1. THE MAJOR LABELS

These have all of the components necessary for full-scale business. Five of these—EMI/Capitol, Warner Brothers, BMG, MCA/Polygram, and Sony—are multinational corporations with their own manufacturing and distribution companies and also distribute labels other than their own. Besides those five multinationals, there are many successful labels with full staffing and big stars. Some, like Arista and RCA, are subsidiaries of the multinationals (BMG).

2. INDEPENDENT LABELS

These are labels operating with independent distribution, sometimes distributed through the multinationals or other direct sources. Some of the bigger independents—Curb and Platinum, for instance—have fully staffed departments for promotion, marketing, development, etc. Most indies make deals for foreign sales through other record companies, on a country by country basis.

3. TELEMARKETING LABELS

Over the past couple of decades, labels specializing in telemarketing have become very successful. Usually these companies license previously released tracks from an artist and repackage them, offering their collection for sale in television spots. They do not put artists under contract, nor do they usually make new recordings themselves. Their success comes from marketing already proven hits or artists. Generally, records released by these companies are only available through their TV ads rather than in stores. (This is called "direct response" marketing.) Big telemarketing labels include Heartland Records, Suffolk, Time-Life, and Reader's Digest.

4. SPECIALTY LABELS

Specialty labels release product for a limited, specialized audience; you'll find speciality companies that concentrate only on jazz (like Pablo or Concorde/Blue Note), or bluegrass (Skaggs Family), or classical (Angel). Ethnic and folk music also have their own speciality labels. Even a genre as far-reaching as comedy has specialty outfits releasing discs and videos.

Some specialty labels will also package and produce "special project" tapes and CDs. These are much like telemarketed albums—usually they're a compilation of hits by various artists, released via special marketing plans. You'll see stacks of these kinds of discs and tapes in places like service stations, convenience stores, and truck stops; a lot of Christmas albums fall into this category. And even major labels will sometimes get involved in this kind of special marketing.

5. PRIVATE LABELS

Certain artists, commercial companies, and organizations make discs intended for their own use. Often, these are done as promotional albums to celebrate, publicize, or tie into some special event. Certain societies have their own private label; an organization like the Knights of Columbus, for instance, might put out a special disc or tape as a fundraiser.

For most—but not all—artists, the big multinational labels are the most alluring, and not just for the obvious reasons. Let's take a look at MCA Records, for instance. MCA Records and MCA Distribution are separate company entities within the MCA Music Entertainment Group, which is owned by the Canadian Seagram's Group.

Under the Seagram's Group umbrella lie these companies:

1. MCA Motion Picture Group
2. MCA Television Group
3. MCA Home Entertainment Group
4. MCA Music Entertainment Group
5. MCA Publishing Group
6. MCA/Universal Merchandising
7. MCA Development
8. MCA Enterprises
9. MCA Recreation Services Group
10. Universal Studio Operations Group
11. Spencer Gifts

And you thought MCA was just a record company? Each of these groups functions as a separate entity under the umbrella with its own president and other officers. With its recent acquisition of the Polygram companies, MCA is even bigger.

Most multinationals have a structure like this, and having all of these connected companies works to an artist's advantage. If an artist and manager are aware of what's potentially available from a record company, they'll be ready for the opportunities that lie beyond simply recording.

Our company, The Jim Halsey Co., Inc., worked closely with all of the record companies in designing and promoting our artists' careers. It was important to us, and for the artists we represented, to maintain a daily working relationship with the different record companies. Many labels became partners on promotions and projects. Sometimes, new artists they discovered and signed also hooked up with us. After several decades in the music business, I have yet to work with a more important record-company person than Jim Foglesong. Jim was president of Dot Records when I met him, and after an uncertain start, we became good friends. He was one of the reasons The Jim Halsey Company became such a successful agency. His vision and creative ideas, coupled with his understanding of the artists' needs and the importance of cooperation between the team members, were all important. But even more than that, he was and is a man of great integrity and a gentleman.

In 1967, I made an independent production deal with Dot Records, giving me the opportunity to deliver a certain number of artists to Dot over a period of years. Our main act at the time was Hank Thompson, and the label required Hank to be one of the artists. Hank was also my partner in the deal, he and I having recently formed the production company Swingin' "T" Productions. In addition to Hank, I was able to get Roy Clark, Rex Allen, Mary Taylor, and other of my acts onto the label.

At this particular time, Roy was a puzzle to record companies. They all respected his ability as a great musician, but instrumentals were not selling, and his previous vocal hits on Capitol Records, "The Tips of My Fingers" and "When the Wind Blows in Chicago," had not been fully promoted and were looked at, in the jargon of the record industry, as "possibly not consistent." Roy could do too many different things. He could sing several different styles of music—pop, country, and blues—and he could play great instrumentals. One of the things record companies do is put a label on an artist, fitting him or her into an identifiable niche, and that was impossible to do with Roy, because he was so multi-talented.

Because of our production deal at Dot, we had a free hand to experiment with Roy's sound. Joe Allison, both a longtime believer in Roy's talents and a good friend, became his producer. (He would ultimately be responsible for Roy's great hit "Yesterday, When I Was Young").

Working at Dot Records, however, was a bumpy ride. Presidents were fired and hired, and our creative energies were simply not being appreciated. With each new president came a new staffing of the sales, marketing, and promotion departments. Chaos seemed to be the order of the day. What was going on here? We needed the cohesiveness of a well-balanced company, but Dot Records was floundering.

Finally, Dot was sold to Gulf & Western. At the time, I was in Las Vegas with Roy Clark, who was performing at the Hughes Landmark Hotel, and I was pretty discouraged with Dot Records. Then I got a call from Jim Foglesong. He introduced himself as "the new president of Dot Records."

I had not met him previously, but he sounded nice enough. He explained how he was going to change a lot of the policies at Dot and bring in a great promotion person, Larry Baunach, to head up marketing and sales. A new distribution system was to be put in place along with a total restructuring of the company. As the conversation came to a close, he once again assured me that things would now be different at Dot.

Then it was my turn.

"Mr. Foglesong," I said, "this all sounds great to me and it's something we've been hoping for. But I must tell you this: within the last two years we have gone through five new presidents at Dot Records, and as many new sales, marketing, and promotion heads. How will we know you'll be around long enough to implement our plans?"

There was a long silence on the other end. But Jim Foglesong recovered enough to give me the assurance he had the mandate. I then pledged my cooperation, and we agreed to work together on what would become one of the most rewarding and personally satisfying relationships in my entire career.

Jim Foglesong believed in our multi-focused projects for our artists. Much of our company's success, and the success of our artists on Dot Records, came because of Jim's cooperation in the marketing and promotion departments. Dot later merged with ABC, and eventually was purchased by MCA. Foglesong and his staff members remained in place through all of the changes, and our friendship and working relationship deepened.

Part of my method in establishing an artist has always been to come up with projects or programs that draw attention, build careers, and sell records. We call these projects *events*! Being the first in a new venue or territory, or with a festival or television show, has long been important to me. I believe that being first establishes the importance of the project. Being the best is important, too, but being first is going to get you more recognition, and it only happens once.

Jim Foglesong helped with the events for many of our artists on his label. We devised unusual, unique events and then worked together to achieve press, record sales, and success. We combined our ideas and sales plans and by teaming up the artists, our company, and the record label, we multiplied our **Power of Performance.** I'll give you some good illustrations in the third part of this book, "Secrets of The Jim Halsey Company."

Before we leave Jim Foglesong and Dot Records, however, I want to acknowledge a woman named Dottie Vance. During all of the change and upheaval before Jim took the helm, there was one believer who managed to remain through each change of command. This was Dottie, a legendary record promoter, who helped make hits out of a lot of early Hank Thompson and Roy Clark songs. She had a great reputation at the radio stations. If Dottie called, she always reached the right people.

Legends like Dottie and Jim remind us that this is still a people business. Even though each company has a certain prescribed structure, its success depends on its people. If the departments are staffed by ineffective personnel and the proper leadership is not involved, all of the other elements will fail. This is why most people picked to head a company bring in many of their own team members. They know that in the pressure cooker of the big-time music business they'd better have people around them they can count on to do the job right, to fit into the team, and to access their **Power of Performance** for the good of everyone involved.

11

The Record Producer

The record producer is the next spoke in the wheel of our Star Team. Usually added to the team at the same time as the record company, the producer works hand in hand with the company, creating recordings calculated to grab the public's interest and make things profitable for both artist and label.

When a record company becomes interested in signing an artist, the big question is: who'll be the producer? The producer goes into the studio with the artist and helps select the material, the musicians, the studio, the engineers, the arrangements, the background singers, and the sound.

You thought the singer did all of that? Sometimes that's true. More often, though, hit records have been more the producer's creation than the artist's. Most of the time it's a collaboration between the two, a meeting of minds and songs and the ways things should be done. Most producers actually work for the record companies, but others have their own studios or produce master discs that they sell or lease to the labels.

You see, cutting a disc is more than just going into a studio, turning on the microphones and machines, and running through the material to be recorded. A lot of thought goes into the production of a record. You have to make sure to get the best songs you can. You must strive to get the best musicians, and the best sound, mixing and balancing correctly, and getting the best performance possible from the singer or singers. It's not uncommon for a producer to ask for several takes of the same song, even as many as 20 or 30. Through this kind of repetition, the producer not only assures himself of a perfect track, but can sometimes get the artist to stretch into new and unexpected levels of performance. This repetition and deliberation is why the process of recording a new 10-song disc can take weeks or even months.

When the musicians and artists are through in the studio, the producer's job continues, as he masters and mixes the recording, often with the help of the artist. That means he takes every track and every take recorded, picks the best, gets the sound he wants, equalizes the selection and flow of material, discovers any hidden mistakes or blemishes, and finishes with a perfect or near-perfect product.

It's a big job. It takes lots of skill and talent. Like the artist he recorded, the producer is looking for a hit!

As I said earlier, most record companies employ their own in-house producers. The part of the company they work for is called the A&R (artists and repertoire) department. Early in the recording careers of Hank Thompson, Wanda Jackson, and Roy Clark, a man named Ken Nelson was an important member of their Star Team. Ken was a producer in the A&R department of Capitol Records. It was his job to discover and record artists exclusively for Capitol.

Remember that the Star Team doesn't always come together in perfect order, with talent followed by manager, then record company, record producer, booking agent, etc. When our company signed as agents for Dwight Yoakam, for instance, he already had a manager—my son Sherman, who served as vice-chairman of The Jim Halsey Company. Although he had no record deal, he did have an important team member, Pete Anderson, in place as his record producer.

It was Sherman's undying belief in Dwight that convinced the rest of the Halsey Company to take notice. Sherman became Dwight's manager, and our company became the booking agent. This also was a little out of sequence, since the record company should have been the next element in place after Sherman signed on as manager. Sherman, however, was so convinced he could get Dwight a record deal that we all got aboard, even if things were a bit out of order.

Dwight is not only a uniquely individual artist, he's a great songwriter. But every time Sherman went to one of the Nashville labels trying to land a record deal for Dwight, he'd get the same kind of negative response.

"Sounds too country," they'd tell Sherman. "Sounds hillbilly."

"If he could just get rid of that glitch in his voice," someone else would say.

"Maybe if he would come into Nashville and record with Nashville musicians instead of his own band," still another would suggest.

This, along with a dozen other turndowns only fueled Sherman's belief that Dwight was an unusual performer, outside the mainstream and different from the norm, who could nonetheless capture the public's attention. Finally he found a Nashville ally, Paige Levy at Warner Bros.

Records, who really believed in Dwight and worked hard to get him on the label. He did sign with Warner Bros., but it was Warner Bros. in Los Angeles where Sherman found two more people who believed in his vision: Mo Austin and Jeff Aroff. Finally convinced of Dwight's potential—in large part because of Sherman's persistence and dedication, as well as Nashville Warner president, Jim Ed Norman and Paige Levy's belief in the project—they gave Dwight a contract.

Sherman's plan also included introducing Dwight to the public in an unorthodox manner. Instead of taking the usual route of putting a new country artist on tour as an opening act for a big-name country star, he booked Dwight as an opener for alternative-rock groups and went after the alternative press. It was unorthodox and extreme! But Warner Bros. liked it, and even more important, it worked.

Additionally, Sherman's vision called for Dwight to do a very stylized, state-of-the-art music video for his first Warner Bros. single, "Honky Tonk Man," a revved-up version of the old Johnny Horton hit. The song was great, Dwight's vocals were superb, and the video—produced and directed by Sherman on 35mm film—set a new standard for visual promotions through videos.

"Honky Tonk Man" launched Dwight's career. The record company had a new hit artist, and the video won countless awards worldwide, including a prestigious New York International Film Festival gold medal for Sherman's directing. Sherman also was named Manager of the Year by *Cash Box* magazine for his innovative approach to launching and managing Dwight's career.

I certainly want to give Pete Anderson, Dwight's creative record producer, a lot of credit for Dwight's success as well, recognizing again that the record producer is one of the nine key members of the Star Team. Pete, from the beginning, saw something unique in Dwight—in his voice, in his songs, and in his style. By using his skills, his **Power of Performance** as a gifted producer, Pete Anderson was able to capture Dwight's own **Power of Performance** in the studio.

The launching of Dwight Yoakam's national career is a good illustration of the power of a team. Although not all the spokes were in place, there were enough to get the wheel rolling: Dwight, the talent; Sherman, the artist manager; Warner Bros., the record company; Pete Anderson, the record producer; Bill Coben, music business specialized attorney; and The Jim Halsey Company, the booking agent. With these, we had the fundamentals of a solid Star Team. As we all worked together, our collective energy produced a collective **Power of Performance**, driving us to success.

Pete Anderson became a part of the Dwight Yoakam Star Team early. This happened because he was an independent producer who recorded material with Dwight "on spec" before the Warner Bros. contract. Sometimes, as in Pete's case, the producer is the first member of a potential Star Team, by virtue of his doing the artist's early demos, as well as the master recordings that make up the finished product.

An independent record producer is a good way for an artist to get his or her material to a record company. If the producer has a good track record of discovering new artists or producing hits, the record companies can make a deal on the producer's reputation alone. It's just another way this essential team member can be important to success in the music business.

When we made our deal with Dot Records in the late '60s, Roy Clark and I wanted an independent producer to do our product. A good friend, Joe Allison, had come to us with material and had been instrumental in some of our previous recordings, so he became our producer at Dot. Joe was creative and a good songwriter himself. He was also ahead of his time, as far as country music was concerned.

While we were looking for material for Roy, a friend named Scotty Turner, who was also a successful record producer, brought us a song left over from another recording session. It just hadn't been right for the artist doing the session. Scotty thought it might be right for Roy.

It was. When Roy encountered the tune for the first time, he said, simply, "This is me." Joe liked it, too, and he produced it as a pop, rather than a country record. When it was released, it became an instant hit on both the pop and country charts, and remains Roy's biggest record to date, having sold more than a million copies.

The song was "Yesterday, When I Was Young" by the great French composer, Charles Aznavour.

Interestingly enough, it was not a No. 1 hit. It had plenty of sustaining power on radio, and because of that it stayed on the charts for a long time, but it never jumped up to the top spot. Instead, it made a slow and steady climb to No. 2 on *Billboard* magazine's country chart, No. 11 on the pop chart. But it was in rotation on radio playlists and in the nation's consciousness a lot longer than many No. 1 records, and because of that it established Roy Clark as a major recording artist.

Joe Allison continued to produce Roy, Hank Thompson, and several other Halsey Company artists for quite a while, scoring other hits and helping to create some great records. Eventually, as often happens, it came time for a change, but before I leave Joe here, I'd like to say to him, "Thanks, Joe, for some good action!"

We were looking for another producer and another hit for Roy. We had considered a number of producers but couldn't seem to find the right combination. By this time, Jim Foglesong had become the head of Dot Records, and when he offered his services as a producer, it sounded like a good idea.

And it was. Jim started a string of records with Roy that would all be successful. In fact, the only No. 1 records Roy has had to date were produced by Jim Foglesong. Those top hits began with "Come Live With Me" by famed songwriters Boudleaux and Felice Bryant, and included such singles as "Honeymoon Feeling" and "Thank God and Greyhound." When you consider the contributions of producers like Jim Foglesong, Joe Allison, Pete Anderson, and Ron Chancey—who's produced 11 No. 1 hits to date with The Oak Ridge Boys—you can understand why I consider a record producer an essential part of the Star Team.

If you're not in the business of making records, it looks a lot easier than it is. One time, when Roy Clark was in Nashville taping the long-running *Hee Haw* TV series, we also had a recording session scheduled. Roy, as many of his fans know, got his start in the music business playing in a band composed of his dad Hester, uncles Paul and Dudley, and several other cousins and family members. The Clarks had continued to play together on weekends over the years, and they were great. As it turned out, Roy's family was in Nashville to do an episode of *Hee Haw*, and we prevailed on Jim Foglesong to cut a family album at the upcoming session.

I remember it well. The session was set for a Sunday evening. All of the members, along with Roy, gathered in the recording studio to run through the songs for producer Foglesong. Roy and his family members did about 45 minutes of run-through with tape rolling, and then Roy went into the control room with Jim, where the two of them listened to the rough tapes, made notes about where to put solos, and what to emphasize in certain places.

Finally Jim said, "I think we have it, Roy. Let's start recording."

Agreeing, Roy left the control room and went back out into the studio—which was now empty! After a short search, Roy found his father and uncles waiting outside in the car, their instruments packed up and put away.

"Come on," Roy said. "We're going to record now."

His father looked at him incredulously. "I thought that's what we just did," he replied.

Indeed, recording an album is more difficult than most people—even some musicians—realize.

♪ ♪ ♪ ♪

How do producers get paid? Those who work within the record-company structure are usually paid by the label. Good producers will always receive a royalty from the company, separate from the artist's royalties.

Independent producers, those who don't work for the label, many times become part-owner of the masters they produce. All kinds of other deals are made with indie producers—sole ownerships, partnerships, joint ventures, royalty sharing, etc.

Most producers are paid an advance sum for their services, based on each side, or song, that they produce. Additionally, they'll receive a royalty payment for each record sold. Normally this royalty is between three and five percent of gross retail sales. Sometimes it's more. Sometimes, in the case of big-name producers, it's a *lot* more.

Finally, whether a producer is an independent or a cog in the wheel of a giant record company, they all share one thing: the evidence of their **Power of Performance** that lies in their finished product, polished and preserved for all to hear.

The Booking Agent

You've probably noticed that this chapter is the longest chapter in the book. That's not only because a booking agent is one of the most important members of the Star Team. It's also because my company, The Jim Halsey Company, was the biggest country music booking agency in the world, and I want to share here some of the things I learned during the Halsey Company's glory years. You'll also note that many of the ideas and theories here touch on several other spokes in the Star Team wheel and can be used by managers, artists, and others.

As a booking agency, our company was in the business of marketing and selling artists. We were famous for our marketing campaigns, individually tailored for each artist. Designed and implemented in a way that maintained respect and appreciation for the art of our clients, our campaigns were still innovative and effective enough to get that "call to action."

When you're selling entertainment, you must condition your buyer—whether a talent buyer for a club or some other venue, or a concert promoter—to make the offer, the *call to action*. To help do that, we made progressive promotions via mail, fax, phone, press and PR, and radio, all reinforcing a concept called "repetitious impressions," which I'll discuss in greater detail later. All of these promotions were part of a marketing plan to build up our artists, a plan coordinated with the overall master career plan established in cooperation with each artist, manager, and record company, and usually put into play around the release of a new record.

As a vital Star Team member, the booking agency contributes important ideas and input. Some people think an agent simply waits for the phone to ring, and then discusses an act's open dates and issues a contract.

To quote the title of a Waylon Jennings hit: WRONG!

Unless you're an agent with a superstar act, you have to stimulate a buyer's interest enough to make him or her call, and then you must negotiate the sale. Most acts don't sell themselves. They have to be sold, and they're sold more effectively with proper marketing. As sales agent for an artist, a booking agent should know all of the important venues, promoters, clubs, television buyers, and the representatives of any other establishments or events that might be able to use the performer's talents. An agent must be a specialized salesperson, knowing all there is to know about both artist and buyer.

If the agent's plans are not carefully orchestrated with the other Star Team members, it can spell disaster. For an artist with a national release, everything must be laid out in a logical order for maximum effectiveness, taking into consideration such things as the disc's release date; sales campaigns in retail outlets; proper cities, venues, and presenters for live shows; a well-devised press and public relations campaign; television and video coverage; radio promotion; and whatever else is needed to make the tour a success.

It may sound to you like the artist manager and the booking agent have similar responsibilities. It's true that their job descriptions often overlap, but they each have a distinct function in the career of an artist.

The manager usually concentrates on a small roster of acts, making sure none of the planning, contracts, and details are overlooked. Remember, it's the manager's job to plan a career and develop the other team members, and for the most part a manager is more long-range in thinking about an artist's career. The booking agent, on the other hand, is responsible for creating a steady cash flow through the artist's touring and personal appearances.

What are some keys to a booking agent's **Power of Performance**? Unique and inventive marketing programs, for one. Also, you can measure performance by the revenue that comes from dates the agent books. Other criteria include the signing of new acts and the servicing of artists and dates. But remember: the main job of the agent is to sell—to book dates for his artists. Most of the creative and esoteric areas of the artist's career are handled by the manager.

If you're an artist, it's very important for you to find a good agent, one who wants you, will work for you, and won't just add your name to a long list of clients. A good booking agency sometimes represents hundreds of artists. If you sign with one of the big agencies, how can you be sure you'll get the kind of personal attention you and your career need?

This is a question answered by one word: *teamwork*. The artist, manager, and booking agent must develop a team relationship—a smaller team, within the Star Team. The manager, because of his job description, will usually have more day-to-day contact with the agent than the artist will, and it's the working together of manager and agent in developing itineraries, accurate fees, and the right venues that will help the agent's own **Power of Performance**. If the artist is a recording act, they'll coordinate touring plans with the release of the latest disc, with tour stops planned to stimulate record play on radio and video play on television, which in turn should help ticket sales for the tour.

See how cooperation between all the Star Team members becomes essential? On the artist's behalf, the manager, booking agent, and record company, along with publicist and promoter, work together on this one touring project. And on a worldwide basis, the big booking agencies will have organizational ties to the top venues, top promoters, and most importantly, the prestigious dates that can be worked by the artist.

The booking agent and the manager should study their artist's potential. What are the act's most marketable attributes? The agent and manager must do research, just as though they were selling automobiles, insurance, or refrigerators instead of talent.

You know I recommend making lists of goals. I also recommend that an agent make a list of reasons why talent buyers would want to buy an act. First, of course, is that the artist will make money for a buyer. A good show is capable of building an audience for repeat dates, and this is important to agents and buyers alike. It's simply not practical always to always be finding new venues and new buyers. An agent needs to establish a following of good, substantial buyers and satisfied customers, and you do that by building a buyer's faith and confidence. As you go along in this business, who you know and who knows you is going to be important.

From the beginning, you must keep it straight and honest. A booking agent's good reputation is worth more than money in the bank, and it stays forever and ever. It is important for an agent not to sell a buyer something not right for him or his venue. Once the sale is made, the buyer has put his faith and trust in the agent and the agent's belief that the act will make money. Happy customers enhance an agent's standing and reputation, which translates into repeat business.

You'll read about promoters in a later chapter, but I want to note now that being a promoter, a talent buyer, a presenter of artists, has many rewards. It's a money-making business that satisfies certain creative needs in a person. But promoting is a very risky business as well. Circumstances and elements that change on a daily basis can mean the difference between success or failure, between making or losing money. It's the booking agent's responsibility to the promoter to provide as many elements as possible to ensure a successful date. That means an agency—in coordination with management and press and publicity—should supply buyers with the essentials, including discs, videos, and photos, to help the buyer get the message to their buying public. An agency should also have the artist available for interviews, if possible.

The booking agent has a responsibility to the buyer, but he also has a responsibility to the artist. For that reason, he should be sure that he's always dealing with reliable promoters, people who'll treat the artists with respect, present them properly, advertise the date correctly, and compensate them for the work.

Most major agencies require at least half of the money in advance once a contract is issued for a specific date. To protect his artist, an agent dealing with a buyer for the first time should get all of the money in advance unless he can gather enough information to convince himself that the buyer is honest and reliable.

If you're an artist or manager, investigate before you sign with a booking agency. Is the agency good at keeping its artists booked? Does it have access to special events, conventions, trade shows, and private parties? Can it fill your particular needs for cash flow and revenue? Does it deal with important promotional venues—halls like the House of Blues in L.A. or the Beacon Theater in New York— that are prestigious for the artist to play and have record-selling cachet?

What are the agency's international connections? How many of the artists on the agency's roster have been there for a long time? What is the agency's reputation for honesty and ethics? Do you like the people?

Having a good individual agent is necessary, but it's not the only reason to sign with an agency. If the agency represents some big acts, that fact can help the once-great, near-great, or the just-getting-started artists, because they'll get sales and opportunities that wouldn't be available if the big acts and their sales strength weren't with the agency. Often a lesser-known act can be sent on tour with a big performer from the same agency, or packages can be put together with several acts supporting the star attraction. For these reasons, it's a distinct advantage to be with an agency that has a number of top, in-demand artists. They give what is known as "accumulated clout."

When working with a new artist, an agent and/or manager can be very effective with a marketing plan that includes an effective website, direct mail, a barrage of faxes, trade and consumer advertising, videos, television guest appearances, and extensive promotions targeted for radio, record stores, distributors, and consumers. The idea of *repetitious impressions* works when one impression after another is made within a short period. This is called "impact enhancing" and creates a measurable increase in the name recognition and identification of the artist or product.

I've seen this work so many times. As you repeat the impressions via your marketing plan, planting the name of the artist over and over, your act becomes hot in the minds of the talent buyers—hotter, in fact, than he or she actually is with the general public. If all of the marketing elements come together at the same time, the promoter will be stimulated to call the agent, ready to buy that artist he's heard so much about—answering the *call to action*.

In a way, the booking agent is a telemarketer. But instead of selling juicers, real estate, or auto wax, he is selling talent, and 90 percent of his sales are achieved over the phone. It sounds impersonal, but if you are giving your artists the proper respect. it's not. It *is* marketing, however, and you can be successful at it by always keeping these six things in mind:

1. *Offer a good product.*
2. *Create the image.*
3. *Fill the need.*
4. *Identify the buyer.*
5. *Make the call.*
6. *Close the sale.*

Our company, representing 40 great artists, never failed to appreciate the fact that we were selling our artists' creative efforts, and that our product—their art—was good. We had respect for our artists, and we demanded that the buyers respect them as well. Our company revolved around the performer.

The Jim Halsey Company was a sales organization; booking acts was our business. Each different sales and marketing plan we devised for our artists exhibited our **Power of Performance** as an agency. It was important to get buyers to call us. If a buyer calls an agent, there is a decided advantage for the agent in making the sale. When the agent has to call the buyer, the advantage switches to the buyer's side. We developed our *call to action* advertising pieces, mailers, faxes, electronic messages, trade magazine ads, and other inventive methods for one reason: to stimulate the buyer to call us. Are you getting the idea?

We became the agents for Clint Black long before Clint Black became a household name. His team, preparing him for stardom, included Bill Ham, his manager; RCA, his record company; and The Jim Halsey Company, Inc., his booking agency. All of us had been working together for nearly a year before RCA released Clint's first single, "A Better Man." When it hit the streets in March 1989, our agency kicked in with the plan that all Clint's Star Team members had agreed on. The goal? To get Clint Black in front of audiences, no matter what the cost, and thereby lend support to his newly released record.

The Jim Halsey Company, RCA, and Bill Ham all worked together toward this goal. We needed every bit of exposure we could get. We needed it within the time frame of the record's release and promotion campaign. Getting an unknown artist to perform in important venues, on important shows, and to open for important established stars is no easy task. But it was the Halsey Company's job.

With that specific goal in mind (along with a very tight time schedule), our company developed a selling and marketing plan, coordinating it with the concurrently running plans of manager Ham and RCA. The action really heated up when "A Better Man" came out. That was the time to call in favors. Every day counted. We had to get as much exposure as possible in a very short amount of time.

Fortunately, Clint is a great artist with appealing looks and a unique sound. Just as important, he's a gentleman, easy to get along with, the kind of man everyone likes. Because Clint had all those attributes, people willingly helped promote him—which made our job a lot easier. Within The Jim Halsey Company, we harnessed our own creative resources and developed a three-part plan, putting our own **Power of Performance** to work for Clint Black.

The plan's three parts involved (1) *power boosters,* (2) *repetitious impressions,* and (3) *impact enhancers.* Here's how it worked:

1. Power boosters. The goal was to book Clint on as many important dates in important markets as we could in a very short period of time, putting him in front of the biggest audiences possible. After many conversations and calling in lots of favors, we had Clint opening 50 major shows—with guaranteed large audiences—in 50 cities, appearing on the same bill with such major stars as The Judds, Reba McEntire, The Oak Ridge Boys, and Alabama.

Soon, we knew we'd need more money to support Clint's tour. Everyone agreed we needed to present Clint with his own band, duplicating the sound he had on record. The problem was that his opening-slot payment for these fifty shows would be $1,000 to $1,500 a night, and providing hotels, meals, and travel for his band members would cost an additional $250,000. Because everyone thought it was imperative for Clint to work these dates with his band, RCA agreed to provide the shortfall—the difference between what he needed and what he was getting paid—even though the company already had big money invested in Clint.

Once the record was out and Clint and his band were on the road, we were in a very critical time period. Every move we now made was very important.

Our collective goal was to make Clint Black a mega-star. The record company was doing its part. Bill Ham, the manager, was doing his. It was up to us, as Clint's agents, to make the final part of the puzzle fit. By mid-summer—three months after the release of the album—we were in the midst of our concentrated promotion. The Country Music Association was sending out ballots for its prestigious awards, with winners announced October 1 on the organization's annual CBS-TV awards show.

We had to work fast, as did the other members of the team. First, we worked to get Clint nominated for a CMA award. If we were able to get his name on the ballot, then we'd have to try to get him elected. Winning an award would solidify what we had built so far and would give him the much-needed **Power of Performance** within the industry.

Even though we had boosted Clint's power by getting him on a lot of big concerts in a short time period, his winning a CMA award was by no means a sure thing. So, to complement the blitz by his record company and management, The Jim Halsey Company developed its own special promotion, putting our particular formula of *repetitious impressions* into action. As I noted earlier, this is one of the most effective methods of establishing name identification and stimulating sales.

2. Repetitious impressions. Our special Clint Black promotion encompassed three ways of securing massive print and direct-mail exposure, all within a 14- to 21-day time period.

First, we developed an artistically designed brochure highlighting Clint, his hit record, and his being destined for mega-stardom. This was mailed to our massive list of over 25,000 industry professionals that included press, TV, and movie people; buyers for fairs, rodeos, performing art centers, casinos, theaters, exhibitions, and festivals; industry executives; and the top promoters and entertainment packagers. Additionally, the brochure was sent to every country music radio station in America—all 3,000 of them.

Then, this same brochure, enhanced with artwork, was paid for and placed strategically by our company in various trade magazines, including *Billboard*, *Variety*, *Amusement Business* and *The Hollywood Reporter*. (*Amusement Business* is read by promoters, theater managers, and buyers for fairs, festivals, and rodeos. *The Hollywood Reporter* and *Daily Variety* are respected daily papers for the motion picture and television industry.)

Finally, as a follow-up to our repetitious impressions campaign, I sent a personal letter to more than 10,000 industry buyers and executives. Yes, I signed them all personally—and then added postscripts to more than a quarter of them!

And that wasn't all I did. Before sending them out, I stacked up all 10,000 letters in the back room of my office building and took a blowtorch to the right edge of the stack! The text of the letters explained that Clint Black was so hot, even the mention of his name would sear paper. Those letters received attention . . . a *lot* of attention!

The personal letters were the final step in repeating the impressions. Designed to arrive after the ads and the printed brochure, the mailings were timed within a 21-day period, coinciding with the time that "A Better Man" was getting its heaviest airplay. It was important not only to identify the record, but also to solidify the name, Clint Black, in the minds of listeners. Too many times a hit record will be so powerful it will overshadow its artist. While it is important to establish both act and song at the same time, you must make sure the artist lives long after the hit record has passed. This is part of the overall building process.

3. Impact enhancers. The impact enhancement method allows you to add to a promotion that's already working, making it even more important—enhancing its impact. With the repetitious impressions part of our campaign working powerfully for Clint, we began booking him on as many television shows as we could, making sure his appearances fell within the time frame of the other elements of our promotion. This impact enhancing part of the promotion kicked off when Ralph Emery introduced him to the vast audience of TNN's *Nashville Now*—Clint's first appearance on a network TV show.

I called Fred deCordova and Peter Lasally, producers of *The Tonight Show with Johnny Carson*. I needed a favor. We needed this show. And we got it! Clint ended up appearing on *Good Morning, America*, too, and other major programs. And because all of these guest appearances appeared within the time frame of our direct mail and print advertising campaign, they enhanced the impact of the repetitious impressions.

By this time, Clint was touring, appearing on stage in 50 major cities, and doing local press and TV along the way. It would be hard to calculate the number of impressions that Clint made during this short period of time, but when it was over, he was a star.

You'll remember that all of this activity from us, management, and record company was timed to give Clint the best chance possible of getting a CMA nomination. We felt that if Clint showed up on the CMA's nominee list for at least one award, it would show that our promotion had been both well-timed and effective. As it turned out, the CMA nominated Clint for *three* awards.

What a break for us! The nominees' names were announced by all the major news services and TV networks, and *USA Today* carried his picture on the cover of its "Life" section.

Our timing with this campaign, coupled with the efforts from RCA and Bill Ham, proved once again the power of collective energies working together as the Star Team, as well as the importance of *power boosters, repetitious impressions,* and *impact enhancers* in stimulating the *call to action.* Buyers, TV producers, members of the press, and radio station programmers began picking up phones all over the country, calling to inquire about Clint Black. So as booking agents, we were helping build another important star for our roster.

You'll remember that in March, when "A Better Man" came out and our campaign began, Clint was getting $1,000 or $1,500 an engagement. Six months later, in September, we booked his first $25,000 gig; and by the first of the year, we were booking him for $125,000 per night.

You may be dealing with personal feelings and artistic temperaments when you're selling a performer, but remember: *selling is the same, no matter what you're selling.*

What a booking agent sells is, simply, people and their art.

♪ ♪ ♪ ♪

An agent's work is never done. Along with the required booking of dates, creating and being involved with events is an important, ongoing part of your daily life.

Reba McEntire was destined to be the mega-star she is today. Sure, she's one of the most talented performers ever to sing a song, or step on a stage, but she also willed her stardom years ago. She has every qualification for it, but more than anything else, she has desire, dedication, determination, and focus! Her **Power of Performance**, both on and off stage, is mighty! Our company was privileged to be Reba's agency for many years, booking her into many prestigious venues and onto a number of important television shows.

The Halsey Company held regular meetings with Reba's manager and her record company, MCA. At one point, we had just finished presenting The Oak Ridge Boys and The Judds at Radio City Music Hall, and we knew the advantages of an important New York date in terms of press, buyers, potential corporate sponsors, television producers, theatrical producers, advertising agencies, etc. Reba was beginning to happen then, and she was going to happen big. I suggested to all concerned that it was time to present her in an important date in New York. She was a star and needed to be presented in a star's venue.

I opted for Carnegie Hall or Radio City and left the decision in the hands of her manager. Logistics were worked out, and finally we were informed that Reba was going to do her Big Apple debut at the Lone Star Cafe, a bar on 54th. It was an "in" place, but its limited capacity didn't allow Reba to be shown off the way she should be—in her great, full show, stuffed with production values.

I blew my stack. Reba was soon to become one of the most important artists in the music business; it was important to present her right in her premier New York engagement. Management and MCA, however, complained about the high costs of Carnegie and Radio City.

I insisted she be presented at Carnegie Hall—and it had to be an event! I got my way, and Judi Pofsky, senior vice president of our company, did an outstanding job of getting the right motion picture producers, advertising agency heads, television producers, and packagers—everybody important to the "music biz"—to attend this event, introducing most of them to Reba for the first time.

These kinds of decisions and the responsibilities that go with them are usually the jobs of managers. But our company, while serving as booking agents for Reba, was also concerned about building her career on a positive, solid footing. The timing of a career-shaping appearance is important. So is not playing the wrong venue. Reba's Carnegie Hall appearance was an important step in the building of her career, coming at a time when she needed to take a giant step forward.

No matter how hard every member of a Star Team—manager, agent, record company, press and PR people, production & staging—works on something like this, it's still up to the artist to deliver his or her most polished and professional **Power of Performance.** Reba did just that, giving a spectacular show only a consummate performer could deliver. If anybody in this business ever understood the necessity of **Power of Performance**, Reba McEntire did!

Our efforts didn't stop once that successful show ended. In fact, they were just beginning . Our job was to follow up on all of the press that was generated and call all the buyers and others who might possibly be able to contribute to Reba's blossoming career. Our "performance" continued throughout the year, with the Carnegie Hall date an important springboard from which to launch other events.

Since that time, Reba has had whom I consider one of the best and most diligent managers in the business, her husband, Narvel Blackstock. Although husbands don't always make excellent managers, he has guided his wife's career with the utmost polish and professionalism.

Again, I stress the importance of teamwork. Working as a booking agency team, The Jim Halsey Company complemented the other essential members of many different Star Teams, all consisting of managers, record companies, producers, music attorneys, press and PR people, promoters, and music publishers. Each of us had our specialized job to do. Mostly we had good chemistry with the other team members, and our collective ideas enhanced the **Power of Performance** for all concerned, including the artist.

♪ ♪ ♪ ♪

One of my favorite managers in the business is Stan Moress. When we first met in the 1960s, Stan was a fledgling PR person employed by the great Jay Bernstein. He left Bernstein for a position with Mike Curb, then the youngest record company president in the business, at MGM. Our careers intersected again in the '80s, when Halsey Company client Tammy Wynette, along with her husband, George Richey, hired Stan to revamp Tammy's image. By this time, Stan had become a big-time manager, handling stars such as Gloria Estefan, Eddie Rabbit, and others. He became Tammy's manager.

As we booked Tammy on specific engagements, Stan stayed in daily touch with me, my agents, and our buyers. Tammy was an important client, and Stan was an effective manager, thorough and inventive, with lots of ideas.

Our company had regular meetings with Stan to plan career strategies and make plans for Tammy's future as an artist. These were held in Tulsa at The Jim Halsey Company conference room, and they usually lasted all day. At the meetings, we presented our company's ideas, discussed certain key dates, and worked with reports from Tammy's PR company, Gangwisch & Associates. All of the Halsey Company team members made a contribution. My chief of television and executive vice president, Dick Howard, would arrive from Los Angeles and focus on TV and commercials. Another senior vice president, John Hitt, our fair and special events chief, would discuss fairs, theaters, and special events, establishing a projected number of dates and the income from them. We'd listen to Stan's ideas and direction and get input from George Richey, Tammy's husband. At the day's end, we would all be coordinated on one central idea. Our goals were established, and everybody knew his or her part.

These types of "summit" meetings were very important. We held them with all our artists and managers, usually once a month. From them, we collectively established goals and set our patterns for the future, putting careers into a "road map," a picture we could all visualize. The meetings gave us a collective direction and put a new charge into all of our selling team; our daily phone calls following the meetings would always be designed to keep the artist's career on the right path.

These get-togethers with other Star Team members were *power boosters*, something every salesperson needs from time to time. *Power boosters* sharpen the **Power of Performance** for everyone on the team, lending collective energy to a specifically designed program.

I loved working with Stan Moress because his vision was the world. There was nothing that couldn't be accomplished with his artist. Stan himself is a little theatrical, a class act who can hold his own with the best of the biggest. Stan has style and flair. At this time in his life, Stan also smoked the biggest cigars I've ever seen, Churchill Havanas, and they put out a lot of smoke.

We also had style. And we, too, were "smoking." When Stan and other associates would come, we'd always pick them up in our Jim Halsey Company stretch limo, fully equipped with phones and VCR. We'd whisk them to our office escorted by four uniformed motorcycle officers, full sirens blowing, stopping all side road traffic along the way.

These weren't Tulsa Police Department officers, though. We used motorcycle escorts specifically licensed to escort funerals. But they wore much the same type of uniform, with helmets, tall riding boots, and black and white cycles with sirens and flashing red lights, and they would stop the traffic and let the limo carrying our important guests pass. Illegal? Yes, but it reflected our "show biz" welcome to our guests.

In addition to our all-day meeting, we'd have a luncheon in the converted boardroom we'd made into a dining room. Our outstanding Tulsa chef, the British-born and theatrical Gerard Campbell, would prepare an elaborate menu in our kitchen. All participants would be presented a printed menu, but the names would be changed to reflect each occasion. During one visit from Stan Moress, for instance, the menu featured Roy Clark Oxtail Soup, Salad with The Oak Ridge Boys' special "Elvira" dressing, Chicken ala Tammy, Potatoes Moress, and, for dessert, Gatemouth Brownies and ice cream.

As I've said, Stan smoked cigars. And even though I'd told him my entire office was a non-smoking area, it was hard for him to refrain. On this day, we all knew it was coming. We were certain he would light up after the meal, when we all relaxed for a little informal conversation.

Anticipating Stan, before the meal I had brought out a box of my very best Cuban Churchills, used just for special occasions, and gave each member of the dinner party (except Stan) one to hide in his or her coat. All had instructions not to light up until Stan did. It was going to be a real sacrifice for all my non-smokers, but we were all eager to see what would happen.

Sure enough, just as expected, Stan asked if we'd mind if he had a cigar. In unison, we said "no" and each person pulled out a Churchill, lit it, and started puffing away. Within two or three minutes, the air was so blue that we couldn't see one another across the room. It was a total smoke-polluted environment. Half of us were coughing, the other half wheezing. It was funny, and good-natured Stan laughed right along with the rest of us.

Stan did a great job for Tammy, and I enjoyed working with him. Tammy's husband, George Richey, eventually took over as her manager, and I must say that he was a great manager, too. As you can see, I've worked with some of the best.

Herb Gronauer was a really fine agent with our company. He'd worked with most of the very big agencies, booking lots of big acts, and before he joined us I'd known him for many years.

Herb was a great telephone salesman, one of the best I have ever known. When part of an artist's itinerary would fall out, he could always find an obscure date to plug in. He was a master of planning tours. Before leaving the office each night, his outgoing mail would be organized to prepare his buyers for his phone calls about artists he was selling.

Sometimes the idea of *repetitious impressions* influences not only the buyers and the public, but the artist as well. Reading newspaper and magazines articles about how great you are, having people line up after shows to tell you how much they love your music, being complimented by TV and radio hosts when you appear on their programs—all of this is *repetitious impressions* in action! If you're an artist, it's easy to start believing all this about yourself. This is when you should remember one of the first rules of the music business: *don't believe all your own press.*

One afternoon, after a particularly hard day, Herb was exhausted from the various problems, phone calls, cancellations, etc. That was the time that a big performer, whom we were representing at the time, called upon Herb in his office. This person, while still a recognizable name, was not currently in demand. His popularity had diminished, and he was very hard to sell, particularly for the kind of money he thought he was worth.

"Listen, Herb," said the aging star. "When these buyers call in for me, I don't think you're asking enough money."

Herb was having a bad day and he didn't need this type of aggravation from an artist—especially one he practically had to beg promoters to buy. "I hate to tell you this," Herb returned. "But I've been with the company for two years, and there hasn't been a 'call in' for you since I've been here. Every sale I've made on you has been a 'call out'."

Sometimes, you just have to explain to artists that they aren't worth the money they're demanding.

Most of the performers we represented at the Halsey Company, however, understood the business. Prices on their concerts were established within the boundaries so all could make money. Again: everybody has to be a team player.

We had a lot of great agents with the company, which was only right. After all, we had a list of important artists who had to stay booked. Another of my favorites, Sol Saffian, had years of big agency experience. He had the ability all good agents possess to pick up a hard-to-get date to fill an itinerary, or to find some obscure venue that would work after an important date canceled, leaving our artist dangling in the middle of nowhere with an open date and the expenses still running.

Sol always had a saying for everything. I wish I had written them all down. In discussing the *Billboard* record charts and some artist who was not in current demand, Sol would comment, "Yeah, their new record came out. It's in *Billboard*—No. 67 with an *anchor*." Of course, the fastest-rising records on *Billboard's* charts are designated by a "bullet," and all agents and managers are concerned about their artists' new record getting a bullet or keeping a bullet, because that means it's still on its way upward. When Sol humorously said a record had an "anchor," you knew he thought it was a loser.

♪ ♪ ♪ ♪

The booking agency is a sales and marketing company. It is no more complicated than that. Remember: the booking agent is the person or company who books dates and events, arranges television shows, and generally creates the cash flow. This will help you differentiate between the agent and the manager.

A lot of times, the booking agent is personified in the movies or television as a fast-talking, cigar-smoking, wheeler-dealer, slapping everyone on the back and calling people "baby" and "sweetheart." Admittedly, some booking agents fit this stereotype. But it's a fading breed. The agent's role today is much more sophisticated than before. The marketplace is more complex, and the tools, the computers and the information with which we work, are also more complex.

Making the sale and booking the date is just part of an agent's job. After getting to know their acts, agents must then research the marketplace; decide on the right territory to play; find the right venues, ticket pricing and percentages; and pick the right promoters. Cash flow created by tours and bookings is what keeps the act going in the beginning. The goal is to make the artist into a sound business property.

An agent has to know music, accounting, geography, sales techniques, and public relations, and be travel agent, negotiator, diplomat, and psychiatrist. As an agent, you must know how to use the tools of your trade just as skillfully as a carpenter, mason, or brain surgeon uses his. Agents also must recognize and call upon their helpers, their teammates about whom we continually talk in this book.

What are the tools needed to be a good agent?

The first one is the agent himself, his knowledge and personality. Before you can sell an artist, you must sell yourself. Having a pleasant personality is a good step. Being able to talk with knowledge about the artist and the business is a must. An agent must do a lot of research on his artist and the artist's style before ever making the first call. Like any good salesperson, an agent must learn both his buyers and his product—the artists—thoroughly. Keeping and maintaining satisfied customers is very important. In this business, *who you know* is very important, but *who knows you* is equally important. A good agent must be versatile and able to sell any type of attraction to any type of buyer.

The next tool an agent needs is a collection of buyers—the promoters, the clubs, the auditoriums, casinos, theaters, arenas, fairs, and various venues. To be in business as an agent, you must know the places to sell your attractions. You acquire these buyers through research and experience.

Another important tool is information. You can't have too much. In this day of computers, the Internet, and web pages, it is easy to assimilate, categorize, and store all types of information. There are a few information sourcebooks that list buyers of attractions on a nationwide basis. *Billboard* magazine publishes several different books with information necessary to help you start selling your attraction. *Pollstar* and *Billboard* magazines offer equally fine collections of special reference books. Research will reveal the type of acts your prospective buyer uses, helping insure that you don't try to sell a rock 'n' roll act to a classical music promoter.

At The Jim Halsey Company, our list of top buyers included 30,000 in America and 15,000 in Europe, the Pacific Rim, and South America. This collection of buyers was an invaluable tool. The more names you have on your list of buyers, the more prospects you have for making a sale. Note that I said "prospects." You still have to contact these prospects and make your sales pitch.

If you are going to be a good booking agent, learn the fundamentals of selling. You can pick up books on creative and imaginative selling in almost every bookstore in America. The same formulas and principles apply to selling performers as to any other product. When I give seminars on the music business, I suggest to all of my attendees that they read all of the sales and self-motivational books they possibly can, because they'll help you establish your own formula, your own plan on how to sell, how to make a pitch, how to promote, and how to advance the career of the artist you represent. Remember, success comes from acquiring satisfied customers.

Our company started every day with a sales meeting. At that time, we would discuss all of the open—that is, unbooked—dates still pending on the various artists we represented. We'd also exchange ideas about where we might be able to fill each date. Every agent within the company had his or her own territory, and our agents knew every aspect of their respective territories—every promoter, every venue, every event that was going on. But sometimes, in dealing with the thousands of dates our artists collectively played in a year, one might overlook something that would be obvious to someone else. Because of being temporarily overburdened with problems or pressures, an agent might forget about a certain venue. It was during this morning meeting that an exchange and networking among all of the agents was valuable, because one agent could make a suggestion that might help another.

Then as now, being a good agent boiled down to being a good salesperson. You had your product, your prospects, and then you made your contacts in a logical order. We had a well-oiled machine. At the sales meetings, we'd also make announcements about a new record product, a television appearance, or something similar. These announcements created what we called "sales burgers," which the agents could use when they went back to their offices. So in a short period of time each morning, 15 to 20 minutes, we accomplished three things:

1. *We started the day with collective energy.*
2. *We all got together for an exchange of ideas.*
3. *We were all stimulated to go out and make that first call of the day.*

The first sale each day is important, because it sets the tone for the rest of the day. To help with our calls, we made various mailings, timing them to arrive just before the agent started calling. When the call came from one of our agents, the buyer would already have that sheet of paper on his desk announcing the arrival in his area of this hot artist, and why it would be advantageous to buy a date. We called this strategy "teeing up your buyer."

We had a good sales force at The Jim Halsey Company, so good that I'm sure I could've walked into the sales meeting one morning and said, "Ladies and gentlemen, we no longer are representing people in the entertainment business. We're selling life insurance. Here are the five policies that we're now selling. These are the specifications on each policy, and why they would be advantageous to certain types of buyers. Now, instead of our regular list of 30,000 concert promoters and nightclub operators, here are names of prospective buyers for this insurance." I guarantee you that the people I had in our company could have left that sales meeting, gone to their desks and made the first phone call, selling life insurance instead of artists.

We were selling art. We were selling people who had great creative ability. But, remember my rule: *no matter what you're selling, selling is the same.*

♪ ♪ ♪ ♪

It is the booking agent's job to book tours. When you're involved in putting together tours, packaging different artists together and working many different venues, it's necessary to keep in mind the building process for a new artist as well as the maintenance of an established artist's career. Maintaining one career is just as important as building another.

Here are three things to remember, whether you're booking a new or a veteran artist:

1. *Don't just put your artist in a venue.*

2. *Don't just go on tour.*

3. *Make everything an event, and make the event happen.*

When you make the event happen, the artist happens, and it's just as easy to create excitement around an entire project as it is to book a date. When Reba played Carnegie Hall, for instance, we put out advertising letting people know that our artist was playing that prestigious venue. Make your show a special event. Make it more than just a date to play. It'll become much more important in the eyes of the public. Call on your **Power of Performance** to make it happen!

Let's say you're in a situation where the Star Team members are hitting on all cylinders. The manager's made a record deal, the record producer has cut a disc with the artist, and everybody's talking about getting the artist on the road. Once the disc is released—on a schedule determined by another team member, the record company—the artist must plan on touring to support his or her product. Touring helps in-store sales, stimulating interest in both the artist and the product on a national level. It helps get radio to play the record. It creates press interest in the artist. It is big-time sales and marketing.

All of these touring benefits don't happen without a well-developed, overall plan—which is where the booking agent comes in. It is an agent's sole function to sell the artist, booking dates into venues and areas requested by the manager, who himself is working with the record company. Each artist will have different interests and requirements for touring. Whatever the demands, it's up to the booking agent to fulfill them.

The specific number of dates that are to be booked within a specified time period is called the *artist's inventory*. This inventory of dates must be sold—that is, an agent must book the artist into a venue for each of those dates. Booking agents usually design a sales and marketing plan for filling each artist's requested itinerary. When these tours are in the process of being booked, the agent talks almost daily with the artist's manager. The more people involved and working collectively, the better the chance for success. So the strategy of the tour is usually worked out between the artist manager, the record company, and the agent.

As I've said, sales and marketing principles are pretty much the same, whether you're selling automobiles or acts, Popsicles or performers. In all cases, you have inventory to sell, prospective customers to sell to, and a method or plan for reaching those customers, explaining the benefits of the product and why they should buy it, and then making the sale.

But there's one big difference. If a salesman selling "real" material, like cars, clothing, or electronic gear, still has inventory after an extended sales period, he then makes the remaining product available at a reduced price. If some still remains, he can make further reductions and, maybe, still cover the cost of the product.

Not so with a booking agent. Once an artist's inventory period has gone by, it's gone forever. You cannot make a sale for a date on last week's calendar. This is why it's imperative that you, as agent, fill the artist's desired itinerary, and why coordination between you and the artist's manager is essential. If an inventory of dates has not been filled, then the tour will be unsuccessful, and the artist and manager will probably be looking for a new booking agent.

When a tour is planned, even before the first telephone call to a prospective buyer is made, the booking agent gets with the manager and the record label and gets the itinerary down on paper. Ideally, together they figure out the ideal tour stops and then determine the exact number of dates for the act to play, taking into consideration the performer's energy level and the amount of territory that can be covered with sensible "jumps"—that is, travel time—between each date. The tour won't always follow this plan exactly, but getting it down on paper helps pull all of the elements into place.

The manager is primarily responsible for putting together this overall plan, setting up the inventory of dates for his act on this particular tour. He then goes to the booking agency and they get out their maps and meet with the manager, record label, and artist. They determine the best area to tour and the best time to do it, with an eye on both selling more discs and making the artist an even bigger name. Once this is agreed on, it's then the booking agent's responsibility to deliver the tour.

Keep in mind that, as the booking agent for a tour, you might not get everything exactly as you want it. A town may not be available—it may not have the right venue, or there may be other reasons. But the town next to it might work. Hopefully, you'll get most of the dates you want to play.

Certain key cities are very important to play, and the chance to play them—even if it means rearranging a tour—should be taken. These key places include New York City, Chicago, Atlanta, Los Angeles, Seattle, and other cities that have at least one big radio station and an important record market. If your act cannot play them when he or she wants to, then you should consider adjusting the tour so these major disc-buying and press centers can still be included.

As a booking agent, you need to know geography, and you must know how to read a map. When you first start planning your tour, draw a line around the states that you want to play. Circle the cities where you have prospective buyers. A lot of times, a record company will know certain promoters, and it can help you in towns you're unfamiliar with. All of this may sound elementary, but it works. Our company did it this way every day, mapping out tours for 35 to 40 artists on an annual basis.

A booking agent's **Power of Performance** is easily judged by the power of the tour he or she has put together—the important cities, promoters, and radio stations involved, PLUS the cash generated! The more knowledge you have about the business and the way it works, the better equipped you are to do a good job for your artist. Learn the functions of all of the other members of your team. Again, it's important to build that teamwork among those team players. It takes a collective effort to push your artist to the top; you need the help of everyone.

In booking a tour for an artist, you, as an agent, have to make a lot of telephone calls to a lot of prospective customers, and you'd better have a good sales pitch once you make the connection. The better the salesperson, the higher the percentage of sales on each round of calling. Recognize, though, that no matter how good you are, if you only make a few calls your chances of making a sale are slimmer. Plan your sales strategy, map out your territory, and make your calls.

The booking agent has the responsibility to secure employment for the artist, but he also has an obligation to the buyer—the talent buyer or promoter. You do not oversell your customers on your product. Instead, you help them make money. As a booking agent, your customers are local, regional, and national promoters as well as talent buyers for clubs, casinos, and other venues. It's in everyone's best interest to keep them in business. So deal with your promoters honestly. Give them value, and help them promote your dates. Remember: *satisfied customers insure repeat business.*

It's like the old story about the chicken and the egg. You have to have the artist to make the tour. But there's no tour if you don't have promoters to buy the dates. So rather than wondering which element comes first, maybe we ought to consider them equally necessary to keep things going.

Keep in mind that the buyer must have a reason to buy. Maybe the artist has a record that's getting good airplay. Maybe the artist has been on television. Or maybe he or she has created a big following some other way.

Let's talk for a moment about an established artist, one who draws a reasonable amount of people and gets a good fee. What's the procedure for booking an act like this?

First, as booking agent, you get input from the record company as to where the artist needs to play to help sell records or, conversely, where the record is hot. It is a good idea to tour in both of these areas in order to maintain or boost sales.

Then, you must carefully consider the tour plans. Will it be a 15- or 20-day tour? Should the traveling be 150 or 300 miles a day? What looks like only an inch or so on the map translates into lots of extra miles for your act to grind out in a bus or van.

Where do you want to go with your artist? Determine what venues are in the territory, which artists have been playing the territory, whether or not they were successful, and what the competition is.

If you're starting out to book a 20-day tour, you don't just write down 20 venues in 20 cities. List 40 or 50, and then realistically pick the most logical routing and the best venues. Every venue is different, and each one has its own particular characteristics. Different artists like different venues. You want to pick the ones where your artist will be the best received, from hardwood-floor honky-tonk to performing-arts center. Take into consideration the record company's ideas on choice of venue. Certain venues have the ability to sell records, and others do not. For instance, it may surprise you that casinos are not regarded as important venues for a record-promotion tour. They're good for cash flow and press, though.

After you've mapped out the ideal tour itinerary, the next step is direct-mail advertising to announce the tour. Then, you start making those telephone calls. Realize that if you want to book a 20-day tour, 50 names of prospective promoters are probably not enough. You may need 120 different names. There's a lot of competition out there on the road, and you won't make every sale, but you have to make every call. Give your prospective buyers the best sales pitch possible, offering good value.

Once a sale is made, try to fit in the other dates, one after another, until the tour is booked. Realize that there's sometimes a key or pivotal date around which the tour will be booked, and it's important to sell that date first. This engagement, for instance, could be in a city the record company feels is so important that it could break your artist into the next level.

Booking the tour is just part of it, of course. Your show's production values are just as important. Agents think that once they've made the sale and issued the contract, the job's done. The truth is that if you want to stay in business, you have to make sure that the best possible technical production is utilized in your artist's appearances. Part of this can be done by including special requirements in the contract rider, such as technical instructions for sound and lights.

Most of the bigger touring shows now carry their own sound and lights and other production equipment. Some even carry their own elaborate sets. They are not going to take the chance of having their show presented improperly because of lack of technical equipment. Several acts hire specific crews or production companies that will work for an entire tour. All of this must be coordinated with the promoters on the tour to insure that each venue can properly handle the production. If you get into an area with an artist and the show doesn't have the proper production, it not only reflects badly on the artist but also the booking agent and the manager for not doing their jobs properly.

There are very few artists, with the exception of standup comedians, who can go out with one microphone and make a proper presentation. So the added value of the production that goes with the presentation is very important for a show. It enhances the audience's interest and excitement. As an agent or manager, it's your responsibility to make sure all the technical requirements are fulfilled on each tour stop. These requirements should be part of the artist's contract with the buyer. But even when they are, unfortunately they aren't always fulfilled. The agent or manager always needs to check and double-check along the way; many times, the artist's road manager has this responsibility as part of his daily duties.

I've often referred to the necessity of having a checklist. This is a good example of what I mean. Just like an airline pilot needs a checklist, the manager-agent needs something on paper that he can use to check everything and not overlook *any* minor details. The production values are part of the artist's **Power of Performance**, reflected on stage. The manager or booking agent's **Power of Performance** lies in the ability to make sure these production values get into every show.

Our tours with The Oak Ridge Boys, Tammy Wynette, Clint Black, and others took so many buses and trucks that they looked like circuses going on the road. Major tours take a lot of people and mean a lot of jobs. Many people get their first start in the business with one of these jobs.

Here are some examples of the services and talents necessary to put a big touring artist on the road:

- The Band/Musicians
- Lighting designer
- Vocalists
- Lighting company
- Background singers
- Lighting director
- Dancers
- Lighting crew/ chief programmer
- Choreographer
- Lighting tech
- Travel agency
- Riggers
- Booking agent
- Video design
- Manager
- Video director
- Tour manager
- Video tech
- Tour accountants
- Camera operators
- Production manager
- Bus company
- Security
- Bus drivers
- Sound company
- Trucking company
- House board mixer
- Truck drivers
- Stage monitors/Mixer
- Record representative
- Audio crew chief
- Sound tech
- Stage techs
- Tour press
- Merchandise/Crew
- Local stage hands
- Wardrobe design
- Wardrobe handler
- Star's valet
- Have I forgotten anybody?
- OH, OF COURSE: THE STAR!

♪ ♪ ♪ ♪

Now, let's talk about territories, which we touched on a little earlier. The Jim Halsey Company utilized its great number of agents by operating in a territorial style. Territories were divided up within the agency, and each agent took a certain territory. A territory could be a number of states or foreign countries. It could even be a certain specialized area, such as television and movies, or fairs and rodeos.

I learned early in my career that *a salesperson with a concentrated area of focus makes more sales.* They're more effective because, if they've done their research, they know their particular buyers and their buyers' needs much more intimately than any other agent. They become specialists.

Many agencies have been accused of throwing darts at a map to determine an itinerary. But if the individual agents know their respective territories and their buyers in those territories, they can coordinate a tour that looks anything but random, and makes sense to all parties concerned. An agency's **Power of Performance** is greatly increased by specialization.

Part of the reason that The Jim Halsey Company developed into a major agency was that I found and hired key people who were skilled in specialized areas. For instance, we wanted to help establish the idea that big-name country artists would do big-time box-office business at fairs and rodeos. I felt that becoming a specialist in the fair and rodeo business would give our company a certain reputation, enabling us not only to do a lot of business with the fairs and rodeos but also to attract other name artists to our company.

From the very beginning, one person—John Hitt—developed the fairs and rodeos for our company. John was instrumental in developing our company into a major agency, one who grew from representing a couple of artists to many. For a couple of years, we even represented an entire agency, the Regency Artists Group, for fairs and rodeos. Regency had some big movie and TV stars on its roster, but it didn't have a fair and rodeo department, and we did.

Tulsa, Oklahoma, was our headquarters. Hank Thompson, Roy Clark, and I, along with Wayne Creasy, Stan Synar, and Mack Sanders, were partners in a number of ventures in Tulsa, including two radio stations and a 2,500-acre cattle ranch south of town in Mounds, Oklahoma.

When John, already a successful music-business figure, came to Tulsa to meet with me, I laid out my plans for the future. What I wanted to build, I told him, was the very best booking agency in the business, one that had skilled agents who secured the very best dates for the artists, and did the very best for the promoter as well. I wanted to do it with integrity and with the philosophy of an artist manager. As I've explained throughout this book, my focus and belief was that the artist was the key to everything. If we focused our agency on the artist and the job we could do for the artist, then everything else would fall into place.

John liked the idea enough to join the company. This was in 1972, and one of the first things we did was lay out a five-year plan, getting down on paper where we wanted to be in 1977. For John, his five-year assignment included the task of helping establish our agency as country music specialists, booking quality dates for our artists and building a name for ourselves. A major part of that was selling to and servicing the fairs as a concentrated sales area of The Jim Halsey Company.

Not only for the first five years, but for 18 of them, John Hitt did exactly what we talked about in that early meeting. Our company built a reputation in the fair business second to none, and John Hitt, for The Halsey Company, became the most respected agent for fairs in America.

With the nucleus of the company established, we attracted other agents, and these other agents attracted other artists. We started building our global territory. We developed effective selling methods for our artists, for our company, and for the buyer these methods tied directly to timing, opportunity, patience, and persistence.

♪ ♪ ♪ ♪

I want to stress that a booking agent or manager's effective use of time, when there are so many things to do and so many details to take care of, is an essential part of the **Power of Performance**.

Because it's not always possible to do everything that you want or plan to do, you must prioritize the elements involved in your work, giving the ones with the highest priority the most attention and "power." If you don't plan your time, you really can't organize properly what you want to accomplish. And how can you organize? We go back to the important method I told you about earlier: *write it all down.*

As a booking agent, you must take care of lots of things every day. The first thing you have to do, of course, is *sell the dates.* Your job not only includes selling, but also taking care of problems on existing dates and servicing the artists.

The dates you've already booked are as important as the ones you're still trying to book, and they can generate problems that must be dealt with. Maybe the promoter hasn't gotten his or her deposit to you. Maybe the tickets aren't selling, or the publicity has gotten lost somewhere. Or perhaps the artist has looked at the time and miles between two dates and told you, "That's too far of a jump for me; I want to change to another date."

To handle all these situations, you must remain organized. You must have your checklist, and you must look at it daily. You have to take care of all your dates and artists—as well as your promoters—to be effective. You must be able to prioritize and divide your time so that you can take care of a number of different facets of the agent's job.

Here are five of the most important:

1. Selling tours and dates—Don't throw darts at the map, literally or figuratively. Working with the manager, the record company, and the artist, collectively decide the most effective times and places to tour.

2. Booking crucial dates—What constitutes a "crucial date"? It's a date in the middle of a major artist's tour that falls out. It's crucial because it's directly related to the tour's cash flow. The act is already on the road and he or she has to stay on tour to keep the money coming in. The record company feels that all the tour dates are important because they're connected with the window of opportunity the artist's new disc has in the market, and the company's territorial managers are already in place with promotions. When a date in the middle of this situation falls out for one reason or another, it becomes a crucial date, and it must be filled. It's an open date, and you must book it, perhaps in a different venue in the same city or area.

Crucial dates are different from career dates. A career date is booked into a venue or market that the record company feels is important because of prestigious promotional opportunities. A New York City date, for instance, can be a career date. Once you get New York City on your itinerary, then you must decide the most important venue for this career date—Radio City Music Hall, Carnegie Hall, the Beacon Theater? Another of the city's venues? Career dates are the ones that are important to the record company and to the overall planning of an artist's career, and they need to be developed as events.

3. Researching for leads—As is true with any sales organization, your list of buyers is important. As an agent, you need referrals. These are the buyers you work with on a daily basis, buyers you cultivate with good deals, special dates, and fair and reasonable prices. They make up what is called your customer base. For you to be successful, they must become satisfied customers.

You should also research and seek buyers with whom you have not worked before. Sometimes you'll read about new promoters or venues in the trades, or a radio station or record company will give you some leads in this area. Our policy at The Jim Halsey Company was to continually build our file of buyers, promoters, clubs, and concert venues, so we could keep more and more of them informed of our artists' availability. We sent out our artists' itineraries, announcing the possibility of their being in a certain area at a certain time. Always, we kept researching, kept developing our buyers' list, picking up information about club openings, new promoters, fairs changing their entertainment policies. It was all part of the research.

This type of information-gathering never ends. This research you do with your conversations, your associations, and your membership in trade organizations (such as the Country Music Association, the Academy of Country Music, the International Association of Fair Buyers and other entertainment buyer associations, the International Federation of Festival Organizations [FIDOF], etc.) can all help you locate and identify prospective buyers.

It's very important that you and everyone working for you, right down to the receptionist, read the trades on a regular basis. The Halsey Company got many leads from newspapers and trades which our secretaries, mailroom people, and receptionists read and brought in, with the salient information circled—information that was new to the rest of us. New leads pop up all the time.

Leo Zabelin, one of my mentors, was director of our public relations for many years. On a regular basis, he would read the newspapers in libraries and retrieve all of the daily papers from the major cities, maybe as many as 40 or 50, bringing them back to our office conference room to go through them. For the next few hours, he'd be busy highlighting new venues, new clubs, new events, and new celebrations.

No other agency had Leo Zabelin, and I don't think any other agency had this service, either. It was invaluable to us.

4. Dealing with problems on existing dates—When you're prioritizing, remember this: take care of problems first. If you don't, they'll not only remain, they'll possibly grow into bigger problems and interfere with your flow of energy. Booking more than 3,000 appearances a year for our stars, we had problems to deal with every day. The tickets weren't selling. The tickets hadn't gone on sale. The promotion hadn't arrived. The advertising hadn't started. There was a conflict with the radio-station presenters. The deposit on the date wasn't in. The venue was closed for remodeling.

You deal with literally thousands of problems over a year's time. But as I told you earlier, I preferred then, and still prefer, to call them *situations*. Every now and then a real problem will arise—remember the MGM Hotel fire from Chapter 4?—and then you can make that distinction. But problems and situations are just part of the business—things that have to be taken care of regularly, just like answering the telephones or taking out the mail.

5. Being the "responsible agent"—Within our agency, we had what was known as "the responsible agent." Not only did each agent have a territory for which he or she was responsible, each agent had three or four artists on our roster that he or she was responsible for. All of our agents booked all the artists on our roster, but the responsible agents had the vital responsibility for their individual acts on a daily basis. Reba McEntire, The Judds, Roy Clark, Tammy Wynette, or any other of our clients knew they could call me or any agent in the Halsey Company. But they also knew that they each had one agent in the company who was their responsible agent, an agent whose job it was to know everything that was going on in their particular career, up to the minute and in-depth.

When we had our sales meetings, it was the responsible agent's duty to go over the artist's itinerary, crucial dates, problem dates, and any other situation specific to his or her particular artist. As we went around the table each morning, we discussed all of the situations for all of our artists. Each performer's responsible agent would tell what was going on, the dates that we needed to fill an itinerary, the status of contracts and deposit checks due on this particular day, special plans for the future, and any crucial dates that needed to be put on the books that day. If someone reported a crucial date, every agent we had would go out and make 10 calls regarding that particular date; with this concentration of effort, we succeeded in getting many crucial dates booked for our artists. In fact, it was highly unusual for The Jim Halsey Company to have an open date on any of our artists.

The responsible agents were the ones who took information from the office to their acts, which was was much more efficient than having every agent in the company calling artists or managers with bits and pieces of information or dates to be cleared.

The term "clearing a date" means getting the artist's okay on an already-booked date. This wasn't always easy. We would give the performer all the details—venue, promoter, number of shows, billing, any support acts—and hope for a quick reply after our recommendation.

The responsible-agent setup made for a consistency in our operations with much less chance for error. The other agents within our company would book dates for an artist, and then take the dates they'd booked to that artist's responsible agent. We'd wait until the end of our daily business, after everybody had gathered all of the dates booked that day, and then make one telephone call to each artist or artist manager, going over everything at one time. (The only exception to this procedure occurred if a date or event came along that needed immediate attention, such as an appearance on *The Tonight Show* or something equally important.)

Looking at the overall situation this way, responsible agents could ascertain which dates made sense, which ones didn't make sense, whether there was enough money offered by the buyer, whether they could get a little more. Instead of making a call every 30 minutes or every hour, the responsible agents made one call to each of their artists at the end of the day and went over the day's business, which was much more sensible and organized, a more effective use of time and energy.

As the head of the agency, I was ultimately responsible for everything. But spreading my duties and responsibilities among the different agents helped me tremendously.

When you begin working as an agent, remember that you must be able to divide your time effectively among the preceding five areas, which is tough enough. But also keep in mind that the constant flow of business provides an equally constant flow of interruptions, which can keep you from spending your time the way you've planned. Something's always coming up, and it's too easy to find yourself farther behind at the end of the day than you were at the beginning.

You know how I feel about the importance of writing things down, be they dreams or responsibilities. As an agent, you should put down all the vital information you've gathered during a day. Then, write down every telephone call that you intend to make, every letter you intend to write. When your morning starts—whether it's with an agency sales meeting or working on your own—you should have an agenda, a list of perhaps 25 or 30 telephone calls you've scheduled to make. Add to that list as the day goes on; in addition to making phone calls, you'll receive them. Some of our agents would make as many as 200 to 250 calls per day, sticking to the plan they'd written down.

The solutions to problems—or, rather, *situations*—are usually a lot more simple than you're willing to admit. It is mostly a matter of controlling your business day, rather than having it control you, of forcing activities into the time available, rather than trying to expand the time to accommodate the activities. Once you really believe that controlling your time is not only more productive but more pleasant, the rest of it is fairly easy.

Here are five work day habits guaranteed to enhance your **Power of Performance**:

1. *Clear your desk of all papers except those relating to the immediate situation at hand.*

2. *Do things in the order of their importance to your planned schedule.*

3. *When you face a problem, solve it then and there—if you have the facts necessary to make the decision.*

4. *Learn to organize*

Again, organize for the next day at the end of the previous day. This gives you peace of mind at night, along with a feeling that you're on top of things. It also infuses you with real excitement about coming into work the next morning. Arrange your next day on paper, defining what you want to accomplish. *Write it down!* Do this, and you'll always feel that you have a head start.

   5. *Return all phone calls.*

Enough said!

A large part of sticking to your schedule is knowing that it's very rare something is so important, or a crisis is so urgent, that it has to be attended to immediately. Treat interruptions as you would any other time commitment. Make sure you program a space in each day for dealing with them.

Our agency customers were buyers for television shows, network producers, prospective corporate sponsors, fairs, rodeos, casinos, promoters, night club operators, theaters, ballrooms, colleges and universities, special events, festivals, city celebrations—*anybody* that used talent. And all of them had one thing in common: they knew their basic needs, which was to present talent and make a profit.

It was our job to help them buy the right attraction.

Then, as now, there were literally thousands of artists in the marketplace. Nashville alone had over 300 touring bands, singers, and recording stars. We had competition! We had lots of competition! And we had a responsibility to create a demand for the artists we represented, and to *sell them*—for a fair and equitable price.

We constantly needed to stimulate our prospective customers to buy *our* talent! The job of our booking agency was to convince the buyer that Halsey Company artists would do a better job, draw more people, get more outside support, be easier to work with, satisfy their ticket buyers, and make them money. It was our agency's **Power of Performance** that determined whether or not we made a sale.

Earlier in this chapter, I used the term *call to action.* It refers to having a buyer call your agency to inquire about one of your acts, and you get it by showing how your act can fill a prospective customer's needs. One of the most effective ways of creating a demand for your act, of activating the "call," is direct mail. Remember how it worked in our Clint Black campaign? It worked for us in many other situations, too. We sent reams of advertising stimuli to the buyers on our preferred list. It was planned. It was organized. It worked.

As an agent, you want prospective buyers to call *you*. Sure, an agent can call up a buyer and make a sale. But what if you have to call 10 buyers before a sale is made, or 20 buyers? Wouldn't it be easier to create some excitement so the buyer calls *you*? Then, all you have to do is negotiate the date and the price. When an agent originates the call, the buyer knows we need the date. No matter how much the buyer might be interested in the act, the fact remains that you're the one who's calling, and he knows that you want to make a sale.

If you instead stimulate that buyer to call you, it's just the opposite. You then know that the buyer wants to buy. Psychologically, you're better prepared to make a sales pitch, to ask for more money and make a better deal for your artist than if you had initiated the call.

Again, I believe in direct mail. I believe in mailing the buyer an advertising piece that stimulates him to pick up the telephone and say, "Yes, I want to buy that attraction. I'm going to call and find out if it's available and how much it costs."

This *call to action* principle is used every day on the infomercial pitches you see on television. They stimulate you to get out of your seat, go to the telephone, and make that toll-free call. In the same way, by stimulating your buyer with an attractive piece that tells about a new record release, a high chart position, a good review, an exciting sales figure, he's stimulated to pick up the telephone and call you.

Also called *direct-response marketing*, this approach saves you a lot of outgoing telephone calls, which can not only be expensive, but time-consuming as well. At the Halsey Company, our effective mailers would include an artist's picture and give his or her history—all positive, positive, positive. "This artist is for you!" "This artist can make you money!" "You should buy this artist!" "CALL US NOW!" Well, it wasn't quite that simple, but that was the gist of our message, and it was very effective for us. You can do it today via regular mail, fax, or even e-mail.

But while we got plenty of incoming inquiries as a result of these calls to action, we still had to make lots of outgoing calls. It's a part of the business, and some agents are better at it than others.

At The Jim Halsey Company, Herb Gronauer constantly impressed me with his telephone skills. Averaging between 200 and 300 outgoing calls a day, Herb was a master at sizing up a buyer's needs and making a deal. He always planned his next day before he left at night, and he always did his own mailings, which amounted to between 100 and 200 pieces each day. His buyers were constantly teed up. Either they'd call Herb about the artist in his mailing, or they'd know about Herb's artist when he called them. Either way, they'd be prepared to talk about a deal. He was one of the best agents I ever worked with.

Ron Baird, another Halsey Company agent, was also methodical and studied with his sales approach. His method of asking for the sale—whether by phone, mail, or in person—was always very intellectual, to the point, and factual. Ron is with Creative Artists Agency now; I consider him one the best agents who ever worked for our company. Ron took the Boy Scout motto to heart: He was always prepared.

Bob Kinkead, a young man who came to our company when he was barely 21, was very aggressive and became one of the best cold-call agents I've ever seen. When our company merged with The William Morris Agency in 1990, Bob went to William Morris for a short time and then became manager of the Nashville office of the Agency for Performing Arts (APA), where he continued to make somewhere between 300 and 350 telephone calls a day, not only in the office, but in his car, on his boat, and in his home. Bob is now in the artist-management business. At our agency, Bob Kinkead made his calls only after he'd stimulated his buyers with effective direct-mail pieces on his artists. He's one of the most dedicated agents I've ever known, and both he and Herb knew the strategy of direct mail followed by a phone call.

Here's some important advice for manager and artist as well as agent: *plan your direct mail*. Target where it's going and the territories it's going into. Recognize early the dates that need to be supported, and start your mailing campaign early, too. Again, I stress that if your mailers and advertising pieces illustrate how the buyers' needs can be filled, you've got a sale. These *impact enhancers* should be so direct and to the point that they stimulate the buyers' *call to action* phone call. How can they pass up the opportunity to present this great artist you've shown them?

Read and reread your advertising copy. Is it to the point? Is it attractively presented? Is it powerfully presented? Will it generate a buyer's *call to action*?

My friend Joe Sugarman, the creator of BluBlocker Sunglasses, has been recognized as the king of direct-response marketing. A long time ago, he told me, "In advertising, the first sentence is the most important. The second most important is the second sentence, and so on." So, make your first sentence important!

Sometimes, you can afford to send your direct mail first class. But when you're mailing 25,000 to 30,000 pieces several times a month, you want to be able to send it bulk mail. It takes more time for bulk mail to get where it's going; sometimes it can take as much as three weeks to get to its destination, while first-class gets there in three or four days. If you're bulk-mailing, plan on when you want the item to arrive, and then work backwards, mailing the piece within the necessary time period so it'll arrive when you want it to arrive.

Part of being an agent is planning ahead. Plan around certain holiday periods when you know there'll be more buying activity than at other times of the year. Start mailing early for New Year's Eve, Halloween, or Fourth of July dates. Fairs usually start buying in the fall for the next season—certainly by the time the big fair-buyers' convention is held in Las Vegas, so plan your mail to arrive accordingly. Make your mailings as creative as possible. As I keep preaching, stimulate your buyer to make the *call to action*.

Use direct mail to sell your ideas. Maybe you have an idea for creative packaging, putting two or three artists together on the same tour. We did it with Roy Clark and Mel Tillis. We did it with Tammy Wynette and George Jones, and several others. It gave the buyer the opportunity to buy a special event. For The Oak Ridge Boys, we put together a gigantic Christmas tour tied in with corporate sponsorship and guest artists. We had support from Larry Jones' Feed the Children charity, Amana Refrigeration, and Totino's Pizza, along with a number of other elements that made the package very attractive to the concert promoter, since it already had a lot of support going for it before the tickets even went on sale. By programming Christmas songs, special staging and effects (including snow on stage), and other elements, The Oak Ridge Boys show became a Christmas event in each city. Because of its initial success, it became an annual "happening."

Other things agencies can do is stimulate hotels to do a series of shows. They can also provide the impetus for community concerts, fundraisers, conventions, and sales meetings; colleges are another good area for agency work. These kinds of dates are booked a long time in advance, so you have to start your promotion many, many months ahead of the show in order to generate buyer interest very early. Maybe it will take more than one mailer to do it. Maybe it'll take two or three But I've seen it happen many times: an artist relatively unknown at the start of a direct-mail campaign becomes, after a series of mailings, big in the eyes of the buyers. Again, that's how *repetitious impressions* work. The buyers have impression after impression put in front of them, and it pays off in increased bookings for your artist.

A lot of times, you can support your mailings with tie-ins to other things, such as television show appearances or ads in trade publications like *Billboard* and *Amusement Business*. Every time a Halsey Company artist appeared on *The Tonight Show* or another popular program, we would send out bulk mailings, usually supported by full page ads in *Holly-*

wood Reporter and *Daily Variety.* If we didn't have time to send our mailings bulk, we'd send them first class.

Faxes and e-mail are other effective ways to notify buyers that something important is going on with the artist. When one of our artists appeared on *The Tonight Show, The Arsenio Hall Show* or *Late Night with David Letterman,* we'd send as many as 500 faxes the morning before the scheduled appearance, saying something like, "Tonight, Clint Black is going to be on *The Tonight Show.* Be sure to watch. He'll be performing his latest single, 'Killin' Time,' which is No. 1 on the charts."

These faxed *impact enhancers* are very effective sales tools. They stimulate the buyer to make that *call to action.*

As a booking agent, you should know everything possible about each of your artists. Remember when we talked about doing research, just like you would if you were selling automobiles or refrigerators? The more knowledge you have about your acts' careers, their records. their backgrounds, the venues they've played, the gross receipts from their shows, the reviews, the crowd receptions, the better equipped you are not only to sell them but get more money for their dates as well. Get the facts in your hand. If an artist made a successful tour of the Northeast, find out the venues he or she played and how many tickets were sold. Were any sold out? If so, use that! If he or she received good press in the area, use that, too.

An agent usually deals with more than one artist, and the bigger the agency, the more acts you deal with. In the Halsey company, I usually liked to keep the ratio of artists to agent at about three to one. When we were representing 35 to 40 artists, I employed between 12 and 14 agents. This didn't overload the agents, but because it was part of my philosophy to go in-depth with each artist, I felt it was the highest ratio of performer to agent that I wanted.

As soon as we signed a new act, every agent had to see it as soon as possible. Then they could honestly say to a buyer, "I have seen this artist. I know what he can do on stage. He can deliver to your audience, and he'll deliver for you at the box office." I don't care how good a salesperson you are. If you haven't seen a performer, you just won't have the natural enthusiasm you get once you've actually watched the act work.

Remember what I said earlier: *Enthusiasm will sell more product than anything else.*

♪ ♪ ♪ ♪

We discussed a lot of things at our morning sales meetings; it was the time for everyone to share information. Early on, before the computer revolution, all of the vital information on our artists was in books. Now, the same info is just as likely to be found on a computer database. Either way, your artist profile should include a picture and vital statistics, the size of the performer's band and its instrumentation, the record label, the albums he or she has had on the charts, the singles that have had chart action, awards received, important venues played, television specials, and production and staging requirements.

In this business—whether you're agent or manager—one of your most important resources is information. When someone calls you about one of your artists, you should be able to punch up your computer—or look in your book—and know instantly about the caller and his or her background. Then, when the callers asks something, you should be able to hit another couple of buttons and pull up the profile of the artist in question.

Remember these three things:

1. *You have to know your artist inside and out.*

2. *You have to know your product.*

3. *You have to know your buyer.*

If you know your artist, your product, you can sell with enthusiasm to your buyer. So write down your information on artist and buyer, put it in your computer or book, keep it at your side. It doesn't hurt to also keep a history of your act's dates, both successes and failures. Make notes of any unusual facts that might help or hinder a sale.

Also remember that booking is selling, and in selling it's not so much what you talk about as how you talk about it. Once you've got the buyer's attention, offering good service is essential. That means expedited delivery of contracts and press material, timely confirmation of dates, prompt responses to any question or request, pertinent information on staging and complete contract-rider requirements, and information on any radio or television appearances that the buyer can use to his advantage. And by all means, be honest with your buyer.

At The Jim Halsey Company, we took great pride in our company's innovative sales approaches. Our mailings were an important way of stimulating buyers—a lot of times, they were pieces of art. We gave our buyers a lot of information; as an agent, you should too. It's another way to exercise your **Power of Performance**.

And now, a few words about the famous *Jim Halsey Company Sell-A-Thon*.

The Halsey Company had a reputation for quality direct mail, featuring good-looking pieces of advertising art. So, at one point, we thought: why not do something that was not quite so tasteful, something that would also create a lot of attention? After all, it's fun to sometimes shake people up.

We always had a lot of dates booked in the fall, which is generally a big time for shows and concerts. On the other hand, January and February of each year are fairly slow because people have spent all of their money during the holiday season, and lots of buyers and promoters think you can't sell hard-ticket shows—that is, shows that require a paid-for ticket—during this time. There's far more sales resistance to dates in the first couple of months of the year than at any other time, and buyers argue much more about paying regular prices for January and February dates.

Let's say you have an artist who wants to work 150 dates a year, which is about average for a recording act. These dates are the artist's *inventory*. Until you book those 150 appearances, spread out over the year with a certain targeted number of appearances per month, there's still inventory left to sell. As I've told you before, once an inventory goes by without selling, it's over. It's not like you've still got it on the shelf, and you can reduce the price and sell it next week. An artist's inventory is tied to time; if the act wants to work a certain amount in the month of March, and March passes with no dates, that artist's March inventory is wasted. You only have so many dates to sell, based on the wishes of the artist.

Although the first of the year is always slow, the artist still needs a cash flow. Many of them give bonuses to their road musicians for the holidays; some take the entire month of December off to be with their families. So, in January and February, there are bills to be paid and salaries to be met—and so dates have to be booked.

To help our artists work more in those months, we came up with a very innovative promotion, taking our cue from automobile dealers. I have a lot of respect for automobile dealers. They know how to sell! They always have a lot of inventory. In order to move it off the lot, they have to come up with hard-hitting deals and competitive prices.

So, with the car-dealer style of advertising in mind, we designed a mailing piece that got more attention than any other mailer I've ever done in my life. At the top, in cartoon-style lettering, was emblazoned the words "The Jim Halsey Company Fall Sale-A-Thon."

"Every Open Date Must Go!" shouted the flyer. "We Must Reduce

Our Inventory!" "Artists Still With Some Dates Available!" "These Dates Must be Booked Now!" "All Offers Considered!" Then we listed each of our artists and the open dates he or she still had.

We sent out a total of 30,000 copies! Using a special toll-free number for the offer, we stayed open for 24 hours a day for all three announced days of the Sale-A-Thon. While we didn't get a lot of action during the middle of the night, the promotion netted us thousands of calls. Some were laughing when they called, some complimented us on the clever promotion, some thought it too "hard-sell." But most had answered the *call to action* and they'd *bought*! Sure, it was a gimmick, but the fact that we were available 24 hours a day during the event showed we were really interested in delivering something for the buyer—and for our artists as well.

Within a week after these mailers hit, we had been deluged with telephone calls and had written several millions of dollars worth of business. We ended up having a lot of fun with the promotion, and the artists and buyers had some fun with it, too.

♪ ♪ ♪ ♪

It is statistically proven that the more calls you make, the better your chances of making more sales. To make calls, you need leads.

At The Jim Halsey Company, we had our own resource base, which included all of the promoters, all of the venues, and all of the buyers we knew. New venues and new buyers crop up all of the time, and these are particularly important in developing new artists. That's because your established acts, the big names you work with, usually have a relationship with the more established promoters and buyers. Sometimes, to get a new artist started, you have to find the out-of-the-way clubs and other venues so you can make an itinerary for them that's meaningful to the record company, which wants an act to play the cities in markets where his or her records are going to be promoted.

Part of our business at the agency every day was scrambling for new leads. We've already talked about the trade papers and Leo Zabelin, who brought in the newspapers every day. Our agents would also call contacts at newspapers and auditorium managers. Sometimes a city's Chamber of Commerce was a good source of information.

Even with those resources, though, we would sometimes get desperate for leads. At those times, we would often call the local radio station.

Radio has been a great source of help to us in our company, and I am grateful to their unselfish giving of information to our agents over the years. A good relationship with radio helped us in many ways, and it can help you as well.

As an agent, you need radio's support. You need radio stations to play your artists' records, because if they don't, it's impossible to have a hit. When you go into a community and book your date with the local promoter, it's important to work with the local radio station as well. Make sure the station gets plenty of material on your artist, and don't rely on the promoter to get it there.

The radio station is a source of information for you. It's also a resource in helping your artist date work. At The Jim Halsey Company, we kept information on radio stations across the country, When we booked an act into a city, we knew what stations could be used as resources. Although our roster carried such diverse acts as James Brown, Roy Orbison, Leon Russell, Rick Nelson, and the Woody Herman Band, the bulk of our clients were country music artists played on country radio stations. The procedure for utilizing radio, however, is the same, whether you're dealing with a jazz act, a rock act, or a country act.

Once you find the radio station or stations whose format fits your act, get the names of the station managers, program directors, and music directors. Not only can they help you with information about their cities, but they can also become talent buyers. Sometimes, big stations sponsor listener-appreciation nights, free concerts for their listeners. Even though a station usually only does that once or twice a year, it's a good way to build your artist in that area by getting him or her in front of a lot of people.

In other situations, a good promoter will get a radio station to be the co-presenter of a show or concert, which means they can use the station and its name as an exclusive promotion vehicle and, many times, use the station's hot air personalities as emcees.

It's also important to know if a station is locally owned or if it's part of a group. Over the years, The Jim Halsey Company developed a lot of friends involved with a group of stations. One was Great Empire Broadcasting Company, headed by Mike Oatman of Wichita, Kansas. Great Empire's holdings included such powerhouse country stations as Wichita's KFDI, Tulsa's KVOO, Omaha's WOW, Shreveport's KWKH and the Branson-affiliated KTTS, out of Springfield, Missouri, along with a number of others in other cities

For many years, Great Empire held listener-appreciation nights. They would buy a package of talent and run it through their different cities, giving the event a concentrated promotion in each one. For 30 to 60 days before each concert, it was nearly all you heard about on the Great

Empire station in that market. These concerts were effective for both Great Empire Broadcasting and the artists doing the shows. The collective **Power of Performance** paid off for everybody.

Although radio can become an important member of your team, I don't list it as one of the first essential team members. Why not? Because it has a very specific role to play in an artist's development. Radio only becomes involved with your artist when—and if—it plays your artist's record. This is a specific, often temporary relationship, but it's an important one. Although there have been a few exceptions over the years, a new recording artist *will not* become a star without radio.

All of the other elements must be in place before radio joins the team. Once it does join, however, it's an essential member with its own **Power of Performance** to contribute to the making of a successful act.

♪ ♪ ♪ ♪

Radio, of course, isn't your only important broadcast medium. Another one that was especially important to the Halsey Company and our performers was television.

At the beginning of my career, I sold an Oklahoma City-based TV show starring Hank Thompson and his Brazos Valley Boys to a regional network. Its **Power of Performance** was amazing, and it didn't take me long to recognize the power of pictures added to audio. Our regional television program enhanced our ticket sales in those areas. Network television, with its ability to instantly reach 30 to 40 million people, became one of our keys in developing our performers' careers.

We had many ways of tapping into TV for our promotional use. Of course, we always notified our buyers when one of our acts had an appearance coming up on a big show. We also worked to get our country stars on non-country shows, crossing them over into another market. We were very successful doing this with Roy Clark in the '60s and '70s, and with the late Minnie Pearl, the wonderful country music comedienne and personality.

Despite her down-home humor and costuming, Minnie (whose real name was Sarah Cannon) was one of the most educated and classy ladies I have ever met. There also was a very hip facet of Minnie's persona that made her equally at home on *The Tonight Show* or *The Bell Telephone Hour* as on *The Grand Ole Opry*.

In the '60s, the standard set for a country music artist's spot on a TV show usually involved bales of hay in front of a barn. Roy Clark helped change that notion. Early on, Roy was appearing on a major network special. When he went out to perform "Malaguena" on his 12-string guitar, he was confronted by corn stalks, bales of hay, and a phony barn. Later, this would be accepted set dressing for a comedy show like Roy's *Hee-Haw*, but it was completely out of context for this performance.

So, I complained to the producer.

"How would you like Roy presented?" he asked.

"Just like any other good artist," I replied. That was it. The set was changed.

Once I saw how fast an artist could gain substantial stardom via television, I knew I wanted to concentrate on it. At the time, John Hitt was already in place for our specialized areas of fairs, rodeos, and conventions. We now needed a television expert, someone who would concentrate on series, specials, commercials, and movies.

Dick Howard, a young man with major agency experience, had worked with our company securing TV guest spots for our artists, and he was known and liked by all. Joining our company in the new position of vice president in charge of television, motion pictures, and commercials, he got the new responsibility of building our television department, securing as many worthwhile television appearances as possible for the artists we represented. He opened and directed our Los Angeles office.

A man of great integrity, Dick had built a fine reputation among television producers and talent buyers as an ethical person. He always wanted to sell the right person for the right show. He also had great vision and imagination and tremendous sensitivity when dealing with an artist's art. Dick had a grasp on the future; I always appreciated his ideas on building our artists as well as our company. He fully understood the Star Team philosophy and the concept of creating *events* with your acts. Both Dick Howard and John Hitt were essential in creating the Halsey Company's success over the next 20 years.

Television was not always a profitable area, because many times an artist would be booked on shows that didn't pay a lot of money. A performer might have to give up a lucrative concert to fly to the West Coast and do *The Tonight Show*—for $356! A guest shot on a major special might get an act seen by 40 million people, but the paycheck for a top-of-the-show guest-artist was only $7,500 or $10,000.

But television exposure had, and has, many other benefits besides the immediate financial ones.

I remember when Roy Clark was making a lot of appearances on *The Tonight Show*. When I was in Nashville, I'd run into other managers and agents, and they'd tell me, "Halsey, you're crazy. You're absolutely crazy to send Roy Clark all the way to California to do a show that pays $356.

You ought to have more pride in your artists than that!"

But the reason I did it is that 40 million people were watching, and the next day our phone would just ring off the wall with buyers and promoters wanting to buy Roy. At that point, some people didn't even know his name. They'd ask for "that guy who looks like Jonathan Winters and plays a guitar."

And It wasn't long before Roy became one of the top five most-recognized people on television, just a few notches under Bob Hope.

Keeping with our company's philosophy, we specialized and focused on a target. We did not have three or four people calling up television producers and directors, giving them a pitch on our different artists, and then three or four others calling next week to do the same thing. It was important to have one person in our company establish a reputation, and then focus on selling our artists on television.

I remain very proud of the professionalism that our company built and practiced over the years, not only in representing our artists, but in our associations with buyers, producers, directors, managers, and fair managers, among others. We were No. 1, and much of the credit goes to two fine gentlemen, John Hitt and Dick Howard.

♪ ♪ ♪ ♪

As a booking agent and manager, over the years I learned not to take "no" for an answer. I always say it's not how many no's you get in your negotiations, but, through persistence and consistency, how many yes's you end up with.

You may remember that in my early days with Hank Thompson, I functioned as both his manager and his booking agent. I had studied sales and marketing in school. I was a consistent salesperson. I knew how to make a presentation, how to negotiate, and how to go for the close. I encountered a lot of problems, of course, but early on, I learned to maintain a positive attitude and not to accept "no."

Here's a wonderful illustration of this attitude.

In those early days, I was taking Hank Thompson and his Brazos Valley Boys across the country, looking for new venues and new events that we could promote. One of the things I wanted to do was find venues that were not specifically country music, but hosted all kinds of different musical acts—venues that were out of the norm for country artists. In those places, I felt, we could create an *event*, exhibit our **Power of Performance** to different kinds of audiences, and build our artist to ever-greater heights.

Hank Thompson and his Brazos Valley Boys had already become a crossover attraction. Although he was a country act, with hits on *Billboard*'s country charts, Hank and his band performed not only country and western swing numbers, but big-band standards as well. Among the songs in their repertoire were the likes of "Tuxedo Junction," "String of Pearls," and "Take the `A' Train." It was a great band, good enough to win the No. 1 Western Swing Band from *Cash Box* magazine for 13 consecutive years. The Brazos Valley Boys also won similar awards from *Billboard*, *Down Beat*, and *Record World,* even as Hank was winning his own awards as a singer and songwriter.

Because of my experience as a promoter, playing the big bands of such top figures as Stan Kenton, Woody Herman, Harry James, Count Basie, and Guy Lombardo, I saw the potential of taking Hank's great western swing band into territories and ballrooms that had only seen big pop bands.

Salt Lake City had such a place. It was a very popular ballroom called the Lagoon, which played only the top big-name bands in the nation. Weekly big-band broadcasts originated from the Lagoon as well. I was determined to get Hank Thompson booked there, helping to expand his horizons, open up new markets, and develop new territories. It would be a good credit for Hank.

The Lagoon was operated by a man named Bob Freed. I put him on our mailing list with the idea of systematically persuading him to buy Hank and the Brazos Valley Boys for his hall. I was convinced they'd do well in his ballroom, and I hoped to convince him as well, by putting into play my method of *repetitious impressions*.

My first few telephone calls to Mr. Freed met with thorough rejection. He didn't just say "no. " He said, "No, not now, and not in the future." He wasn't interested in Hank Thompson—or any other country music performer, for that matter.

I've talked before about overcoming rejection. You'll encounter it in any kind of sales business; you cannot take it personally. Instead, you have to somehow discover a way of getting that "no" turned around into a "yes." You have to discover why you were turned down, revise your strategy, and try a different approach, a different sales angle.

The point is not just to convince your prospective buyer to buy what you have for sale. You have to make the sale right for a buyer's situation, so he can profit by it. You have to convince him that it is right for him and his customers. Many times that's a big job, and it's where you lose a lot of sales people. They get discouraged. They lose their focus on their goals.

My focus, however, was solidly on my goals. I was following my plan, but Bob Freed at the Lagoon in Salt Lake City was hindering my progress toward achieving those goals by refusing to buy. My **Power of Performance** was not effective with Mr. Freed. So, I came up with an exercise that worked for me then, and continues to work for me today. It will work for you, too.

I put myself in Mr. Freed's shoes. I examined what it would take to convince him to buy. In making a sale or in representing a client, you don't need to use hype or an exaggerated sales pitch. Just be normal, and logically give every reason that you can think of as to why this sale, this deal, should take place.

That's what I did. Over a period of three months I sent a series of letters to Mr. Freed about Hank and the band, each one telling of a recent success or containing a positive review of a new record. I sent along *Billboard* charts to show him that Hank had a record climbing the charts every week. I mailed him stories from metropolitan newspapers about Hank's appearances, and I notified him about upcoming television appearances that Hank was going to make.

After beginning this campaign, I heard nothing from Mr. Freed. No letters. No telephone calls. So I called *him*—and got another emphatic "no." I decided that before I made another call to him, he'd have so much information at hand that he couldn't say no again. I was determined to change his "no" to a "yes."

Three months after I implemented this *repetitious impressions* plan, I arrived at work to find a letter on my desk postmarked Salt Lake City, with the return address of the Lagoon. The message inside was simple and to the point. Bob Freed had answered the *call to action*. He'd decided to try Hank Thompson at the Lagoon, and for the date and the price I'd suggested. He wrote that he'd become so sick and tired of my insistent barrage of phone calls, letters, mailing pieces, and advertising on Hank Thompson that he considered booking Hank as his only way of getting rid of me. My *repetitious impressions* had worked! He further stated, however, that if the engagement was not successful, he never wanted to hear from me again, and that I was to take his name, address, and telephone number out of my Rolodex forever.

So, there was a lot riding on the date. But I knew that date—or, rather, that *event*—would be a huge success, and it was. It surpassed my expectations, and it certainly surpassed the expectations of Bob Freed. He played Hank Thompson at the Lagoon many, many more times after that, and we became great friends. My persistence and perseverance had paid off. My **Power of Performance** was evident.

♪ ♪ ♪ ♪

As an agent, you should always be trying to find new and inventive ways of marketing your roster of artists. It's just as though you have a retail store with lots of good merchandise: a lot of what you sell goes to the same satisfied customers, so sprucing up the displays, arranging several items together, or doing something new and different can create excitement. In the Halsey Company, we sometimes packaged two of our biggest stars together to make a super show aimed at Las Vegas casinos. For tours, we'd creatively package several of our artists and send them out on one bill in an effort to draw larger crowds, generate more excitement in the press, and make every tour stop an *event*.

I love events. And they don't get much bigger than the one the Halsey Company got involved with in the early 1980s when, after much work, negotiating, and deal-swapping, we announced that we were presenting, for a very limited number of engagements, a reteamed *George Jones* and *Tammy Wynette*. It was the first time they'd toured together since their highly publicized divorce, and they'd be singing their big duet hits, live, once again. What a natural! What an event! The press and television news went crazy, and radio was ecstatic. The George and Tammy tour was going to be one of the biggest musical events of the year, and the Halsey Company was presenting it.

The promoters and the press gave us a lot of credit for working the magic necessary to reunite these two country music giants, and I wish we could take the credit. We *were* the agents, the ones selling this colossal tour, but Tammy's husband, George Richey, was the mastermind. A multi-talented individual, Richie is a songwriter, musician, and a great producer; but I think his talents as an artist manager surpass everything else. He has an astute ability to guide an artist's career, and he had done so superbly with Tammy for years. He knew the potential **Power of Performance** of a Tammy and George tour, but nobody thought it possible to bring these two legends back together again professionally. George Richey made a deal and he made it work. Our part was easy. The hard part was in creating the event.

The pre-tour press was terrific. Promoters lined up to be among the chosen few who'd present these historic dates. Many of them, however, were skeptical of Jones. He'd been going through some rough times in the past several years, earning the well-deserved nickname of "No-Show Jones" for his failure to make all of his bookings.

To everybody's relief, however, he showed up for all the George and Tammy dates and did a terrific job. In fact, both Tammy and George were terrific, receiving glowing reviews wherever they played. With the help and inspiration of George Richey, we'd had the honor of presenting one of the most historically important touring events in country music.

We should have stopped there.

After the tour, George Richey's brother Paul became Jones' manager. He asked that we stay on as a part of the George Jones Star Team. I've always been a fan of Jones' talents, and we were excited about representing this superstar. So we signed an exclusive, three-year booking-agent agreement with Mr. Jones and announced to the world we were selling dates on this legend.

It was a booking bonanza! Dates were going on the books faster than we could issue the contracts. But as soon as we had Jones' itinerary filled for several months in advance, things started going askew for George again. He started missing dates again. Sometimes he even showed up at the venue but refused to get off his bus and go on, leaving thousands of irate customers scrambling for ticket refunds.

Naturally, after each blown date, the promoter would file a lawsuit against George Jones to try to recover the losses involved in advertising, building rental, and all of the other expenses involved with promotion of the date.

Our contracts clearly stated that The Jim Halsey Company functioned only in an agency capacity, and were not responsible for any of our artists' actions. Nevertheless, every date that George missed brought us a lawsuit. We had to hire local legal counsel in every city where he missed a date. Although the actions against us would always be dismissed, since we were not liable, it still cost our company a couple of thousand dollars each time to get our liability legally cleared. Because of this, when we were only three months into our three-year contract with the legendary George Jones, our legal fees totaled more than $30,000.

Representing George Jones hit us in the pocketbook in other ways as well. Because of his erratic behavior, all of my agents were now feeling the heat from their good buyers. Everyone who'd lost money on a Jones date now wanted a favor, a good break on the other acts he or she was buying from us.

Finally, I called a meeting with Paul Richey, Jones' manager. I explained to him that I had the greatest respect for George Jones' talent, but I could no longer afford to be involved with booking him. I returned their three-year contract with thirty-three months remaining. Richey understood. The lawsuits we were getting hit with were embarrassing for him, too.

I'd had the honor of representing the historic reuniting of Tammy and

George. I'd represented George Jones, the legend, and for a short period of time his name and picture had graced our artist roster. In all, it had been a very rewarding experience for me.

About a year later, I was backstage at Opryland for a television event. A number of our artists were making guest appearances, and so was George Jones. I hadn't seen him since we parted company. Although this was still during a time when he was having some personal difficulties, he was very cordial and we had a nice visit. At one point, though, the talk turned to business and he started to chastise me. "Halsey," he said, "when your agents are booking my dates, tell them not to make the jumps so far."

I had to tell him we hadn't represented him for over a year.

I'm happy to report that since our time with George, his wife, Nancy, has helped him turn his life around, and he's doing very well, thank you. Nancy Jones has worked successfully not only to restore his personal life, but his professional life as well. Fans and promoters alike have been forgiving and have supported George's rehabilitation. By the way, I'm still a big George Jones fan and respect him immensely.

The lesson I learned from my experience with Mr. Jones just reinforced my belief that an agent needs to do a good job for all concerned. It's not a good deal unless all parties benefit. And if you're an agent with more than one artist, your dealings with the buyers and promoters will reflect on your entire roster and all their shows, not just a single engagement.

Because it involves selling and marketing, the agency business is a business of details. Details can make the difference between mediocrity and greatness, failure and success. And details can get you in trouble. Again, remember to keep and consult your checklist of details!

As an agent, you have to depend on information from other people to complete your own schedule of events. I've adopted a very important rule about this, and I suggest you adopt it also.

It is: *never assume*!

Never assume *anything*. Get out that checklist. Check it and double-check it. Make it a habit. It's a very important protection against mistakes and missteps.

Here's a checklist of general business procedures to provide you with an example for your own:

Never assume . . .

- *someone remembers your name*
- *someone has the correct dates*
- *someone has returned the contract*
- *someone has your correct phone number and address*
- *someone has sent the deposit*
- *someone has sent the advertising*
- *someone has placed the advertising*
- *someone has sent the promotional material for the show*
- *someone has received the promotional material for the show*
- *your act is booked for only one show*
- *your act is booked for two shows*
- *the bus driver knows the way*
- *it's only an hour's drive*
- *everyone remembers the contract details*
- *the buyer's check is good (this is a big one)*
- *the check is in the mail*
- *the date is firm*
- *your act is getting proper billing*
- *your act is getting billed at all!*
- *your act's name is spelled correctly in the billing*
- *food and beverages are furnished*
- *hotel rooms are complimentary*
- *"it's been paid for"*
- *"it's been picked up"*
- *it'll be furnished when you arrive*
- *the sound is good*
- *the piano is tuned*
- *the lighting's adequate*
- *stagehands will be there*
- *everybody speaks English*
- *the car is full of gas*
- *a spare tire's in the trunk*
- *the luggage will arrive with your flight*

- *the airline's ticket price is the same as before*
- *the airplane is on time*
- *these are "first class" tickets*
- *the opening act is good*
- *the closing act is good*
- *the act does no "blue" material.*
- *the record-release date is firm*
- *plenty of rental cars are available*
- *the food is good*
- *the kitchen is clean*
- *the hotel is good*
- *that anybody knows what he or she is talking about!*

Beware of . . .
- *home cooking*
- *free breakfast*
- *all you can eat*

It's trouble when you hear . . .
- *"probably . . . "*
- *"it'll be a piece of cake . . . "*
- *"any moment now . . ."*
- *"you can't miss it . . ."*
- *"certain winner . . ."*

BEWARE WHEN YOU'RE TOLD
- *"no problem . . ."*

AND WORST OF ALL
- *"I assume so . . ."*

I'm sure you can think of lots of other examples. Just remember, *have a checklist*, and check and double-check it. It'll make your life easier with less chance for error.

♪ ♪ ♪ ♪

It is up to the agency to continually research and develop new markets. Since The Jim Halsey Company represented many artists with global appeal, it was our responsibility to do everything within our power to open overseas markets. Our agency was the first to go international with country music, which is now a global enterprise. Remember: you should always try to be the best and to strive for perfection, but . . .

Being *first* is always important! And it only happens once!

The recognition an artist receives from being first on a television show, at a festival or other event, in a certain venue, at a live recording, or in a country that has never had that kind of act opens a lot of doors. In this business, there's always a carrot dangling. Go for it.

Hank Thompson was the first to open my eyes to the potential of global record sales and international touring, both of which were virtually untapped by country music acts at the time. Together, Hank and I opened a lot of the international doors for the first time.

I made some mistakes, however. But I learned from them.

Roy Clark's 1976 concert tour in the Soviet Union was a great education. The first Soviet tour ever made by a major country music artist, it not only activated whole new opportunities for marketing country music, it also brought forth a lot of hazards and potential hazards that had to be corrected on the spot. Even though we were furnished good escorts and interpreters by Gosconcert, the official USSR concert bureau, the language barrier was almost impenetrable at times. I had failed, in all of my negotiation, to include the provision of a bilingual crew. Our interpreters spoke excellent English, but they were unfamiliar with much of the technical language we needed to use to communicate with our all-Soviet production crew, who spoke only Russian. After that experience, I vowed that next time, wherever we went overseas, I would insist on a bilingual crew.

♪ ♪ ♪ ♪

You can achieve a lot of success in this business by doing something completely unexpected—and by being the first to do it.

Roy's Soviet tour was important because it was a first. Country music in the USSR was something unexpected, and we were the first to do it. We accomplished it and it was a press and cultural bonanza.

Nobody had ever tried to do country music at an international jazz festival, either—especially the most prestigious one in the world. Country music at the Montreaux Jazz Festival in Switzerland? Why not? It would really be a first, and certainly worthy of worldwide press.

You can measure **Power of Performance** in many ways, but it all boils down to accomplishment. Ideas and dreams are great, but they have to be followed and implemented.

This dream was totally off the wall—a superstar-driven country music package, playing the stage of the Montreaux Jazz Festival.

Claude Nobs has for years been Montreaux's imaginative and capable creator/impresario. His consideration for his artists and his audience is tops. His striving for quality artistic entertainment is constant and ongoing.

I met Claude Nobs at the annual music convention, MIDEM, in Cannes, France. This meeting, held each January, brings together all of the top recording and publishing executives to exchange ideas and sell product. Many managers, artists, and impresarios attend. Each night during the five-day conference, the record companies present a gigantic gala, studded with their biggest stars.

In 1979, our company, in conjunction with Jim Foglesong and ABC Records, presented a country music gala at MIDEM—another first. Roy Clark, The Oak Ridge Boys, and Don Williams gave one of the best gala performances ever staged at the convention, and I had Claude Nobs in the audience. The performers followed that with still another first—a gala for Princess Stephanie of Monaco at the Sporting Club in Monte Carlo.

After seeing our acts perform, Claude caught the vision The Jim Halsey Company had for Montreaux. We made a deal to present, for the first time ever, a country-music show at the Montreaux Jazz Festival, which was coming up in six months. Once again, I needed support from the record company. And once again, Jim Foglesong got on board.

Sensing Claude Nob's attention to detail and commitment to excellence, I made a trip to Switzerland to finalize our show for the coming summer. We put together a huge concert studded with quality performers: country superstars Roy Clark, The Oak Ridge Boys, and Barbara Mandrell as headliners, packaged with legendary acoustic performers Doc and Merle Watson and enhanced with special appearances by blues and R&B stars B.B. King, Gatemouth Brown, Taj Mahal, Lonnie Brooks, Little Milton, and James Brown, Buck Trent, and Jana Jae.

Wow! What a show!

It was very important for me to give Mr. Nobs and the Montreaux Festival audience a top-quality concert, so during my advance trip to Montreaux, I investigated *everything*: stage facilities, sound and lights, hotel accommodations, transportation from Geneva to Montreaux, food facilities, stagehands. My own **Power of Performance** was on the line here. I wanted to be respected for my thoroughness and professionalism and, as the saying goes, I left no stone unturned.

When I returned to the United States, I found out that my L.A. associate, Dick Howard, was going to be able to sell this concert for television, which meant it was going to be an event, for sure. But it also meant even more logistical details to check out and firm up. I made a checklist of everything that needed to be accomplished.

Jim Foglesong was excited. Three major acts on his ABC Records label were the show's stars. Together, we anticipated the grand breakthrough we were about to accomplish. Our press and public relations company, Gangwisch & Associates, and the ABC Records press department worked hand in hand to make this a big press event, as well. Again, all of the Star Team elements were coming together to deliver a consolidated performance.

I felt so clever. My attention to detail extended to the smallest components of the event: specially designed bags, stickers, and luggage tags, and special shirts and tour jackets, posters, stage passes and other paraphernalia tied in with the event. We put together a tour book that included every piece of information anyone could possibly want, from the beginning flight numbers to our exact arrival time back home. It was a terrific compendium of information, and we gave it to every person on the tour.

Because I had done other international shows—particularly those on the Soviet tour—I'd picked up some useful experience. This time I was pretty smart. I wasn't going to experience the same difficulties as I had in Moscow and Leningrad, where Russian was the only language spoken by the stage and technical crew. This time, I insisted to the Montreaux producer, that the crew—from stage manager to floor manager—had to be bilingual.

That was just one of the details we took care of. We had transportation waiting when we arrived at the airport. When we got to the hotels, we were already registered and our rooms were already assigned. Bouquets of fresh flowers awaited our stars. Meals were arranged. Luggage and instruments were handled precisely and accurately. Nothing was misplaced or lost. Everything was fine, until we reached the stage for rehearsal. Then I learned one of the greatest lessons of my life.

Fred Woods, my dependable tour and production manager, strode excitedly toward me as I arrived at the auditorium for the first rehearsal and camera run-through. I waited for him, anticipating our fantastic spectacle, feeling pretty proud of the way things were going.

"We've got a problem," Fred said.

"What's wrong?" I asked.

"Nobody speaks English," he replied. "Not the stage manager, not the hall manager, not the TV director, none of the stage hands—nobody."

"Fred, get your contract out," I said. "Read what it says."

He looked at me. "Oh, they've followed the contract to the letter. We certainly have a bilingual crew. But the languages they speak are *French* and *German!*"

Well, it hit me. I had failed to make English one of the required languages. They'd followed the instructions in the contract, certainly, but I'd been too smug to realize that not everyone speaks English. We overcame the problem by an ingenious method of sign language. It was hard, but it worked.

I was embarrassed, but I'd learned a good lesson. *Always have a checklist, and always double-check everything!*

You cannot check the details too many times in your negotiations. You must double-check even the things that seem obvious. Go over the details of the plan with your associates, and check each other! It's all part of being a good impresario, and a part of your expected **Power of Performance**. Attention to detail puts you on the road to excellence, and certainly keeps you from making some very, very humiliating mistakes.

The biggest hit of the Montreaux Festival was Roy Clark, as always the master showman. Interestingly enough, the Montreaux audiences seemed disappointed with the more poppish, modern sounds of the Barbara Mandrell show and The Oak Ridge Boys. They wanted pure, down-home, American country music. That meant, of course, that Doc and Merle Watson's set was a big success. Roy, of course, tailored his show to fit the audience, and his joint performances with Doc and Merle were well-received.

While our country-pop acts didn't go over as well as we planned in the first ever country show at Montreaux, country music has since expanded considerably throughout Europe, and all kinds of country music are now well received overseas.

A London-based impresario named Mervyn Conn was instrumental in helping establish country music in Europe. Mervyn's festivals, held throughout the U.K. and Europe, were for many years "the place" to get an artist started overseas. At this time, I wanted to build an international demand for artists like Don Williams, Tammy Wynette, Roy Clark, The Oak Ridge Boys, Donna Fargo, Freddy Fender, and Hank Thompson, and

I wanted to expand it beyond the traditional European ideas of what country music was.

I liked Mervyn and got along well with him. I also saw the importance of what he was developing—even though, at his early festivals, his audiences were the real hardcore country-music devotees, not the crossover audiences coveted by the record companies. A great promoter, Mervyn had established a successful annual event in London, the Wembley Country Music Festival (later shortened to simply the Wembley Festival), and he drew large audiences not only in the U.K., but also in the Scandinavian countries, Germany, Holland, and eventually some of the Eastern European nations. I felt it was important for us to tap into this base audience, and then add our own special touch.

Mervyn was difficult in negotiating deals, always haggling over some of the most minute details, right down to the last plane ticket or hotel room. But with Mervyn, whatever was negotiated and agreed upon was always fulfilled. He had his **Power of Performance** fine-tuned.

In 1980, The Jim Halsey Company had more artists on tours with Mervyn Conn than any other booking agency in the world. Seeing an opportunity to achieve some great worldwide press, Mervyn and I decided to announce our 1981 booking agreement by holding a large international press conference at the prestigious Mayfair Club in London. Our agreement, officially drawn on parchment and done in calligraphy, stated that in 1981 The Jim Halsey Company would supply and Mervyn Conn would accept a combination of artists to appear in the U.K. and Europe, with a total guaranteed amount in excess of $2 million. At the time, this was the largest contract for country music outside of the United States ever written.

Many contracts are simply sent through the mail, signed by all parties, and put into force. But this was something much more than just the signing of a personal appearance contract. When we announced this new association, our press conference was jam-packed, and the news reverberated around the world. A large contingency of worldwide press witnessed the actual signing. It was a monumental association, and the impact it had on country music reflected the **Power of Performance** of The Jim Halsey Company, Mervyn Conn, and Gangwisch and Associates, our PR company.

Our story broke in the global press, giving us all an international **Power of Performance** before any of the artists involved had even set foot on a foreign stage in fulfillment of the contract. This is the way it's supposed to work. We had called attention to this record-breaking contract through the press. There was **Power** in this collective **Performance**.

A chapter is upcoming on press and public relations, but I want to note here that we would usually invite the press to an elaborate cocktail party, exclusive of Mervyn's press receptions, when our own artists were working overseas. Gangwisch had established an association with a U.K. press outfit called Byworth-Wooten, comprised of two energetic and accomplished young PR pros, Tony Byworth and Richard Wooten. Between Gangwisch and Byworth-Wooten, we were able to garner enormous amounts of press for our artists. One gathering, in fact, was so well attended by British and other European media that we had continual stories for the next three months on Roy, Tammy, George Lindsey, Hank Thompson, Freddy Fender, Donna Fargo, Don Williams, and The Oak Ridge Boys. We usually held these parties in the Roof Garden of the Royal Garden Hotel in London, inviting press and entertainment VIP's. (And our company picked up the tab for these costly events, not the artists.) We'd arrange individual interviews with the stars we represented, achieving a press coup and giving our performers some extra punch.

The Wembley Festivals were the stepping stones to Europe and individual tours and concert appearances overseas. They also afforded us opportunities to establish relationships with television producers. As a result, our Dick Howard—working his **Power of Performance** on an international level—was able to sell a number of TV specials, and even a series of six 30-minute shows starring Don Williams, and three starring Roy Clark.

Mervyn Conn was successful in many ways, not only for our company and our artists, but for all of country music. He deserves more credit than he gets for helping to establish the success of American country music in Britain and the rest of Europe today.

We also worked with another important impresario, Jeffrey Kruger. Jeffrey flung his promotional net wide; he was the one to establish both Glen Campbell and Don Williams as huge international stars. Over the years, Jeffrey and Mervyn Conn have taken turns in promoting a lot of our acts. Jeffrey, for instance, was the first to introduce Dwight Yoakam to the European market through his Peterborough (UK) International Festival.

As I've said, we wanted to get our stars in front of European audiences that weren't exclusively country fans. At this point, I'd already presented our stars in a lot of the world's most prestigious venues, from Las Vegas casinos to the Montreaux Jazz Festival, Carnegie Hall to Moscow's Rossiya Theater. I was looking now for an important, prestigious venue in the U.K. for The Oak Ridge Boys. Of course, the *most* prestigious would be the Royal Albert Hall in London, a venue reserved almost exclusively for the biggest stars in the world. What better place to exhibit the **Power of Performance** of our stars?

Impresario Jeffrey Kruger took the lead in this case. He was presenting Johnny Mathis in concert at the Royal Albert; we convinced him to put The Oak Ridge Boys in to do the show's first half.

As we've discussed, an important part of any event is the press it receives. After all, while only 6,000 people would actually attend the concert, we needed to let the whole world know about it, thereby boosting the power of the act. We accomplished this through teamwork, with our important team member Kathy Gangwisch and her press and PR company going into action, coordinating with the promotion team from The Oak Ridge Boys' record company. We made the event larger than life with press parties and conferences, interviews in both the US and in London, and a combined **Power of Performance** contributed to by every involved team member. The Oak Ridge Boys did their part, too, and the show was a huge success!

I might add that both Mervyn and Jeffrey would often have special events or tours, or would top one another by offering us better money and amenities. Those things determined which one we signed with each time around. I have a lot of respect for and I'm enormously grateful to them both for helping us establish our artists internationally. We continued to view Europe as a great opportunity, not just for personal appearances, but also for television, records and music publishing. And we continued to introduce our artists to European audiences through those two fine impresarios, as well as others.

The UK and Europe became such a big market for us that we eventually opened an office in London, becoming the first country music agency ever to do so. Records, TV, personal appearances, specialized tours, and music publishing all needed immediate attention in this region, and a young, energetic record-company executive, Charles McCutcheon, became our man in London, doing a great job for us.

When we were starting to develop Dwight Yoakam, we looked for an impresario who was working with younger, more contemporary alternative acts. We chose to work with an aggressive and capable young man named Paul Fenn, who ran a company named ASGARD. For Dwight, we took a totally different approach than we had with our other, more established artists. We played him in more alternative venues and went for coverage in the alternative rather than mainstream press. Paul Fenn did his job thoroughly, and Dwight became a successful international act.

Why was it so important to me to reach out around the world? You may remember that even when I was a beginning impresario with my very first artist, Hank Thompson, I believed that the world was linked by artists and their art. I saw no barriers or restrictions, no boundary lines that an artist couldn't cross. Even language couldn't deter music, the universal language.

Over the years, I'd often recall reading about Sol Hurok, whose story had reached out to me, a high school boy in Independence, Kansas, inspiring me to become an impresario. For Sol Hurok, the world truly was his stage. I was developing it to be Jim Halsey's, too!

♪ ♪ ♪ ♪

In summing this chapter up, I'll tell you that becoming a successful booking agent boils down to a simple formula. It's called the *Three "S" Principle*, and it's as important as it is simple.

THE THREE "S" PRINCIPLE

1. Sign `em

2. Sell `em

3. Service `em

I have seen a lot of booking agency offices with a simple framed sign that states, "Remember the three S's." When I see that, I see a dedication to where that company is going. We can sometimes get so complex with our explaining of theories, methods, formulas, and philosophies that we overlook the fact that it's really a simple, straight-ahead business that yields many rewards to its successful practitioners.

When I give lectures and seminars, I often conclude with a story that brings our lofty discussions back to earth. It's about a friend of mine who was walking down 57th Street in New York one busy noontime. He saw, approaching from a distance, a veteran of one of the big booking agencies named Irv Dinkin. Now Irv Dinkin is the personification of what a booking agent is all about; he works at selling tours and one-nighters for his acts just about every day of his life. You know he has problems. You know he has open dates on his mind.

As my friend passed Irv, he said, "Hi, Irv. How're you doing?"

Without hesitation, Irv answered sharply, "Looking for a Tuesday night," and passed on by.

I think that says it all.

♪ ♪ ♪ ♪

I'll finish this chapter with some wisdom from an agent I consider one of the very best, Bill Elson. The former executive vice-president of International Creative Management (ICM), Bill is now a partner with Ascendant Management Consultants.

Not long ago, I did a lengthy video interview with Bill. We discussed agents and agentry from all sorts of philosophical, intellectual, and methodological standpoints. But finally, he said, it boiled down to this: "If somebody wants to be an agent, they just need a telephone and someone who's out of work who plays the guitar."

That may sound simplistic and even arrogant, but it's really what being a booking agent is all about. It's about seeing economic opportunity and personal fulfillment in finding somebody a job. And that's something you can do anywhere in America.

13

Press and Public Relations

If you've ever studied journalism, you've heard about the five W's: *Who? What ? Where? When?* and *Why?* These are the five questions a newspaper reporter must answer in every story.

The five W's are also very important to another member of the Star Team, the press and public relations (PR) person. In the last chapter, we talked a little about this important team member. Now, it's time to examine the role in detail.

Please keep in mind that at the beginning of an artist's career, press and PR is sometimes handled by the artist manager or the artist's record company. Performers, in fact, may have to handle their own press until they're financially able to hire a specialist. So everyone involved in an artist's career needs to learn how it's done.

First, a simple definition: a press person, also known as a publicist and still occasionally called a press agent, is the member of the team whose job is to get your artist's or company's name in newspapers and magazines and on radio and TV, to spread "the good word" about your clients. Publicists are also helpful in designing media campaigns for events and causes.

These team members are important during all phases of an artist's career. In the beginning, the stories they release to the media will help build the performer's name recognition—getting, in a sense, free advertising for an act, free advertising that sells the public on your performer. In the beginning, people need to know about an artist, and the publicist must release interesting stories to the media.

Recognizing the value of using a publicist is important, but understanding *how* to use one is essential. You must include your publicist in the overall planning of an artist's career. As we've said before, involving all the team members in the master plan gets everybody's energy working in the same direction and opens the channels of communication, which leads to the reception of more helpful ideas. When you're directing the publicity for an artist, you must determine your overall goal and desired results.

Generally, publicists generate news stories to the media so the public will become more aware of the artist. An upcoming tour, a new record release, a television appearance, a major contract with a corporate sponsor, or an outstanding sold-out performance are all worthy of stories, and should be publicized.

After the publicist writes the story, he or she releases it to a media list. In addition to the traditional electronic and print media, the Internet has become another media outlet—and perhaps even fax and computer networking can be included. A good publicist will have personal contacts in all media, which helps him or her get stories placed. And when you're developing a campaign to build an artist, a publicist's stories can be used effectively in conjunction with paid advertising and personal appearances.

Hank Thompson was responsible for many "firsts" within the country music business. He was, for instance, the first country music artist to record a "live and in person" album. In fact, Hank did three live albums, all big successes: the award-winning *Hank Thompson at The Golden Nugget* (produced by Ken Nelson for Capitol Records), *Live at The Texas State Fair* and *Live at The Cheyenne Frontier Days*. These weren't just records by an important act—acting in accordance with my philosophy, we turned each one into an event.

Hank was a unique talent, and so was Roy Clark. At this time in my career, I represented them both. Hank was established, but Roy wasn't. I knew that what we did early in Roy's career would be essential in helping determine how far and how long his career would go. I also knew the career of the famed Grand Ole Opry comedienne Minnie Pearl, whom I was also handling, could be expanded to a larger audience.

I felt that if we could reach beyond the country music audience, Hank, Roy, and Minnie all had a good chance of breaking into the mainstream. I visited with several people who did press and PR for country stars, but they couldn't grasp what I envisioned for Hank, Roy, and Minnie. Finally, I told my artists I wanted to hire a "Hollywood press agent," someone who could get their names in publications besides the country music magazines. Of course, it was important not to lose our country music press, but I wanted to get stories in mainstream publications all over the country. A story picked up by a major newspaper syndicate—the *New York Times, Los Angeles Times,* or *Chicago Tribune*—would be ideal. At that time, you simply didn't see syndicates like those running stories on country artists.

I wanted to hire the best, and we did. We hired Jay Bernstein in Beverly Hills. He was expensive, but he was worth it. It was the first experience Hank, Roy, Minnie, or I had with a press and PR person, outside of what we did in-house or what was furnished by the record company, and our association with Jay Bernstein opened my eyes to the importance of using a top mainstream professional. Through Jay's office, I also met a couple of other impressive young men.

Stan Rosenfield did a lot of the groundwork on Hank, Roy, and Minnie's behalf, working the trade publications *Hollywood Reporter* and *Daily Variety* and making daily visits to various television shows. Stan also worked closely with our television agent, Dick Howard.

Hey, we were beginning to build a team!

Stan was an important part of our building process, getting Minnie, Roy, and Hank lots of press. Now Stan Rosenfield heads his own Beverly Hills-based PR agency, and it's a very big one.

Stan Moress (remember the cigar-smoking incident?) was also with the Bernstein office at the time. He was just beginning his career. Later, he'd move to record companies and then to his own business, working as a personal manager for many big stars in both the pop and country fields. I consider him one of the best managers in the business. He is bright, imaginative, dedicated to his artists, and best of all, he's a person of integrity.

Jay Bernstein has since become a super-important manager and producer, a true Hollywood star-maker.

See how this business works? You start by building relationships. As you grow in the business, most of the people you come in contact with also grow. If you're in the music and entertainment business, you're in the relationship business as well. As a beginning manager, agent, or promoter, you often have to be your own publicist. That happened to me. As a young promoter in southeast Kansas, I knew that when I was bringing a show or dance to town, advertising was important. But I also knew it was important to have newspaper stories—ideally with pictures—giving the who, what, when, where and why as a complement to the advertising. It was the same thing with radio.

I knew I had to establish personal relationships with people in the media, so I would always personally take my news releases to the editors and always with a generous supply of tickets for good seats to the event. This was not "payola." The shows I would bring to town were always worthy of a good story, and the tickets served as a common courtesy, a means of saying thanks. It was equally important to get good press reviews from the show, which would help build audiences for my next event.

A competitor in a neighboring town once asked how I got so much press on the shows I was promoting. In his hometown, he said, the papers never mentioned his shows. I asked if he took good complimentary tickets to the newspaper. He said he hadn't thought of it, but he'd try it the next time.

A couple of months later, we visited again. He was really unhappy with me. He'd given out comp tickets to the newspaper, and it hadn't worked. Not one story in the local paper. Not even one mention.

I told him I couldn't believe it.

It was true, he insisted. "I gave good complimentary seats to every newspaper delivery boy, " he said heatedly. "I gave tickets to all 35 of them, and still no story."

I had to explain to him that the tickets should go to the people responsible for getting his stories in the paper: the editor, the managing editor, anyone who writes columns, specializes in music, or has a lot of influence over what stories run. Believe it or not, he was so disgusted that he never tried to place a story again, choosing to rely only on paid advertising. And that brings us back around to a point I made earlier. In promoting a show or building an artist, paid advertising is important, but you enhance the power of advertising with editorial copy, copy not paid for. It authenticates the event or product.

It's the same thing with radio. Stations and air personalities can enhance the power of your paid advertising with on-air plugs or comments about your forthcoming show or artist. Perhaps they'll even do an interview with the artist. Everything doesn't have to be paid advertising. And getting publicity, which is essentially free advertising, is part of the publicist's job.

Throughout this book, I've emphasized how important it is to have a goal, have a purpose, and then establish a plan. Publicists needs to know the master plan for an artist's career. They need to know when stories are to be released, and where they should go, and why this publicity is important.

They always need to keep the five W's in mind: *Who? What? When? Where?* and *Why?*

By knowing the master plan, and the direction of a performer's career, and by utilizing the five W's, publicists can creatively unleash their own **Power of Performance**.

They can increase the dimension of an event. They can even *create* one.

I'm not saying that a publicist should exaggerate or blow things out of proportion, although that sometimes does happen. A good press and PR person, however, can craft a story that emphasizes an event's importance and makes it appear to be bigger than life.

Positive images of artists or a company can be built by using a good press agency and getting the story in front of the targeted audience. Accumulating a lot of stories, advertisements, and television appearances in a short period of time, combined with effective direct mail, telemarketing, and use of electronic media, will create the *repetitious impressions* that are so important in launching an artist's career, or taking it to the next level.

♪ ♪ ♪ ♪

In the first part of this book, we talked about putting together a press kit. Whether you are a publicist, a manager or an artist doing your own publicity, one of the first things you must make available to the media is a good press kit. Think of it as a business card you can leave with your media contacts—a short, concise package of information. When they open it, they should have all the vital information on your artist, material that answers the questions raised by the five W's: *Who? What? When? Where?* and *Why?*

In addition to media, the press kit is used to service concert buyers, prospective corporate sponsors, and others you want to tell about your artist or company.

The most effective press kit for an artist contains:

1. *At least one good 8 x 10" picture.*

2. *A brief biography of no more than two pages.*

3. *A discography (listing the artist's recorded work).*

4. *Reprints of reviews and articles and/or quotes from important figures.*

5. *A current tour itinerary (if applicable).*

6. *A business card or the printed name and address of the publicist*

7. *The current CD or tape.*

Because most newspapers and magazines now use lots of color, it's also advisable to include at least one color photo of the performer. Also, electronic press kits, or EPKs, are being used more and more to introduce acts. EPKs are videotapes that usually include a song or two plus an interview with the act. Not meant to take the place of the regular press kit, they instead complement it.

All these materials (except the EPK) should be packaged attractively in some sort of folder. The established attractions have custom-designed press kit folders; those just getting started can go to a discount or office-supply store and find inexpensive, attractive folders in a variety of styles and prices.

♪ ♪ ♪ ♪

Like the press kit, a good press release addresses the questions *Who? What? When? Where?* and *Why?* It should do that in a simple and effective way.

Remember my telling about Joseph Sugarman, creator of BluBlocker sunglasses? As you'll recall, when Joe creates advertising, his theory is to always put your most important statement in your first sentence, the second most important in your second sentence, and so on. That method applies to press releases as well. If you can grab the readers' attention in the first sentence, they'll stay with you for the rest of the text. Positive first sentences such as "Roy Clark will appear at Carnegie Hall" or "The Oak Ridge Boys have scheduled a concert at Royal Albert Hall to kick off their spring tour" sets your readers up for the rest of the pertinent information.

Before sending out your press release, always check and double-check for accuracy, spelling, and grammar. Double-space the printed message so editors and others will be able to read it easily and can make additions or deletions in the copy before they print their own version. Always include the name or names of people who can supply more information, if needed. Put all of that right below the letterhead, before the main body of the release: *Contact* (Name, address, telephone number)

Below that should be the release date, either

For Immediate Release

or

Release On (date)

or

Release After (date)

A good press and PR person will have a specialized list of contacts. Usually, these are broken down into several areas:

1. *The trades* (papers and magazines dealing with the music and entertainment business, including *Billboard, Amusement Business, Hollywood Reporter, Variety* (in both weekly and daily editions), *Gavin Report, Radio & Records, Pollstar*

2. *Local newspapers*

3. *Newspaper syndicates* (i.e. *Los Angeles Times, New York Times, Chicago Tribune, Knight-Ridder*)

4. *Magazines* (*Rolling Stone, Entertainment Weekly, People*)

5. *Wire services* (Associated Press, Rueters International)

6. *Broadcast media* (TV and radio)

7. *Cable news conferences* (interactive)

8. *Direct mail*

9. *Electronic distribution* (faxes, e-mail, Internet, etc.)

Although a beginning publicist may not have, or even need, contacts in all of these areas, it's important to use the contacts you do have and to build more as you go along.

♪ ♪ ♪ ♪

The Jim Halsey Company, Inc. had a press department. Even though we had Gangwisch & Assoc., an outside press and PR company, under contract, we needed our own department as well. After all, we represented 40 artists, and daily handled requests from the press and other media. And whenever a Halsey Company contract was signed for a date, we immediately sent out a full press kit on the artist.

Press kits are constantly updated, and it's as important to delete old material as it is to add new material. When you're sending a press kit to a promoter, always include more than one picture; this kit will be one of his basic tools for promotion, advertising, and publicity, and he'll need extra photos for his newspaper and other ads.

Working with their artists, publicists can come up with other ways to help a promoter. Some artists will be willing to make custom advertisements on audio and video for each engagement. Most will do interviews with local newspapers, radio, and television. It's the publicist's job to set up these interviews, which are usually done by telephone in advance of the date.

Another way to get coverage from newspapers, television, and radio is to hold a press conference. This is an invitation for the press to meet at a designated time and place for an important announcement—a special tour, an upcoming big event, the signing of an artist to a new record contract or to a new agency—and it's always more effective to have the artist present for the conference. It gives the press a chance to ask the artist questions, and there's always something magical about the in-person handshakes and greetings.

The publicist organizes these press conferences, notifying his or her media contacts and following up with phone calls to make sure the invitations got where they were supposed to go.

Press conferences should be short and to the point. You should announce the reason for the conference, refer to the handouts given the attendees, and have the act on hand to answer questions.

For many years, we did a very successful series of Christmas dates with The Oak Ridge Boys. Then we decided to go the extra step and make the next Christmas tour an event. We held a press conference in Nashville to proclaim just that, and when the press showed up and asked what made this particular tour any different, we were prepared with our list:

1. We'd added new Christmas music as well as traditional favorites to the regular show.

2. We'd added special production numbers with sleighs, animals, and snow.

3. Special guest star Marie Osmond had been added to the concert.

4. Santa and his elves would appear in person.

5. We'd tied the entire tour in with Larry Jones' Feed the Children charity. (We not only gathered tons of food each night for the effort, but distributed it to the needy in the cities we played the next day, which was a media event in itself.)

Because of these things, each of The Oak Ridge Boys dates turned into a fantastic holiday event. Pre-concert news conferences in each city we played insured us of additional press.

None of The Halsey Company events in this book would have been as successful without the effective use of the press. Press is a *power booster*. Unless you are trying to create some sort of mystery about an act by not doing press, you must make your artists accessible to the media.

There are electronic, interactive news conferences organized via satellite. These can be especially effective when announcing a major concert tour by a big artist. An increasingly popular way of bringing news to a multitude of people is via the Internet. While not nearly as personal as a press conference, it still gives people opportunities to ask questions of a performer and find out news about a tour or other event.

A website on the Internet can be very effective, too, if you remember to update it daily, and to make it personal.

Press and PR people are specialists, most of whom work on a contract basis. Some are hired for specific jobs or tours. Others remain as part of the essential team on a year-round basis.

It takes an imaginative and creative person to do this job. Good publicists are experts who've accessed their **Power of Performance**. If they have—and you don't want them if they haven't—you will see absolute magic happen.

♪ ♪ ♪ ♪

For more than 25 years, the same press and PR person represented The Jim Halsey Company, Inc. It was Gangwisch & Assoc. in Kansas City and Nashville, headed by Kathy Gangwisch. A person who understands the value of team energy, she worked with many of our artists—including The Oak Ridge Boys, Roy Clark, Mel Tillis, Tammy Wynette, and Don Williams—and was involved with almost every event project our company has conceived.

While the terms "publicist" and "public relations" seem synonymous, they are really two different things. Public relations involves work, projects, or events that enhance an artist or company's image in a positive way. Most of the artists represented by our company were involved with public relations endeavors that would elevate their status as human beings: collecting food for Feed the Children, playing in golf tournaments for charities, and lending their name to worthwhile fundraising events.

Several years ago, our company launched a major campaign on The Oak Ridge Boys that included extensive press, radio, promotion, and advance on all dates. It was just like a circus promotion. As The Oak Ridge Boys' public relations firm, Gangwisch & Assoc. was getting enormous amounts of major national and regional press on the group. At the same time, we were heavily involved in doing the same types of promotions with Roy Clark, Reba McEntire, Mel Tillis, The Judds, and some of our other superstar attractions. It was a busy summer.

We were heading into the fair and rodeo season, with these artists playing the biggest fairs and rodeos in the nation. It was going to be a very big-grossing time for us. Naturally, all avenues were covered, and press releases went to all the big national magazines, including *Time, Life, Esquire*, and *People*. We were trying to saturate them with the fact that country music was happening, and that our names were the biggest names in country music, the ones making the biggest grosses, playing the biggest venues, drawing the biggest crowds.

Pouring all of your energies into a campaign like this is a little like blowing up a balloon. You hope you do the things that can make your project fly while avoiding the things that will make it blow up in your face.

If you believe in yourself and the value of your project, and you've accessed your **Power of Performance**, you know it's going to fly. You know the "big call" will come.

One hot summer evening, the "big call" came. I was working in the yard some distance from the house. It was just beginning to get dark when my wife, Minisa, called excitedly to me from our second-floor balcony.

"Jim," she shouted, "*Time* magazine is calling from New York!"

Time magazine from New York! We both knew what *that* meant.

I dropped everything and hurried up the hill. As I jogged toward the house, my mind raced through all of the possible reasons for the "big call."

"Is it about The Oak Ridge Boys?" I wondered frantically. "Roy? Reba? The Judds? Maybe it's about *me*. *Time* magazine—hooray!"

I teased myself with the possibility of stories on more than one of my acts, knowing that at least one Halsey Company client would be the lucky recipient of some Time magazine ink. I hardly dared to dream of a cover piece—but I did. Time seemed to stand still as I hurried along, all these possibilities flashing in front of me. *Time* magazine . . . from New York. All the years of hard work and dedication, all of the artists' sacrifices of time and energy, was about to pay off. *Time* magazine would not call at nine in the evening for a casual quote. No, nine p.m. meant something *big*. When I finally reached the top of the hill, I was out of breath—not just from the physical exertion, but from the excitement and anticipation. I could feel my heartbeat in my mouth, throat, and fingertips. I felt almost giddy. Leaping up the front porch steps two at a time, I ran into the house. My wife, who seemed just as excited as I was, handed me the phone.

"Hello?" I gasped.

"Mr. Jim Halsey?" asked a pleasant voice that seemed to hold promise of wonderful news.

"Yes, this is Jim Halsey."

"Good evening, Mr. Halsey. I'm Nancy from Time magazine in New York City, and I have good news for you."

Time *magazine in New York has good news for me!*

"I'm calling to offer you our very special subscription bonus," she continued. "Thirty-six weeks of *Time* magazine at half the price. No money now; we'll bill you after you receive your first issue."

Suddenly, the cover story with Roy Clark, The Oak Ridge Boys, Reba, The Judds or Mel, exploded and fluttered away in my mind like so much confetti.

"And what's even better," Nancy from Time magazine in New York said, "if you give me your order right now over the phone, we'll give you a *free pocket calculator.*"

I took a deep breath and gathered the strength to decline the offer, then I returned the phone to its cradle.

I sat down.

I laughed. Hard. And my wife joined me. It was a good joke on us both.

I share this story with you because I'm a dreamer. I always have been and always will be. Our dreams take us places where other people are unable to go. Being able to accept a disappointment or rejection with a good laugh is part of making your dreams into realities. For a dreamer, nothing is impossible, even a *Time* magazine cover.

♪ ♪ ♪ ♪

Advertising and promotion is not the same as press and public relations, but it all ties together. Effective use of the media, in both paid and unpaid forms, builds your artist, band, or project. In fact, in the music and entertainment business, effective use of the media is essential to success. Press is an *impact enhancer* for any campaign. Whether it's career building, tour planning, record promotion, or the maintenance of a career, how effective you are is determined by how well you've employed the media in your overall plan.

At The Jim Halsey Company, my plans included using every media opportunity, along with an in-depth advertising campaign. Together, they created the *repetitious impressions* you've heard so much about in this book.

Please understand the term "impressions." When one person sees or hears an advertisement or a media mention, that's one impression. If the same person sees or hears it again, that's two impressions. If a thousand people see one ad, that's a thousand impressions. When you hear advertising agencies talking about a certain campaign getting, say, 10 million impressions, that means through ads and other mentions in the media, their product was seen or heard 10 million times.

To get the maximum number of *repetitious impressions*, we'd design campaigns for our artists using every method we had available, including guest appearances on television, radio interviews, newspaper and magazine stories, record releases, and direct mail. A typical campaign would bunch together as many as six to eight television guest shots, with our artist appearing on everything from network series to local shows within a three- or four-week period. Usually, these appearances would be coordinated with a record release or some other important event. During this time of concentrated television exposure, our press and PR people would schedule as many interviews as possible with national publications, important daily newspapers, radio shows, cable news shows, magazines, etc.

Additionally, this activity would be designed to tie in with a specific record company promotion aimed at rack jobbers (record distributors who have racks in a variety of stores), distributors, and giant retailers such as Wal-Mart, Border's, Blockbuster, Hastings, or Tower Records. During this time, our method of *repetitious impressions* would also include a systematic direct-mail campaign regarding that particular artist.

To maximize the effect, direct-mail advertisements using three different artistic treatments should be mailed to the same list, so that the buyers and promoters receive these three different pieces spread over a six-week period—the same period that encompasses your artist's concentrated TV appearances, the accompanying flurry of press, and the record-company promotion. The first piece of mail should arrive at the beginning of the campaign, and the third, or last, piece about two weeks after the campaign has peaked. If you time everything right, for that four to six weeks it will seem like there is nobody more important in the world than your artist.

I developed this method of *repetitious impressions* early in my career and have used it effectively with every one of my artists at one time or another.

In the early days of building Roy Clark's career, for instance, I used it quite effectively. For some artists, you actually have to be careful about having too many *repetitious impressions*, especially too many television appearances in a short time, because of overexposure. If your performer is one-dimensional, too many appearances too close together could have a negative effect instead of a positive one. This, of course, wasn't true with Roy. He could do so many different things that the audience never got tired of seeing him.

I remember one campaign we did in which Roy started with an appearance on *The Tonight Show with Johnny Carson*, followed it up with a guest shot on Mitzi Gaynor's special, and made additional appearances with Merv Griffin, Dinah Shore, Mike Douglas, Joey Bishop, and the *Hollywood Squares*. During this time period he also did interviews with a writer for the Associated Press, with Jack Hurst for Hurst's syndicated column in the *Chicago Tribune*, and with such major daily newspapers as the *Detroit Free Press*, *Kansas City Star*, and *Las Vegas Sun*. He had a new album out and a current show at the Frontier Hotel in Las Vegas. While Roy always had a lot going on, this was an especially good time for us to maximize his efforts with a *repetitious Impressions* campaign.

The Jim Halsey Company used *repetitious impressions* on a year-round basis, making more direct mailings than any other agency in the business. I took great pride in developing our list of talent buyers and promoters not only nationally, but internationally as well. I firmly believed that if my target list of buyers could be kept informed on a regular basis of the artists we represented and what they were doing, they would be more stimulated to buy.

It worked. They called, we called, and they bought!

Our direct mail would go out at least twice a month to every name on the list. Special campaigns or new record releases might bump it up to once a week. It was sometimes directed, sometimes generic, but always on a regular basis.

This was a lot of mail. We always hit at least 60,000 pieces a month, and sometimes sent out 120,000. The cost was considerable, but we had help, with the artist, the record company, or the music publisher often helping financially. We also complemented our mailings with full-page ads in *Billboard, Amusement Business, Cash Box, Radio & Records,* and other trade publications.

One time I took out a two-page spread in *Billboard* to announce that our combined artist roster had achieved, through the press and television in the past 12 months, total impressions of 280 *billion,* a phenomenal amount of impressions that illustrated the importance of our agency as well as the artists we represented. The advertisement also noted that somewhere in the world, every minute of every day, one of our artists was being played on the radio.

This two-page announcement was targeted toward advertising agencies, prospective corporate sponsors, and television and cable TV programmers. We specifically targeted other promotions as well, including ones for annual events such as the Fair Buyers Convention in Las Vegas, held at the end of November.

While these were advertising campaigns, you can understand how they became much more effective when coordinated with a press and PR campaign. Advertising is paid media exposure; publicity and public relations is unpaid media exposure. Together, they work hand-in-hand.

The Music Publisher

At this point, we've attached almost all of the spokes to our Star Team wheel. Beginning with the artist—the hub of the wheel—we've added the artist manager, the record company, the record producer, the booking agent, and the publicist, all necessary components of any Star Team.

Now it's time to add another essential member: the *music publisher*. Although many people would be hard-pressed to explain exactly what this team member does, a music publisher is often one of the main ingredients in developing a star.

A music publisher represents the songs created by a songwriter, collects the revenues for their use, and splits it with the songwriter. What usually happens is that the publisher collects 100 percent of the revenue generated by a song, and then gives 50 percent to the songwriter.

The music publisher copyrights the material, registers it with a performing-rights organization (BMI, ASCAP, or the smaller SESAC), stays up to date with the current compensation policies, and negotiates licensing fees for the songs. Publishers are a crucial part of the business, although I must add that they—along with the rest of us—wouldn't be necessary if there were no songwriters.

In many ways, the relationship of a music publisher to a song is like the relationship between a booking agent and a performer. The publisher, in other words, represents a song. It is the publisher's responsibility to get a song recorded. It is the publisher's responsibility to get a song in commercials, on television, in a film, or on stage. When the music publisher obtains a song from a songwriter, the publisher gains full control of that song, taking the responsibility for promotion and deciding where the song's potential can best be utilized. Publishers have the ability to make money off a song in many, many ways!

Music publishers have great resources at their command. They also stay on top of national and international regulations regarding the use of songs. These regulations can change rapidly, and a publisher helps the songwriter by always being aware of the parameters that define the way a song can be used.

Publishers can also be very instrumental in helping a new singer/songwriter get a record deal. Some have their own publicity department, which can supplement the record company's promotion on a new release. That's just one way a music publisher's **Power of Performance** can and should be coordinated with that of the rest of the Star Team.

Music publishers are found in cities where there is a lot of musical activity, places like Los Angeles, New York, Nashville, Austin, Atlanta, Chicago, and Seattle. You can find their addresses in the yellow pages of the telephone book. Most local phone companies have books for other cities; you can also check your local library or Chamber of Commerce.

The Internet is also an excellent source of information on music publishing, copyrighting, and songwriting. Much of the information an up-and-coming songwriter needs is out there for the finding.

Good music publishers are busy. Many are reluctant to accept unsolicited new material. If you know anybody in the business who can give you a referral, that would be a great help. Sometimes, attorneys who specialize in the music business (we'll talk about these in the next chapter) will, for a fee, represent you and your songs to a music publisher or record company.

Write letters! Try to see publishers. Do anything you can to see anybody, even if it's the secretary, the security person, or another office worker. Many times, people like these can introduce you to a publisher or recording executive. Once again, it's up to you to actualize your **Power of Performance**.

♪ ♪ ♪ ♪

Now let's discuss how you will make money with your songs.

As we've said, the music publisher functions for your song or songs in much the same way that a booking agent works for a performer. Publishers represent your music and pay you a portion of what your song earns. Their efforts on your behalf are important.

We mentioned BMI, ASCAP, and SESAC earlier. These are not music publishers, but organizations that license copyrighted music to users and collect fees for the writer and publisher. These users include radio and television stations, nightclubs, casinos, arenas, amusement parks, hotels, and any other commercial establishment in the US where music is played publicly. The form of payment to the publisher and songwriter is called a *royalty*.

The term has an interesting origin. Music publishing started in 15th century Italy. Because all musical compositions were printed at the time, the term "music publishing" came into use. The kings, princes, and other members of royalty bestowed exclusive rights to musicians and composers to print sheet music. Those musicians and composers, in return, paid their benefactors from the proceeds of their work, and since they were paying *royalty*, that's how the term came to be.

Today, songwriters and publishers have a number of potential sources for royalty income. Here are eight of the most common:

1. **Mechanical Royalties-** These are paid by the record company. Mechanical royalties are paid either by song or by song length. If the song is less than 5 minutes then the royalty rate is 7.55 ($0.0755) cents, and if the song is greater than 5 minute then the royalty rate is 1.45 ($0.0145) cents per minute. The mechanical royalty rate for each copy of the record, CD, or tape made and distributed are as follows:

Royalty Rate by Year

Year	Per Song	Per Minute (if song is greater than 5 minutes)
2000 – 2001	7.55 cents	1.45 cents
2002 – 2003	8 cents	1.55 cents
2004 – 2005	8.5 cents	1.65 cents
2006 & greater	9.1 cents	1.75 cents

Royalty Rate by Song (2000 – 2001 rates)

Song Length		Royalty Rate
Less than	**5 minutes**	7.55 cents
	6 minutes	8.70 cents
	7 minutes	10.15 cents
	8 minutes	11.6 cents
	9 minutes	13.05 cents
	10 minutes	14.5 cents

Royalty Rate by Album (2000 – 2001 rates)

Number of Songs per Album	Royalty Rate (All songs under 5 min.)
1	7.55 cents
2	15.1 cents
3	22.65 cents
4	30.2 cents
5	37.75 cents
6	45.3 cents
7	52.85 cents
8	60.4 cents
9	67.95 cents
10	75.5 cents

Example: If there are ten songs on a CD or cassette, each running five minutes or under, the total payment by the record company to the music publisher (or publishers) would be 75.5 cents per CD & cassette sold. If this album goes platinum and sells one million copes, then royalties would equal $755,000. The music publisher, in turn, then pays the songwriter a portion of the revenues. This portion is usually a 50/50 split, depending on the arrangement between the songwriter and music publisher.

2. Performance royalties—These are divided into two categories: *broadcast performance* and *non-broadcast performance*. These royalties are collected and paid by the performing rights organizations mentioned earlier: BMI, ASCAP, and SESAC.

Radio and TV broadcasters have a system in which the songs they play are periodically logged. From this, they compute a song's average airplay. Every broadcaster pays a blanket licensing fee to all three performing rights organizations for the right to broadcast copyrighted material. Each organization then pays its songwriters and publishers a portion of the fees collected as *broadcast performance royalties*, based on the average airplay reported by the stations .

Keep in mind that a songwriter can only belong to one performing rights group, either BMI, ASCAP, or SESAC. The organization a songwriter belongs to is responsible for paying his or her broadcast-performance royalties.

A *non-broadcast performance* occurs whenever copyrighted material is played in public for profit. This covers both recorded music and live performances, and it can happen almost anywhere: theaters, arenas, auditoriums, fairs and rodeos, concert halls, restaurants, theme parks, casinos, night clubs—even elevators and funeral homes. BMI and ASCAP have been very successful in compelling every one of these venues to comply with the federal law and secure a license to play copyrighted material. They, of course, must pay for the privilege, which assures songwriters and music publishers more revenue.

3. Jukebox royalties—Another important source of revenue licensed by BMI, ASCAP, and SESAC, royalties from jukebox play are paid out to publishers and member songwriters.

4. Sheet music royalties—When there were more pianos than stereos in American homes, sheet music sales were an important part of a publisher and songwriter's income. Sheet music has become less and less important over the years, but some is still being created on a mass-market basis, mostly in the form of songbooks and folios by popular artists.

5. Grand rights royalties—This isn't one of the better-known sources of songwriter income, but it generates a lot of revenue for certain writers. The term *grand rights* refers to Broadway shows and musicals. Once a writer has music in a hit show, these royalties can last a long time. Shows can travel for years following a Broadway run, with "bus and truck companies" crisscrossing America on tours and repertoire and college theaters picking up a show. They all have to pay the publisher grand rights before the curtain can go up.

Look at the continuing popularity of such shows as *Guys and Dolls, Showboat, Oklahoma!, Music Man, Annie Get Your Gun,* and, of course, all of the Andrew Lloyd Webber shows. They will be around for years, making money for those who created their songs.

6. Synchronization royalties—When your music is used in movies or on a television show, you get a synchronization fee. Generally paid to the publisher (who splits it with the writer), it's not a set fee. Instead, the fee amount is negotiated with whoever wants to use it.

7. Special permissions royalties—Now this is an interesting one. These are licenses worked out with merchandisers that want to use a song in a disc or tape for a special marketing program.

Companies often put together special albums to be sold through service stations, convenience stores, or large supermarket chains. You've seen these around, especially at Christmas and other holidays. Like synchronization royalties, the fee for this kind of song use is usually negotiated, and the songwriter and publisher—along with the artist, of course—get the money.

8. Foreign rights royalties—A lot of songwriters today have universal appeal: their songs have the potential to become popular all around the world. So foreign rights can be very important. As a songwriter, you must try to get a publisher with experience in making deals outside the US so that you can have your songs promoted internationally, with international royalties the result. Revenue can be exceptionally good in the European market, as well as in South America and the Pacific Rim countries.

A beginning songwriter may not have access to a publisher with worldwide offices, but a savvy publisher can make sub-publishing deals with other publishers to license your material abroad.

We should also note that the performing rights organizations, BMI, ASCAP, and SESAC, have reciprocating agreements with other performing rights societies around the world, which helps when it comes to international performance royalties.

Let's step away from the publisher for a moment and answer the question most asked by beginning songwriters: how do you protect your original material?

Under the Revised Copyright Act of 1976, you have an automatic copyright on your song the moment you have completed your material, either on paper or on tape. For further protection, you may register your copyright with the Library of Congress. To do that, write the **Copyright Office, Library of Congress, Washington, D.C., 20559** and request Form PA, returning it with the required payment.

Realistically, it's usually not necessary to register your copyright until your song has been recorded; however, it's always a good idea to put the copyright symbol, that little "C" with the circle around it (©), along with your name, address, and date, on each of your lyric sheets or on any label of cassettes that contain your songs. Under the most recent copyright laws, a copyright is good for the life of the writer plus 70 years.

♪ ♪ ♪ ♪

There are pitfalls that await you in this business. At every turn, unscrupulous operators are, ready to take advantage of the unwary. When you're assembling your Star Team, be very careful about the people you add. Make sure you are getting value received for any money you pay out, and be very careful when paying anyone *anything*.

Let's take the music publisher as an example. A legitimate music publisher will publish your song and try to generate income from it, royalties that will be split with you. *Never* pay a publisher to publish your song. The publisher should be earning money *for* you, not *from* you.

This is generally true in the recording business, as well.

If you have a song or a performance that is worth being recorded, a record company will, in most cases, advance the money for the recording session, hoping to get a return on its investment in the form of marketable music. If you are asked to pay for the recording or for the manufacturing of so many cassettes or CDs, watch out—that's a red flag!

Examine what you're getting in the deal. Is it up to you to pay the recording costs? To get your product manufactured and distributed to the record stores? To promote your records on radio? If you are paying for everything, you have gotten into the record business, and your chances of succeeding are slim indeed.

Here's one of the most common ripoffs. A songwriter or singer sees an ad In a newspaper or magazine soliciting "new songs and new artists." The address on the ad gives the name of a record company in some major recording center—New York, Los Angeles, Nashville. So the artist sends in some material.

Unfortunately, no matter how good or how bad the material is, a glowing report soon arrives from the "record company." It says, this could be the next big hit. All you need is to record it professionally and get it on radio stations. And, of course, that's where they come in.

They'll tell you what they're going to do, and they'll do exactly what they say they will. They'll record your song, and they'll get it to radio stations. But it's going to cost you. And your cost to record with them will almost always be much more than if you simply went to a recording studio of your own choice and hired a bandleader and musicians yourself.

They'll send your song to a certain number of radio stations, just to remain legal. But the program directors and music directors at radio stations don't usually listen to new material from a record company that's not in the mainstream. They're also familiar with these kinds of labels and know what they represent. And what's more, they don't usually listen to anything on cassette, which is the way many of these companies distribute your material.

So before paying anyone anything, find out who you're dealing with. Get some recommendations from other people who have worked with them. Check with the Better Business Bureau, the Chamber of Commerce, music publishers, or trade organizations. It may save you thousands of dollars.

♪ ♪ ♪ ♪

Remember that part of my method for success is being persistent and consistent? Well, I've found over the years that songwriters, to their credit, are a *very* persistent lot. If songwriters are really serious about their craft and believe in their songs, hardly anything will discourage them. And the most persistent ones have an uncanny ability to penetrate even the most secure backstage areas of giant superstars. I know. It has happened on some of my own shows.

The backstage has been tightly secured, with no friends, no family, no business associates allowed. There's not enough room and the show's on a tight schedule. And there I'll be, standing in the wings, watching my superstar Oak Ridge Boys wow an audience. Then suddenly, a tug on my sleeve, the feel of a cassette tape pressed into my hand, and the familiar words:

"Excuse me, Mr. Halsey. I've written this song especially for The Oak Ridge Boys. Would you see that they get it after the show?"

This is one of the lessons of this book, and of the Halsey method: If you are persistent, if you want it badly enough, you will make your own breaks. You will open the doors that seem to be closed.

This kind of tenacity is what gets songwriters into closed recording studios and sessions and onto the sets of TV shows. For a persistent songwriter, every meeting with a music-business person is an opportunity to get his or her songs heard. I have been pitched songs by bankers, doctors, and college professors. Waiters and waitresses have brought me material in restaurants. I've been slipped tapes at funerals, weddings, concerts, movie theaters, on airplanes, and even late at night by an undiscovered songwriter who had discovered my home address.

These are the ones who will remain enthused about their songs after suffering untold rejection. These are the ones who, after having been turned down dozens of times, will still submit their songs with the firm belief that they are hits waiting to happen. These are the ones with a good, strong pair of shoes who can take them down endless pavements in search of success, who can get their feet inside of doors. These are the ones who won't quit until they have a legitimate publisher and are seeing royalties from their work.

These are the ones who will make it.

♪ ♪ ♪ ♪

This same guidelines, by the way, apply equally as well to performing artists as they do to songwriters. I remember presenting one of my seminars in Tulsa back in 1992, where I talked to the crowd about the same things I've just told you here: make the calls, get your foot in the door, and don't be afraid you are bothering someone by pitching your song or your talent—it's the persistence that will pay off.

About a quarter to seven the next morning, the phone in my hotel room rang. "Good morning, Mr. Halsey," said the masculine voice on the other end. "I attended your seminar last night, and I have three talented sons who write and play music. They want to become stars."

I said, "Fine. Send me a tape and I'll listen and give you my opinion."

"Mr. Halsey," he returned. "I paid 50 dollars to hear you last night. I'm following the advice you gave. I'm getting my foot in the door, so to speak. I have my three sons downstairs in the lobby. Would you please come down and hear them?"

Well, what could I do but say yes. He was, after all, following the method I'd given him the night before.

Twenty minutes later, in the lobby of the Tulsa Marriott Hotel, I was watching and listening to one of the greatest young groups I'd seen in a long time. The three boys were brothers, and each boy had *star* written all over him. Their father, Walker Hanson had told me over the phone that his sons were talented; Zach, Isaac, and Taylor proved him right. It was a winning act.

Walker asked me if I'd be interested in helping his boys, and I gave him the name of my Los Angeles attorney, Bill Coben, along with lots of encouragement. I knew they'd make it. Coben became their lawyer, and an important part of their Star Team, helping Walker assemble the other team members. The Hansons, as they were known when I saw them that morning, became Hanson—a household name in millions of homes all over the world, a huge teen-idol band, and a multi-platinum-selling recording act.

I feel fortunate to have been there at the beginning with advice and encouragement for them, and I'm proud that they thank me in their official biography for helping them along the way. They persevered, they got a foot in the door, and they made it.

The Music and Entertainment Attorney

Our Star Team is coming together now, with only two more elements to add. Have you found your place on the team yet, or are you still looking?

Next chapter, we'll talk about the promoter, the final spoke in our Star Team wheel. Now, however, it's time to talk about the music and entertainment attorney. As we begin dealing with contracts, record deals, videos, royalties, guarantees, and percentages, the team needs somebody to look over each of these deals, to check the contracts, and maybe even to help negotiate a contract, or at least fine-tune some of its language. Remember how important my attorney, Bill Coben, was to the success of Hanson, helping Walker and the boys build their own Star Team.

It's important to make sure that this music and entertainment attorney is a specialist. I don't care if your uncle is the most famous attorney in Cleveland—if he doesn't know the music and entertainment business, he is basically useless to your Star Team. Get somebody with experience. Good music attorneys are not going to cost that much more than any other good attorney without the necessary specialized knowledge. Because they know the nuances of the music business, and know about the kinds of deals made in it, a music and entertainment business attorney will be worth what he or she costs. Many good music attorneys deal with record companies on a daily basis. They have close relationships with decision-makers within the companies, so they might even help an artist get a record deal.

At the very least, a music attorney is essential in dealing with contracts. An emerging artist will usually have to forge contracts with a manager, a booking agency, a record company, and a music publisher—all members of the Star Team. Contracts may also come up for music videos, commercials, product endorsements, and corporate sponsorships, among many other things.

Dealing with these contracts calls for the in-depth knowledge of a music and entertainment attorney. There are, in fact, whole law firms that concentrate their expertise in these areas. Most entertainment lawyers work on an hourly fee basis. Some may become more involved and require a monthly retainer. Others may take a personal interest in the artist's career and work for a percentage of the artist's earnings. And sometimes, if an attorney believes in the potential of a new artist, he or she will help the artist assemble a Star Team—as Bill Coben did for Hanson. Accessing the specialized music attorney's **Power of Performance** can play a major role in the success of an artist.

Since 1967, I have been blessed with good attorneys. Dan Sklar and Bill Coben, based in Los Angeles, negotiated many entertainment-business contracts for The Jim Halsey Company. Warren Jackman and Eric Grimshaw, of Tulsa, represented us in corporate and other areas of business. Ralph Gordon has represented some of my Nashville business, and Joel Katz and his firm have worked with me in other specialized areas. It's been a good combination.

As a manager, I've negotiated a lot of record contracts, but I've always been smart enough to include my attorneys, Bill Coben and Dan Sklar, in the process. Record contracts can be several hundred pages in length, and they're *always* tilted in favor of the record company. To get the best deal possible, the manager and the artist must be knowledgeable and very alert, and the music attorney must be on board to help protect the artist's rights.

♪ ♪ ♪ ♪

Many performers, upon getting their first recording contract, are so eager to seal the deal that they forget about their rights. They'll sign anything just to start recording.

Obviously, this is a bad idea. At the very least, an artist must be able to recognize the basic language of a recording contract and to understand things enough to ask questions. So it's in every Star Team member's best interest to know the meanings of the following words:

TERM: This is the length of time for which the record company is signing the artist, expressed in a number of years and/or number of albums. But this can be deceptive. There's a big difference between a firm term and a term with options. That is, an artist may think he or she has a seven-year, seven-album deal, but it may only be firm for the first year and first album, with an option for the remaining six. The option can also be expressed only by year *or* album, instead of both. A lot of people think they've signed a long-term deal, only to be cut loose when their first one or two discs don't perform up to expectations and the company decides not to pick up their option.

Remember this: whether or not to pick up an option is *always* the record company's choice.

GUARANTEES AND ADVANCES: These terms represent the amount of money the record company pays the artist. In most cases, this amount is usually *recoupable* (see below) against sales. In other words, if an artist gets a $40,000 guarantee or advance for a recording session, that artist won't get any more money until he or she has earned more than that $40,000 back from *royalties* (see below).

RECOUPABLE: If an artist sees the term "recoupable against royalties" on a contract, it means that the record company will recover everything it advanced or spent on the artist's behalf before the artist receives any more money. Areas where the record company might spend money include tour support, independent promotion (to supplement in-house promotion), videos (sometimes split 50-50 with the artist), transportation, wardrobe, supplemental musicians, and almost anything else it wants to charge an artist for. The company will withhold all funds from the artist until its expenditures have been recovered.

ROYALTY: This is an amount, either a percentage of sales or an exact dollar amount, paid to the artist based upon the number of records sold. And the artist may not receive money for a long time if all of his or her disc sales are *cross-collateralized* (see below).

CROSS-COLLATERALIZED: What this means is that *all* of an artist's recorded product must be paid for before the artist receives any money. One disc's costs are charged against, or crossed with, the costs of all of the others. If the artist has one good-selling album and one poor seller, the sales of the two are added together, and nothing is paid to the artist until the total sales of both albums are enough to cover costs.

RESERVES: Before a record company will pay an artist for album sales, it will put an amount of the money owed the artist into reserve for a specified period of time—sometimes as much as 12 months or even longer. So the artist won't be paid all the monies actually owed him or her until the record company is absolutely certain this money won't have any encumbrances against it.

FREE GOODS: Free goods are supposedly product used for radio-station promotions, press and PR, or as a sales incentive to move the artist's product with retailers. Since the artist's contract calls for payment on product sold, there's no payment for product given away—free goods. If, to sell 100,000 CDs, the record company gives away 10,000 copies, does this mean the sale of 110,000 copies has been discounted or that full payment of royalties will be paid only on the 100,000 and no payment on the 10,000 free copies? In a worst-case scenario, the record company sells 100,000 copies of one artist's disc, but gives away 10,000 free copies of another artist's CD. The "free goods" provision on any contract should always be carefully examined by a qualified music attorney!

PACKAGING CHARGE: This is the amount deducted for the cost of packaging each CD or cassette into a case with cover photo, liner notes, etc. This cost is deducted before royalty payments are made to an artist. We should note that this charge is usually inflated in favor of the record company.

CUTOUTS AND DELETES: Cutouts and deletes are old albums that have outlived their sales potential, the discs and tapes you see in "bargain bins" of just about any music store. Usually, the record company stipulates in a contract that no royalties will be paid on these albums.

But shouldn't there be some form of payment to the artist on these, especially if they're discounted to someone overseas, or to stateside dealers who buy junk? And if an artist sells merchandise on the road, as most do, he or she should always have the contractual option to buy their own cutouts and deletes at the same deeply discounted price the record company offers to anyone else.

CONTROLLED COMPOSITIONS: These are songs controlled by the artist, either as a writer, co-writer, or publisher. In some cases, if more than 70 percent of the songs on an album are controlled by the artist, the record company will pay the music publisher a reduced rate. Consequently, the songwriter receives less.

Also, some record companies now pay publishing royalties for only ten songs on a CD. If an artist wants more than ten, the publishing royalties will be divided among however many songs are on the CD. This has nothing to do with the royalty the artist receives as a singer or performer, just any songwriting royalties he or she may have as composer.

BEST-OF ALBUMS: Most recorded product is cross-collateralized, but a "Best-of" album can be treated as a separate venture. If the artist is hot enough and has had a lot of hits, the record company may treat the "Best-of" CD as separate, not "crossing" it with any other of the artist's albums, so the artist could receive payment for just that disc. This is something, however, that has to be negotiated at the time of an artist's initial contract with the recording company.

JOINT RECORDINGS: These may prove artistically interesting and quite commercial—just ask Willie Nelson—but they should always be done at the artist's discretion. An artist should look for a "favored nations" clause in a contract. This assures the artist payment and billing equal to that of whomever he collaborates with on a joint recording.

RECORD CLUBS: Since record clubs sell albums for less than retail price, royalties will be less. An artist needs to be careful about promotion and free goods here as well. Most ads for record clubs let you pick so many CDs for free, or for a penny, when you join the club. The record club doesn't pay royalties on those records—they're considered free goods to the record clubs. Thousands of your CDs can be given away to promote someone else's catalog.

In most circumstances, I'm opposed to that. I recently negotiated a contract for a one-album deal, and the label included the stipulation they would be able to give so many thousand copies of the disc to a record club for use as giveaways in attracting new members. We did not accept this.

If you have a big catalog—if your act has, say, 15 or 20 albums in the catalog—you've got a chance to make that back, because people will order something else recorded by that act. But if you've got only one album in the record club, and people can get it free, there's no way they're going to order a second one and pay for it.

Record clubs can sell a lot of product for an artist, and in a lot of ways they're good. But you have to be careful of what you're giving them when you negotiate a contract.

DIRECT-RESPONSE SALES: Any contract should include a provision for payment for CDs offered for sale in TV ads, whether it's an artist's entire CD or individual tracks included on a compilation disc with other artists. A lot of product can be moved by direct-response marketing programs on television—many of us remember the successful TV promotions for albums by the likes of Andy Griffith, Tennessee Ernie Ford, and Slim Whitman, or have seen spots for the endless repackagings of classic rock 'n' roll hits. If an artist has other discs in stores, television-sales albums will usually stimulate their sales.

VIDEO: The contract should stipulate the number of music videos to be made and the cost. It should also tell who's going to pay for them. Often the record company will advance the money for a video and then recoup it from the artist's royalties. Sometimes the company will recoup half the cost and pay the other half itself. Maybe it'll even pay the whole cost of the video. It depends on how hot the artist is.

The record company will always own the copyright to the video. An artist should check a contract carefully to see who has creative con-trol—who can pick the production company, producer, director? Does the artist have a choice? And what about the royalty structure for sales of music videos?

FAVORED NATIONS: We've mentioned this in the "joint recordings" section. It means that an artist's payment, treatment, and billing will be equal with the highest ranking contract in a collaborative artistic venture.

TOUR SUPPORT: In a first-record deal, it's usually not known how much, if any, tour support will be needed. Once an artist is established, however, tour support is absolutely part of any record deal. This sup-port, which comes from the record company, can involve promotion, advertising, additional musicians, travel arrangements, tour press, lights, sound, production, costumes, instruments, and anything else necessary to make the artist's presentation acceptable and that he or she can't afford to pay up-front. The tour-support portion of a recording contract can be flexible, but it is necessary. The dollar amount can be fixed or it can be advanced per tour; but either way it will probably be recouped from the artist's royalties. In other words, it's a loan the record company makes to the performer that has to be repaid—but only by royalties from the sales of the artist's records.

ACCOUNTING, RIGHT TO AUDIT: Artists are entitled to an accounting of their album sales at regular intervals. They are also entitled to audit their record company's books. Both of these rights need to be spelled out in the contract.

MERCHANDISING RIGHTS: Most record companies now want the right to sell the artist's merchandise, and they'll try to get that privilege in their contracts. Many record companies have their own merchandising arms; the artist still gets paid for merchandise sold, but only a percent-age. If possible, a performer should keep his or her own merchandising. This is called the *right of choice,* and it means that the artist must approve anything with his or her image on it, including such things as T-shirts, photos, and tour books. Sometimes, the artist can make a more advanta-geous merchandising deal, getting an advance directly from the merchan-dising companies and recouping it through sale of merchandise instead of records. A merchandising company might give a star, say, $250,000 for merchandising rights, which all has to be recouped by the company through sale of the merchandise.

In some cases, that money comes from the merchandising company in the form of a personal loan, and the artist has to be very sure that what he or she signed to get the advance is not going to have to be repaid. If it is, and the artist doesn't sell enough merchandise, he or she can be on the hook for thousands of dollars. That's a very important point, and it's another reason why performers need good managers and lawyers.

PROMOTION BUDGET: This is the money the record company is willing to spend itself to promote a record via such things as ads, special promotions, graphic arts, in-store displays, special sales bonuses, and television, newspaper, and radio campaigns and contests. Establishing a budget for this is the responsibility of the record company, but many times the amount is not spelled out in the contract. A disc might need more promotional input than the record company believes is necessary. Or worse, the company could drop the ball and do nothing. For both these reasons, a specific promotion budget must be in the contract.

INDEPENDENT PROMOTION: Sure, the record company people are always convinced they have everything covered, so promotion outside of the company won't be needed for a disc. This, though, is debatable. In many instances, once a record starts to happen the artist needs all of the help he or she can get, and fast! Performers should ask for a contractual provision guaranteeing a certain amount of money for "independent promotion," jointly administered by the artist's manager and the record company.

OWNERSHIP OF MASTERS: Unless an artist is a superstar, and is leasing his or her master recordings to the record company, or the record is being done through a production deal, the record company always owns the masters. Of course, if the company wants an artist badly enough, deals can be made in which ownership of the masters reverts back to the artist or production company after a certain length of time or when the company's investment has been recouped.

Sometimes a record company may be interested in releasing an artist's master recording, but not interested enough to pay for the session or advance the money. The company may then opt to license the songs on the master recordings and pay the artist a royalty.

So a lot of times a producer will have enough faith in an artist to go in and make a whole album without knowing where he or she is going to sell it. The producer, or the artist and producer together, invest the money, do the session, then go out and shop the masters to see if some company wants to release it. But a company may say, "We're not going to give you money up front for this, but we'll pay you a royalty." That's licensing a master, and it's usually done for a specified period of time, after which the producer and artist get the masters back and the company no longer has any interest in the masters. They're leased for a period of time for a percentage of royalty. It's a good way to get an album out there, too, if you know what you're doing and you believe in yourself.

FOREIGN PAYMENTS AND RIGHTS: Many times royalty payments will be different in each foreign territory that sells an album. If artists aren't with a multinational company, their record companies will have to negotiate with other companies for pressing and foreign distribution. Because we're living in a global marketplace, with almost any product today carrying the potential for worldwide sales, it's important to have a music attorney on the job here.

ASSIGNMENT OF CONTRACT: This is almost always the right of the record company, but there are certain restrictions that may well apply, and artists must understand them. They must know whether the company has the right to assign their entire contract (if the company sells out to another record company, does the artist have to go to the new company?) or just certain masters or tracks. In the case of a buyout or merger, artists should have the opportunity to decide where they go themselves.

Keep in mind that a record-company contract can be assigned to almost anything—not just another record company, but a bank or some other entity. Record masters and publishing contracts are almost like chattel these days, traded like stocks and bonds. An artist may not have much to say about whether or not his or her catalog can be sold to someone else, but the company shouldn't be able to piecemeal it out without the artist's approval.

BREAKAGE: Are they kidding? In this age of CDs, cassettes, and DVDs, are there still massive broken shipments? Many record companies think so. Some will pay only 90 percent, even 85 percent, of royalties on sales, deducting 10 or 15 percent for breakage.

This practice goes back to a time when records were fragile and easily broken. It hasn't really had any validity since the advent of the vinyl LP, and certainly not since the introduction of cassettes and CDs. If the artist is big enough, he or she can usually negotiate for payment on 100 percent of the sales.

Finally, an essential piece of advice: *Never sign any agreement or contract until your specialized music and entertainment attorney has examined and approved it.* Usually, there'll be a lot of changes.

In this chapter, I've identified some of the basic contractual terms; it may be just enough information to be dangerous! Again, any Star Team needs a specialized attorney. Don't be without one. I never have been!

16

The Promoter

There's a reason I've listed the promoter as the final Star Team member. It's because he or she is usually the last component to be plugged into an artist's master plan, the last spoke in the wheel. All of the other Star Team members, from manager to attorney, should be in place first. Collectively, with their combined **Power of Performance**, they give the promoter something to promote.

What does a promoter do? He or she puts the artist on stage, in front of an audience. He or she presents the artist. Usually relying on ticket sales for payment, the promoter is the risk-taker, a team member whose performance relies on time, money, ingenuity, energy, and friendships. Without the promoter, there would simply be no show.

Many music-business professionals have started out as promoters. I'm one of them. When I was 19 and still a college student, I began bringing every imaginable type of show, band, artist, and production to my hometown of Independence, Kansas. The city had a great auditorium, and I took it upon myself to fill it.

When I started, I knew enough about the retail business to see an analogy that helped me make the transition to the entertainment business. I saw the auditorium as my store, the attraction as my merchandise. I would notify my customers—the potential ticket buyers—and try creatively to convince them they would like my show; that it was a good value, and that they should make the decision to come—to answer the *call to action* and purchase a ticket. It sounds simple, and it was. All I had to do was my homework on the attractions I was bringing in and figure out the potential audience for them.

You've read earlier how important I think it is to create an *event* with your shows. I learned instinctively how to do that. The first show I promoted featured regional western swing star Leon McAuliffe and his

Cimarron Boys band. My finances dictated that I had to be inventive about my advertising and promotion. So I examined every possible way to inform the public: radio, newspapers, posters, handbills, mailing lists, special contests. I left absolutely no avenue unexplored.

I will never forget the night of the dance, my first night in show business. I wasn't sure how it would go. In those days you didn't do a lot of advance ticket sales; the people who heard about an event would just show up at the box-office right before it was supposed to start. On this night, there was a long line waiting to get in by the time the box office opened. In fact, the dance had been going for 30 minutes before the last person in line could buy a ticket. That place was jam-packed with people; my first promotion was a success. Somehow, I'd done enough things right. And I realized right then that I was in the music business for good!

Early on, I established some important criteria for my business. Good ethics was one, the continual pursuit of the satisfied customer was another. I gave the people what they wanted: a good show at a good value. Truly, the **Power of Performance** was there.

Then, when I was 20 years old—with a number of successful promotions under my belt, but still learning—I had the **Power of Performance** dramatically demonstrated to me. It also was something I'll never forget. Neither will I ever forget the man involved, legendary big-band leader Woody Herman, who would later become my client and mentor.

I had been very successful in my first year and a half as a promoter. But since I was still in college while I was operating the business, I was using every penny I made, and everything I promoted had to be cost-effective. I was always looking for great deals, ones that offered small risk but high potential profits.

I got my opportunity when Woody Herman and his great 19-piece jazz band came through. They were playing the major cities in Kansas and Oklahoma: Wichita, Topeka, Kansas City, Tulsa, and Oklahoma City. What was most important was that they had an open date during this time—and they'd be close to Independence.

Usually when there's an open date, the agent will offer promoters in the area a special price, below the normal asking price, just to fill in the date and help meet some of the road expenses.

That's what happened to me, and that's how I got Woody Herman. I'll always remember the date: February 21. It was shortly after the New Year holiday, I was short of money, but the deal was so good that I couldn't resist. Under regular circumstances I wouldn't have been able to afford him, but with this special "routing" price, Woody's guarantee was low and I could see myself making some pretty good money.

I did one of my most thorough jobs promoting this date, turning it into an event, working my **Power of Performance** as a budding impresario. I made sure that everybody in southeast Kansas and northeast Oklahoma knew that the great Woody Herman and his band were coming to Memorial Hall in Independence, Kansas. Local merchants offered special "Woody Herman" sales prices. The mayor proclaimed February 21 "Woody Herman Day" in Independence.

Most managers call the promoter the day before an engagement, requesting that the promoter have the guaranteed amount , in cash, ready for the act. When Woody's manager called, I assured him there wouldn't be any problem. I was sure myself. In fact, I was sure that after Woody got his guaranteed amount, he would also pocket lots more money on his percentage of the take. (Most big acts get a percentage of the gross from box-office receipts, after the guaranteed amount is reached.) We were getting calls from all over the territory inquiring about tickets.

The day of the concert, Woody was coming in from Topeka, 125 miles to the north. Since I'd taken the date on short notice—one of the reasons I got a good price—I hadn't sold a lot of tickets in advance. But I had literally hundreds of people asking me to hold their tickets at the box office. It was going to be a big success.

Then the unexpected hit, and it was a promoter's worst nightmare.

Just a few hours before the show was to begin, a huge blizzard and ice storm hit northern Kansas and roared southward, right toward Independence.

My heart sank.

By the time I opened the box office at 7 p.m., it was snowing so hard I couldn't see across the street. The storm was becoming one of the worst blizzards Kansas had seen in 20 years, and my event was turning into a disaster.

No cars moved on the streets. A few loyal Woody Herman fans braved the weather and walked to the auditorium. But I could see what was going to happen. There would be hundreds of reservations for tickets that would not be picked up. The elements had displayed their own **Power of Performance!**

I was sick to the soul. All my hard work, all my great promotion, all my time—wasted. Minutes before showtime, fewer than 100 hardy Herman fans had trekked through the blinding storm to get to the concert. At least they were warm inside the auditorium.

I checked the time. At 8 p.m., when the show was scheduled to start, I planned to take the stage and explain that Woody and his great band weren't going to make it. I knew everyone would understand. There wasn't anything moving in southeast Kansas that night. I knew some people had braved the elements that night hoping that Woody had arrived earlier in the day, but that's not the way things work with traveling musicians. They work late, sleep late, and travel late, usually arriving just in time to set up and play.

I was going to take a big loss on the night, as well as learn a good lesson: a promoter should *never* promote a show or enter into an obligation unless he has the funds to pay it off. Although I wouldn't have to pay Woody Herman his guaranteed fee, I was still financially obligated to the hall and the stage hands, and to my advertising and promotional expenses. I had enough to pay these costs, but barely. At least, I thought, I wouldn't be buried by the blizzard.

At 8 p.m., I started for the stage, ready to tell the sparse audience that Woody couldn't make it because of the storm, and all tickets would be refunded. Then, suddenly, I saw two large headlights barely visible through the falling snow. It was the sole vehicle moving on the streets. It could only be the bus!

Sure enough, it was Woody Herman and his Thundering Herd fighting the elements, and, like the U.S. Post Office, making their appointed rounds despite the weather, arriving at Memorial Hall in Independence at exactly 8 p.m.

My heart sank!

Now the concert would go on as advertised—but with only a bare handful of brave souls there to see it. Much more important, I was now again obligated to pay Woody Herman his guaranteed fee. How could I do it? Where was I going to get the money? I'd counted on the box-office receipts to pay off, but with this record-breaking winter storm, I'd collected only few hundred dollars in ticket sales.

Woody Herman was one of my musical idols. How could I tell him I couldn't pay him?

The only option I had was to try and get a loan for the amount at the local bank the next day. But I knew that wouldn't happen. My banker, Mr. Ernest Sewell, was conservative, and he didn't much approve of the risks involved in promoting shows.

I finally realized this could be my last date as a promoter; I guessed I might as well enjoy it. So when the lights went up and Woody's great band struck its first note, I was sitting in the audience. And did I enjoy it! In spite of everything, that night was one of my finest musical memories.

Woody's powerful concert that night did just what it was supposed to do; his **Power of Performance** transformed me, put me in a different space. And when it was over, I pulled my spirits together, got my positive attitude in shape, and swallowed hard, mustering up the courage to tell Mr. Herman I only had a few dollars on hand to pay him. I'd have to try to raise the money the next day.

Had it been only yesterday that his manager had talked to me, insisting that the guarantee be paid in cash? Everything had seemed so rosy then, and I'd been so confident about raising plenty of money on the date. Now, just a day later, my whole world had turned around.

I stood in the box office, waiting uneasily for Mr. Herman. I had to tell him the truth.

Then he entered the room. It was the first time we'd met. In a gruff voice, he asked for the promoter.

"I'm that person," I blurted out, desperately working up my courage.

He looked surprised to find that he was working the date for a 20-year-old kid. And before I could say anything else, Woody asked in that matter-of-fact style that was his trademark, "How much did you take in tonight, kid?"

"About $350, Mr. Herman," I answered.

Without hesitation, he said, "Listen, kid, why don't you give me that, and we'll call it square."

I almost fell on the floor.

Was this man a mind reader? Did he really understand that because of him, a miracle had just happened? Woody Herman had not only just exhibited masterfully his **Power of Performance** on the stage of Memorial Hall; he'd also encored with that power to me, a grateful audience of one, in the box office.

Because of Woody Herman, I was still a promoter—and a wiser one. The lesson I learned that night is an important one: *never extend your resources beyond what you can pay.* And remember, while it's good to look at all the possible scenarios, never forget weather as a possible trickster on the day of your event.

Instead of ending my career as a promoter, this potentially disastrous meeting foreshadowed a relationship between Woody Herman and me that would last for decades. Later on, I promoted many more of his dates; I even became his agent in the 1980s, almost exactly 30 years after we first locked eyes in that Independence, Kansas, box office, with the blizzard raging outside. I found Woody to be a man of great integrity, with the ability to pick promising young musicians from around the country—recognizing their potential **Power of Performance**—and shape them into real players. I enjoyed being his agent and was proud to have represented this great musical organization.

I learned a lot from Woody Herman, beginning with that encounter in Memorial Hall. Decades later, when our business relationship had blossomed into a personal one as well, I finally told him that the young promoter for that long-ago date had been me. I explained that, because of his grace in accepting a far lesser amount than his guarantee, my career had probably been saved.

Woody remembered the date well, and he confessed that he was surprised that the impresario had been only 20 years old. He'd sensed that it would be bad news for me if he demanded his full amount. So on the spur of the moment, he saved everyone embarrassment, and more, by asking for only the box office receipts. He told me he was glad to get that much "gas money" from the job.

We both had some good laughs about our first meeting, but it set the tone for a major part of my philosophy when I later formed my booking agency: *it's in everyone's best interest to keep a promoter in business.*

Perhaps even more important, I learned from Woody Herman on that icy night that the **Power of Performance** is just as important off stage as on.

Since then, I have worked to develop my own **Power of Performance** as a manager, agent, impresario, businessman, and human being. And as I built my own company, which would employ many people and represent many fine artists, I always tried to pass on the theory of the **Power of Performance**, and how accessing it will put you on the road to success.

♪ ♪ ♪ ♪

My next few years as a promoter provided a good education for me. I promoted everything—concerts by jazz groups, big bands, and symphony orchestras; classical events; wrestling matches; circuses; ice shows; and performances by rhythm & blues and country acts. I learned by doing— by making mistakes and failing as well as by getting things right and creating events with my shows. By starting as a promoter, one of the essential Star Team members, I was able to learn all of the facets of the business, and what made them all work.

Very early in my career, I learned that it takes a lot of cooperation from all concerned. Almost instinctively I began finding out who the important team members were and observing how they all worked together. I was learning how to be successful, developing my Star Team method, exercising my **Power of Performance**.

As a promoter, you learn about cutting the right deals with the venues, and about the right venues for an artist. You must know about whatever or whomever you're promoting. Who's the audience for what you have? How do you reach that audience? If you have a choice of venues, what is the best venue for this particular act?

Here's a simple formula every promoter should remember. First, figure expenses carefully, taking into account the cost of the venue, the artist, any co-headliners, advertising, promotion, the stage crew, staff salaries, box-office commissions to the agencies that sell your tickets, ticket sellers, lights and sound, possible traveling expenses, and taxes, and fulfilling all of the requirements of the artist's contract.

Add all of these up. This amount represents your *expenses*.

Next, find out the number of people your venue will hold. You can now establish the ticket price. My own advice is to base the ticket price on how much it will take you to make a reasonable profit (the amount after your expenses) if you sell enough tickets to fill three-fourths of the venue's capacity, or three-fourths of what you anticipate your artist will draw. Of course, if you sell more, so much the better.

This is a reasonably safe formula. But, as you know, if you sell far fewer tickets than you need to make a profit, you not only lose money, but a lot of time and energy as well. For this reason, being a promoter carries a certain amount of risk.

In dealing over the years with a lot of music-business professionals, including agents, managers, and record company and music publishing executives, I've found that many of them started as I did, as a promoter on a local or regional basis.

I think Sol Hurok, the legendary impresario who was my first inspiration, would approve.

A large part of this book is about creating events, and every good promoter must know how to produce one. To create an event, you take something special, add a number of complementary elements, and transform this something special into something *extraordinarily special*, expanding it far beyond what it would be if the extra elements were absent— and many times exceeding even your own expectations. How do you create a true event? My experience has taught me that you can do it best if you do it in these eight stages:

 1. Inspiration
 2. Goal and Purpose

3. Planning

4. Expanding the Elements

5. Implementation

6. The Event

7. Review

8. Follow-up

Let's illustrate the method with an event that meets the criteria of something extraordinarily special. In the early 1970s, when we were establishing The Jim Halsey Company in Tulsa, we convinced our client, partner, and friend Roy Clark, to join us in Oklahoma. He and his wife, Barbara, moved from Annapolis, Maryland, and established a home in Tulsa. Meanwhile, our group of partners—including Hank Thompson, Wayne Creasy, Mack Sanders, and Stanley Synar—had many investments in the community. We owned and operated two radio stations and a large apartment complex, built several office buildings, and purchased a large ranch south of Tulsa. Because of our high profile—and highly leveraged financing—we had been able to acquire many businesses and properties; because of our high visibility, we were the subject of much press, both local and national.

Most of the investments we made fit within our philosophy of synergy, in which one plus one can sometimes equal not two, but 20. We were all contributing to an overall plan, and among the things we were trying to do was build Tulsa into a music center.

Tulsa had our support, and we had Tulsa's support. Now, with our collective energies and high visibility, was the time for a community public-relations event. Not simply something that would get us press, but something that would benefit the whole community. And so, we began thinking in stages:

1. Inspiration: While I'm not especially sports-minded, I had a vision of establishing a major sporting event in the name of Roy Clark. The sport was golf; the idea was a celebrity golf tournament. Many of our friends within the music and entertainment industry had heard so much about our projects in Tulsa, they were eager to see for themselves. This would give them a great excuse to visit.

2. Goal and Purpose: Establishing a golf tournament in Roy's name would be an opportunity to invite any industry-related associates to Tulsa, to have a good time playing golf, to give our community high national visibility, to raise some money for a local charity—and to do some business as well.

3. Planning: Since the organization and planning tasks fell mainly on The Jim Halsey Company, this signaled the beginning of the hard-work phase. Roy, a good golfer, liked and supported the idea. My main man in Tulsa, John Hitt, was also a good golfer; he became an important member of our planning team. Warren Jackman, our attorney, got on board early. When we needed a good local charity, he got Children's Medical Center (CMC) of Tulsa involved. That worthy hospital was not only a beneficiary, it supplied us with our golf course as well.

We planned to end the weekend of celebrities and golf with an all-star celebrity concert. Famed Tulsa evangelist Oral Roberts contributed by furnishing his beautiful, state of-the-art, 10,000 seat Mabee Center on the campus of Oral Roberts University for the concert event. Dr. Roberts and his son Richard have always supported us, and we them. They're good golfers, too!

We were beginning to roll, and we were still six months away from the event. That sounds like plenty of time, but there's no such thing as too much time. The more time you have to plan and work, the more elements you can add.

4. Expanding the Elements: We were set with the Roy Clark Celebrity Golf Tournament, our dates were scheduled, our goal and purpose in place. Now, it was time to expand the elements.

With a special event like this, it's always good to get as many prominent citizens involved as possible. We established a big committee, staffing it with community leaders, members of the board of Children's Medical Center, media executives, bankers, lawyers, automobile dealers, and others. There was a lot of work to be done, and a lot of volunteer help was needed. One of the best moves we made was getting the Women's Auxiliary of the CMC involved. They had some great ideas and made important contributions.

For nearly six months the office staff of The Jim Halsey Company was involved daily with the planning and work. Everyone contributed to the team effort that turned this into an extraordinarily special event. As we went along, we invited a lot of major talent buyers to our weekend extravaganza, people we dealt with all year long: television producers; fair and rodeo buyers; casino operators from Las Vegas, Reno, and Tahoe; club operators; and concert promoters.

We brought these folks into Tulsa as our guests for two reasons. Number one, it was a way of saying "thanks" for the business they had given us over the preceding year. Number two, we were going to have most of the artists we represented involved with the tournament. Subliminally, having the buyers on hand worked as our own private sales opportunity for our artists' upcoming dates.

Since we had so many of our artist roster involved—Roy Clark, Hank Thompson, The Oak Ridge Boys, Mel Tillis, Freddy Fender, and others—we enlisted the support of their record companies. Since most of our artists were with ABC Records (later to become MCA), that label became our most active record-company team member. ABC Records' president Jim Foglesong, whom I talked about earlier, always supported our events when they made sense to him and his company. (I must add that he was also a good golfer.) He came on board for the tournament, and ABC Records invited many top radio personalities and performers from across the nation to spend the weekend in Tulsa. Some would play golf, some would just play, but all would have a good time, rubbing shoulders with TV and movie stars, country and pop music greats, and Tulsa's industry and community leaders in a relaxed and informal atmosphere.

Now for the press. As we continued expanding the elements, the time came to plug in Kathy Gangwisch, our press and PR person extraordinaire! With Kathy providing input, we invited a number of national and international press representatives, getting leading newspapers and magazines to cover the golf tournament. In addition, many of the visiting radio personalities planned remote broadcasts to their home stations from the golf course, our headquarters hotel, or backstage at the Mabee Center during the all-star celebrity concert we had dubbed "Star Night." Ralph Emery, America's No. 1 country-music radio personality, would be doing live interviews with the stars over Nashville's clear-channel WSM as well as for the stations that carried his syndicated shows.

5. The Implementation: All of the ideas were in place. We prepared a written manifesto covering all of the elements. Included in it was a chronological schedule of events; where they were to take place; schedules for various artists and celebrity rehearsal times and appearances; airport pickups and hotel times; scheduled parties and receptions; interview appointments; tee-off times—every minute detail. We hoped fervently we hadn't left anything out.

The week of the event, the Halsey Company offices were like the nerve center of a military operation, with every single member of our staff armed with a full list of instructions. Our office was the focal point for all of the weekend's business, and it took our entire staff. We were, of course, only one of several elements, each with its own responsibilities. Also on the team were the local committees, the local board of directors, Jim Foglesong's group at ABC Records, and Roy and Barbara Clark, who were acting as hosts.

6. The Event: If the first five stages are completed well, an event should run smoothly, even though unexpected situations will always arise. This event unfolded and played itself out like a great circus, with everything happening and everyone functioning at full capacity. For a great three-day weekend everybody was working, playing, having a good time, and doing some good for the Children's Medical Center! It was a success!

I'm sure some people think something like this just happens. They have no idea of the hours, days, weeks, and even months that go into planning a three-day event, and the teamwork it takes to pull it off. We couldn't have done it, nor would it have been the huge success it was, without the effort of hundreds of Tulsans working and contributing their time and money . . . or the six-month-long efforts of many of The Halsey Company employees . . . or the stars with their talents and time . . . or the contributions of many sponsors. We had a particularly special relationship with Amana Refrigeration, who supported with money and hundreds of prizes.

In return, many Halsey Company artists—including Roy, The Oak Ridge Boys, and Mel Tillis—lent their support to Amana's annual charity tournament. Roy played golf, signed autographs and, with Barbara, hosted a dinner and reception for the contributors and celebrities; he remained busy the next year returning favors to many of the celebrities who came to play in his tournament. Bob Hope, for instance, has probably given us more "free" dates than any other celebrity. Roy, in turn, would give a "free" date to any request Bob would make for his own celebrity tournaments and events. That's how it works.

7. The Review: Here's the test. Did the event meet the criteria of your goal and purpose? To find out, review all of the elements involved. Have a meeting of the principal planners and workers as soon after the event as possible—at least within the following week. That way, everything will still be fresh in their minds. Note mistakes both large and small, and get suggestions for improvement. If you plan for your event to be an annual one—as the Roy Clark Celebrity Golf Tournament and Star Night turned out to be—it's not too soon to start planning for the next one.

Annual events are good for a couple of reasons. First, so much energy goes into the initial start-up of any event that subsequent annual events get the benefit of residual planning. Second, any event can be improved and enhanced every year that it's staged.

Regardless of what kind of event you have, always answer these questions:

1. Was it a success with the audience?

2. Was it a success within the business?

3. Was there good media coverage?

4. Did the event meet your own critical criteria and standards?

5. Did it bring great recognition to the artist or artists involved?

6. Did it bring great recognition to sponsors or charity involved?

7. Did it have a lasting cultural effect?

8. Did it represent all concerned with integrity?

9. Was it financially successful?

10. Were the customers satisfied?

In the case of The Roy Clark Celebrity Golf Tournament the answer to all 10 questions was "yes."

8. The Follow-up: A lot of the important work is done after a successful event's over. Among the things you must do is make sure there are follow-up stories for the press, that the money pledged is collected for your charity, that thank you's go out to all concerned.

In most music industry-related events, many of the important business contacts are not made until the actual event occurs. Acquaintances made at performances and the accompanying receptions can be the starting place for follow-up meetings with prospective buyers, corporate sponsors, or potential television projects.

By the time the Roy Clark Celebrity Golf Tournament came along, I had further developed my theory of the **Power of Performance**, and I was learning how the combined energy of each element, each member of a team, is essential for success. The golf tournament illustrated perfectly both of these ideas, as well as showing the benefits a promoter reaps when he or she is able to create a true, real *event*.

♪ ♪ ♪ ♪

The Jim Halsey Company created another huge event in Tulsa. In fact, you could call it our Event of All Events. It incorporated everything we've talked about in this book: the *call to action*, the *power boosters*, the *impact enhancers*, the *repetitious impressions*, plus a sophisticated level of other sales and marketing techniques, all fueling an event of gargantuan proportions!

Let's start by reiterating that an important part of all sales and marketing is maintaining satisfied customers and building repeat business, and that an agent or agency constantly has inventory of an artist's dates to fill. As you've already read, The Jim Halsey Company was constantly keeping our buyers informed through direct mail, trade ads and good and ongoing press and public relations campaigns. It was also very important for us to develop events for our artists and our company—just as it's important for a promoter to transform his shows into events wherever possible.

With that idea in mind, we developed a combination event and promotion of such magnitude that it almost defies description. Dubbed the Tulsa Ranch Party, it was not only a gigantic thank-you celebration for our best customers—the promoters and other talent buyers—but also the biggest three days of the year for selling our artists.

What we did was invite talent buyers, television producers, record company executives, and radio personalities to spend a weekend in Tulsa as our guests. While they were there, we showcased new talent for them, and each of our major stars also gave a tasteful performance at some time during the big weekend.

The Tulsa Ranch Parties were held south of Tulsa at the 2,500-acre Circle R Ranch, which my partners—Roy Clark, Hank Thompson, Wayne Creasy, and the late Stanley Synar—and I jointly owned. Although we were raising cattle there, none of us lived in the ranchhouse, which looked like something out of the *Bonanza* television series. Instead, we used it for entertaining. When you sat on top of the hill overlooking the swimming pool, patio, and thousands of acres of beautiful, rolling Oklahoma pasture land sprinkled with contentedly grazing cattle, the atmosphere was super-conducive for relaxation, informal socializing—and *big-time sales*.

The 2,500-acre spread included a natural amphitheater, which provided a memorable place to present our artists. We had chairs available, but most people ended up sitting on the ground, enjoying the fantastic barbecued ribs, brisket, links, turkey, and chicken expertly prepared by our partner Stan Synar—whose profession was real estate, but whose specialty was outdoor cooking. Proud of my Cherokee heritage, we had Indian tepees scattered around the property with Native American art also on display. We always featured Indian dances as part of the weekend's entertainment.

This was no set created by a Hollywood designer. It was our place, a real place, a place to bring and entertain our guests.

We held our Tulsa Ranch Parties in early autumn. The timing was designed not only to take advantage of the beauty of the season in Oklahoma and celebrate the harvest, but to entertain all of the important state fair buyers before their annual late November meeting in Las Vegas.

A lot of fair buyers decided on their headliners for the following year during Ranch Party festivities, and my ably equipped *chargé d'affaires* of the fair department, John Hitt, along with his staff, was always on hand to arrange the bookings.

In this unique setting, our buyers enjoyed live shows from the likes of Roy Clark, Hank Thompson, The Oak Ridge Boys, Mel Tillis, Tammy Wynette, Minnie Pearl, Freddy Fender, Donna Fargo, Don Williams, and Jimmy Dean. By the time our guests were heading back to their respective homes in Los Angeles, New York, Las Vegas, Reno, Nashville—and London, Tokyo, Moscow, Sofia, Budapest and Prague—our artists would have much of their coming year's itineraries already booked.

There was nothing high-pressure about our sales methods, but who wouldn't be in a mood to buy after a weekend at the Tulsa Ranch Party? The Jim Halsey Company hosted a good party, and everyone on our staff knew who was coming and how important these guests were to our artists and to us. No one lived in the ranchhouse, but it was fully furnished, with the bedrooms outfitted as offices. Those were used for private sales meetings, where my expert agents would get down to the business of discussing itinerary and money for the artists who had caught the eyes and ears of our Ranch Party guests.

Dick Howard was in charge of inviting our guests from the television industry. During the event, his staff was equally busy booking television deals, guest spots, guest-host jobs, and commercials. What a bunch of deals were made during the gigantic Tulsa Ranch Party weekend! The tally of future bookings *always* ran into the millions of dollars.

And you never knew what other benefits might come out of that colossal weekend.

In one of our early Ranch Parties, for instance, we presented a show by The Oak Ridge Boys. Many of the buyers for the big state fairs were seeing The Oak Ridge Boys for the very first time, and it's an understatement to say that The Oak Ridge Boys wowed 'em. Before the weekend concluded, John Hitt had written The Oak Ridge Boys deals for more than 30 major fairs!

At this point, The Oak Ridge Boys had recently made the transition from gospel to country music; Columbia Records had just dropped them, and I hadn't yet been able to get them a new record deal. I wanted them at ABC-Dot where we had Roy Clark and Hank Thompson, but Dot president Jim Foglesong wasn't convinced they'd succeed as a secular act. That afternoon, however, as he stood with me under the autumnal Oklahoma fall sun, a gentle breeze blowing around us, watching The Oak Ridge Boys doing their superb job of performing, he turned to me and said, "I'm convinced. Let's make a deal." We hammered out the basics of The Oak Ridge Boys' new record deal right on the grounds of the ranch, each of us holding one of Stan Synar's great BBQ sandwiches.

That was the magic of the Tulsa Ranch Parties. Deals were struck left and right. Nothing was left to chance. We were all prepared with our sales plans before any of the guests arrived—what we wanted to sell, who we wanted to sell, where and for how much was all in our heads. We all had our artists' routing books in our hip pockets. When a buyer expressed the slightest interest, we were ready. If interest wasn't forthcoming within a sufficient time period, we tactfully made suggestions. We didn't want to force anything, but we wanted to be effective. We had our inventories of dates for the following year, and the Tulsa Ranch Party was the big sales event that filled our artists' itineraries.

It was a sales event without parallel in the industry, a private showcasing of Halsey Company artists before the most important buyers in the world. And it upset many of our competitors, because we had the first opportunity to book our acts with fair buyers for the coming year.

We covered many, many different bases with this one gigantic weekend. We invited members of the press in from everywhere, and got stories for the next three months in return. A limousine company from St. Louis, Jed's, asked to be included, so our guests were greeted by 25 new white Cadillac limousines to transport them from Tulsa hotels to the ranch.

Ralph Emery's broadcasts from the Ranch Parties reached all across the country. Dick Howard sold a taping of Ranch Party highlights every year as a syndicated TV special. To further gild the lily, Hank Thompson, Roy Clark, Mack Sanders, and I were owners of two radio stations in Tulsa, one AM and the other FM. We invited our very best sponsors to this invitation-only affair, and many advertisers helped with party supplies. Pepsi furnished the soft drinks, Pringles the chips, Hunts the ketchup, local auto dealers the cars; the list goes on and on. Nowhere in America could a Tulsa radio advertiser see such shows and rub elbows with stars of such magnitude. Our radio stations booked a lot of heavy advertising dollars for the coming months. The Ranch Party worked for everyone.

There was magic at the Ranch Party. Not only sales and marketing magic, but the real thing as well. One of our frequent guests was the Amazing Kreskin, the renowned mentalist. He wasn't represented by our company, but he was a good friend and welcome at our gatherings. He did a lot of one-on-one entertaining and was a delightful addition to the event.

I'll never forget when one of our guests inappropriately asked Kreskin if he was going to do any tricks.

"I don't do tricks," Kreskin replied. "I do magic."

This he does, and so did we at the Tulsa Ranch Parties.

The overwhelming success of these events illustrates how planning carefully, setting a goal, and having a distinct purpose will result in success far beyond anyone's imagination. Each Tulsa Ranch Party took a year of planning and included the thoughts and ideas of everyone within our company. It took coordination with our in-house PR Director, Leo Zabelin, and our Company's PR firm, Kathy Gangwisch and Associates, which was able to bring in a large contingency of quality press representatives from around the world for this event every year.

It took thought, planning, and coordination, much as you would see in a military campaign. Our goal was the same: to win. We always won, but in our case the winning made our world a better place to live.

Wrapping It Up

Finally, the Star Team wheel is complete: the talent at the center; the eight spokes, each representing a different team member, radiating out from it, forming the support that enables the wheel to roll down the road to success.

As you go along in your music-business career, you'll see that others will become members of your team from time to time. These will be extended-team members. The ones we've discussed in this section, however, are the essential nine. The order that they're brought in will not always be the same as we've listed here, and some members of a team will often perform more than one function, as I did when I was both the booking agent and manager for Hank Thompson. The important thing is that, to be successful, each member of the team must combine his or her energy with that of the other team members. This is what the team's **Power of Performance** is all about.

No matter which one of these Star Team members you want to be, it's important for you to know about them all. With what you've learned in this section as a guide and foundation, continue to educate yourself on the functions of each team member. That way, you'll know what to expect from everyone involved. You'll know what to look for, and you'll be able to determine if the other team members are doing their parts. If you decide to be a promoter, you'll have a leg up on this; promoters and other talent buyers usually have the most well-rounded knowledge of the team, simply because they routinely work with *all* members of a Star Team.

Whatever job you choose, learn it better than anyone else. If you do, there'll always be a place for you in the music business

♪ ♪ ♪ ♪

While most of what we discuss in this book is about business, *all* of it is about life. No matter what you do for a living, you should learn to pay attention to things going on around you, to signals that indicate change, or acceptance. A lot of what we learn comes simply from experience. Education and discovery comes when you try new things and do new things—when you live.

As you know, I'm a great believer in lists. Establishing a plan with chronological timetables gives you a path to follow in any endeavor. When you've written it down, step-by-step, go back over it, do research, flesh out details. Make sure to put your list where you can see it several times a day, to refresh your memory about what it contains. And then remember that if you strive to go beyond your projected plan, you may even surprise yourself with your own abilities.

Be ready to make sacrifices, extend your energies, take chances, and put a lot at risk. Be ready even to take a new direction in the middle of a project. And then, follow your dreams. Pay attention to them, give them respect, and believe them possible.

Maintain faith in yourself and your projects.

Let *nothing* discourage you from following your dreams and reaching your goals.

Twelve-year-old "General" Jim Halsey (extreme right) reviewing his junior marines-Washington School grounds, Independence, KS 1942.

Jim and Minisa Halsey.

Photo by Kathy Gangwisch

Jim Halsey and daughter Gina Halsey.

Photo by Kathy Gangwisch

Impresario Sherman Halsey with Impresario Jim Halsey.

The Tulsa Partners, Tulsa, Ok. 1972 left to right- Hank Thompson, Wayne Creasy, Roy Clark, Jim Halsey.

1976 Tulsa Ranch Party Aerial Shot. All Halsey Company artists performed, and were filmed for TV. Ranch owned by Roy Clark, Jim Halsey, Hank Thompson, Wayne Creasy, and Stan Synar.

Neewolah Celebration, Independence Kansas. Jim Halsey, country music star Don Williams, celebration chairman "Generalissimo" Jerry Webb.

1982-The Oak Ridge Boys celebrate a new multi-million dollar contract with MCA. Leading the song is MCA (Nashville) President Jim Foglesong, with Duane Allen, producer Ron Chancey, Joe Bonsall, Richard Sterban, William Lee Golden, Mickey Baker (Oak's Office), and Manager Jim Halsey.

Oral Roberts, Las Vegas entertainment czar Walter Cain, and Jim Halsey during Roy Clarks' Celebrity Golf Tournament, Tulsa, Oklahoma.

Left to right: Sherman Halsey, Roy Orbison, Jim Halsey prior to Orbison's Bulgarian tour, 1982.

Bandleader Woody Herman receives ceremonial Indian blanket from Impresario Jim Halsey (Cherokee).

Leo Zablin, friend and mentor.

Impresario Jim Halsey, Minisa Halsey with Bulgarian Stars (left) Atanas Kosef and (right) Bisser Kirov.

BMI Country Music Awards dinner, 1985. left to right-Ed Cramer-Special BMI Consultant, Minisa Crumbo-Halsey, Francis Preston–BMI President/CEO, Jim Halsey.

Halsey talks to client Reba McEntire backstage at her Universal Amphitheatre performance. Looking on: Narvel Blackstock, Reba's husband and manager(left) and Halsey Co. executive Terry Cline (right).

Photo by Ray Pilszak

Left to right: Jim Halsey, Dick Howard, Roy Clark, Joe Bonsall.

Photo by Minisa Halsey

Jim with daughters Gina and Crissy. Occasion—Halsey receiving Doctor of Fine Arts Honoris Causa Bakers University, Kansas.

Recording of "Making Music" with Gatemouth Brown, Roy Clark and producer Steve Ripley.

Celebrating 25 years together, 1984. left to right- John Hitt, Herb Gronauer, Joe Hupp, Jim Halsey, Steve Pritchard, Roy Clark, Terry Cline, Steve Dahl.

Photo by Gina Halsey

Soviet Life

Left to right: Roy Clark Friendship Tour cast, Moscow, USSR Thanksgiving Day-1988. Fred Woods, Bridget Dolan, Roy Clark, Jim Halsey, Minisa Halsey, Chris Carter, Judy Pofsky, and Gina Halsey.

Photo by Gina Halsey

Entertainer Roy Clark and manager Jim Halsey (far left) picked up a few health tips during Roy's concert tour of the Soviet Union when they met up with these Soviet Cossacks at their hotel in Moscow. In town for a convention, these Soviet gentlemen, all 100+ years, agreed to pass on their youthful secrets — "vodka once a day, a fur hat ten months out of the year, and a closed mouth."

Jim Halsey receives the Hubert Long International Award, presented by Impresario Mervyn Conn, Wembly Festival, London 1982.

Jim Halsey meets with Frederico Mayor, General Director of UNESCO (The United Nations' Organization for the Exchange of Science and Culture), and presents a limited edition lithograph "Sun Hawk, Taos" by Halsey's wife, Native American artist Minisa Halsey.

Tulsa International Festival left to right- Miss Jean Shoo (Korea), Professor Armando Moreno-Secretary General FIDOF- UNESCO, Jim Halsey, Kenny Rogers. back row- Tessy Sol Allen- Nigeria, Nigerian Group.

White House Entertainment. left to right: Sound Generation from John Brown University, Siloam Springs, Arkansas, President Gerald Ford, Jim Halsey, Roy Clark, Singer Diana Trusk, banjoist Buck Trent.

Radio City Music Hall — Follow your dreams and visions, I did with this one.

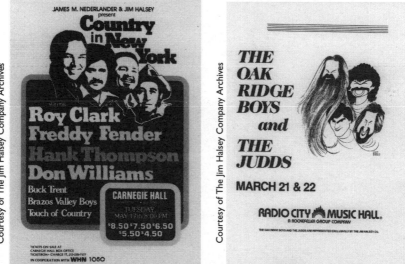

Working with artists involved in restoring of Ford's Theatre, President Bush greets Impresario Jim Halsey and his wife, Minisa Crumbo-Halsey.

Jim Halsey presents President Jimmy Carter and First Lady Rosalyn Carter with his famous rose (note lapel).

Photo by Travis Caperton

Jim Halsey receives Oklahoma Governor Frank Keating's award for "Excellence in Art and Education," recognizing Halsey as director of Oklahoma City University's program for Music and Entertainment Business.

Courtesy of The Jim Halsey Company Archives

Vying for an entertainment industry record, The Jim Halsey Company was proud to announce the renewal of the near 40 year management/booking relationship between Jim Halsey and Texas cowboy Hank Thompson. Thompson was Halsey's first client in 1951. The two posed for this photo with Minnie Pearl in 1952 backstage at the Grand Ole Opry. On a 1989 get together at Halsey's corporate headquarters in Nashville, the three reenacted the scene for the camera.

Photo by Kathy Gangwisch

May 1977- Jim Halsey receives the Jim Reeves Memorial Award from the Academy of Country Music on ABC network telecast, presented by Roy Clark.

Photo by Jan McCaffrey

Students in Halsey's Music and Entertainment Business Program at Oklahoma City University attend the awards ceremony as Halsey receives the Governor's Award for Excellence.

PART THREE

Secrets of The Jim Halsey Company

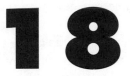

The Halsey Method

In the rest of this book, we'll look at some of the methods and secrets I used to make The Jim Halsey Company, Inc., the biggest country music agency in the world. To paraphrase what my friend the Amazing Kreskin told a guest at one of our Tulsa Ranch Parties, these are not tricks. We didn't do tricks. However, many times we did magic. And with the knowledge in this book and your own **Power of Performance**, you may be able to do some magic yourself.

♪ ♪ ♪ ♪

A couple of pages ago, at the close of the last section, I briefly mentioned four things: *goals, research, timetables,* and *following your dreams*. Because these have all been important components of my career and my life, I now want to take a little more time on each one of them.

First, *goals*. You know that I advocate writing down your goals and putting the list into a place where you can encounter it every day. I caution you to make sure that the goals you set are your own. Many people get off the path by trying to achieve goals someone else has set for them. You must build your future on where *you* want to go and on what *you* want to do.

Make your goals realistic and reachable, and put a timetable on them. Start out marking time in increments of 6, 12, 18, or 24 months and then expand to three-year and five-year goals. Your plan *begins* when you get it down on paper—this is part of the Halsey method.

The large staff I directed at The Jim Halsey Company always represented at least 40 different artists. This roster included the high-caliber, big-name performers I've mentioned throughout this book. Each had his or her individual desires and goals, and it was up to us to implement a plan that would help these stars achieve what they wanted. In every case, we would consult with the artists—and sometimes with the performer's other Star Team members, especially managers and record-company executives—to determine where they wanted to go with their careers. We'd write down all of the desires, potential opportunities, realistic—and sometimes seemingly unrealistic—goals, and, most important, their dreams. By writing down each artist's "want list," we had something tangible to focus upon. We then had the opportunity to build a plan, using the idea of "events" and the talents of other team members for achieving those goals.

Here's a secret: My method requires that 90 percent of the goals you write down have to be realistic. You also need to have a certain number of goals that are attainable in a short period of time. Early in life, I learned that establishing a lot of unrealistic or unattainable goals will discourage even the best salespersons, so you need to make sure that most goals are always within reach. That makes it easier to eventually attain the unattainable.

At The Halsey Company, our lists always contained goals that could be achieved, many of them relatively quickly. There was a lot of the possible, and a little bit of the impossible. When my salespeople and agents achieved the possible, all that was left was the impossible. As a result, we were always achieving the impossible.

The specific goals and timetables were important; they made the list a guidebook, a road map giving everyone the right direction to follow. At the Halsey Company, we always shared these written directions with each artist involved.

Again, *put your goals in writing*. The reason I stress this so many times in this book is that writing down goals is one of the most important parts of my method.

Now, to *research*. Once you get your goals down, pursue a diligent pattern of research. Investigate every means that might possibly help propel you to the conclusion of your plans. If a lot of avenues of research aren't immediately available to you, do as much study as you can and then start to work. As you work toward your goals, you'll hit some roadblocks. Solutions to these problems will often present themselves as you continue to work; research can help you get past some of the pitfalls as well.

Always pay attention to what's happening with your plans. Many times, a new direction will present itself in the middle of the project. Sometimes a complete change of plans or a new direction will be necessary.

As I said, you should establish *timetables* at the beginning. Remember that it's not necessary to follow these down to the second. They do, however, give you important guidelines for achieving your goals.

Finally, I again stress the importance of *following your dreams*. Following dreams is a very effective way to access your personal **Power of Performance**. My own dreams have been a source of expansion for my life, for The Jim Halsey Company, and for the artists we represented. Dream your dream of dreams. Nothing is too great to conceive. I sincerely believe that anything is possible when you follow your dreams.

I have always been a dreamer, relying upon my visions to identify where I wanted to go with my life and my career. These include visions about developing projects and events as well as going to unexpected places. Dreams have fueled my life and provided much of what this book is about.

Building Identity

As we continued our direct-mail campaigns, our coordinated promotions with record companies, regular TV and cable appearances, and identification with corporate sponsors, we found that our *repetitious impressions* were creating an identity for The Jim Halsey Company as well as for our artists. I wanted us to be known as a major company that represented major stars, but I also wanted the company to be remembered on its own.

In order to do this, I used a couple of methods, both with the idea of creating a kind of instant identity. I learned one way to do this from my good friend, Walter Kane, entertainment czar for the Howard Hughes-owned hotels in Las Vegas. Walter had a gimmick of affixing a little embroidered rose on the lapel of every person he encountered. I believe he first used this as a means of identifying people who were cleared to go backstage at his shows; however, it quickly grew past that into one of his trademarks, one of the things he was remembered for.

When we made the first Soviet Union tour in 1976 with Roy Clark—an important landmark not only for country music but for diplomatic relations as well—Mr. Kane gave me hundreds of these roses to take along.

"A rose is a symbol of friendship," he told me. "Pass these out in the USSR. " And I did. As I met various officials and government dignitaries and exchanged greetings, I'd make a point of sticking one of Mr. Kane's little roses on the front of their clothing. That instant communication, that personal touch, was an instant success. Truly, our hosts saw the roses for what they were: small, sincere symbols of friendship. Opening night in Moscow's Rossiya Theater was packed full of government dignitaries, medal-bedecked officials, television crews, and all of the top representatives from Gosconcert, the official concert agency that was handling our visit. By that time, we were a week into our trip, and many of the officials sported the friendship rose—sometimes right next to their rows of military medals.

At the official reception before the concert, Madam Butrova, the Minister of Culture, was our host. We exchanged greetings and I ceremoniously pinned her with what had now become "The Official Rose of Friendship." As I did, I felt the importance of what the rose was becoming—a way that two people could communicate personally, physically, and spiritually, without having to speak each other's language. I think the first full significance of the rose came home to me at that moment.

That night at intermission, a Ministry of Culture attaché came backstage, seeking me out.

"Excuse me, Mr. Halsey," he said in excellent English. "Madam Butrova would like to know if it would be possible for you to give her 12 more roses?"

While part of the magic was the personal contact of putting the rose on somebody, I was flattered by her request and certainly honored it.

I continued using the rose in my extensive travels around the world, becoming known as not only an impresario, but as the man who carried the Friendship Rose. Always, the rose instantly broke through social or political barriers, magically bringing everyone involved into an immediate area of peace and harmony.

I became quite well known for my roses. People who hadn't yet gotten a rose from me would come up and ask for one. At conventions and trade shows, buyers would come to our booth seeking both me *and* a rose. People in elevators would spot the rose on my lapel and ask if I was Jim Halsey. Of course, I would always extend the rose of friendship.

One day, my wife Minisa and I were having lunch at New York's Plaza Hotel, in its crowded Oyster Bar. I couldn't help noticing that a gentleman sitting a few tables away kept staring at us. Finally, he got up and came over.

"I noticed the rose on your lapel," he said. "Do you know Jim Halsey?"

I told him I *was* Jim Halsey.

It turned out to be Gil Cates, brother of Joe Cates. The Cates brothers were big producers of TV specials, and they were fond of Roy Clark, The Oak Ridge Boys, Minnie Pearl, Mel Tillis, Tammy Wynette, and many of our other stars. I had worked mainly for Joe, who knew about my roses. However, I'd never met Gil, even though Roy had sung the title song for a Gil Cates-produced movie, *I Never Sang For My Father*, for which stars Gene Hackman and Melvyn Douglas and writer Robert Anderson received Academy Award nominations.

Gil Cates knew about the rose, too, and I was happy to extend one to him at the Plaza Hotel Oyster Bar.

Another Halsey secret is to establish something you'll be remembered for. It can be an unforgettable advertisement, a hit song, a great performance—in my case, it was the Friendship Rose.

All of those roses out there illustrate my method of *repetitious impressions*. The rose was an *impact enhancer*, with its own **Power of Performance**.

All of that was important to me, because when it all boils down to the essentials, I'm a salesperson. I have good product for sale and I want to make a deal. I'm also the man with the rose. Remember me?

Yes, they did—and it worked! I still use the rose today! Thank you, Walter Kane!

♪ ♪ ♪ ♪

When you're in the music and entertainment business, it's important to become known and remembered within the industry. It's just part of selling yourself, your artists, your company. The Friendship Rose was a very personal gift—and people always like receiving gifts. The little lapel roses became worldwide symbols of our company, and significant examples of the **Power of Performance**.

After I had been giving out the roses for quite a while, I began looking for something extra to give out on our trips abroad. I wasn't trying to detract from the power of the roses, but wanted something in addition that would be fun and remembered by people, something that would cause talk and attention. The roses had become my personal gift, my identification. Now people expected them from me.

I wanted some new pass-out promotion that we could tie in with one of our artists, or with some of our events. The idea I ended up using didn't come immediately, but it came naturally.

One of my favorite condiments in the world is McIlhenney's Tabasco, the famous brand of hot pepper sauce. Whenever I traveled out of the country, I would always purchase miniature bottles for my own personal consumption, since it was hard to find overseas. I always ended up sharing it, too. Members of my traveling entourages constantly requested the Tabasco; diners at neighboring tables in some of the finest restaurants in France, England, Hungary, Russia and Bulgaria, upon seeing me produce a bottle, came over and asked for samples. The piquant sauce was so popular overseas that, as I was preparing to leave on a European tour with Roy Clark, I requested a thousand miniature Tabasco bottles from McIlhenney to give away. After the company graciously granted our request, we placed small stickers on the backs of the bottles that read, "Roy Clark, The Hot One," and took off on tour with something that would get us more notice than a full-page ad in an international magazine.

The miniature bottles of Tabasco sauce didn't just make for a good promotion. It was a *great* promotional idea. All of our artists liked it, and we used the miniature bottles many times for specific promotions: The Oak Ridge Boys, The Hot Ones; Tammy Wynette, The Hot One; The Hot Show, Hilton Hotel and The Judds. We used these little bottles everywhere. McIlhenny furnished them, and in return got its own publicity as well as implied endorsements from the artists whose names were used on the bottles. For a long time, the company didn't charge us for the Tabasco, and we didn't charge them for the implied endorsements. Finally, we were using so many miniatures that McIlhenny asked if we would pay a small charge. We did. It was still a good deal, and everyone benefited from the *repetitious impressions* created by the promotion.

We ended up using Tabasco in lots of different ways. As a radio promotion for one of The Oak Ridge Boys' singles, we once sent 2,500 miniature bottles to stations through the mail. On several other occasions, I purchased giant, commercial-sized bottles of Tabasco from restaurant-supply houses and put them in specially constructed wooden boxes lined with velvet, where they looked like bottles of fine, rare wine. When one of our acts performed in a foreign country, we would give these as gifts to high-ranking officials. I'll bet some of those large bottles still have a few drops left. As long as they do, and for a time afterwards, we will still be remembered as "The Hot One."

The practice of the **Power of Performance** works in wondrous ways. All you have to do is use your imagination and proceed. The Tabasco promotion shows that it's more important for a promotion to be inventive and creative than it is to be expensive. Those little bottles were simple, but effective.

What were we looking for? Identification, pure and simple. The Tabasco promotion is a good example of the techniques we've discussed in earlier chapters: *repetitious Impressions, power boosters*, and *impact enhancers*. The promotion was used to sell our artists, to sell our company, to be remembered so that we'd get the *call to action*.

I love Tabasco sauce. It's the **Power of Performance**—with a bite.

Logo and Trademark:
Our Spiritual Shield

A good company logo or trademark should not only represent your company's philosophy, it should also have personal meaning for you. It is, in a symbolic way, your shield.

An effective logo or trademark will help others remember you. It's an important part of your **Power of Performance**, and it should be powerful itself. I believe that I have one of the best logos in the business: Woody Crumbo's *Eagle Dancer*.

I should explain that my own heritage is Cherokee. In 1999, I was a recipient of the Cherokee Medal of Honor; of all the awards I've received in my life, it means the most to me. For many of my events, including overseas tours, I have included Native American dancers on the program.

I also love Native American art; I've collected it for a long time. In fact, it was through my love of this art that I met my wife, Minisa Crumbo, who is one of the finest of the Native American artists herself. Through Minisa, my interest in this art form was expanded even further.

Then, because of my association with Madam Butrova, the Soviet Minister of Culture who loved my embroidered roses, Minisa had the opportunity to do a one-person exhibition in the USSR. I brought Minisa's art to Madame Butrova's attention, and she became very interested, inviting Minisa to Moscow to talk about a possible Soviet showing. After the ministry examined samples of Minisa's work, looking for a hidden political agenda and finding none, she received an official invitation to show her artwork in Moscow, Leningrad, and Kiev.

She exhibited her art for nine months, to great public and critical acclaim, becoming only the second American artist to be extended an invitation for a one-person show by the Soviet Union. (The other was the acclaimed artist Jamie Wyeth.) Minisa and her work were featured extensively in television and press throughout the Soviet Union. She was even on the cover of *Soviet Life* magazine.

Of course, since there is no longer a Soviet Union, she was also the final American artist to be accorded this great honor.

Minisa's father, Woody Crumbo, was the dean of American Indian artists; his work is exhibited in museums all around the world. I was a big fan of Woody's—not only because he was such a fine artist, but a great man as well.

One series he did that I was particularly fond of showed dancers in various costumes, performing different dances. Three paintings of Eagle Dancers, each facing a different way, were a part of this series.

Very few of Woody's originals were available. Most of his art was available as limited-edition lithographs, silkscreens, and etchings. Over a period of time, however, I was able to find and purchase two of the three original paintings of the Eagle Dancers, and one of them became the logo trademark of The Jim Halsey Company, gaining fame throughout the world. I used Woody Crumbo's *Eagle Dancer* in our ads and on posters, pins, and business cards. I knew we had something very special when people began asking us for several of our business cards at once.

The *Eagle Dancer* image gave us another way for people to recognize and remember us. Whenever I gave my business card to someone for the first time, I got reactions that reminded me of Joe Sugarman's famous TV ads for his BluBlocker sunglasses: "Wow! Look at this!" "Can't believe this!" "I've never seen a business card like that!" "This card is beautiful!" The *Eagle Dancer* trademark has become so well-known and so identified with me that the recognition is there forever.

Because of our extensive collection of Native American art and the number of people who identified with Woody Crumbo's *Eagle Dancer*, our company for years published a calendar reproducing 12 beautiful pieces from our original art collection, which further enhanced our identification with Native American artwork.

When you design a logo or trademark, make it something that's important to your company, and something that not only identifies you, but with which you identify. To me, the *Eagle Dancer* had a deep spiritual significance, augmented by the fact that it was created by a member of the family. It is a great piece of art, one that has not only made a deep impression for The Jim Halsey Company, but is a well-known and respected work from a major American artist. I'm very proud to have this *Eagle Dancer* as the logo that identifies our company.

Eagle Dancer, Woody Crumbo

The Art of Negotiation

In the music and entertainment business, negotiating deals is an art. In this chapter, I'd like to give you some examples of the art of negotiating—both good and bad—taken from my own experience.

In the building stages of Roy Clark's career, it was my strategy to expose him to the largest audience possible. Even then, Roy possessed enormous and varied talents. In addition to his mastery of many different instruments and his distinctive vocal style, he had an engaging stage presence and an innate flair for comedy. I wanted people to experience the whole package. We had Roy on records, we did press and public relations, we packaged him with other artists, we did radio benefit appearances and other free shows with him, just to get him seen and heard. Of course, his multiple talents made him a natural for television—and he did *lots* of it.

In the beginning, though, when we were both novices in the business and I was serving as both his manager and agent, it wasn't always easy to get our message across to the important television producers.

In 1967, Roy's "Yesterday When I was Young" hit the top of both the pop and country charts, enabling us to place him on a lot of television shows. At the same time Roy's song was going through the roof, movie star Mitzi Gaynor was contracted to host a network television special, which would also feature other big-name stars. To me, this special would be the perfect vehicle to enhance Roy's career and help him find an audience beyond country music.

The producer was Jack Bean, Mitzi's husband. But after several meetings with him, sincerely pitching Roy and all of his comedic, musical, and acting abilities, I could see that I wasn't getting anywhere. Finally, because I wanted this show for Roy so badly and knew how we needed it, I resorted to a little hard-sell—which definitely is not my style. That's when I made the mistake that dooms many salespeople. I focused too hard on making the sale, on selling Roy, rather than concentrating on filling the need of my customer, the buyer, who in this case was Jack Bean.

I finally played my trump card and used my last sales tool. I told Jack Bean that Roy Clark's current single, a Top Ten record, had just reached sales figures of over *one million* copies. I felt that if all the other reasons I'd given to make the sale had failed, this one would be the one that changed his mind.

After I dropped that bomb in Mr. Bean's office, there was a long silence. Finally, he leaned back in his chair.

"Sold a million copies, huh?" he asked.

"That's right," I returned.

Folding his arms behind his head, he looked me straight in the eye. "I guess that means he's only going to appeal to a little over two percent of our audience," he said.

The room fell silent again. A little uncomfortably, I pondered his words.

"We are very interested in Roy Clark," he finally added. "But it's not because he's sold a million records. We have to appeal to 40 million people. That's our audience. We like Roy's talents and think he will appeal to this 40 million."

I was embarrassed, but I'd learned a valuable lesson. Being overanxious to close a sale, I had almost blown the whole deal by not sizing up my buyer properly. I'd deviated from my normal style and become impatient, overlooking the very basic point of selling that I'd been teaching my own salespeople for years: fill the needs of your customer and you've got a sale. If I'd been graded on my **Power of Performance** in this negotiation, I don't know if I would've passed.

Fortunately, Mr. Bean saw the qualities in Roy. He'd just been slow in making a decision because so many other pieces of the production had to fit into place.

The Mitzi Gaynor special turned out to be a major showcase for Roy's talents. He sang "Yesterday When I was Young," he played "Malagueña" on the 12-string guitar, and he did some comedy. He even danced a little.

This experience taught me that an important element of being a good manager, agent, promoter, or any other member of a Star Team dealing with contracts, obligations, selling, marketing, advertising, or promotion is knowing the art of negotiation. Good deal-makers understand the fundamentals of sales and marketing, as well as knowing and applying simple rules of etiquette. They know their product, understand the needs of all involved, and organize their presentations. They're concise and truthful, they listen to concerns, compromise when needed, and they ask for the sale.

There are two key words in any deal-maker's vocabulary: *patience* and *persistence*. And remember: *It's not a good deal unless it's a good deal for everybody.*

♪ ♪ ♪ ♪

Every person in the sales business has a style. Some are forceful, some are bombastic, some are high-pressure, some merely make a presentation.

What are The Jim Halsey secrets of selling and negotiation? First of all, be a good listener. Find out your prospective customer's needs and then determine how to fill them. Get your buyers to open up. Learn their priorities, time frames, budgets, and special requirements, Then you can make an intelligent presentation.

Remember the Scout motto: *Be Prepared.* Do your homework. Present to your buyer an artist and a program that will be to his benefit. Never use high-pressure tactics. Never sell something your buyer does not need or that won't benefit all the parties involved.

It's simple: if you can fill the need, you can make the sale. Make your presentations, ask for the sale, and trust your **Power of Performance** to make it happen.

♪ ♪ ♪ ♪

I've written earlier about my long-term relationship with the Howard Hughes-owned hotels in Las Vegas, including the Frontier, Desert Inn, Sands, Landmark, Castaways, and the Silver Slipper. And you've also already met my friend Walter Kane, the originator of the Friendship Rose, in these pages.

In 1971, Hughes asked Kane, his friend and business associate for half a century, to become the entertainment director for all of his Vegas hotels. In taking over as "entertainment czar" for the six hotel showrooms, Walter Kane became one of the most influential and powerful entertainment buyers in the world.

Mr. Kane was a promoter, an impresario of the first magnitude. He deserves a whole book. Describing him as a "colorful show-business impresario" doesn't begin to indicate the spectrum of color and energies this unique character exuded.

Walter Kane was a master negotiator. He liked nothing better than to make a deal. Much of my learning in selling, marketing, and negotiating came from my experiences with Mr. Kane. He was an absolute master of the **Power of Performance**, always giving a better performance than any of the big stars he hired for the main showrooms. He was one of my teachers, one of my mentors, and certainly a valued friend.

You can usually count the individuals who created turning points in your life and career on the fingers of one hand. For me, Walter Kane is one of those people. Through all the years I was associated with him, over countless hours at dinners and show openings, we had many discussions that transcended business. Some of the best were about his personal history. His stories and life were so interesting to me that spending even a few hours with him was always the high point of a trip to Las Vegas. Many times, while we were enjoying a dinner together, it would be interrupted by a telephone call for "Sir Walter," originating from the Bahamas. That would be the big boss man, Howard Hughes, inquiring about the show counts, how the showroom audiences were receiving various stars, etc. I never met Howard Hughes, never spoke to him, but I was impressed with the detailed information he'd always request about the artists and the shows in his hotels. I was intrigued that this mysterious man, who ruled such an empire, wanted to know things like how many people Roy Clark had in the showroom that night, their reaction to him, and whether or not he got a standing ovation. He always did. Plus, it was energizing just to be across the table from a man who was talking directly to Howard Hughes.

After one of these important calls, Walter Kane and I would get back to business as usual. But the whole aura of the evening would invariably be changed, the air charged by the call from Howard Hughes. I was there, and I experienced it. Talk about a **Power of Performance**!

Even today, many a manager and agent is mumbling to himself about his dealings with Mr. Kane. Because of his age—he was 82 at the time of his death, in 1983—many of the agents he dealt with underestimated his fine memory. I learned early in my dealings with him that his so-called "bad memory" was a convenience he used at the negotiating table, and always to his advantage.

From the beginning, Mr. Kane and I were friends, with mutual respect for each other. He made deals the way a good musician plays his instrument: with grace and beauty, and as often as possible. His countless stories about his different deals and negotiations over the years were invaluable to me in creating some of my own style, and I'll confess now that on our countless evenings together, I'd usually lead him into talking about his deal-making secrets.

Upon first taking over the entertainment-buying responsibilities for the Hughes hotels, Mr. Kane inherited a number of contracts with performers he was obligated to honor. One of these contracts was for a two-week playdate with Roy Clark. Walter was not a country music fan, so you can imagine his surprise when he first saw Roy's show-stopping performance. But even that show and its reception by the Landmark Hotel audience didn't change his mind about country music. He just wasn't interested in buying any more country artists. He wasn't even interested in seeing me so we could talk about more time for Roy. When Roy finished his obligated two weeks, Kane wanted to change the entertainment policy at the Landmark to one that would not include Roy, or anybody else considered "country."

As strange as it sounds, Las Vegas wasn't aware of the entertainment world outside its own city limits. At this time Roy was already a big star, guest-starring on network television shows, drawing big crowds nationwide, and cutting records that invariably climbed the charts. But in Las Vegas, with Walter Kane, he was still a hard sell.

At this time, Kane was looking for a musical format that would work consistently at the Landmark. I knew if I could ever establish a working relationship with him, I could sell him not only Roy, but a lot of the other artists on our roster. He didn't want country music. I thought I could change his mind by applying one of the basic principles of selling and marketing: *educate your buyer*.

Remember my advice about having a good pair of shoes, strong enough that you can get them in the door without getting your foot mangled? I wore out a pair or two of those trying to get established in the Hughes hotels. I was seeing some success selling other artists to different Vegas hotels and clubs, but not in the ones owned by Howard Hughes. Walter Kane wouldn't even see me. I would always call ahead for an appointment, only to be told that he had no appointments available. Furthermore, he let it be known that he wasn't interested in any of the artists I represented.

Did that stop me? No. Every trip I made to Vegas would include a visit to his office in the Sands Hotel.

Walter Kane had six secretaries. Eleanor Grasso, Carolyn Wallace, and Barbara Kelly were the three in charge. They all sat in one large room, which contained the entryway to Kane's plush office. Every time I came in and reintroduced myself, they would restate the fact that it would be impossible to see Mr. Kane. He had an opening that night. He had a meeting with an act. He was tied up. He just wasn't interested in my artists. And all the while, I could hear him through the door to his office, talking energetically on the phone, sometimes shouting, making deals. I had to get into Mr. Kane's inner sanctum. If I could just meet him face to face, I knew I could sell him.

After I'd visited Kane's office a few times, Eleanor, Carolyn, and Barbara began recognizing me. I'd always bring them gifts—flowers, or boxes of Godiva chocolates. Once, I filled up a big five-gallon canister with hard candies and took it in; other times, I'd bring in a five-gallon can of popcorn and leave it for them. After awhile, they began to chat informally with me. I began to know them. In a way, they were glad to see me each time, because I always brought them a little something.

Still, I couldn't get in to see Walter Kane.

Finally, on one of my visits Eleanor Grasso—the head secretary—stopped me as I was leaving the office. "Wait just a minute," she said.

I stood stock still as she opened the door to Mr. Kane's office and slipped in. Listening intently, I heard her say, "Mr. Kane, can't you give Mr. Halsey just five minutes of your time? He's come here every week for the last six weeks. You've refused to see him. I think, as a courtesy, you could give him five minutes."

The door opened. Had I made it? Yes! With a smile, she beckoned me in, and in a moment I was standing in front of the entertainment czar of Howard Hughes' hotels. Finally, I had my chance. And I knew I'd better not mess it up.

At the time, there was a little ray of hope for country music acts at the Landmark. Jimmy Dean had been successful at a number of Las Vegas venues, and he currently had a Landmark contract. But although he was a country music recording artist, he was also a television star and wasn't really considered "country" by the Vegas buyers. I told Mr. Kane that Roy Clark had the same kind of crossover appeal. Mr. Kane wasn't really familiar with Roy, even though Roy had just finished playing two weeks for him. But I gave him my best sales pitch, and he listened intently.

We spent little more than five minutes together at our first meeting. But somehow, we connected right then, beginning the long relationship we would have. From the first, we each recognized that the other had a "performance" to give.

I did not, however, immediately get an additional two weeks for Roy at the Landmark. That was what I'd wanted, but Mr. Kane wasn't ready. I'd done my best. He wasn't buying.

But I wasn't discouraged. In fact, I was elated! I had made contact. I had made my presentation. I had given my **Power of Performance**. And I knew that one of the formulas for a successful sale was persistence. I would be back (and sooner than I thought).

At the end of our meeting, I excused myself, thanked him for the time, and headed back to my office in Tulsa. That's when a strange thing happened—the first of many that would occur throughout our relationship.

I had no sooner returned to Tulsa when I got an urgent call at my office. It was Walter Kane. He wanted me to sit down with him in his office in Vegas and talk about a Roy Clark deal at the Landmark Hotel!

I had to make a decision. Did I want to get right back on a plane and travel another four hours back to Las Vegas, without even unpacking my bags? Or could I try to do it by telephone, or set it up for a later time?

In the business of selling, you have to be able to recognize an opportunity for a sale when it's presented to you. It was a time to act, not hesitate. It was my opportunity to sell Roy Clark to Walter Kane and the Hughes hotels.

So I hauled myself and my unpacked bags right back to the airport, got on a plane, and returned to Vegas where I met with Mr. Kane. That meeting began a long relationship between Roy Clark—and the other artists I represented—and the Hughes line of hotels. It also began my educational experience with Walter Kane.

One of the most important things I learned from Mr. Kane is that learning by experience is one of the best ways to learn. In the business of entertainment, it's sometimes the *only* way to learn. That's why this book is autobiographical, telling you about some of my experiences in the music and entertainment fields. I learned from these things; you can too.

Out of our meeting came two more weeks for Roy at the Landmark Hotel—exactly what I'd hoped for. The crowds there loved him. He sold out his shows, and the Landmark was always getting calls and letters, wanting to know when he'd be back. Prior to his playing the Landmark, Roy had co-headlined with Petula Clark at Caesar's Palace for two weeks, but no long-term deal was forthcoming. We couldn't get the money we needed, or even any interest, from a lot of the other big Las Vegas hotels because they didn't think country music would sell on the Strip.

The Landmark was actually two blocks off the Strip, but it was still considered a major hotel and showroom, even if it didn't have quite the same stature as the rest of Hughes' hotels. However, as long as we did good business at the Landmark, and my relationship with Mr. Kane continued to grow, I felt that sooner or later our Landmark successes would open the door to the Strip for us.

Walter Kane was always thrilled with Roy's sold-out business at the Landmark, and I eventually convinced him to put Roy at the Frontier Hotel, one of the major venues on the Strip. But I couldn't convince his superiors. They all liked Roy, but they were afraid country music just wouldn't make it there. Walter Kane knew it would. Roy Clark knew it would. *I* knew it would. Still, no sale.

Then our big break came. You always have to watch for these times, and when they come, you have to act.

During one of Roy's opening-night engagements before a capacity crowd at the Landmark, Walter Kane and I were enjoying Roy's show in Sir Walter's private booth, complete with a red hot-line telephone.

Suddenly, it rang.

Mr. Kane answered and turned ashen in color, visibly upset with the information he was receiving. After he hung up, he turned to me.

"What will I do?" he asked. "Robert Goulet is opening tonight at the Frontier, but he's unexpectedly become ill. The showroom is packed and dinners are being served; in fact, customers are eating right now, waiting for the show to start.

"We can't cancel now, and the opening comic can't carry the show beyond thirty minutes."

Goulet probably wasn't nearly as sick as Mr. Kane was at this moment. There was no time for a replacement. Or was there?

Without asking Roy if it would be acceptable to him, I suggested we whisk Roy to the Frontier—two blocks from the Landmark—by limo immediately following his show, so he could fill in for the stricken Goulet. If our timing worked, the staggered showtimes would allow Roy just enough time to get from the Landmark to the back stage of the Frontier as the opening comic was finishing his act.

There wasn't time to ask Roy or even explain the situation. He just had to trust Mr. Kane and me. And he did. Just as Roy finished his Land-mark show, we ushered him into a limo—guitar, amp, and all. As we sped the two blocks to the Frontier, we explained the situation briefly, and Roy understood. He got out of the limo, his guitar and amplifier were rushed to the Frontier stage by Jack Yenchek and his great stage crew, and Roy Clark, without rehearsal, stepped center stage to present one of the best shows of his life.

He winged it. The band winged it. And the audience loved it. When he finished his show, with "Malagueña," he got a standing ovation.

What a show! It had worked!

That night was a turning point in our Las Vegas career. Roy Clark had proved once and for all that he could entertain anybody, anywhere. The powers that be believed it now, and suddenly we were talking multiple weeks and a long-term deal. Now it's a part of entertainment history. Strange to think that so many people were afraid to take a chance.

But Roy Clark wasn't. I wasn't. And thank God, Walter Kane wasn't.

This situation, once again, proved that patience is a virtue in this business. It also illustrated the value of cooperation between all parties—manager, artist, and buyer. In this case, as it should be in all cases, we had one common goal—the satisfied customer!

Our relationship with the Hughes hotels lasted for many more years, ending only when the chain started selling off its properties. We played to capacity audiences in all of their main hotel showrooms, including the Frontier, Desert Inn, and Sands, but we still fondly remember those early sold-out days at the Landmark, where our Walter Kane association began.

♪ ♪ ♪ ♪

Later, after Roy had graduated to the Frontier Hotel, where he headlined for many years, the Landmark became a source of frustration to Mr. Kane. He'd tried several different entertainment policies for the Landmark, but none had been really successful, and there was no continuity in the programming. I'd suggested several artists I thought could be successful there, but none had been acceptable to him.

At this time, I was constantly in Las Vegas working with Roy and two of our other artists, Mel Tillis and Tammy Wynette, at the Frontier, Desert Inn, and the Sands. I had a lot of meetings with Mr. Kane, trying to figure out a solution for his Landmark situation. I couldn't come up with the right idea for him, even though I made a number of suggestions. After one completely frustrating session, I returned to my office in Tulsa, knowing I had the right answers for a successful Landmark show, but unable to sell them to Mr. Kane.

Soon after I'd arrived back home, I received a frantic call from Mr. Kane requesting my immediate return to Las Vegas. Colleagues of mine at other agencies thought it was ridiculous that I would make these long flights, do a turn-around, and return to Las Vegas. They told me if it were them, they wouldn't give Walter Kane any more time. But I'd proved over and over again that it was worthwhile for myself, my company, and my artists. Once again, I saw an opportunity to be of service to Walter Kane and Howard Hughes' six Vegas venues, so I caught the first flight out.

As I flew to Las Vegas I tried to put a picture together, using everything I knew about the situation. I knew I hadn't yet been able to come up with the entertainment idea Mr. Kane would buy for the Landmark Hotel. I knew the kind of problems he might be facing. I knew the kinds of venues our artists needed for best exposure. Finally, I knew if I could find the right solution to his problem, I could provide a real service to both our artists and the Hughes hotels.

I knew all of that. But the question was, what could I possibly pitch him that I hadn't pitched before? What could I offer Mr. Kane that would be unique to his Landmark operation? Most of all, how could I be of service to him?

That last question seems obvious enough in any situation, but its importance is often overlooked by an over-zealous salesperson. Too often, we forget that we're in the service business—service to our buyers, to our artists, and to our public. And when I viewed the Landmark problem from that perspective, I finally saw the solution. It was an idea I've put forth several times in this book: Don't concentrate on simply trying to sell an act to headline somewhere. Instead, put together an *event*.

Arriving in Las Vegas, I knew what I wanted to sell. Now, all that had to be done was sell it, and between the airport and Mr. Kane's office, I got my "performance" together.

When I arrived at his office in the Sands Hotel, I was very excited about presenting my plan for an event in the Landmark. But I didn't start right in with my presentation. Instead, I did something very important to any negotiation. I *listened*. He told me his needs and what he wanted to accomplish. He complained about the high cost of artists, of production, of advertising. As he talked and I listened, he was, in essence, preparing himself for my presentation. When he finally finished, I explained my plan for the Landmark. It was no accident that I said exactly what he wanted to hear. He had let me know what he wanted, and I'd heard him and responded with a plan.

My idea for the event was a production show called Country Music USA It would feature country music stars on a rotating basis, showcased in a Las Vegas-style production, allowing for variety as well as stability.

Mr. Kane bought it. It became our opportunity to prove that country music would work in Vegas, and it did. Country Music USA was good for the Landmark, and it gave major hotel-showroom exposure to established country music artists. It also became a developing ground for many emerging artists. Running two years straight at the Landmark (except for three months at the Silver Slipper while the Landmark underwent remodeling), it was great for all concerned.

Because of Country Music USA, many Halsey Company artists got their first Vegas exposure in a big-name showroom. These included The Oak Ridge Boys, Ferlin Husky, Hank Thompson, Freddy Fender, LeRoy VanDyke, Bob Luman, Mel Tillis, Johnny Paycheck, Tommy Overstreet, Skip Devol, Ray Price, and "Hee-Haw" TV regulars Guinella Hutton,

Grandpa Jones, and Archie Campbell. It was a good illustration of how a good deal can be good for everyone involved, and it showed that putting elements together to create an *event* creates something far more special than just packaging some acts together for a show. It also demonstrated another point, one that I simply can't stress enough: *never underestimate the value of your product.*

Give the person sitting across the table a chance to tell you his or her needs. Listen to the problem, then give your solution. That, in a nutshell, is the secret to successful negotiating.

♪ ♪ ♪ ♪

After the success of Country Music USA, country music became a staple of the Las Vegas entertainment market. Once our show broke the ice, it wasn't too long before big-name country stars were being asked to headline venues on the Strip. Because many of our artists were not only there in the first wave, but successful there as well, we were able to move into other hotels, including Caesar's Palace, Bally's Grand, The Hilton International, Sahara, Desert Inn, and the Sands. Continuously, The Jim Halsey Company had one or more major stars headlining at these big Strip hotels. We were the only ones booking name country artists into Vegas. We were specialists.

And always, we tried to make each date an event. Whenever we played our big stars at these major hotels, we would try to tie in a promotion or a contest. Working with radio stations in Arizona and California, we'd promote free trips into Las Vegas for listeners to win. We came up with the idea of offering "Have Dinner with the Star" contests. We'd negotiate with the hotels for free rooms and bargain with airlines for free tickets. We'd work with the record companies and various corporate sponsors. Somehow, each engagement had to be more than simply a date; it had to be an *event.*

A Vegas date with one of our acts became something customers and fans anticipated with excitement. They knew The Oak Ridge Boys' show at Bally's Grand or Caesar's Palace, or the Vegas shows with Roy Clark or Mel Tillis, wouldn't just be plain old *shows.* There'd always be something unique to go along with them, a special event or new promotion. On several occasions, for instance, we cut live albums with our acts at the hotel showrooms. Other times, we'd broadcast over a radio network. Always, we'd invite press from around the world to view our major artists' shows, which usually assured us glowing reports and reviews.

All this, as you can probably see, was simply another manifestation of my philosophy of the **Power of Performance.**

The casino areas of Las Vegas, Reno, Lake Tahoe, and Atlantic City are not for every artist, but they were important and right for our company. These showrooms helped us develop such acts as Roy Clark, Mel Tillis, The Oak Ridge Boys, Freddy Fender, Dwight Yoakam, Tammy Wynette, Ray Price, Reba McEntire, The Judds, and Clint Black into major stars. They also provided good cash flow. And perhaps most important, they gave us the chance to showcase the Halsey Company star roster under the most favorable production situations, with good lights and sound, special production facilities, big flashy marquees, and lots of press. And because we were able to bring in television and motion-picture buyers, fair producers, rodeo producers, special events producers, prospective corporate sponsors, and convention buyers to see these great artists in very comfortable situations, these dates were springboards to many more sales.

The Las Vegas Event

Imagine a glittering showroom, abuzz with quiet conversation and the clinking of glasses. Then suddenly the lights dim, the spangled curtain shimmers, and the announcer's voice booms from the speakers: "Ladies and gentlemen, Bally's Grand Hotel is proud to present . . .The Oak Ridge Boys!"

If your act is good, it will only be better in Vegas.

Casino areas are always well covered by the local press and major news services. The reviewers for papers in places like Las Vegas and Atlantic City have important voices; usually seasoned entertainment writers and journalists whose reviews and comments are respected throughout the country and the world. Most of them bring years of seeing what works and what doesn't work to their reviews and stories, and they are usually very consistent with their standards. A good review from one of them can be used as an endorsement for your artist's talents. A bad review gives *you* something to work on. Even negative reviews can contain a good comment or two, and those can be used in your news releases and other publicity material for your acts.

Las Vegas, Atlantic City, and other casino areas are better than normal places for creating promotions and making your shows into *events*. As an artist, manager, or booking agent, you shouldn't just accept a booking in one of these places and rely on normal avenues of promotion. Las Vegas, for instance, is a great place for a presentation, but you also have more competition. There are all kinds of promotional avenues to examine, including airlines, bus benches, taxi stops, billboards, newspapers, and special television and radio campaigns. A big Vegas or Atlantic City engagement is a great opportunity to market an artist internationally, and you should let the world know that your act is appearing in one of these showrooms. If you're a booking agent, invite everyone on your buyer's list, even if you know some or most can't attend. While these areas usually aren't of major importance when it comes to record sales, bookings in major casinos and hotels are impressive and should be publicized.

♪ ♪ ♪ ♪

For artists, managers, and booking agents, Las Vegas takes on a special importance each November. The last week of that month is the date of the annual convention of the International Association of Fairs and Expositions, when all the fair and rodeo buyers from across the United States and Canada gather to exchange ideas and select attractions for the coming year.

The Las Vegas convention is much like any other trade show, with various booths where agencies and other fair vendors display their wares. Our Jim Halsey Company booth held pictures of and pamphlets about all our artists. A lot of times, we gave away merchandise, including tour jackets and T-shirts, to various fair buyers. We prided ourselves on having a unique marketing program on display at the convention—always something different, something spectacular.

The Jim Halsey Company was an entertainment agency, of course, but first and foremost, it was a sales organization. We had to devise ways of attracting attention so we could sell our artists for the coming season. For that week in November, our **Power of Performance** had to be the best. We expected it from ourselves. Our artists expected it from us. And the attending fair buyers always expected it, too!

One of our more successful ways of standing out from the crowd was our use of a jumbo slot machine, which Bally's—where the convention was held—was always kind enough to loan us. One of these slots stands as high as a human being, and that in itself was an attention-getter. But it was the way we used it that made it such a great promotional tool.

What we did was allow every fair manager and talent buyer to have a pull on the machine. If any of them proved lucky enough to line up the three bars and hit the jackpot, he or she would win a performance from any one of our stars—absolutely free!

Imagine having a chance at a free show from Roy Clark, Mel Tillis, The Oak Ridge Boys, Minnie Pearl, Tammy Wynette, Reba McEntire, The Judds, Ronnie Milsap, or Merle Haggard, among many others. If you were a talent buyer, wouldn't *you* be interested?

The slot-machine promotion, needless to say, captured the imagination of the attendees, with a constant line of the top fair buyers in the United States and Canada in front of our booth, waiting for a turn at the slot. Those who didn't win a free show—which, of course, was almost all of them—were able to win records, videos, jackets, T-shirts, and other paraphernalia belonging to the different artists.

The Halsey Company booth was always the most popular one at the convention, and the slot machine was a wonderful promotional tool, year after year. But as good as that was, we came up with an even greater promotion. We were able to book most of the big casino showrooms with Halsey Company artists during the run of the convention, which created a real event. What better way to sell your stars than to have them playing Vegas, at one of the main venues, with all those buyers in town? Each year, we concentrated heavily on getting as many of our artists as we could into these showrooms while the convention was going on. Once, in the six major hotels that were presenting headline attractions at the time, our acts were in five of them. It made Vegas look like a Jim Halsey Company town. Those arriving in Las Vegas for the International Association of Fairs and Expositions convention were hit from all sides with the names of our artists, the marquees of major hotels advertising them in letters as big as those on billboards. At Bally's Grand, it was Roy Clark and Reba McEntire plus the great comedy of Williams and Ree. The Hilton offered The Judds and The Nitty Gritty Dirt Band; Caesar's Palace, The Oak Ridge Boys and the Forrester Sisters; the Frontier Hotel, Lee Greenwood and Bill Medley; and the Sahara Hotel, Mel Tillis and the Statesiders.

What an array of entertainers, and all Halsey Company artists!

If we'd put the names of our stars on every billboard in town, we couldn't have launched a more impressive campaign. These major marquees advertised our headliners 24 hours a day, and when the fair buyers hit town for the week, all they could see were the major acts we'd be selling them for their coming fair season. It took almost a year to put that multiple-act event together. It was a major coup for us, one that no other agency had done before—or has done since.

Besides being impressive to all the fair buyers, this multiple-venue event attracted a lot of flak from our competitors, especially after Joe Delaney, the important entertainment-business columnist for the *Las Vegas Sun* , wrote, "Jim Halsey's most recent Las Vegas accomplishment deserves a place in the *Guinness Book of World Records*."

It was all part of promotion, of creating events. It was a perfect example of the **Power of Performance**.

♪ ♪ ♪ ♪

Our company developed an outstanding rapport with fair buyers and fair managers around the country, and fairs became a major source of revenue for our artists. John Hitt, who you'll remember headed The Halsey Company's fair department, built us into the No. 1 fair booking agency in the world. Some of that ranking came because of the big stars we handled, but much of it was because of the great service that John and the rest of the Halsey Company associates gave to the fair buyers. A born salesperson, John knew the eternal value of a satisfied customer.

John and his sales crew always did a tremendous business at the fair buyers' convention in Vegas. With Halsey Company acts headlining in the main showrooms, we had the opportunity to entertain the fair buying committees and make sales at the same time. John and his staff always prepared several months in advance, arranging personal interviews with the fair buyers during the convention. It took a lot of preparation to make all those connections, but when John and his crew hit Vegas, they were set up for one meeting after another—and one sale after another.

Once again, one of the keys to success is planning, planning, and *more* planning. Not only were the names of our artists shouting out from marquees, but also from ads, pamphlets, promotional pieces, and billboards. If you were a talent buyer, you couldn't miss them. And as icing on the cake, before any fair buyer arrived in Las Vegas, he or she received a personal invitation from us to one of the showrooms where our artists were appearing, or to play our giant slot machine for a chance to win his or her fair attraction for the next year.

We had confidence in our product. We had confidence in our promotion. And we had confidence in our presentation. We were always successful at gatherings like the International Association of Fairs and Expositions convention because we maximized every promotional element available to get our artists in front of the buyer as well as the public. In this case, the bookings in these top Vegas venues provided prestige, international recognition, and cash flow, and helped us develop new artists, which we used to open the shows for our headliners.

It's always advantageous to sellers to present their wares to prospective buyers in the most favorable light. Automobile dealers do it. Furniture and appliance dealers do it. They present their cars or sofas or stoves in beautiful settings, with lighting designed to enhance whatever special features of a product might be especially noteworthy.

Any manager or agent can apply this same principle. Selling your act to a prospective buyer can be aided by lighting, staging, and special presentation. Las Vegas was the perfect place to bring buyers, television producers, record-company executives, columnists, and magazine writers to see our shows. Any of the big showrooms offered a well-dressed stage with special effects, an impressive strip marquee with our star's name, comfortable seats, and of course, the best sound and lights. A deal could almost always be closed in one of the comfortable booths at one of these shows as the buyer watched Mel, Roy, Tammy, The Oak Ridge Boys, Reba, Lee Greenwood, The Judds, Freddy Fender, Merle, or any other of our star artists play to a receptive full house. There was something about the glamour of Las Vegas, with the lights going, the neon flashing, and our artists' names in big letters on the marquees, that enhanced the **Power of Performance** and set the mood for deal-making.

In the '70s and '80s, country stars were not always easy to sell to network television shows, because some L.A. executives were still unconvinced of their drawing power. Taking advantage of the easy access from Southern California to Las Vegas, we often flew in TV producers and talent coordinators who we knew were in the process of putting together network shows. When these people saw our country acts in a Las Vegas atmosphere, we were able to close many a television deal.

The Jim Halsey Company was a pioneer in getting country acts on mainstream television programs. Thanks to my associate and executive vice president, Dick Howard, selling country music artists to non-country TV shows was a constant goal of The Halsey Company. Running our L.A. office, Dick not only made a name for himself as the expert country music agent in Southern California, but also established our company as the No. 1 agency for getting country artists on network television—and kept us there.

Nice is Nice

A good project or promotion should have a worthy conclusion—a fulfillment of the goal and purpose I've spoken about before in this book. If things work out right, many will have benefited, including all of the artists and companies involved.

Any good manager or impresario is always looking for the right date or promotion to present itself, so it can be turned into an event. Remember: Most events start out as simply concerts or personal appearances, and the difference between something ordinary and something spectacular is based on the degrees of imagination and inventive planning involved. As you know, I was always looking for some type of happening that could be turned into an event for one of my artists. Sometimes, one just fell into my lap.

That was the case with one of our best Halsey Company promotions. It began with a casual meeting in the lobby of the Carlton Hotel in Cannes, France, during the MIDEM Music and Entertainment Convention. Jacque Mediciene, mayor of Nice (pronounced "niece"), France, Oak Ridge Boys principal William Lee Golden, and I were discussing the MIDEM convention, and Jacque Mediciene suggested that The Oak Ridge Boys would be perfect to open the new convention center in Nice, a state-of-the art creation called the Acropolis. Projected to be the most modern facility in the south of France, it was to house a concert stage, exhibit halls, a shopping center, recording studios, and broadcast facilities.

We arranged a meeting the next day with Mediciene, who would make the final decision about The Oak Ridge Boys. After meeting and negotiating with him, we got an official invitation.

Everything about the deal was good. The Oak Ridge Boys were to play one show for a fee of $50,000. In addition, we would get deluxe hotel accommodations and meals; 35 round-trip, first-class airline tickets on Air France; sound and lights for the show, and all internal transportation. The problem was fitting the date into The Oak Ridge Boys' itinerary. It was isolated, and there was not enough time to book any other meaningful dates on either side of it.

Still, I hated to pass up this opportunity to further expand our European visibility and potential record sales. If we couldn't turn this booking into something meaningful and practical, it would be just another personal appearance.

We contacted an old friend, Larry Jones, whose Oklahoma City-based Feed the Children charity does such outstanding worldwide work. "Any suggestions?" we asked him.

He had a good one. At the time, Kenya, Africa—where Larry's charity was helping feed the people of the Riff Valley—was in the midst of a long, severe drought. If water could be obtained in the area, the people could begin planting crops and start growing some of their own food.

Larry asked us a question. If he could deliver matching funds, would The Oak Ridge Boys donate their $50,000 performance fee to Feed the Children for the express purpose of drilling a water well in the Riff Valley?

Duane Allen, Joe Bonsall, Richard Sterban, and William Lee Golden, the four members of The Oak Ridge Boys, readily agreed. Everyone liked the idea of putting the performance fee into drilling a well for a drought-stricken area. One of the most satisfying things about it was that the event would, in a significant way, live for a long time after the actual concert concluded. The well would stand as its symbol .

As the opening of the Acropolis grew near, it was becoming an event in itself. Press members from all over Europe were invited to witness the opening. Television was going to cover it, and many TV news departments were sending crews for live "bites" of the event .

The Halsey Company did its own brand of promotion, inaugurating a 90-day campaign built around the slogan "Nice is Nice!" All of our promotional material was geared to this phrase. Our news releases, special press kits, radio packages, T-shirts, and anything else dealing with the concert went out imprinted with the slogan, The Oak Ridge Boys' logo, and the image of crossed American and French flags.

Kathy Gangwisch, our PR person, was on a roll, getting lots of TV, radio, and newspaper interviews. The television magazine shows were all covering the event. Halsey Company senior vice president Judi Pofsky, working out of Los Angeles, sold the live gala broadcast internationally and to ABC radio in America. The coverage was worldwide and enormous! It was a media event, just as we'd wanted.

Prior to the performance, the city of Nice held a press conference and reception. As Larry Jones made prayers for the opening of the Acropolis and the success of the concert, he gave a startling announcement: instead of one water well in the Riff Valley—our goal—Feed the Children had been able to raise enough money to drill *four* wells! Further, he said that each well would be named after one of The Oak Ridge Boys!

There were many other welcoming remarks, but nobody could top that.

Joseph Rael, a Picuris and Mountain Ute medicine man who had accompanied our entourage to France, performed a beautiful blessing of the new Acropolis building and the concert. Larry Jones videotaped the entire proceedings and the concert for inclusion on his own television show, carried in 110 markets. Portions of the event were broadcast over Eurovision and on almost every TV network and channel throughout the world.

This is a magnificent example of what can happen when you practice **Power of Performance**. Everyone concerned combined their talents and, working together, turned an ordinary concert date into an event of monumental proportions. To this day, the four wells are producing precious water for the residents of the Riff Valley.

See how important projects are born? Sometimes they can come from something as casual as a conversation in a hotel lobby. You should always listen closely to the details of *any* proposal or idea. There may be some hidden benefits beneath the surface.

Learn to use and expand your imagination. Recognizing the potential of an idea is at the heart of perfecting your **Power of Performance**. And remember also that when an opportunity is presented to help people, we are always helped in the process. It is possible to have fun, take care of business, and do good all at the same time. Our experiences in Nice once again showed The Jim Halsey principle that a deal is good only when it's good for all concerned. Nice *was* nice!

The First Soviet Tour

In May 1974, an event took shape that would change my life.

Roy Clark was headlining in Las Vegas, doing one of his two-week engagements at the Frontier Hotel. Late one afternoon, he and I were sitting around in his hotel suite, watching the evening news, when a segment appeared about a group of Soviet dignitaries at the Seattle World's Fair. They were on an official visit to America, and the TV interviewer asked them if there was any place in the US not on their official itinerary that they'd really like to see.

"Yes," immediately answered Alexi Stepunin, the delegates' leader. "We had hoped to visit Las Vegas, but it was not included in our trip."

I think Roy and I both got the idea simultaneously.

"Roy" I said, "let's invite them to Vegas to see your show, as your guests."

Roy was all for it. Both of us, however, figured it would be impossible. The main thing was that it would have to be done on very short notice and there obviously would be a lot of—if you'll excuse the expression— red tape.

Nevertheless, I made the call the next day to our State Department. I'd already talked to the Frontier Hotel, and, seeing the possibilities of some great press, hotel management had agreed to fly the Russians from Seattle to Las Vegas and return them to Los Angeles via Hughes Air West. (This was a regional airline owned by Howard Hughes, who also owned the Frontier Hotel.) Further, the delegation would be housed at the Frontier and would be guests at Roy's dinner show.

To our surprise, the State Department approved. It turned out that the Soviets had an open date in their itinerary, and it was okay with the US officials as long as it didn't cost the government anything extra. I don't think any deal between the US and USSR had ever been struck so fast.

Two days later, 18 Soviets—doctors, scientists, economists, farm specialists, and other dignitaries—arrived in Las Vegas, the guests of Roy Clark and the Howard Hughes organization. When we met them at the Vegas airport, a string of Hughes-provided limousines was waiting. Upon the delegation's arrival at the Frontier Hotel, each member was given a bag of $25 worth of quarters to play the slot machines—and they dispersed through the casino like mercury hitting a slick surface.

That's when I began to doubt the wisdom of our invitation. Would we see our Russian friends again? Would they show up for Roy's dinner performance? Would they *defect*? Our brainstorm and the swiftness with which we carried it out hadn't left much time to consider any possible negative outcomes.

Thankfully, any fears or doubts were alleviated at the opening of Roy's dinner show, when all 18 showed up right on time. We seated them front and center, waiting to see how they'd react to his performance.

Roy always does a great show. I don't know if this show was greater than usual, but his **Power of Performance** on stage that night could have been felt all the way to Moscow! After he concluded the show with a rousing performance of "Malaguaña" on his Ovation twelve-string guitar, the Soviets, along with everyone else in the sold-out showroom, gave him a standing ovation.

After the show, Roy received all 18 Soviets in his dressing room. The delegation, under the leadership of Mr. Stepunin, presented Roy with many gifts—the best of which was an official invitation for him to present his concert in the Soviet Union!

Although Roy's journey to the Soviet Union was a long way from starting at this point, the story of his initial invitation to the Soviet Union, their attending his show, and their subsequent return invitation for him to perform in the USSR garnered enormous amounts of international press in those Cold War times. Once again, our **Power of Performance** was enhanced by plugging in a Star Team member—publicist Kathy Gangwisch. We all worked together to get as much press and PR as this unusual set of circumstances warranted.

Then, after that initial flurry of publicity, the real work began.

Our first step was to deliver our official proposal to State Department officials, who were delighted with the idea. Through the US government's cultural-exchange program, they'd had presented many American shows to Soviet audiences. But even with all of the artists involved in the State Department's program, they'd had few stars the magnitude of Roy Clark to work with—and they'd *never* presented an American country-music artist in the Soviet Union.

But the whole thing was going to take months of negotiations, beginning with financial ones. The State Department's cultural-exchange program wasn't heavily funded, and the Soviets had only rubles, which couldn't be exchanged for American dollars. Roy agreed to go for no fee, but he insisted that all his musicians and crew be paid. The Oak Ridge Boys were invited to go as well, becoming important *impact enhancers* for the event.

In addition to working out the financial details, we had to jump a lot of other hurdles to make the tour happen. At one point, the Soviets sent three different delegates to view Roy's show, and then asked that he delete one number from his show before presenting it in Russia. The offending song? It was the main theme to the hit movie *Doctor Zhivago*, which had been a staple of Roy's concert for years. It offended the Soviets because its Russian *emigre* author, Boris Pasternak, was *persona non grata* in the USSR, and Soviet officials wanted no reference to him or his works.

Much of the time between the actual invitation, which came in May 1974, and the tour, which began in January 1976, was spent in negotiating details to the minutest degree. It was also spent in utilizing the upcoming tour as a wonderful vehicle for press and public relations.

From the time it was conceived, the Roy Clark Soviet Union tour represented a milestone—not just for country music, but in the realm of human relations. I have never seen the personification of our **Power of Performance** philosophy more dramatically demonstrated than during Roy's first performance in the USSR.

It began on January 18, 1976, when we arrived in Moscow. Many hours earlier, we'd had a sendoff from Tulsa International Airport with press and television in attendance, and evangelist Oral Roberts asking God for a blessing of safety, harmony, success, and friendship. Now, we were suddenly facing a Moscow temperature of 25°F below zero and heavy snow. Our path from the plane to the airport was lined on both sides with Soviet soldiers carrying wicked-looking Kalishnakov machine guns, each soldier holding his finger on the trigger! After an 18-hour flight, that was quite a reception.

Then we found out there'd been a change in schedule. We weren't starting the tour in Moscow at all, but in Riga, Latvia, 14 hours north of Moscow by train. After an 18-hour flight, we were greeted with the prospect of a 14-hour train ride. What a drag!

(I should mention here that, at this time, the political relationship between our two countries was at a low ebb. Later, we found out that the Soviets were afraid the US was going to bomb them at any time—which would make anyone a little nervous, I guess.)

Taken to the Moscow train station directly from our flight, we boarded the midnight train to Riga. None of us had ever been this far from home, and in the kind of environment where Americans didn't appear to be particularly welcome. Wearily, Roy and I looked at each other. Had we made a mistake? Although we didn't say it, I'm sure we both thought it: *Will we ever see home again?*

As we all boarded the train, however, we began to experience a revelation of the human spirit.

There had been enormous publicity in the Soviet press and on Russian television about Roy and his upcoming shows. And the passengers in the crowded train knew who we were. Not long after the train pulled away from the station, one of the Russians broke out a guitar and started playing Hank Williams' old classic, "I'm So Lonesome I Could Cry." Other passengers joined in. Members of our entourage started taking out their instruments. The Oak Ridge Boys began singing some harmonies.

Power of Performance? You bet! Our troupe and the Russians on the train couldn't communicate—except through performance. And it was *powerful*! For that entire 14 hours, as the train pulled us slowly through the Russian night, music rang out from singing hillbillies—both American and Russian. By the time our train arrived in Riga, I may have been a lot sleepier than I wanted to be, but I was also feeling much better about our reception in the USSR.

♪ ♪ ♪ ♪

Our premier Russian concert, the first of 18 sold-out shows, was set to begin promptly at 8 p.m. the night after our arrival in Riga. Despite a busy day of setting up, rehearsal, and time with the Soviet press, everybody was up for this debut—and, truth to tell, a little apprehensive as well.

The concert began with a cold audience, and the well-below-zero temperature outside had little to do with it. You could feel the attitude rising off the entire opening-night crowd. *Okay, Americans,* they seemed to be saying, *prove to us how good you are. Make us enjoy it.*

This was going to be the test. Our first night. Our first concert. And before they even heard the first note, the audience was hostile. Those old misgivings about this whole trip began creeping back in.

What happened next is impossible to describe adequately. As I stood backstage, watching, Roy came out and began the show. Within *30 seconds*, he'd changed the entire audience's mood from cold, impassive hostility to warm, loving friendship. A few more minutes into the show, and he was getting the kind of reception and acceptance these Soviet citizens would've given their country's biggest hero. He was not only entertaining them; he had won them over!

That audience loved Roy Clark, calling him out again and again for encores when his regular concert concluded. He introduced The Oak Ridge Boys in the middle of his show, and they got the same kind of response. It was a magical night for everyone.

In all my years in show business, I have never seen any performance move an audience more than those performances did. And their reception was a portent of things to come, because the same kind of thing happened *every* night, at *every* performance, on our Russian tour.

It was, simply, the pure essence of the **Power of Performance.**

Do you see how it works? Sure, we all understand how a gifted artist can give a powerful performance on stage. But this goes beyond the simple musical or entertainment aspects of a show into an even vaster territory, and it has to do with the obligation of everyone involved to evoke all the individual power that comes with performance.

In this case, it was our mission not just to entertain, but to show people through music and art that we all have a common heritage. All of us can live in peace and harmony together; the first step is to meet on the common ground of performance. Roy and The Oak Ridge Boys had a responsibility not only to themselves to give the best performance they could give, but to our country, the United States of America, to be the best representatives and goodwill ambassadors they possibly could be. Through these kinds of efforts, we all make a contribution toward a better world.

♪ ♪ ♪ ♪

By the time the tour concluded three weeks later, at the Rossiya Theatre in Moscow, it was a tremendous success by any standards. Journalist A. Agisheva, writing in the national paper *Pravda*, gave the concert a glowing report. He concluded his front-page review with this statement: "In one of the songs ["Orange Blossom Special"] sung by the ensemble, they tell about a train, which carries from Florida to the North fruit, turkeys and various things, in which the fertile land of this state is rich. Figuratively speaking, one could say that today this train makes stops in Moscow, Leningrad and Riga. The American guys and girls sang here of their striving for peace, happiness and love. And this is the best confirmation, that people of good will always understand one another."

This Roy Clark-Oak Ridge Boys tour opened lots of doors, culturally as well as diplomatically. And it doesn't just make a good story; it also provides an example of how, when all elements are working together, you can achieve success in anything.

The elements involved in this Soviet tour were legion. Roy Clark and The Oak Ridge Boys, of course, were the talent. Then there was The Jim Halsey Company as booking agent and management, and Kathy Gangwisch for press and public relations. (Kathy came up with the idea of having all the performers' bios and other press material translated into the Soviet language before we left America, which made everyone's job easier.)

In addition, the team included our music-business attorneys Bill Coben and Dan Sklar to review the contracts; ABC-Dot Records head Jim Foglesong, for whose label Roy Clark and The Oak Ridge Boys recorded; and the musicians, road crew, and sound and lights people. That was the Star Team, and it worked with lots of other elements: the US State Department—which could be seen as the promoter—the American Embassy, the Voice of America radio network, the Howard Hughes organizations (including the Frontier Hotel and Hughes Air West), the Soviet Embassy, the Soviet Ministry of Culture, Gostel Radio, Gosconcert, Intourist, Alexi Stepunin, and the thousands of newspapers, radio and television stations, and magazines that carried stories about this tour before, during, and after the trip. In addition, the makers of Clark candy bars (no relation to Roy) gave us plenty of their product to pass out along the way, as did the Wrigley company, providing packets of Juicy Fruit gum. Everyone worked in harmony, using his or her individual talents and skills to enable the Soviet tour to become a history-making event—not just for country music, but for American music!

See how the **Power of Performance** philosophy works? We didn't just go to Moscow for a concert; we created an *event* that the whole world knew about. When everyone's performance works together, it produces a spectrum of power. When all team members work together, the power takes on a life of its own. It's a power that should be used only in the most wholesome and positive of ways. And when it is, it produces results greater than anything imagined or planned.

It worked for the Soviet Tour event. From conception to implementation, it took 18 months to get it done, but it was worth all the effort and planning. Its success lifted the Iron Curtain, helping other American artists to enter eastern Europe and make their own contributions to harmony and peace in the world.

25

Orbison Magic in Bulgaria

Around the time of the first Roy Clark Soviet tour, I became interested in FIDOF, the International Federation of Festival Organizations, and its charismatic founder and leader, Professor Amando Moreno. Founded in 1967 in Cannes, France, simultaneously with MIDEM (the Music Business Industry Conference), FIDOF's umbrella expanded to include more than 360 major music festivals in 80 countries.

FIDOF introduced me to festivals and organizations that were not familiar with country music (but soon would be). As the organization broadened my scope, I became more active in pursuing my goals on an international basis. In fact, I served as FIDOF's president from 1984 through 1990 and currently hold the title of president of honor, in recognition of my service to FIDOF.

Many of my artists, aware of Roy Clark's then-recent great success in the USSR, were interested in the world festival arena. One of them was the legendary rock 'n' roller Roy Orbison. Already a big international record seller, he had at the time toured extensively in Asia, Great Britain, and Western Europe, witnessing the effect of his own **Power of Performance** on international audiences. He had not, however, appeared in any Communist countries.

We were able to secure Mr. Orbison an invitation to perform in Bulgaria.

From his Nashville home, Orbison would travel halfway around the world to give a show. That wasn't so different for him, a seasoned traveler and international performer. What *was* different was that this would be his first-ever concert behind the Iron Curtain. He was to be the headliner at the final gala performance at the Golden Orpheus Festival in Sunny Beach, Bulgaria—the prestigious talent showcase of the Communist world. Outstanding young talent from Bulgaria, the Soviet Union,

China, Hungary, Romania, Poland, East Germany, Czechoslovakia, Albania, Cuba, North Vietnam, and Yugoslavia made up the festival's roster, along with a handful of performers from outside the Soviet bloc—England, Holland, France, and West Germany.

But now, for the first time, it would be an American artist who had the honor of closing the festival's final night, the Gala Performance. Roy Orbison wasn't a communist, of course. But he knew music was the international language, and he also knew that through music and art, an atmosphere of peace and harmony could be created and perpetuated.

Although The Jim Halsey Company was known as the largest country-music agency in the world, with many superstars on our roster, we also represented other major artists from other musical genres, including rockers Leon Russell and Rick Nelson, R&B icon James Brown, and big-band legend Woody Herman, who had helped me through that snowed-in Independence, Kansas, date at the beginning of my career. All of us were bound by one common thread: we believed peace and harmony could be achieved through music and art, and that the **Power of Performance** could change lives.

At the time, The Jim Halsey Company had become involved with many international projects. We had been, for instance, producing an international festival in Tulsa and Oklahoma City (at Oklahoma City University), as well as at Independence (with the Neewollah Festival) and Baldwin (at Baker University), Kansas. Through these events, we became aware of fine Bulgarian singers like Bisser Kirov and Nelly Rangalova, each of whom took our grand prize in successive years.

Now, for the first time, America was coming to Bulgaria—in the person of Roy Orbison, creator of such immortal songs as "Crying," "Pretty Woman," and "In Dreams."

It was a long and grueling trip for him. As we got closer to Sunny Beach, the airplane and airline changes grew more and more frequent, and the planes seemed to get smaller each time. Finally, arriving in Sofia, Bulgaria, 24 hours after the start of the trip, we got into a Balkan Airlines twin-prop job of near-antique vintage, which was to take us to Bourgas. From Bourgas, it was on to Sunny Beach by official government limousine.

Finally, we made it to the festival site. Exhausted from hours of flying, no sleep, irregular food, and the constant changing of planes, Roy Orbison emerged from the limo and looked around a moment. Then, in an uncharacteristically gruff manner, he asked me, "Halsey, where are we?"

"Sunny Beach, Bulgaria, Roy," I answered. "You are the first American to ever perform here."

"*Bulgaria?*" Orbison said incredulously. "You told me we were going to *Bavaria.*"

I never found out if he was kidding.

♪ ♪ ♪ ♪

As I've said before, it's always important to be the first at something, and our company liked to be first with programs, events, and projects. Our artists liked to be first, too. Roy Orbison was the first artist to represent America as a performer in the prestigious Golden Orpheus Festival, and he did a superb job.

Before sound check on the afternoon of Orbison's performance, he and I, along with officials from both the American Embassy and the Bulgarian Ministry of Culture, were walking down the Avenue of Flags in front of the concert hall in Sunny Beach. Flags from all of the nations represented at the festival flapped in the sea breeze. There was the Bulgarian flag, of course, as well as those from the Soviet Union, East Germany, Hungary, Romania, Poland, Czechoslovakia, Albania, Yugoslavia, North Vietnam, Cuba, and China. And for the first time ever, we saw Old Glory flying proudly over Sunny Beach, right next to the Soviet flag.

The Deputy Minister of Culture, who was hosting our sight-seeing walk, turned to Roy.

"Look, Mr. Orbison," he said. "Because you are here, your American flag is flying today in Bulgaria."

I don't need to tell you that this was goosebump time for all of us Americans, walking on the Avenue of Flags that day, far away from home.

Roy's performance that night may be one of the best he ever gave. In Europe, audience members will often bring flowers to the stage when they particularly respect and appreciate an artist's performance, and I have never in my career seen as many flowers as I saw that evening. The entire stage—and it was gigantic— was totally buried in flowers, all brought to the stage by members of the enthusiastic crowd. And Roy's ovations were tremendous. After each song, the audience would break into rhythmic clapping that lasted for many minutes. His show was delayed so many times by the delighted crowd that I didn't think he'd be able to finish.

Perhaps the most touching thing about his concert, however, was that everyone in the audience knew all of his songs, singing along with most of them and making for a very emotional evening.

The concert attracted press from all over the world, and the entire show went out over Eurovision, which broadcast to an audience of 200 million viewers in Western Europe. In addition, Soviet TV beamed it to more than 500 million Eastern Europeans, giving Orbison's performance a potential audience of more than 700 million people!

Again, it's easy to understand the importance of the **Power of Performance** by a great artist on a prestigious stage, but the performance we have to give in our everyday lives is equally important, because that performance can change lives as well.

After the gala concert, my wife, Minisa, and I hosted a dinner at the leading hotel in Sunny Beach. We had champagne and caviar, *shopska* salad, and virtually everything else we could get on the menu. After all, we were celebrating Roy Orbison's overwhelming success—a success for America!

Our party included several guests from the American Embassy as well as Eastern European superstars Bisser Kirov of Bulgaria, Alla Pugachova of the USSR, and Iosif Kobson, known as the "People's Artist of the USSR." We were also honored by the presence of the Bulgarian Minister of Culture, who had become an instant Roy Orbison fan. We witnessed magic that night, with American, Bulgarian, and Soviet performers and artists all sitting at one table, talking music and art, transcending their political boundaries, respecting and enjoying one another.

As a result of the banquet and Roy Orbison's fantastic success at the festival, some very positive things happened. The cultural attaché with the American Embassy had been in Bulgaria for three years without ever being able to get an appointment with the Minister of Culture. Now, here they were together at the same table with the rest of us, making champagne toasts to Roy Orbison's success, to each other's countries, to peace, to art and music, to expanded friendship, to those who were not with us, to everything that came into anyone's mind.

The final toast? As is the custom, we all made it to our mothers—an appropriate finish to this magical, emotional, joyous evening.

The next week, the cultural attaché had an appointment with the Ministry of Culture. Interestingly enough, they discovered that they lived in the same apartment complex. Meanwhile, we had made a deal for Bisser Kirov to tour in the United States, and we'd started the wheels in motion for another American superstar, Roy Clark, to perform at Sunny Beach.

All of this and more happened because of Roy Orbison's **Power of Performance**, and all that went with it..

Let me stress again that I really believe art and music can make the world a better place to live, a place of peace and harmony. The artists and musicians of the world can contribute greatly to this process, but those of us who don't take a stage to make our living can make contributions of equal value. It doesn't have to be a monumental event happening halfway around the world, like the concert at Sunny Beach. It can happen in your home, your neighborhood, your local concert hall, your church or temple.

Music is a feel-good profession that can change lives. Those of us on the presenting and business side have just as much obligation—and can get just as much gratification—as the artists themselves. We must find out how to be the best we can possibly be, learning by experience to be bigger and better than our last performance.

26

The Second Soviet Tour

In November of 1988, Roy Clark returned to the Soviet Union.

There were a lot of reasons it took so long to get him back there. For one thing, the Soviet Union was in a constant state of financial flux, and hard currency—that is, currency exchangeable on the international money market—was becoming more and more scarce there, because of less and less trade with other countries. Of course, the Russians wanted Roy back—but they wanted someone else to pay for it. Also, funding for the State Department's cultural-exchange program, never lavish by any standards, had dried up completely as far as the Soviet Union was concerned. (This was, you'll remember, an era of harsh diplomatic relations between our two countries.)

We were going to have to be resourceful in funding our event this time, but we couldn't even begin looking for funds until we had the official invitation from the Soviets, and at least some idea of what they could offer.

For more than a decade, between 1976 and 1987, I made numerous trips to Moscow, trying to get both the invitation and a deal that would work for everyone. It proved to be a unique and unprecedented deal-making experience for me. Setting up a major tour usually follows a pattern: you find a promoter, establish the venues and dates for your act, coordinate any record releases, set up a TV show, and start to work. With the Soviets, though, I had tried to delicately mesh all the government organizations, the times, and the events.

All tours came under the direction of the Ministry of Culture. But it was necessary to coordinate things not only with the Ministry of Culture's concert bureau, Gosconcert, but also with the government-owned Gostel Radio (for TV and radio broadcasts). Then, all of these agencies had to work with Intourist, the USSR's official hotel and travel agency.

Since the officials at every one of these agencies constantly disagreed with one another, putting the tour together was a lot harder than just finding venues, getting the dates approved, and arranging the logistics of the tour.

It took a great deal of negotiation to even get the invitation. Several times, I flew to the USSR to make formal negotiations only to get home and find that the heated political differences between the US and the USSR had caused the cancellation of the State Department's cultural-exchange program. These cancellations were always temporary, but they were maddening, and when the ban was lifted I'd have to start over again at square one.

I don't think most people would have kept going with it, but, knowing how important this would be to Roy's career—among other things—I called upon one of my big helpers: patience.

Finally, in late 1986, after four days of steady meetings with top Soviet officials, we got the invitation for Roy to do a two-week series of concerts, with one week in Moscow venues, and one week in Leningrad. The kicker was that the Soviets had no hard currency—nothing available that would convert to US dollars; they had only rubles to pay for the tour, and rubles weren't worth anything outside the USSR. They would finance all internal travel, hotels, allowances for meals, and certain other logistical items—but in rubles, not dollars.

All along we had been negotiating for dollars, but Soviet circumstances had changed drastically, and dollars were no longer available for artist exchange. What few they did have were needed for wheat and other goods essential to the Soviet people—not entertainment. Remember, that on our 1976 tour, the State Department, through its cultural exchange program, had paid the band members and bought the airline tickets. By this time, however, that funding had dried up. If we wanted to tour now, we'd have to finance it totally, without a penny from either government.

After the years of negotiations to set this tour and the thousands of dollars our company had invested in trips for me to the USSR, this event had become too important for me to drop. I had to figure some resourceful way to make the trip happen and to make it pay off. How could I do it?

Finally, I made another trip to Moscow. If I couldn't get it done, I'd already decided to put the Soviet tour on the back burner. But I had to make it work.

Meeting with Mr. Ostakovitch, director of Gostel Radio (the television branch of the Ministry of Culture), I explained the circumstances and insisted that we be given the television rights to our shows. Normally, the Soviets kept the rights, did their own taping, and sold the product. I wanted to work a compromise that would allow them to save face and still give us the deal. We finally agreed that they could televise the event for the Soviet Union and its satellite countries, and let us have broadcast rights to the rest of the world. They would furnish us certain live-concert footage, and we would have total access to anywhere we wanted to film, within reason. It was a great meeting with Mr. Ostakovitch, a true gentleman and a good negotiator. I think we both ended up with what we wanted.

Now I had everything we needed from the Soviets to make the tour—except money. Which, of course, meant my work was really just starting. It would be another two years before Roy Clark set foot on a Moscow stage, because it took that long to coordinate all of our efforts. We had to do some real planning, because *we had to pay for the tour ourselves: transportation, salaries, hotels, meals, and all.* As he had with the previous tour, Roy agreed to go without a fee. But everything else, including the salaries of his musicians and crew, had to be paid.

The total amount needed was somewhere around $200,000, which would pay for our airline tickets, our excess baggage, and the salaries for our musicians and crew. All the USSR could pay for were our hotel bills.

Now the real planning began, and we did it according to the Halsey method of using eight distinct steps, in the same way we created the Ranch Party events I wrote about in Chapter 16.

1. Inspiration: This was already in place. Inspired by the tremendous success of our first Soviet tour, we would call this one the "Friendship Tour."

2. Goal and Purpose: The goal was to create a self-financed tour. The purpose was to create peace and harmony through the musical performance of Roy Clark, with a secondary purpose of providing a vehicle for an enormous amount of press and PR for Roy.

3. Planning: In this stage, my main associates—John Hitt, Judy Pofsky and Sherman Halsey—met with me to lay out what we hoped to accomplish. The major question: how were we going to get it paid for?

We had four ideas to put on the drawing board.

1. Get several corporate sponsors.
2. Sell the show for US broadcast.
3. Enlist the aid of Roy Clark fans and other American citizens.
4. Stage a fundraising banquet in Nashville

The very first corporate sponsor we signed came from a "cold call," which in the sales business means calling up a prospective buyer who doesn't know you and trying to make a sale. I decided to write a letter—to make, if you will, a cold call—to a person I considered the foremost marketing expert in America: Joe Sugarman. I didn't know him personally and he didn't know me. I had been impressed, however, when I'd read the text of a speech Mr. Sugarman had given—the one in which he'd said that the most important sentence in any piece of advertising was the first one, followed in descending importance by the second, the third, etc. And I'd been a fan of Joe Sugarman every since I'd first read and ordered from his JS&A advertisements in the airline magazines. I was, in addition, truly mesmerized by his inventive and creative new form of marketing, the television infomercial—a half-hour ad that looked like a regular program—which a marketing genius Richard Sutter had invented for Joseph Sugarman to sell BluBlocker sunglasses. And sell them he did. BluBlocker became and still is the top-selling sunglasses brand in the world, and Sugarman's infomercial started a revolution in telemarketing.

In my letter to Mr. Sugarman, asking him to become one of our corporate sponsors, I tried to use the principle I'd read about in his speech. Here, then, are the first two sentences of my letter to him:

"Dear Mr. Sugarman:

Obviously, you are the most inventive salesman in America today. I think you will have a great appreciation for the patriotic marketing program I am proposing in this letter. . . ."

I think you'll agree that I was quick to learn his technique—and it worked! We heard back almost immediately. Yes, he would come on board, providing funding in the dollar amount we had asked for. In addition, he would give us 5,000 pairs of BluBlocker sunglasses, specially imprinted with the words "Roy Clark Friendship Tour." These sunglasses normally cost $69 a pair, but these would not be for sale. They'd only be used to promote Roy's tour.

Wow! In addition to helping finance the tour, Joseph Sugarman had provided us with nearly $350,000 worth of BluBlocker sunglasses.

His gift of sunglasses gave us another idea. Now we wanted to involve all of America in this tour, using the vehicle of country radio.

We formed the Friendship Radio Network, designing a large Friendship Book with pages three feet high and two feet wide, which Roy would take with him to the USSR. Loose pages for the book were sent to radio stations, who in turn asked their listeners to sign one of the pages. For a gift of two dollars, those signing would receive a postcard sent by Roy from Moscow during the Friendship Tour! Four thousand pairs of the special BluBlockers would be sent as gifts to the stations on the Friendship Radio Network (which would leave us 1,000 to take to the USSR as gifts). The stations were free to use the glasses in promotions, but BluBlocker had to be mentioned.

Nearly 500 radio stations across America became part of the network, each collecting signatures for the pages of the Friendship Book. When it was time to take the book on tour, it contained more than 25,000 signatures—and the signees had given us a total of $50,000, a full one-quarter of the money we needed to raise.

We displayed the Friendship Book with its 25,000 signatures, at each concert, making sure the Soviets understood that the tour was made possible by a combination of contributors, including the 25,000 Americans who'd signed the book. This show of goodwill and support, seen in page after page of signatures, was a big hit with the Russian people.

It was a hit with us, too. We were very grateful—frankly, we hadn't expected such a huge response. And now we were obliged to send 25,000 Roy Clark postcards from Moscow!

We found a good photo of Roy, taken in front of Moscow's St. Basil's Cathedral during his previous Russian trip. It made a great visual for the postcards. We put that photo on 25,000 postcards, addressing each one before we left. When we got to Moscow, we figured all we'd have to do is put on stamps and drop them off at the nearest post office.

That was what we figured. Unfortunately, it was easier said than done. When we arrived in Moscow, our trusted Gosconcert tour manager, Inna Sonovich, informed us it would be impossible to get that many stamps. They just were not available.

But we had to have them! She had to get them! We explained the situation, and she understood.

To this day we are not sure how Inna, as resourceful as she was, came up with 25,000 Russian stamps. But she did, and for the next two weeks—at every rehearsal, every show, every news conference, every place where more than two people with two hands and a wet tongue gathered—we drafted anyone we could find to help us lick and stick 25,000 stamps on the 25,000 postcards. On the last day of the tour, we finally finished—only to have Moscow's Central Post Office refuse to handle the cards. But once again, the invaluable Inna Sonovich prevailed, and most of the cards arrived in the US about six weeks after we did.

It was a great promotion. People still talk about receiving Roy Clark postcards from the Soviet Union, and they have become keepsakes in thousands of homes. Thanks go to Joseph Sugarman for inspiring this great promotion and, with his BluBlocker sunglasses, helping make it possible.

4. Expanding the Elements: Even with the great assistance of Joe Sugarman and the Friendship Book signees, we still needed more cash— or more help. We got the latter from American Airlines, which had helped us fly in celebrities to our golf tournaments. A sizable portion of our budget was set to go toward the almost 50 international round-trip airline tickets we needed. To help with that budget item, American agreed to give us round-trip tickets from Nashville to Frankfurt, Germany, where we would have to buy tickets to get from Frankfurt to Moscow. In return, American Airlines would be a part of the television show arising from the event.

Another of our long-time corporate friends, Amana Refrigeration, came aboard. Amana had helped us in numerous other projects, including the Roy Clark Celebrity Golf Tournament, where the company was a major sponsor. Liberty overalls and jeans, a first-time sponsor, gave us major help as well some cash and blue jeans.

Meanwhile, Judi Pofsky, the senior vice-president in our Los Angeles office, was busy pitching this tour for television. A big TV sale was important for several reasons. First, the only money Roy would take would come from the television show. Second, we needed it for documentation of the tour. Third, its use as a vehicle for generating press would further enhance Roy's image as an international peace diplomat.

Jim Owens Productions of Nashville became the buyer and producer. The Nashville Network (TNN) agreed to multiple runs. The musical documentary would be a co-production between the Owens and Halsey companies.

Things were coming together pretty fast now, but our tour dates were also fast approaching—and we were still $50,000 short of our projected budget. So we created another event to help kick off the main event. We envisioned it as a black-tie banquet, at $150 a plate, to be held in Nashville, and asked Bob Hope to emcee. He agreed, provided we furnished him a private jet. Industrialist Armand Hammer, who had earlier turned down our requests for help with the tour, furnished his Oxy Petroleum Jet as transportation for Hope and his entourage.

Preparation for the Friendship Tour banquet was a masterful project in itself, taking everyone in our company to make it happen. When it did, everyone in Nashville's music and entertainment business turned out.

Our own entertainment was superb that night, as well as being unusual for a Nashville banquet. Among the acts performing were the

Ellis Island Band, a klezmer group from Los Angeles that performed East-ern European music. Roy's friend, the classic entertainer Phil Harris, also took the stage, and there wasn't a dry eye in the place when he finished his version of Tom T. Hall's, "Old Dogs, Children and Watermelon Wine."

Many entertainment and sports personalities who'd supported Roy's Celebrity Golf Tournaments in Tulsa were surprise arrivals, including actor David Huddleston (of *Santa Claus* fame), who was not only a friend, but a recruiter of many of the celebrities for the tournament. In addition, every star and up-and-comer in Nashville attended. Opryland gave its full support. Frances Preston, president of BMI, had several tables. Tennessee congressman Bob Clement, along with senator Jim Sassor and Senator— and future Vice President—Albert Gore.

The reception progressed, with a wonderful job of emceeing from Bob Hope, who, after talking about the funds that were being raised for the Roy's tour, asked, 'Wouldn't deporting him be cheaper?" And then, midway through, came the biggest surprise of the night. I'd reached back into my bag of tricks to come up with it, and I knew it was a sure-fire show-stopper.

For years, at our Tulsa Ranch Parties, golf tournaments, and a few of our international festivals, we'd hired a marching band to come through at a certain time, and it always grabbed attention and brought everything to an absolute halt. The marching-band stunt hadn't, to my knowledge, ever been done in Nashville, and things did screech to a stop when the Tennessee State University Marching Band came parading through the party. They were sensational and a great surprise to the guests.

It was a fun time. Roy and Barbara Clark were perfect hosts and, with the banquet and party, we raised the final amount we needed to cover tour expenses—not to mention getting tons of international press cov-erage from the event.

5. Implementation: Now our expenses were covered, the logistics taken care of, and we were ready to go. We had our special touring cases, suitcases, hanging garment bags, patches, stickers, posters, bag tags, tour books, and matching all-weather slickers—everything embla-zoned with the Roy Clark Friendship Tour logo. As we were making final preparations to leave, Christie Cookies of Nashville—whose owner, Jim Christie, was a big supporter of the tour—delivered numerous tins of outstanding cookies for us to to take along as presents for the Soviets.

6. The Event: Finally the day arrived for our departure from Nashville International Airport aboard American Airlines. A big crowd came to see us off, and those who showed up had a final chance to sign the

Friendship Book, in case they'd missed the opportunity before. Then we were airborne, and with a different sense of anticipation than before.

This was truly an event, and not just because it had taken six years to plan it. One of the biggest reasons was the participation of the Voice of America radio network. Listening to VOA broadcasts had been officially forbidden in the USSR since 1976, but, in conjunction with Roy's tour, Soviet officials had lifted the ban. Judy Massa's popular VOA country music program was going to be broadcast live from Russia featuring music from Roy's concerts. His playing and singing would circle the globe in this historic, first-time broadcast. Just as Roy Clark had blazed cultural and diplomatic trails 12 years before in his earlier Soviet trip, he'd be setting some new "firsts" on this trip also.

7. The Review: It's important to understand the preceding six steps in creating an event. Even if your event is of a much more modest nature than a trailblazing international tour, the steps still apply. And it still goes that any event can be extremely important to the career of an artist, as the Roy Clark Friendship Tour was to Roy's career.

It's essential for Star Team members to review any promotion, campaign, or event after it concludes. After all, something like this is part of the history, and our futures are based on our history. After the Roy Clark Friendship Tour was finished, every single person involved with it met and examined what had happened in minute detail. We all studied, talked, and contributed notes (which are still in my files, just in case I ever want to mount this type of tour again), deeming the tour a success in virtually every phase.

8. The Follow-up: This step prolongs the benefits of the event and opens the door to other elements in an artist's career. Because of the Roy Clark Friendship Tour, Roy was now fully recognized as a world-class entertainer and diplomat. This recognition opened the doors to countless press and TV interviews and kept Roy in the public spotlight in more ways than just as a performer. Because of his great humanitarian works, his involvement with the Children's Medical Center, his charity golf tournaments, and the world-wide recognition he'd earned from his global tours, UNICEF, the United Nations International Children's Fund, named him a special ambassador for the organization, and even sponsored his next Tulsa golf tournament. I also served for years on UNICEF's board of directors.

See how all of this works? What started out to be just a tour of one-night concerts in the USSR ended up as a life-changing and career-enhancing experience. It was an important tour from the beginning, but its importance grew exponentially through exhaustive planning and development.

I've only covered its high points here. There could be a whole book written about the two Soviet tours, and I may just write it someday.

Many rewards come from a successful project. They can be emotional, material, financial, and spiritual. Sometimes, you get them all.

Many of Roy's rewards from his Friendship Tour came as recognitions of a job well done. Before the fund-raising banquet, I wrote a letter to every US Representative and Senator telling them about the upcoming trip, noting that Roy had given both his time and his celebrity endorsement to the US State Department's cultural-exchange program.

Nearly every member of the US Congress sent a note of support to Roy; he received almost 500 different messages from political figures. I had them all bound in a book and gave the book to Roy so he'd be able, in future years, to reflect on how much his efforts were appreciated.

Here are some excerpts from that one-of-a-kind book:

More than the universal language of music, though, your big heart and winning ways will touch many lives and create friendship that spans the globe.

—Vice President George Bush

It is the creative spirit that nourishes the roots of our culture in order that we may have a more human world and it is through the arts that we will be remembered by those who will come after us. It is those strains of music, lines of poetry, the words and colors running through our minds which bind us together. Your generosity in sharing your talent across the sea will help create and foster a climate encouraging the release of that spirit on earth which is a need as profound as the need to speak.

— Senator Bob Dole (Kansas)

I've often thought that you, like Will Rogers, have never met a man you didn't like.

— Senator Nancy Landon Kassebaum (Kansas)

The world has long known that music is an international language and the voluntary contributions of artists like yourself often does more to strengthen the understanding between its many peoples than any number of official meetings.

— Senator Jeff Bingaman (New Mexico)

If this incredible reception you received on your tour in 1976 is any indication, I'm sure this trip will be a great success in a number of ways—in sharing country music with the Soviet public, in exploring new avenues for this entertainment industry, and in establishing a closer cultural exchange between our two nations.

— Senator Don Nickles (Oklahoma)

Your efforts have served to broaden the cultural exchange between the US and the USSR during a time of new found openness between these two countries. You should take great pride in the lives that you have enriched through your many years as an entertainer.

— Senator Robert C. Byrd (West Virginia)

The Friendship Tour is a great idea and a fine way to improve relations between Russia and the United States. Bon Voyage!

— Representative Patricia Schroeder (Colorado)

I am confident the Soviet people will joyously relish your music, as have the American people for many years. Good luck in this terrific endeavor.

— Representative Dan Glickman (Kansas)

Best of luck in your upcoming tour. Your efforts on behalf of peace and understanding are most appreciated here in the Congress.

— Representative Bill Richardson (New Mexico)

I cannot think of a better representative to the Russian people than someone with your talents and abilities.

— Representative Bob Clement (Tennessee)

Thank you for promoting peace and understanding around the world through your concerts.

— Governor Bill Clinton (Arkansas)

I am confident your down-to-earth country style will be well received and that you will be an immediate Soviet star, as you are here in the USA.

— Governor Henry Bellmon (Oklahoma)

Roy, I cannot think of a more appropriate emissary to represent our great state and nation to the people of Russia.

— Governor Ned McWherter (Tennessee)

♪ ♪ ♪ ♪

As you know, much of my philosophy has to do with following your dreams and visions. Again, it's important to note that some will work, and some won't. But the important thing is to follow them all, and to learn to work with them.

The event I've just written about, one of my best, started with just that: a dream. And as the rest of the Star Team and I worked with it, it grew into an event of such magnitude and lasting impact that it's still talked about.

It was a major event, but it began with a dream. And when you start with the raw and exciting material of your own dreams and visions, and follow through with my eight-point plan, you'll be able to create your own events, as important and unique to you and your Star Team as the Roy Clark Friendship Tour was to us.

So get started!

27

Vision to Reality: Radio City Music Hall

I can point to many projects and events—and even artists—that have been developed as a result of dreams and visions. As I've noted throughout this book, it's important to recognize dreams for what they are: inspirations that come to us to tell us how something could be. With good and careful planning, we can turn them into reality.

Years ago, I had a vision of developing an important event in New York City, something that would attract the attention of advertising agencies, commercial producers, convention producers, prospective corporate sponsors, television and radio executives, record company executives, members of the press and media, and concert, casino and fair buyers. It was a vision of a showcase that would elevate the image of my artists and pay off for years to come.

My vision? To put The Oak Ridge Boys and The Judds into Radio City Music Hall.

Our company had already done a number of shows at Carnegie Hall, another internationally recognized venue. Even The Oak Ridge Boys had played there. But my vision this time called for Radio City Music Hall.

At this point, our company was just beginning to break The Judds. Wynonna and Naomi had two successful records under their belt, they'd won some awards, and we felt a prestigious engagement with The Oak Ridge Boys at Radio City Music Hall would give them a big boost. We figured it could even be the push they needed to catapult them into bona fide stardom.

As you know from previous chapters, part of the secret of developing artists into stars is getting them seen and heard by people who can do something for them. A lot of times, you can do this by packaging shows, putting a developing act on the front half of a big superstar's concert. This was what we did with The Oak Ridge Boys and The Judds, figuring that the combination of the two would not only be dynamite for the New York market, but also something that could explode The Judds' career. In addition, it would be an *impact enhancer* for The Oak Ridge Boys, who were launching both a new album and a new tour.

Before any work began on this project—before, in fact, anyone else knew anything about it—I started my meditation and prayer, formulating exactly what it was I wanted to accomplish. As I had seen Radio City Music Hall many times before, I knew exactly what the stage and the exterior, marquee and all, looked like. During my meditation, I envisioned The Oak Ridge Boys on Radio City's giant stage, with all of the lights, sound, and production imaginable. I also imagined The Judds on that stage, standing and performing in warm, perfect, lighting. I visualized a sold-out hall with thunderous applause and standing ovations. I then envisioned that wonderful neon marquee of Radio City Music Hall with the names of my artists, The Oak Ridge Boys and The Judds, emblazoned in white-reverse across the front.

I was determined to make this date happen, and I was determined to make it an event.

It became one.

We actually did the date—the *event*—almost a year later. It took that much time to work it out properly. First of all, we needed the support of The Oak Ridge Boys' record company, MCA, and The Judds', which was RCA. We convinced both companies of the merits, and long-term benefits of doing a gigantic promotion. They understood exactly how important this date could be and pledged full support.

Our next step was to coordinate the dates of the two groups along with the venues with the proposed record release schedules for both artists. We planned to book them together for not only Radio City Music Hall, but other selected dates.

The Radio City date would be most effective if it coincided with the release of their new albums. We scheduled planning meetings between The Oak Ridge Boys and The Judds and Kathy Gangwisch and Assoc., our PR firm.

We all knew that this was our opportunity to showcase our two acts in one of the most prestigious venues in the world, in one of the most important entertainment cities in the world, something that wasn't expected of country music performers at the time. So the promotion from all aspects had to be enormous and elaborate.

First I contacted Margo Fieden, the agent for the great caricaturist, Al

Hirschfeld. I wanted a centerpiece, if you will, a symbol to speak for the event. A Hirschfeld caricature of The Oak Ridge Boys would be exactly that, something that could be used constantly to create *repetitious impressions* in posters, program books, newspaper ads, billboards, invitations, and, eventually, in a live album recorded by The Oak Ridge Boys on the Radio City Music Hall stage.

In fact, we had plans for Hirschfeld's masterful caricature to continue to work after the event was history. We arranged with Felden to do a limited number of serigraphs of the piece; our idea was that Hirschfeld would sign and number and The Oak Ridge Boys would autograph each copy. This limited edition would then be sold, with proceeds going to our favorite charity, the Oklahoma City-based Feed the Children.

Remember how, in Chapter 12, I told you never to assume anything? You'd have thought that a project like this, with proceeds going to a good charity and everyone involved benefiting in various ways, would be easy to accomplish. Unfortunately, it wasn't. In fact, it never happened. The difficulties that grew out of The Oak Ridge Boys' personality differences were reaching critical mass at the time, and shortly after the engagement, William Lee Golden left the group. The limited-edition serigraphs were never sold, the charity funds never raised, and the great Hirschfeld caricature was used only for the Radio City event. Thank goodness William Lee Golden returned to The Oak Ridge Boys in 1996.

Still, the promotion became enormous and was a great success. Press, radio, the record and publishing companies, management, and our PR firm all had a synergistic effect on one another and on the event itself.

Ron Delsner, one of New York City's finest promoters, handled the concert (along with Radio City Music Hall), and he took care of all of the public promotion. Equally as important to us, however, was promoting the event within the industry. We started working on press many months before the date in order to obtain space in the weekly and monthly publications. Both The Oak Ridge Boys and The Judds made themselves available for press, radio, and television interviews.

On a broader basis, we ran ads using the Hirschfeld caricature in many national and international magazines and newspapers, plus all of the trades. We knew that most of their readers were not going to flock to New York City from around the world for our concert, but we wanted to make a "prestigious announcement," letting everyone know this was an important event with two important acts.

At the same time, radio was being worked on a nationwide basis. MCA Records held contests over many country radio stations, flying the winners into New York City for the show. Also flown in were important talent buyers from around the world, whom we specially invited.

One of the major pre-concert events was a party and reception held in the Time-Life Penthouse directly across from Radio City. Five hundred of the biggest music, broadcasting, advertising, and press and media executives from around the world attended, along with heads and chief executives from some of America's top corporations. It was a big success. The artists' "performance" at this reception was as important as what they would later do on the Radio City stage, and I'll bet The Oak Ridge Boys and The Judds shook hands with every single one of the 500 invited guests.

Time finally came for the concert, and it was just as I'd envisioned it nearly a year earlier. Radio City Music Hall, with the names of our acts emblazoned across its marquee, was completely sold out, and both The Judds and The Oak Ridge Boys received thunderous applause and standing ovations. In every sense of the word, it was an *event*.

Sometimes, after everybody has worked so hard for so long on a project like this, there's a letdown feeling after it's over, a sense of disappointment in knowing that the euphoric space occupied by the event is no more. That wasn't the case for me. Sure, I was tired, but I was filled with a wonderful feeling of satisfaction and success.

Still, there was one more thing I wanted to do.

The Oak Ridge Boys and The Judds were packed and gone. The audience members, carrying their own memories of this marvelous show, had all dispersed when Minisa, Kathy Gangwisch, and I walked out the front door of Radio City Music Hall into the neon night of New York City. We looked back at the marquee, still ablaze with "The Oak Ridge Boys and The Judds." It was a symbol of a dream and vision I'd had almost a year earlier, and I wanted Kathy to take a picture of it.

She did, and that picture still hangs prominently in my office, an illustration of the power of a dream that comes true, an example of how to go from dream to vision to reality.

Again, the Radio City Music Hall show is a graphic illustration of what an *event* should be. We created it by following the right steps and revising our plans over and over again, perfecting them, tuning them, until we finally put them into operation. We had our goals established. We focused upon them. We were successful.

You can do the same thing. As I've told you before, part of the secret of success is to constantly strive to go beyond what you might think of as your limits. Extend your energies and abilities to achieve new goals and broaden new horizons. Project your goals. Put them in writing and look at them frequently. Then, formulate your plans for achieving them.

Most of all, have the courage to follow your dreams, because that is where it all starts—for you, for me, for everyone who wants to succeed in this business.

PART FOUR

NOW IT'S YOUR TURN

The First Job–
Your Power of Performance

Now that you've finished this book, you should have a good understanding of the elements that make up the music and entertainment business. And you should know by now that it all boils down to *sales* and *marketing*.

This business is about people. It is about common sense. It is about getting as much knowledge and education as you can. It is about discovering your own **Power of Performance**, how to access it, and how to master it.

There's a lot of vital information in this book, things I've learned over the decades I've been in the business, and I suggest that you reread the chapters you're most interested in, marking or underlining the points you feel are important. I hope you found the personal stories I told to illustrate some of these points both entertaining and educational as well.

One of the keys to making it in this business is knowing that it's never a one-person show, but a team effort. Another key is knowing that you're probably not going to step directly into the team-member role you want, despite your training and education. That doesn't matter! The important thing is to get into the business. Get your foot in the door, get past the receptionist, get on the inside. Then you will be able to start working toward the job you really want.

Some years ago, a young law-school graduate came to see me. He wanted to be an agent, and he wanted to work for The Jim Halsey Company. But even though he had a law degree, he had no agenting experience, and I was looking for a seasoned agent at the time.

"We'll keep your application on file," I told him, giving him the time-honored, polite turndown. "If something comes up, we'll call you."

Just as he was getting ready to leave my office, my assistant interrupted the meeting. It seemed we had a "situation" that needed attention. Our company always maintained a limousine and a full-time driver to pick up important guests, artists, and visiting buyers and executives. But the driver had just quit—and ABC Records president Jim Foglesong would be arriving at the airport shortly!

"What should we do?" my assistant asked.

Before I could offer any suggestions, this young law-school graduate jumped to his feet. "I can drive the limousine for you!" he announced.

He was hired "on the spot" because he was *on the spot*—in the right place at the right time. It may not have been the job he came to our offices looking for, but it was an opportunity for a music-industry job. Knowing instantly he'd be better off learning the business from the inside, he accepted the challenge.

For the next few months, this young man chauffeured artists, record company presidents, promoters, nightclub operators, casino managers, and fair and rodeo buyers for us, coming in contact with nearly every important person the Halsey Company was dealing with then. He listened and he learned, and after those months we hired him to start training as an agent.

His name was Terry Cline. He was capable and ambitious, and he stayed with The Jim Halsey Company for 15 years, becoming one of our major executives.

See how important it is to be able to recognize opportunities, and to act on them? They may not always seem right at the moment. They may not even seem to be anything you want. But you must examine all of them closely. If there's a possibility one will open the door to other opportunities, give it lots of consideration.

It's now time to put your own plan into action. Decide where you want to go, and whom you have to contact to get there. Use this book's description of essential Star Team members as a map. Then determine the real-life team members, the players you want to contact. Write their names down on a piece of paper. This sends a subliminal message to them, telling them you want to make connections.

How can you find these people? How can you get to know them? For starters, read the trades, which tell you about the major executives of record companies, booking agencies, management companies, and publishing companies.

Then make lists of these names. Study them. Find out all you can about who they are and how they operate.

Once you determine who it is you need to see to advance your career, the next challenge arises. How do you get an appointment with them? How can you make them notice you and pay attention to you?

Remember *persistence*? It's one of the 10 keys to the **Power of Performance**. And being persistent in making your contacts, or trying to make your contacts, comes into play at this time. Frankly, it's very unlikely that you'll get to see the executive you want to see on your first try. You must call on all of your history, education, and memory, and on what you've learned from the trades and the books on the business you've read—including this one—to finally get through the door and past the receptionist or secretary. That's the first person you'll meet in an office, which means that he or she is your first hurdle. It's very important to be clear and straightforward when you approach this first contact.

When you encounter the receptionist, be very courteous and state exactly what you want. Be positive and firm. Show him or her that you have self-confidence, but also show respect. Stand up straight, look him or her in the eye, and project the image of being both focused and grounded. Have your resume and a photo with you. *And don't be afraid to make a cold, in-person, call.*

It's very easy to be turned down over the telephone. The person you're calling may have a full schedule, there may be no positions available, etc. If you walk instead into an office, projecting positively and clearly, you stand a much better chance of seeing the person you want to see.

If you cannot see that person, try to see someone else in a position to help you. At least try to get past the receptionist so you can get inside.

Once you're inside, make your presentation as short and concise as possible. Do not take a lot of time. Don't hang around, lounging in a chair. Sit up straight. After you have said what you want to say, stand up, thank the person for seeing you and for the time, and see if another appointment is called for. Then leave. You aren't there for conversation, and it's usually a good idea to depart before the person begins signaling you that the meeting is over.

When you exit the office, always leave your name and telephone number, as well as a business card. Next, make call-backs. Keep the person informed about what you're doing. Remember the idea of *repetitious impressions*. Without being overbearing about it, make a repetitious image in the mind of that person. It will help you when he or she is looking for someone to fill a position.

There are a lot of ways to try to make your entrance into this business. Do not overlook the opportunity of getting into the business you want by accepting a lesser, more menial, job—as Terry Cline did with us. Once you are in the door and begin to know people, you can show them your abilities and skills. If you're actually working for a music or entertainment company, no matter what your position, you stand a thousand-percent better chance of advancing within the company than somebody from the outside does. An entry-level job that gives you the opportunity to meet people—in a mail room, as a delivery person, as someone who runs errands or chauffeurs a car, or even as a waiter or waitress in a restaurant frequented by music-industry people—can be a real asset. Who you know and what you learn are equally important in this business.

If you still can't land a job, try to find someone who knows a person in the company where you've interviewed. You don't want to be just another name in a file drawer full of resumes; making someone on the inside of the company aware of you can help you stand out from the pack.

Remember, when you call on the people you want to work for, your first impression may be your last. So make that first impression good—good enough to be a stepping stone to successful future contacts. Make them want to see you again, or at least let them investigate you and see what you are about and what opportunities you may hold for them as an employee. Your **Power of Performance** may never be needed as much as it is on your first interview.

♪ ♪ ♪ ♪

The **Power of Performance** is really what this book is about. In these pages, I've told you about the way I've built my life in show business, music, and entertainment—utilizing my own **Power of Performance,** and that of the other members of the Star Team, to achieve my goals.

This concept can just as easily be used by those interested in any other career involving sales and marketing: electronics, real estate, insurance, furniture, banking, computers, automobiles, advertising—anything where success is derived from interaction with people and teams.

There are thousands of creative, stimulating, and financially rewarding jobs in the music and entertainment business. The better educated and better prepared you are, the more knowledge and experience you have, the more available you are to success. Learn, study, work, concentrate, have a goal with a purpose— and *stay focused!* Learn about your **Power**

of Performance and access it to make your personal dreams and visions into your own realities.

Learning how to use your personal **Power of Performance** will help you understand success and where to find it. Most important, the **Power of Performance** is the key to life and how to live it! It is a gift. It is your gift. You have it now. *Use it!* The path from your dreams to your goals may sometimes be difficult to navigate, but the trip will never be dull.

Take it from another dreamer.

Good Luck!

Jim Halsey

Appendices

A
Record Company Administrative Chart

B
Glossary of Music Business Terms/Jargon

C
Suggested Reading Materials

D
1000+ Important Contacts

THE RECORD COMPANY
ADMINISTRATION

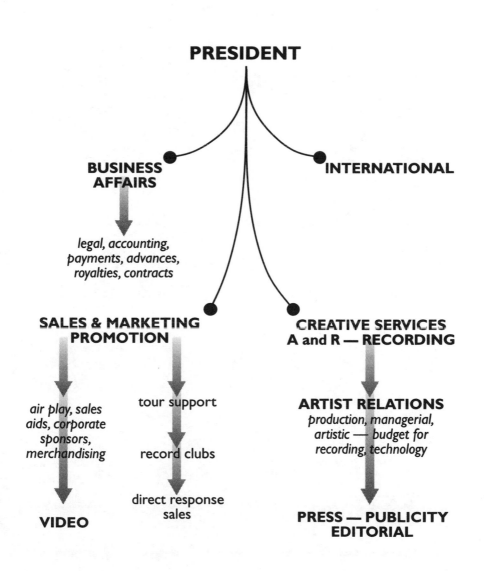

PRESIDENT

BUSINESS AFFAIRS

legal, accounting, payments, advances, royalties, contracts

INTERNATIONAL

SALES & MARKETING PROMOTION

air play, sales aids, corporate sponsors, merchandising

tour support

record clubs

direct response sales

VIDEO

CREATIVE SERVICES A and R — RECORDING

ARTIST RELATIONS
production, managerial, artistic — budget for recording, technology

PRESS — PUBLICITY EDITORIAL

Glossary of
Music Business Terms/Jargon

Acetate Dub: An individually cut record (as opposed to pressed records).

Administration: The supervision of all financial, copyright and contractual aspects of either an entire catalog or a particular song.

Advance: Money paid before the recording or release of a song, to be deducted against future royalties of that song.

AF of M: American Federation of Musicians; unions for musicians, arrangers, copyists, contractors and orchestras.

AFTRA: American Federation of Television and Radio Artists; union for singers, actors, announcers, narrators, and sound effects artists.

AGAC: American Guild of Authors and Composers; a songwriter's protective association.

Angel: The financial backer of a play.

A&R Director: Artists and repertoire; record company employee in charge of selecting new artists, songs and masters.

Arrangement: The adaptation of a composition for performance by other instruments and voices than originally intended.

Arranger: One who adapts a musical work to particular instruments or voices.

Artist: Individual or group under recording contract.

ASCAP: American Society of Composers, Authors and Publishers; a performing rights organization.

Assignment: The transfer of rights to a song or catalog from one copyright proprietor to another.

Biography: A concise account of an artist or group's industry related experience or background.

BMI: Broadcast Music, Inc.; a performing rights organization.

Booking Agent: One who finds employment for artists from buyers of talent.

Bootlegging: The unauthorized recording and selling of a performance of the song.

Bullet: Designation of a record listed on the charts, referring to increased record sales.

Casting: The selection of actors, musicians, or dancers for an artistic project.

Catalog: All the songs owned by a music publisher considered as one collection.

Charts: Lists published in the trade magazines of the best-selling records. These are separate charts for pop, soul, country, western, etc.; musical arrangements.

Chord: Three or more notes sounded simultaneously that imply a harmonic function.

Chorus: A section of the song that repeats itself at certain intervals.

Clearance: The right of a radio station to play a song.

Clearance Agency: See performing rights organization, ASCAP, BMI, SESAC.

Click Track: A perforated sound-track that produces click sounds that enables one to hear a predetermined beat in synchronization with the movie.

Collaborator: One of two or more partners in the writing of songs.

CD (Compact Disc): Digital audio recording

CMA: Country Music Association; organization devoted to promoting country music.

Commercial: The potential to sell; that which has mass appeal.

Common-Law Copyright: Natural protection of a song based on common laws of the various states. To be superseded by a single national system effective January 1, 1978.

Composer: One who writes the music to a song.

Composition: A musical work; the art of writing music.

Co-Publishing: The joint publication of one copyrighted work by two publishers.

Compulsory License (Phonorecords): Statutory mandate given to a copyright owner to permit third parties to make sound recordings of the copyright owner's song after it once has been recorded.

Consumer Publication: Entertainment oriented periodicals written and published for a general public readership i.e., Rolling Stone, Spin.

Copyright (n): The exclusive rights granted to authors and composers for protection of their works; a song or musical composition.

Copyright (v): To secure protection for a song by filing the proper registration forms with the Copyright Office.

Copyright Infringement: Stealing or using somebody else's copyrighted song.

Copyright Notice: Notice comprised of three elements:

1. The symbol of copyright, the word "copyright," or the abbreviation "Copr."

2. The year the song has been registered for copyright or the year of first production of the work.

3. The copyright owner's name.

Copyright Office: Federal government department, one of whose main purposes is to file and supply information regarding copyrights.

Copyright Owner: The owner of any one of the exclusive rights comprised in copyright.

Copyright Royalty Tribunal: A committee created by Public Law 94-553 to determine adjustments starting January 1, 1978, of royalty rates with respect to compulsory licenses for educational television, cable television, jukeboxes, and sound recordings.

Cover Record: Another artist's version of a song already recorded.

Co-Writing: Joint authorship of one work by two or more writers.

Cross Collateralization: Means of recouping the money spent on one song or recording against the earnings of another song or recording.

Crossover: A song which receives airplay in more than one market.

Cut: To record; a recorded selection.

C&W: Country and Western

Date: A recording session or live engagement.

Demo: A demonstration recording of a song used to show its potential to music industry personnel.

Demo Firm: An organization specializing in the production of demo tapes.

Distributor: Company that exclusively handles the sale of a record company's product to jobbers and retail outlets for a certain territory.

D.O.R.: Dance-Oriented Rock; a categorization of popular music utilized by radio stations.

Employee For Hire: Contractual basis whereby a motion picture producer or company employs a composer or lyricist to create music or songs for a movie with copyright ownership to be retained by the producer or company.

Engineer: Individual who operates studio equipment during the recording of a song.

Exclusive Songwriting Contract: A contract which prohibits the songwriter from writing for more than one publisher.

FIDOF: The International Federation of Festival Organizations.

Folio: A collection of songs offered for sale to the public.

Gold Album: Certification by the Recording Industry of America that an album has sold half a million units.

Gold Single: Certification by the Recording Industry of America that a single has sold half a million units.

Grammy: Music industry awards presented by the National Academy of Recording Arts and Sciences (NARAS).

Groove: Rhythm or tempo that helps create the "feel" of the song.

Harmony: The combination of musical notes to form chords that serve to enhance the melody line; the art of combining notes into chords.

Harry Fox Agency: An organization which represents music publishers in connection with the mechanical reproduction of their copyrights as well as the use of their compositions for motion picture synchronization.

"Head" Arrangement: An arrangement devised spontaneously. No charts are prepared for instrumentalists and vocalists. Instead, they read off lead sheets and an arrangement is made from various experimental styling devised at the studio.

Heads Out: Manner in which a reel-to-reel tape is stored, with the loose end at the beginning of the tape, enabling the tape to be played immediately.

Hit: A record that sells many copies; a description applied to records that achieve top 40 status.

Hook: A phrase or melody line that repeats itself in a song; the catchy part to a song.

Heavy Metal: A category of popular music characterized by high-volume, maximum guitar presence.

Impresario: An entertainment entrepreneur

Ink: To sign a contract.

Jingle: A short phrase of music usually accompanied by lyrics used to convey a commercial message.

LP: A long-playing record played at 33 1/3 revolutions per minute (rpm).

Label: A record company

Leader: Conductor or person in charge of the band.

Lead Sheet: A musical notation of a song's melody along with the chord symbols, words, and other pertinent information.

Leader Tape: Reel-to-reel tape which contains songs separated by white tape for easy access.

License (n): A legal permit.

License (v): To authorize by legal permit.

Lick: A brief, improvised musical interpolation.

Logo: An artistic design found on records and album covers that identify the company issuing the product.

Lyrics: The words to a song.

Lyric Sheet: A (typed) copy of the lyrics to a song.

Lyricist: The writer of the works to a song.

Manager: One who guides an artist in the development of his/her career. Same as artist or personal manager.

Market: Selling place; medium where only one type of record is played (i.e., pop, R&B, C&W, etc.)

Master: A finished recording of the song from which records are pressed and distributed to radio stations and record stores.

Mechanical Right: Right granted by the US copyright law to copyright owner to profit from the mechanical reproduction of his song.

Mechanical Rights Organization: Collection agency for copyright owners of money earned from the mechanical reproduction of their songs.

Mechanical Royalties: Moneys earned for use of a copyright in mechanical reproductions, most notably records and tapes.

Mix: Blending together the tracks of a multitrack recording.

Modulate: To change from one key to another in a song.

MOR: "Middle of the Road"; songs that may be classified as easy listening.

Motif: The shortest significant melody of a song or theme.

Moviola: A projection machine that reduces film to a small viewing screen.

Music Publisher: The individual or company who:
1. Screen songs and gets them commercially recorded.
2. Exploits the copyrights.
3. Protects the copyrights.

4. Collects income from performance, mechanical synchronization, and printing rights both in the United States and in foreign countries.

Neutral Demo: A demo that doesn't sound like it's for one particular artist, but best represents the song whereby it can be recorded by anybody.

One-Stop: Wholesale record dealer that sells the records of several manufacturers to jukebox operators and record stores.

Overdub: The addition of instruments or voices to pre-existing tracks.

Packager: One who selects and combines talent for shows.

Payola: Secret payment to broadcasters to play certain records.

Pen: To compose or write.

Performing Right: Right granted by US copyright law which states that one may not publicly perform a copyrighted musical work without the owner's permission.

Performing Rights Organization: Society whose purpose is to collect monies earned from public performances of songs by users of music and to distribute these to the writers and publishers of these songs in a proportion that reflects as accurately as possible the amount of performances of each particular song.

Performance Royalties: Monies earned from use of one's song on radio, television and other users of music.

Phonorecord: Any device which transmits sound other than that which accompanies a motion picture or other audio-visual work.

Photo-Offset Reproduction: Reproduction of musical manuscript by printing press.

Pick: A song that has been reviewed by the trades and projected to have success.

Pirating: The unauthorized reproduction and selling of sound recordings (i.e., records and tapes).

Pitch: To audition or sell; the position of a tone in a musical scale.

Platinum Album: Certification by the Recording Industry Association of America that an album has sold a minimum of one million units.

Platinum Single: Certification by the Recording Industry Association of America that a single has sold a minimum of one million units.

Plug: Broadcast of a song; to push for a song's performance.

Plugola: Secret payment to broadcasters for free mention of products on the air.

Points: A percentage of money producers and artists earn on the retail list price of 90 percent of all records sold.

Press: The manufacture of a large quantity of records duplicated from a master for commercial sale.

Printed Edition: A song published in the form of sheet music.

Professional Manager: The person in charge of screening new material for music publishers and of obtaining commercial recordings of songs in his company's catalog.

Producer: The individual who oversees the making of a single or long playing record, radio, television or stage show from inception to completion.

Production: The technical aspects of the music industry, including sound systems and lighting requirements as well as video and recording processes.

Program Director: Radio station employee who determines which songs shall be broadcast.

Promoter: One who secures talent from an agent for the production and presentation of a performance; the primary risk taker in the event.

Prosody: The marriage of words and music.

Publication: the printing and distribution of copies of a work to a public by sale or other transfer of ownership, or by rental, lease or lending.

Public Domain: Unprotected by copyright due to an expired copyright or caused by an invalid copyright notice.

R&B: Rhythm and blues; "soul" music.

R&R: Rock and Roll.

Rack Jobber: Dealer that supplies records of many manufacturers to certain retail outlets such as drugstores, variety stores, and supermarkets.

Release: The issuing of a record by the record company.

Road Manager: Traveling supervisor hired by artist to coordinate details of concert tours on behalf of the artist.

RIAA: Recording Industry Association of America.

Royalty: Money earned from use of the record or song.

Self-Contained Artist: An Artist who writes and performs his own material. Also refers to artists who require no production or personnel assistance from promoters.

SESAC: A performing rights, mechanical rights, and synchronization licensing organization.

Session: Meeting during which time musicians and vocalists make a recording.

Sheet Music: Printed editions of a single song offered for sale to the public.

Showcase: A presentation of new songs and/or talent.

Single: A small record played at 45 rpms containing two selections, one on each side; record released because of the expectation by the record company that "A" side would achieve success.

Song Plugger: One who auditions songs for performers.

Song Shark: One who profits from dealing with songwriters by deceptive methods.

Speculation: The recording of a song with payment to be made to the recording studio, musicians and vocalists when a deal is consummated.

Split Publishing: When the publishing rights to a song are divided among two or more publishers.

Staff Writer: One who writes exclusively for a publishing firm and earns a salary in this capacity.

Standard: A song that continues to be popular for several years.

State-Of-The-Art: Contemporary or current.

Statutory Copyright: Status acquired by a composition when it is registered with the Copyright Office or is published with the proper copyright notice.

Studio: Place where a song is recorded.

Subpublisher: The company that publishes a song or catalog in a territory other than that under the domain of the original publisher.

Subpublishing: When the original publisher contracts his song or catalog to be handled by a foreign publisher for that territory.

Sweeten: The addition of new parts to existing rhythms and vocal tracks such as strings and horns.

Synchronization: The placing of music in timed-relation to film.

Synchronization Right: The right to use a musical composition in (timed-relation to) a film or video tape.

Tails Out: The manner in which a reel-to-reel tape is stored, with the loose end at the end of the tape, requiring the tape to be removed before playing.

Time Reversion Clause: Contractual agreement in which a publisher agrees to secure recording and release for songwriter's material within a certain period of time. Failure to secure recording and release triggers reversion of the song rights to the writer.

Top 40: Radio station format where records played are only those contained in lists of the best-selling records.

Top 100: Lists published in the trades of the top-selling singles for a particular market.

Track: One of the several components of special recording tape that contains recorded sounds, which is mixed with the other tracks for a finished recording of the song; the recording of all the instruments or vocals of a particular music section; music and/or voices previously recorded.

Trades: Music industry publications, i.e., Billboard, Pollstar, Variety, Hollywood.

Union Scale: Minimum wage scale earned in employment by members of AFTRA, AF of M, SAG, etc.

Verse: The selection of a song that precedes the chorus or is the A section in AABA pattern songs.

Writer's Signature: Unique style of the writer.

& GUESTS
Mark Morris' L'Allegro,
il Penseroso ed il Moderato
Poems (1974-2000)
UNION SQUARE · 2:00 - 3:00 PM

26 · monday

**A CELEBRATION of
TENNESSEE WILLIAMS
featuring MEL GUSSOW,
CHERRY JONES
& LAILA ROBINS**
Collected Plays of
Tennessee Williams, Vols. 1 & 2
LINCOLN TRIANGLE · 7:00 - 8:00 PM

NINA BERNSTEIN
The Lost Children of Wilder:
The Epic Struggle to Change
Foster Care
UPPER WEST SIDE · 7:30 - 8:30 PM

27 · tuesday

BIBA CAGGIANO
Biba's Taste of Italy
LINCOLN TRIANGLE · 7:00 - 8:00 PM

28 · wednesday

CAROLE WILBOURN
The Total Cat
CITICORP · 6:30 - 7:30 PM

AUGUST WILSON
King Hedley II
LINCOLN TRIANGLE · 7:00 - 8:00 PM

ELISSA SCHAPPELL
Use Me
PARK SLOPE · 7:30 - 8:30 PM

**CHRISTIANE
NORTHRUP, M.D.**
The Wisdom of Menopause

PETER BALAKIAN
June-tree: New and Selected
Poems (1974-2000)
ASTOR PLACE · 7:30 - 8:30 PM

JOHN BANVILLE
Eclipse
CHELSEA · 7:30 - 8:30 PM

DOROTHY GALLAGHER
How I Came Into My Inheritance
and Other True Stories
LINCOLN TRIANGLE · 7:00 - 8:00 PM

CHRISTIANE BIRD
Neither East Nor West:
One Woman's Journey through the
Islamic Republic of Iran
UPPER EAST SIDE · 7:30 - 8:30 PM

ANDREI CHERNY
The Next Deal:
The Future of Public Life
in the Information Age
UPPER WEST SIDE · 7:30 - 8:30 PM

20 · tuesday

LOUISA ERMELINO
The Black Madonna
ASTOR PLACE · 7:30 - 8:30 PM

PAUL LEVINSON
Borrowed Tides
CITICORP · 6:30 - 7:30 PM

CAST DISCUSSION
The Rocky Horror Show
LINCOLN TRIANGLE · 6:00 - 7:00 PM

**AYANA D. BYRD
& LORI L. THARPS**
Hair Story:
Untangling the Roots of Black
Hair in America
PARK SLOPE · 7:30 - 8:30 PM

Breaking in to the Music
Business

- Siegel, Alan

$14 Paper

Appendix C

Suggested Reading Materials

Baskerville, David, Ph.D. *The Music Business Handbook and Career Guide*. Los Angeles/Denver: The Sherwood Company, NA.

Biederman, Donald E. *Law and Business of the Entertainment Industries*. New York: Prager Publishers, 1992. (Revised Edition)

Brabec, Jeffrey & Todd. *Music, Money, and Success*. New York: MacMillan Publishing Company, 1994.

Braheny, John. *The Craft and Business of Songwriting*. Ohio: Writer's Digest Books, 1987.

Brillstein, Bernie. *Where Did I Go Right?: You're no one in Hollywood unless someone wants you dead*. New York: Little, Brown, 1999.

Burton, Gary. *A Musician's Guide to the Road*. New York: Billboard, 1981.

Carter, Walter. *The Songwriter's Guide to Collaboration*. Ohio: Writer's Digest Books, 1988.

Citron, Stephen. *Songwriting*. New York: Limelight Editions, 1992. (Revised Edition)

Dannen, Frederic. *Hit Men: Power Brokers & Fast Money Inside the Music Business*. Vintage Books, 1991.

Davis, Sheila. *The Craft of Lyric Writing*. Ohio: Writer's Digest Books, 1985.

Eisner, Michael. *Work in Progress*. New York: Random House, 1998.

Frascogna, Xavier M., Jr. & Hetherington, H. Lee. *Successful Artist Management*. New York: Watson-Guptill Publications, NA.

Gates, Bill. *Business @ The Speed of Thought: Using a Digital*. New York: Warner Books, 1999.

Gillette, Steve. *Songwriting: The Creative Process*. Pennsylvania: Sing Out Corporation, 1995.

Goldstein, Jeri. *How To Be Your Own Booking Agent, and Save Thousands of Dollars*. The New Music Times, Inc., 1998.

Hamm, Charles. *Music In the New World*. New York/London: W.W. Norton and Company, NA.

Iacocca, Lee. *Iacocca: An Autobiography*. New York: Bantam Books, 1984.

Krasilovksy, William M. & Shemel, Sidney. *This Business of Music*. New York: Billboard, 1995.

Lathrop, Tad & Pettigrew, Jim, Jr. *Music Marketing and Promotion*. New York: Billboard, 1999.

Lawhon, John F. *The Selling Bible*. Tulsa: J. Franklin Publishers, Inc., 1995.

Lawhon, John F. *Selling Retail*. Tulsa: J. Franklin Publishers, Inc., 1986.

Ligget, Mark and Cathy. *Songwriting: An Insider's Guide to Making it in the Music Industry*. New York: Plume, 1985.

Martin, George. *Making Music*. New York: Quill, NA.

McDougal, Dennis. *The Last Mogul: Lew Wasserman, MCA, and the Hidden History of Hollywood*. Crown Publishing, 1998.

Monaco, Bob & Riordan, James. *The Platinum Rainbow*. California: Swordsman Press, 1980.

Passman, Donald S. *All You Need To Know About The Music Business*. New York: Simon & Schuster, 1994. (Revised Edition)

Rachlin, Harvey. *The Songwriter's Handbook*. New York: Funk & Wagnalls, 1977.

Rapaport, Diane Sward. *How To Make & Sell Your Own Recording*. New Jersey: Prentice Hall, 1999. (Revised 5th Edition)

Rose, Frank. *The Agency: William Morris and the Hidden History of Show Business*. New York: Harper Collins, 1995.

Sanjek, Russell. *Pennies from Heaven: The American Popular Music Business in the Twentieth Century*. New York: Da Capo Press, 1996.

Shemel, Sidney & Krasilovsky, M. Williams. *This Business of Music*. New York: Billboard Publications, 1995. (Revised Edition)

Shemel, Sidney & Krasilovsky, M. Williams. *More About This Business of Music*. New York: Billboard Publications, 1982.

Siegel, Alan H. *Breaking into the Music Business*. New York: Fireside, 1990.

Slater, Robert. *Ovitz*. New York: McGraw Hill, 1997.

Sugarman, Joseph. *Advertising Secrets of the Written Word: The Ultimate Resource on How to Write Powerful Advertising Copy from One of America's Top Copywriters and Mail Order Entrepreneurs*. Las Vegas: DelStar Publishing, 1998.

Sugarman, Joseph. *Marketing Secrets of a Mail Order Maverick: Stories & Lessons on the Power of Direct Marketing to Start a Successful Business and Create a Famous Brand*. Las Vegas: DelStar Publishing, 1998.

Sugarman, Joseph. *Television Secrets for Marketing Success: How to Sell Your Product on Infomercials, Home Shopping Channels & Spot TV Commercials from the Entrepreneur Who Gave You BluBlocker Sunglasses*. Las Vegas: DelStar Publishing, 1998.

Wacholitz, Larry E. *Inside Country Music*. New York: Billboard Publications, NA.

Whaley, Julie Wesling. *1987 Songwriter's Market: Where and How to Market Your Songs*. Ohio: F&W Publications, NA.

Williams, Roy H.. *The Wizard of Ads: Turning Words Into Magic and Dreamers into Millionaires*. Austin: Bard Press, 1998.

Wolf, Michael J. *The Entertainment Economy*. New York: Random House, 1999.

Zyman, Sergio. *The End of Marketing As We Know It*. New York: Harper Collins, 1999.

55 Publications

1. Acoustic Guitar
P.O. Box 767
San Anslemo, CA 94979
(415) 485-6946
(415) 485-0831 fax
E-Mail: editors.ag@stringletter.com

2. Acoustic Musician
1065 River Rd.
New Market, VA 22844
(540) 740-4005
(540) 740-4006 fax
E-Mail: acoustic@shentel.net

3. Alternative Press
6516 Detroit Ave., #5
Cleveland, OH 44102
(216) 631-1510
(216) 631-1016 fax
E-Mail: cherry@altpress.com
Website: www.altpress.com

4. American Country
P.O. Box 68052
Grand Rapids, MI 49516
(616) 458-1011
(616) 458-2285 fax

5. Bass Player
411 Borel Ave., Ste. 100
San Mateo, CA 94402
(650) 358-9500
(650) 358-8278 fax
E-Mail: bassplayer@mfi.com
Website: www.bassplayer.com

6. The Beat
5015 Eagle Rock Blvd., #302
Los Angeles, CA 90041
(323) 257-2328 phone
E-Mail: getthebeat@aol.com

7. Big City Blues
P.O. Box 1805
Royal Oak, MI 48068
(313) 872-BLUES
(248) 543-9415 fax
E-Mail: BCityBlues@aol.com

8. Billboard
1515 Broadway, 14th Floor
New York, NY 10036
(212) 764-7300
(212) 536-5358 fax
Website: www.billboard.com

9. Bluegrass Unlimited
P.O. Box 111
Broad Run, VA 20137
(800) BLU-GRAS
(540) 341-0011 fax
E-Mail: info@bluegrassmusic.com
Website: www.bluegrassmusic.com

10. Boom!
2699 Collins Ave.
Miami Beach, FL 33140
(305) 532-8841
(305) 532-8864 fax
E-Mail: kike@boomonline.com
Website: www.boomonline.com

11. Circus
6 West 18th St.
New York, NY 10011
(212) 242-4902
(212) 242-5734 fax
E-Mail: circusrave@aol.com
Website: www.circusmagazine.com

12. CMJ Weekly
11 Middle Neck Rd.
Great Neck, NY 11021
(516) 466-1992
(516) 466-7159 fax
E-Mail: cmj@cmj.com

13. Contemporary Christian Music
107 Kenner Ave.
Nashville, TN 37205
(615) 386-3011
(615) 386-3380 fax
Website: www.ccmcom.com

14. Country Music
49 E. 21st St., 11th Fl.
New York, NY 10011
(212) 260-7210
(212) 260-7445 fax
E-Mail:
comments@countrymusicmag.com

15. DJ Times
25 Willowdale Ave.
Port Washington, NY 11050
(516) 767-2500
(516) 944-8372 fax
Website: www.djtimes.com

16. **Details**
632 Broadway, 12th Fl.
New York, NY 10012
(212) 598-3710
(212) 598-3774 fax
Website: www.condenast.com

17. **Down Beat**
102 N. Haven Rd.
Elmhurst, IL 60126
(630) 941-2030
(630) 941-3210 fax
E-Mail: downbeat@worldnet.att.net
Website: www.downbeatjazz.com

18. **Electronic Musician**
6400 Hollis St., #12
Emeryville, CA 94608
(510) 653-3307
(510) 653-5142 fax
E-Mail: girlabout@aol.com
Website: www.emusician.com

19. **Fiddler Magazine**
P.O. Box 125
Los Altos, CA 94023
(650) 948-4383 phone/fax
E-Mail: Fiddlemag@aol.com
Website: www.fiddle.com

20. **Gavin**
140 Second St.
San Francisco, CA 94105
(415) 495-1990
(415) 495-2580 fax
E-Mail: editorial@gavin.com
Website: www.gavin.com

21. **Gig Magazine**
460 Park Ave. S, 9th Fl.
New York, NY 10016
(212) 378-0400
(212) 378-2160 fax
E-Mail: Gigmag@psn.com
Website: www.gigmag.com

22. **Guitar Player**
411 Borel Ave., Ste. 100
San Mateo, CA 94402
(650) 358-9500
(650) 627-8701 fax

23. **Hits**
14958 Ventura Blvd.
Sherman Oaks, CA 91403
(818) 501-7900
(818) 789-0259 fax

24. **Home Recording**
6 E. 32nd St., 11th Fl.
New York, NY 10016
(212) 561-3026
(212) 251-0840 fax
E-Mail: homerecmag@aol.com

25. **Jazz Times**
8737 Colesville Rd.
Silver Spring, MD 20910
(301) 588-4114
(301) 588-5531 fax
E-Mail: jazztimes@aol.com
Website: www.jazztimes.com

26. **Latin Beat Magazine**
15900 Crenshaw Blvd., Ste. 1-223
Gardena, CA 90249
(310) 516-6767
(310) 516-9916 fax
E-Mail: LBMAG@aol.com

27. **Magnet**
1218 Chestnut Rd.
Philadelphia, PA 19107
(215) 413-8570
(215) 413-8569 fax
E-Mail: magnetmag@aol.com

28. **Modern Drummer**
12 Old Bridge Rd.
Cedar Ridge, NJ 07009
(973) 239-4140
(973) 239-7139 fax
Website: www.moderndrummer.com

29. **Music Biz Magazine**
1745 Jefferson Davis Hwy.
Arlington, VA 22202
(703) 416-5664
(703) 416-4675 fax
E-Mail: jeff.cohen@musebiz.com
Website: www.musebiz.com

30. **Music Connection**
4731 Laurel Canyon Blvd.
N. Hollywood, CA 91607
(818) 755-0101
(818) 755-0102 fax
E-Mail: musecon@earthlink.net
Website: www.musicconnection.com

31. **Music Reviews**
1514 Wealthy St.
Grand Rapids, MI 49506
(616) 458-1011
(616) 458-2285 fax
E-Mail: wvster69@aol.com

32. **Music Row**
1231 17th Ave. South
Nashville, TN 37212
(615) 321-3617
(615) 329-0852 fax
E-Mail: news@MusicRow.com
Website: www.countrycool.com

33. **New Age Voice**
52 Executive Park S.
Atlanta, GA 30329
(404) 636-9040

(404) 636-5051 fax
E-Mail: editor@newagevoice.com
Website: www.newagevoice.com

34. **Paper**
365 Broadway, 6th Fl.
New York, NY 10013
(212) 226-4405
(212) 226-5929 fax
E-Mail: chrism@papermag.com

35. **Planet Jazz**
1 Westmount Sq.
Montreal, Quebec H3Z 2P9
(514) 485-7746 phone/fax

36. **POPsmear**
50 W. 23rd St., 6th Fl.
New York, NY 10010
(212) 328-2212
(212) 328-2213 fax
E-Mail: contact@popsmear.com
Website: www.popsmear.com

37. **Pulse!**
2500 Del Monte St.
West Sacramento, CA 95691
(916) 373-2450
(916) 373-2480 fax
E-Mail: pulsemag@aol.com
Webstie: www.towerrecords.com

38. **Rap Pages**
8484 Wilshire Ste. 900
Beverly Hills, CA 90211
(323) 651-5400
(323) 655-2339 fax
E-Mail: rapbag@lfp.com
Website: www.rappages.com

39. **Real Blues**
302-655 Herald St.
Victoria, BC V8W 3L6
(250) 384-2088 phone
E-Mail: rblues@ampsc.com
Website: www.realbluesmagazine.com

40. **Rhythm**
928 Broadway
New York, NY 10010
(212) 253-8872
(212) 253-8892 fax
Website: www.rhythmmusic.com

41. **Rhythm and News Magazine**
P.O. Box 678
Wappingers Fall, NY 112590
(914) 691-9505 phone/fax
E-Mail:
webmistress@rhythmandnews.com
Website: www.rhythmandnews.com

42. **Rockrgrl Magazine**
7683 SE 27th St., #317
Mercer Island, WA 98040
(206) 230-4280
(206) 230-4288 fax
E-Mail: rockrgrl@aol.com
Website: www.rockrgrl.com

43. **Rolling Stone**
1290 6th Ave.
New York, NY 10104
(212) 484-1616 phone

44. **Rude International**
P.O. Box 1302
Cambridge, MA 02139
(617) 267-2360 phone
E-Mail: rude@rudeinternational.com
Website: www.rudeinternational.com

45. **Sing Out!**
P.O. Box 5460
Bethlehem, PA 18015
(610) 865-5366
(610) 865-5129 fax
E-Mail: info@singout.org
Website: www.singout.org

46. **Smug Magazine**
511 Canal St., 2nd Fl.
New York, NY 10013
(212) 219-7624
(212) 219-7627 fax
E-Mail: smugnyc@aol.com
Website: www.smugmagazine.com

47. **The Source**
215 Park Ave. S, 11th Fl.
New York, NY 10003
(212) 253-3700
(212) 253-9343 fax
Website: www.thesource.com

48. **Spin Magazine**
205 Lexington Ave.
New York, NY 10016
(212) 231-7400
(212) 231-7300 fax
E-Mail: whemes@spinmag.com
Website: www.spin.com

49. **Trace**
476 Broome St.
New York, NY 10013
(212) 625-1192
(212)(265-1195 fax
E-Mail: jon@tracemag.com
Website: www.tracemag.com

50. **Vibe**
215 Lexington Ave.
New York, NY 10016
(212) 448-7300
(212) 448-7430 fax
E-Mail: sjenkins@vibe.com

51. **Country Weekly, Inc.**
118 16th Ave. South
Nashville, TN 37203
(615) 259-1111

52. **Amusement Business**
BPI Communications, Inc.
1515 Broadway
New York City, NY 10036
(212) 764-7300
(212) 382-6001 fax
Website:
www.amusementbusiness.com

53. **Pollstar**
4679 W. Jacquelyn Ave.
Fresno, CA 93722-6413
800-344-7383
(559) 271-7900
(559) 271-7979 fax
E-mail: info@pollstar.com

54. **Variety**
5700 Wilshire Blvd. Suite 120
Los Angeles, CA 90036
(323) 857-6600
(323) 857-0494 fax
Website: www.variety.com

55. **The Hollywood Reporter**
5055 Wilshire Blvd. 6th Floor
Los Angeles, CA 90036
(323) 525-2000

100 Radio Stations with Local Talent Shows

1. **WJAB 90.9 FM**
P.O. Box 1687
Normal, AL 35762
(256) 858-4051
(256) 851-5907 fax
E-Mail: mburns@aamu.edu
Website: www.wjab.aamu.edu

2. **WRAX 107.7 FM**
244 Goodwin Crest Dr., Ste. 300
Birmingham, AL 35209
(205) 945-4646
(205) 942-3175 fax
E-Mail: suzy@wraxfm.com
Website: www.wraxfm.com

3. **KDKB 93.3 FM**
1167 W. Javelina Ave.
Mesa, AZ 85210
(480) 897-9300
(480) 491-8482 fax
E-Mail: rock@kdbd.com
Website: www.kdbd.com

4. **KEDJ 106.3 FM**
4745 N. 7th St., Ste. 410
Phoenix, AZ 85014
(602) 266-1360
(602) 263-4844 fax
Website: www.kedj.com

5. **KUAF 91.3 FM**
U of Arkansas
747 W. Dickson, #2
Fayetteville, AR 72701
(501) 575-2556
(501) 575-8440 fax
E-Mail: kuafinfo@comp.uark.edu
Website: www.kuaf.com

6. **KABF 88.3 FM**
2101 S. Main St.
Little Rock, AR 72206
(501) 372-6119
(501) 376-3952 fax
E-Mail: kabf@igc.rog
Website: www.kabf.aristotle.net

7. **KCXX 103.9 FM**
740 W. 4th St.
San Bernardino, CA 92410
(909) 384-139
(909) 888-7302 fax
E-Mail: x1039@local.net
Website: www.x1039.com

8. **KIOZ 105.3 FM**
5745 Kearney Villa Rd., Ste. M
San Diego, CA 92123
(619) 565-36006
(619) 560-0742 fax
Website: www.rock1053.com

9. **KCME 88.7 FM**
1921 N. Weber St.
Colorado Springs, CO 80907
(719) 578-5263
(719) 578-1033 fax
E-Mail: kcmeinfo@oldcolo.org
Website: www.kcme.org

10. **KTCL 93.3 FM**
Clear Channel
1380 Lawrence St.
Denver, CO 80204
(303) 893-3699
(303) 534-7625 fax
Website: www.ktcl.com

11. **WKZE 98.1 FM/1020 AM**
67 Main St, Box 1020
Sharon, CT 06069
(860) 364-5800
(860) 364-0129 fax
E-Mail: wkze@snet.net

12. **WAPJ 89.9 FM**
UCONN-Torrington
855 University Dr.
Torrington, CT 06790
(860) 622-6813
(860) 626-6847 fax

13. **WMPH 91.7 FM**
5201 Washington St.
Wilmington, DE 19809
(302) 762-7199
(302) 762-7042 fax
E-Mail: radio@wmph.org
Website: www.wmph.org

14. **WSTW 93.7 FM**
P.O. Box 7492
Wilmington, DE 19803
(302) 478-2700
(302) 478-0100 fax
E-Mail: wstw@aol.com
Website: www.wstw.dpnet.net

15. **WAUR 96.3 FM**
529 Bryant St., NW
Washington, D.C. 20059
(202) 806-3500
(202) 806-3549 fax

16. **WPFW 89.3 FM**
2390 Champlain St., NW
Washington, D.C. 20009
(202) 588-0999
(202) 588-0561 fax
E-Mail: louhankins@aol.com

17. **WDNA 88.9 FM**
4848 SW 74th Ct.
Miami, FL 33155
(305) 662-8889
(305) 662-1975 fax
E-Mail: wdna@paradise.net
Website: www.wdna.org

18. **WFIT 89.5 FM**
150 W. University Blvd.
Melbourne, FL 32901
(407) 674-8950 phone
E-Mail: wfit@iu.net

19. **WPUP 103.7 FM**
1010 Tower Pl.
Bogart, GA 30622
(706) 549-6222
(706) 353-1967 fax
E-Mail: rock1037@aol.com
Website: www.rock1037.com

20. **WNNX 99.7 FM**
3405 Piedmont Rd
Atlanta, GA 30305
(404) 266-0997
(404) 364-5855 fax
Website: www.99x.com

21. **KBSU 90.3 FM/730 AM**
Boise State U
1910 University Dr.
Boise, ID 83725
(208) 426-3663
(208) 344-6631 fax
Website: www.boisestate.edu/bsuradio

22. **KECH 95.3 FM**
P.O. Box 2158
Ketchum, ID 83340
(208) 726-5324
(208) 726-5459 fax
Website: www.kech.com

23. **WEFT 90.1 FM**
113 N. Market St.
Champaign, IL 61820
(217) 359-9338 phone
E-Mail: weft@prairenet.org
Website: www.prairienet.org/weft

24. **WGCI 107.5 FM**
332 S. Michigan Ave.
Chicago, IL 60604
(312) 427-4800
(312) 322-3032 fax

25. **WJAA 96.3 Fm**
1531 W. Tipton
Seymour, IN 47274
(812) 523-3343
(812) 523-5116 fax
E-Mail: wjaa@compuage.com

26. **WRZX 103.3**
6161 Fall Creek Rd.
Indianapolis, IN 46220
(317) 257-7565
(317) 253-6501 fax
Website: www.wrzx.com/x103

27. **KWIT 90.3 FM**
4647 Stone Ave.
Sioux City, IA 51106
(712) 274-6406
(712) 274-6411 fax
Website: www.kwit.org

28. **WOI 90.1 FM**
Iowa State U
Communications Bldg.
Ames, IA 50011
(515) 294-2025 phone
E-Mail: woi@iastate.edu
Website: www.iastate.edu/~woi

29. **KLZR 105.9 FM**
3125 W. 6th St.
Lawrence, KS 66049
(785) 843-1320
(785) 841-5924 fax
E-Mail: dodger@lazer.com
Website: www.lazer.com

30. **KFDI 101.3/1070 Am**
P.O. Box 1402
Wichita, KS 67201
(316) 838-9141
(316) 838-3607 fax
Website: www.kfdi.com

31. **WKQQ 100.1 FM**
1498 Trade Center Dr.
Lexington, KY 40509
(606) 252-6694
(606) 255-0981 fax
Website: www.kqq.com

32. **WFPK 91.9 FM**
301 York St.
Louisville, KY 40203
(502) 574-1640
(502) 574-1671 fax
Website: www.wfpk.org

33. **WBRH 90.3 FM**
2825 Government St.
Baton Rouge, LA 70806
(225) 388-9030
(225) 379-7685 fax

34. **WWOZ 90.7 FM**
P.O. Box 51840
New Orleans, LA 70151
(504) 568-1238
(504) 568-9267 fax
Website: www.wwoz.org

35. **WCDQ 92.1 FM**
P.O. Box 631
Sanford, ME 04073
(207) 324-7271
(207) 324-2464 fax
E-Mail: wcdq@wcdq.com

36. **WCLZ 98.9 FM**
1 City Ctr.
Portland, ME 04104
(207) 773-2504
(207) 773-2703 fax
E-Mail: wclz@wclz.com

37. **WIYY 97.9 FM**
3800 Hooper Ave.
Baltimore, MD 21211
(410) 889-0098
(410) 467-FAX1
Website: www.98online.com

38. **WRNR 103.1 FM**
112 Main St., 3rd Fl.
Annapolis, MD 21401
(410) 626-0103
(410) 267-7634 fax
E-Mail: info@wrnr.com
Website: www.wrnr.com

39. **WAAF 107.3 FM**
200 Fiberg Pkwy., Ste. 4000
Westboro, MA 01581
(508) 836-9223
(503) 366-0745 fax
Website: www.waaf.com

40. **WHMP 99.3 FM**
P.O. Box 268
Northampton, MA 01061
(413) 586-7400
(413) 585-0927 fax

41. **CIMX 88.7 FM**
30100 Telegraph Rd
Bingham Farms, MI 48025
(313) 961-9811
(313) 961-1603 fax
Website: www.89xradio.com

42. **WDET 101.9 FM**
Wayne State U
4600 Cass Ave.
Detroit, MI 48201
(313) 577-4146
(313) 577-1300 fax
E-Mail: wdetfm@wdet.org
Website: www.wdet.org

43. **KFAI 90.3/106.7 FM**
1808 Riverside Ave.
Minneapolis, MN 55454
(612) 341-3144
(612) 341-4281 fax
E-Mail: music@kfai.org
Website: www.kfai.org

44. **KMSU 89.7 FM**
Mankato State U
DMSU MSU 153, Box 8400
Mankato, MN 56002-8400
(507) 389-5678
(507) 389-1705 fax
E-Mail: kmsu@ms1.mankato.msus.edu

45. **WJSU 88.5 FM**
P.O. Box 18450
Jackson, MS 39217
(601) 968-2140
(601) 968-2878 fax
Website: www.jsums.edu

46. **WSTZ 106.7 FM**
1375 Beasley Rd.
Jackson, MS 39206
(601) 982-1062

(601) 9362-8270 fax
Website: www.z106.com

47. **KKFI 90.1 FM**
P.O. Box 32250
Kansas City, MO 64171
(816) 931-3122
(816) 931-7078 fax
E-Mail: kkfi@aol.com
Website: www.gazlam.com/kkfi

48. **KDHX 88.1 FM**
3504 Magnolia
St. Louis, MO 63118
(314) 664-3955
(314) 664-1020 fax
Website: www.kdhx.org

49. **KGPR 89.9 FM**
Montana State U
2100 16th Ave. S.
P.O. Box 6010
Great Falls, MT 59406
(406) 761-8292
(406) 761-8296 fax
E-Mail: kgpr@msugf.edu

50. **KZOQ 100.1 FM**
P.O. Box 4106
Missoula, MT 59806
(406) 728-5000
(406) 721-3020 fax
E-Mail: Z100@kzoq.com

51. **KEZO 92.3 FM**
11128 John Galt Blvd.
Omaha, NE 68137
(402) 592-5300
(402) 596-9428 fax
Website: www.z92.com

52. **KTNP 93.3 FM**
5010 Underwood Ave.
Omaha, NE 68132
(402) 561-2000
(402) 556-8937 fax
Website: www.thepoint933.com

53. **KXPT 97.1 FM**
4660 S. Decatur Blvd.
Las Vegas, NV 89103
(702) 876-1460
(702) 876-6685 fax
Website: www.point97.com

54. **KXTE 107.5 FM**
6655 W. Sahara Ave., #C-202
Las Vegas, NV 89146
(702) 257-1075
(702) 889-7595 fax
Website: www.kxte.com

55. **WGIR 101.1 FM**
P.O. Box 101
Manchester, NH 03105

(603) 625-6915
(603) 625-9255 fax

56. **WHEB 100.3 FM**
P.O. Box 120
Portsmouth, NH 03802
(603) 436-7300
(603) 430-9415 fax
Website: www.wheb.com

57. **WHTG 106.3 FM**
1129 Hope Rd.
Asbury Park, NJ 07712
(732) 493-2000
(732) 493-0813 fax
E-Mail: feedback@1063.com
Website: www.1063.com

58. **WDHA 105.5 FM**
55 Horsehill Rd.
Cedar Knolls, NJ 07927
(973) 455-1055
(973) 538-3060 fax
E-Mail: rock@wdhafm.com
Website: www.wdhafm.com

59. **KBAC 98.1 FM**
2021 Pinon St.
Santa Fe, NM 87505
(505) 989-3338
(505) 989-3881 fax
Website: www.kbac.com

60. **KTAO 101.5 FM**
P.O. Box 1844
Taos, NM 87571
(505) 758-5826
(505) 758-8430 fax
Website: www.ktao.com

61. **WBFO 88.7 FM**
U of Buffalo
3435 Main St.
Allen Hall, Rm. 205
Buffalo, NY 14214
(716) 829-6000
(716) 829-2277 fax
E-Mail: mail@wbfo.org
Website: www.wbfo.org

62. **WQBK 103.5/103.9 FM**
4 Central Ave.
Albany, NY 12210
(518) 462-5555
E-Mail: wqbk@wqbk.com
Website: www.wqbk.com

63. **WRDU 106.1 FM**
3100 Smoketree Ct.
Raleigh, NC 27604
(919) 876-1061
(919) 876-2929 fax
Website: www.rdu.citysearch.com

64. **WXRC 95.7 FM**
Box 940
Newton, NC 28658
(704) 322-9472
(828) 464-9662 fax
E-Mail: bestrock@957xrc.com
Website: www.957xrc.com

65. **KJKJ 107.5 FM**
505 University Ave.
Grand Forks, ND 58203
(701) 746-1417
(701) 746-1410 fax

66. **KQWB 98.7 FM**
2501 13th Ave. SW
Fargo, ND 58103
(701) 237-5500
(701) 237-5400 fax
Website: www.q98.com

67. **WOXY 97.7 FM**
5120 College
Corner Pike
Oxford, OH 45056
(513) 523-4114
(513) 523-1412 fax
E-Mail: woxy97x@fuse.net
Website: www.wxy.com

68. **WKSU 89.7 FM**
Kent State U
1613 E. Summit St., P.O. 5190
Kent, OH 44242
(330) 672-3114
(330) 672-4107 fax
E-Mail: blum@wksu.org
Website: www.ksu.org

69. **KATT 100.5 FM**
4045 NW 64
Oklahoma City, OK 73116
(405) 848-0100
(405) 848-1915 fax
E-Mail: jakedaniels@katt.com
Website: www.katt.com

70. **KSPI 93.7 FM**
P.O. Box 1269
Stillwater, OK 74076
(405) 372-7800
(405) 372-6969 fax
E-Mail: thespy@ionet.net
Website: www.kspi.com

71. **KLCC 89.7 FM**
4000 E. 30th Ave.
Eugene, OR 97405
(541) 726-2224
(541) 744-3962 fax
Website: www.klcc.org

72. **KINK 101.9 FM**
1501 SW Jefferson

Portland, OR 97201
(503) 226-5080
(503) 226-4578 fax
Website: www.kinkfm102.com

73. **WZZO 95.1 FM**
P.O. Box 9876
Allentown, PA 18105
(610) 434-1742 phone
E-Mail: wzzo@fast.net
Website: www.wzzo.com

74. **WPLY 100.3 FM**
1003 Baltimore Pike
Media, PA 19063
(610) 565-8900
(610) 565-5578 fax
Website: www.y100.com

75. **WTPA 93.5 FM**
P.O. Box 9350
Harrisburg, PA 17108
(717) 697-1141
E-Mail: radio935@935wtpa.com
Website: www.935wtpa.com

76. **WBRU 95.5 FM**
85 Benevolent St.
Providence, RI 02906
(401) 272-9550
(401) 272-9278 fax
Website: www.wbru.com

77. **WAVF 96.1 FM**
1964 Ashley River Rd.
Charleston, SC 29407
(843) 852-9003
(843) 852-9041 fax
E-Mail: comments@96wave.com
Website: www.96wave.com

78. **WTPT 93.3 FM**
223 W. Stone Ave.
Greenville, SC 29609
(864) 242-4660
(864) 271-5029 fax

79. **KDDX 103.1 FM**
2827 E. Colorado
Spearfish, SD 57783
(605) 341-6009
(605) 642-7849 fax

80. **KUSD 89.7 FM**
P.O. Box 5000
Vermillion, SD 57069
(605) 677-5861
(605) 677-5010
Website: www.sdpb.org

81. **WUTC 88.1 FM**
615 McCallie Ave.
Chattanooga, TN 37403
(423) 755-4756
(423) 755-4174

E-Mail: mark-colbert@upc.edu
Website: www.wutc.org

82. **KXHT 107.1 FM**
6080 Mt. Moriah Rd.
Memphis, TN 38115
(901) 375-9324
(901) 375-5889 fax
E-Mail: leecagle@hot107.com
Website: www.hot107.com

83. **KAZI 88.7 FM**
8906 Wall St., Ste. 302
Austin, TX 78754
(512) 836-9544
(512) 836-1146 fax
Website: www.kazi.citysearch.com

84. **KDGE 94.5 FM**
15851 N. Dallas Pkwy.
Addison, TX 75001
(972) 770-7776
(972) 385-1211 fax
Website: www.kdge.com

85. **KPFT 90.1 FM**
419 Lovett Blvd.
Houston, TX 77006
(713) 526-4000
(713) 526-5750 fax
E-Mail: mary@kpft.org
Website: www.kpft.org

86. **KBZN 97.9 FM**
257 E. 200 South, Ste. 400
Salt Lake City, UT 84111
(801) 364-9836
(801) 364-8068 fax
E-Mail: breeze@kbzn.com
Website: www.kbzn.com

87. **KXRK 96.3 FM**
57 W. South Temple, #700
Salt Lake City, UT 84101
(801) 524-2600
(801) 521-9234 fax
Website: www.x96.com

88. **WNCS 104.7 FM**
P.O. Box 551
Montpilier, VT 05601
(802) 223-2396
(802) 223-1520 fax
E-Mail: pointfm@together.net
Website: www.pointfm.com

89. **WEQX 102.7 FM**
P.O. Box 1027
Manchester, VT 05254
(802) 362-4800
(802) 362-5555fax
Website: www.weqx.com

90. **WCDX 92.1 FM**
2809 Emerywood Pkwy, Ste. 300

Richmond, VA 23294
(804) 672-9299
(804) 672-9316 fax

91. **WROV 96.3 FM**
3807 Brandon Ave., Ste. 2350
Roanoke, VA 24018
(540) 725-1220 phone
Website: www.96-3rov.com

92. **WTJU 91.1 FM**
U of Virginia
711 Newcomb
Hall Station
Charlottesville, VA 22904
(804) 924-0885
(804) 924-8996 fax
E-Mail: wtju@virginia.edu
Website: wtju.radio.virginia.edu

93. **KMTT 103.7 FM**
1100 Olive Way, Ste. 1650
Seattle, WA 98101
(206) 233-1037
(206) 233-8979 fax
Website: www.kmtt.com

94. **KNDD 107.7 FM**
1100 Olive Way, Ste. 1550
Seattle, WA 98101
(206) 622-3251
(206) 682-8349 fax
Website: www.kndd.com

95. **KAEP 105.7 FM**
1601 E. 57th St.
Spokane, WA 99223
(509) 448-1000
(509) 448-7015 fax
Website: www.1057thespeak.com

96. **WVPN 88.5 FM**
600 Capital St.
Charleston, WV 25301
(304) 558-3000
(304) 558-4034 fax
E-Mail: wpvr@wvpubrad.org

97. **WMMM 105.5 FM**
7061 Ganser Way
Madison, WI 53719
(608) 826-0077
(608) 826-1245 fax
E-Mail: 1055triplem.com
Website: www.1055triplem.com

98. **WORT 89.9 FM**
118 S. Bedford St.
Madison, WI 53703
(608) 256-2001
(608) 256-3704 fax
E-Mail: wort@terracom.net
Website: www.netphoria.com/wort

99. KMTN 96.9 FM
P.O. Box 927
Jackson Hole, WY 83001
(307) 733-4500
(307) 733-7773 fax
E-Mail: kmtn@blissnet.com
Website: www.kmtnksgt.com

100. KUWR 91.9 FM
U of Wyoming
P.O. Box 3984
Laramie, WY 82071
(307) 766-4240
(307) 766-6184 fax
Website: www.uwyo.edu/wpr

26 Amusement Parks

1. **The Magic Kingdom at Walt Disney World**
P.O. Box 10040
Lake Buena Vista, FL 32830
(407) 824-4321 phone
E-Mail: wdw.guest.communications
@wda.disney.com

2. **Disneyland**
P.O. Box 3232
Anaheim, CA 92803
(714) 781-4560 phone
Website: www.disneyland.com

3. **Epcot Center at Walt Disney World**
P.O. Box 10040
Lake Buena Vista, FL 32830
(407) 824-4321 phone
E-Mail: wdw.guest.communications
@wda.disney.com

4. **Disney-MGM Studios at Walt Disney World**
P.O. Box 10040
Lake Buena Vista, FL 32830
(407) 824-4321 phone
E-Mail: wdw.guest.communications
@wda.disney.com

5. **Universal Studios Escape**
1000 Universal Studios Plaza
Orlando, FL 32819
(407) 363-8000 phone
Website: www.uescape.com

6. **Disney's Animal Kingdom at Walt Disney World**
P.O. Box 10040
Lake Buena Vista, FL 32830
(407) 824-4321 phone
E-Mail: wdw.guest.communications
@wda.disney.com

7. **Universal Studios Hollywood**
100 Universal City Plaza
Universal City, CA 91608
(818) 777-1000 phone

8. **Seaworld Florida**
7007 Sea Harbor Dr.
Orlando, FL 32821
(407) 363-2200
Website: www.seaworld.com

9. **Busch Gardens**
P.O. Box 9158
Tampa Bay, FL 33674
(813) 987-5212 phone
Website: www.buschgardens.com

10. **Seaworld California**
1720 S. Shores Rd.
San Diego, CA 92109
(619) 226-3845 phone
Website: www.seaworld.com

11. **Six Flags Great Adventure**
P.O. Box 120
Jackson, NJ 08527
(732) 928-1821
(732) 928-2775 fax

12. **Knott's Berry Farm**
8039 Beach Blvd.
Buena Park, CA 90620
(714) 220-5200 phone
Website: www.knotts.com

13. **Paramounts Kings Island**
P.O. Box 901
Kings Island. OH 45034
(513) 754-5700 phone
Website: www.pki.com

14. **Cedar Point**
1 Cedar Point Dr.
Sandusky, OH 44870-5259
(419) 627-2350 phone
Website: www.cedarpoint.com

15. **Six Flags Magic Mountain**
P.O. Box 5500
Valencia, CA 91385
(818) 992-0884 phone
Website: www.sixflags.com

16. **Santa Cruz Beach Boardwalk**
400 Beach St.
Santa Cruz, CA 95060
(831) 426-7433 phone
Website: www.beachboardwalk.com

17. **Six Flags Great America**
542 N. Route 21
Gurnee, IL 60031
(847) 249-1776 phone
Website: www.sixflags.com

18. **Six Flags Over Texas**
P.O. Box 99192
Arlington, TX 76199-0192
(817) 530-6000 phone
Website: www.sixflags.com

19. **Adventuredome at Circus Circus**
2880 Las Vegas Blvd. South
Las Vegas, NV 89109
(702) 734-0410 phone

20. **Six Flags Over Georgia**
P.O. Box 43187
Atlanta, GA 30378
(770) 739-3400 phone
Website: www.sixflags.com

21. **Knott's Camp Snoopy**
Mall of America
5000 Center Court
Bloomington, NJ 55425-5500
(612) 883-8600 phone
Website: www.campsnoopy.com

22. **Hershey Park**
100 W. Hershey Park Dr.
Hershey, PA 17033
(717) 534-3900 phone
Website: www.hersheypa.com

23. **Busch Garden The Old Country**
1 Busch Gardens Blvd.
Williamsburg, VA 23187-8785
(757) 253-3350 phone
Website: www.buschgardens.com

24. **Silver Dollar City**
HCl Box 791
Branson, MO 65616
(417) 338-2611 phone
Website: www.silverdollarcity.com

25. **Worlds of Fun**
4545 Worlds of Fun Ave.
Kansas City, MO 64161
(816) 454-4545
Website: www.worldsoffun.com

26. **Frontier City**
11501 NE Expressway
Oklahoma City, OK 73131
(405) 478-2412

50 Disc & Tape Manufacturers

1. **AAAA A/V Duplicators**
4609 N. 12th St.
Phoenix, AZ 85014
(800) 988-6424
(602) 212-1769 fax

E-Mail: sales@voiceconnection.com
Website: www.voiceconnection.com

2. **A&R Musician's Services**
2209 W. 1st St., Ste. 104
Tempe, AZ 85281
(888) 343-9359
(480) 303-9369 fax
E-Mail: claytonews@aol.com

3. **Abbey Tape Duplicators**
9525 Vassar Ave.
Chatsworth, CA 91311
(818) 882-5210
(818) 407-5900 fax
Website: www.abbeytape.com

4. **Aggressive Records Audio Duplication**
P.O. Box 6163
Minneapolis, MN 55104
(612) 645-7805
(612) 645-7805 fax
E-Mail: sales@aggressive.com

5. **Allied Digital Tech.**
13011 6th Ave., 14th Fl.
New York, NY 10019
(212) 757-6800
(212) 757-5230 fax
Website: www.allied-digital.com

4364 35th St.
Orlando, FL 32811
(407) 649-0008
(407) 649-9005 fax

11835 W. Olympic
Los Angeles, CA 90064
(310) 473-9253
(310) 473-9238 fax

6. **Alshire Int'l Inc.**
1015 Isabel St.
Burbank, CA 91506
(800) 423-2936
(818) 569-3718 fax
E-Mail: alshire@alshire.com
Website: www.alshire.com

7. **Artist Development Concepts**
983 Osos St.
San Luis Obispo, CA 93401
(805) 781-6886
(805) 781-6886 fax
E-Mail: ron@adc.cc
Website: www.adc.adc.cc

8. **ASI**
316 Newbury St., Ste. 32
Boston, MA 02115
(617) 424-0065
(617) 424-7253 fax
E-Mail: asidisc@xensei.com

9. **Atlanta Manufacturing Group**
83 Walton St., #202
Atlanta, GA 30303
(404) 230-9559
(404) 230-9558 fax
E-Mail: info@amgcds.com
Website: www.amgcds.com

10. **Audio Duplication and Services, Inc.**
3 Manor Lane
St. Louis, MO 63135
(314) 965-8895
(314) 909-1337 fax

11. **BMG Studios**
1540 Broadway
New York, NY 10036
(212) 930-4800
(212) 930-4679 fax

12. **Cassette Express**
116 17th Ave. South
Nashville, TN 37203
(615) 244-5667
(615) 242-2472 fax

13. **CDs For You**
816 Auto Mall Rd.
Bloomington, IN 47401
(800) 237-1811
E-Mail: cdsforyou@aol.com
Webstie: www.vivientertainment.com

14. **CD Labs, Inc.**
10643 Riverside Dr.
N. Hollywood, CA 91602
(818) 505-9581
(818) 985-7088 fax
E-Mail: cdlabs@earthlink.net
Website: www.cdlabs.com

15. **CD Man**
7791 Montcalm St.
Vancouver, BC V6P 4P1
(604) 261-8314
(604) 261-3313 fax
E-Mail: info@cdman.com
Website: www.cdman.com

16. **CDS**
634 W. Broadway
Glendale, CA 91204
(800) 599-9534
(818) 240-7927 fax
Website: www.cdsg.com

17. **CD Sonic**
273 Commonwealth Ave.
Boston, MA 02116
(888) CD-SONIC
(617) 424-0657 fax
E-Mail: cdsonic@cdsonic.com
Website: www.cdsonic.com

18. **CD Source**
327 W. Fayette St.
Syracuse, NY 13202
(305) 242-3656
(305) 242-1114 fax
E-Mail: tommy@cdsource.net
Website: www.cdsource.net

19. **Chicago Masterworks**
P.O. Box 1519
Crystal Lake, IL 60039
(800) 675-9454
(815) 356-9066 fax
E-Mail: cmasterw@aol.com

20. **Cinram, Inc.**
2153 Mass. Ave.
Cambridge, MA 02140
(617) 547-2828
(617) 547-2622 fax
E-Mail: jackiewhelan@cimram.com
Website: www.cimram.com

4905 Moores Mill Rd.
Huntsvill, AL 35811
(800) 433-3472
(256) 852-8706 fax

21. **Cleveland Data-Sound Solution**
9821 Olde Eight Rd., #1
Northfield Center, OH 44067
(330) 467-4100
(330) 467-4236 fax

22. **Color Film Corporation**
100 Maple Ave.
Stoneham, MA 02180
(781) 279-0080
(781) 438-7957 fax
Website: www.colorfilm.com

23. **Corporate Disk**
8212 Hwy. 33 E
Freehold, NJ 07728
(630) 616-0700
(630) 616-9171 fax

24. **Cosmo**
2633 S. King St., #103
Honolulu, HI 96826
(808) 949-2811
(808) 949-5998 fax
E-Mail: manager@cosmo-media.com
Website: www.cosmo-media.com

25. **Cravedog Records**
P.O. Box 1841
Portland, OR 97207
(503) 233-7284 phone
E-Mail: cravedog@teleport.com
Website: www.cravedog.com

26. **Creative Sound Corp.**
25429 Malibu Rd.
Malibu, CA 90265

(310) 456-5482
(310) 456-7886 fax
E-Mail: csound@csoundcorp.com
Website: www.csoundcorp.com

27. Crown Magnetics
1223 Bitter Blvd.
Lebanon, PA 17046
(800) 736-9001
(717) 274-3615 fax
Website: www.crownmagnetics.com

28. Crystal Clear Sound Audio Manufacturing
10486 Brockwood Rd.
Dallas, TX 75238
(800) 880-073
(214) 349-3819 fax
E-Mail: cdtape@crystalclearsound.com
Website: www.crystalclearsound.com

29. Cyberdisk Manufacturing
69 Brunswick Ave.
Moosup, CT 06354
(800) 894-3472
(860) 564-5654 fax
E-Mail: peter@wagarassoc.com

30. DB Plus Digital Services, Inc.
250 W. 57th St., #725
New York, NY 10107
(212) 397-4099
(212) 397-2207 fax
E-Mail: info@dbplus.com
Website: www.dbplus.com

31. DigiRom
130 W. 42nd St.
New York, NY 10036
(800) 815-3444
(212) 730-8820 fax

32. Disc Makers
3445 Cahuenga Blvd., W.
Los Angeles, CA 90068
(800) 731-8009
(323) 876-6724 fax
E-Mail: info@discmakers.com
Website: www.discmakers.com

7905 N. Rte. 130
Pennsauden, NJ 08110
(800) 468-9353
(856) 661-3450 fax

1219 Westlake Ave. North, Ste. 200
Seattle, WA 98109
(800) 553-8906
(206) 285-2394 fax

11 W. 17th St., 2nd Fl.
New York, NY 10011
(800) 446-3470
(212) 353-0573 fax

33. Disk Manufacturing
27 Copernicus Blvd., Unit 6
Brantford, ONT N3P IN4
(888) 256-DISC
(519) 756-8641 fax
Website: www.ballmedia.com

34. Disc Plus
11434 Ventura Blvd., #100
Studio City, CA 91604
(818) 761-8870
(818) 761-8877 fax

35. Disctronics
3800 Barham Blvd., Ste. 102
Los Angeles, CA 90068
(323) 851-7300
(323) 851-7579 fax

36. Doc Data California
8960 Eton Ave.
Canoga Park, CA 91304
(818) 341-1124
(818) 341-9131 fax
E-Mail: clara@docdata.com
Website: www.docdata.com

37. Dreams Factory
2246-F Dabney Rd.
Richmond, VA 23230
(804) 358-2828
(804) 358-4512 fax
Website: www.dreamsfactory.com

38. Duplication Factory
4275 Norey Dr.
Chaska, MN 55318
(612) 448-9912
(612) 448-3983 fax
Website: www.duplicationfactory.com

39. Earth Disc
5900 Wilshire Blvd., 26th Fl.
Los Angeles, CA 90036
(800) 876-5950
(323) 692-7840 fax

40. Eastco
3646 California Rd.
Orchard Park, NY 14127
(716) 662-0536
(716) 662-3360 fax
E-Mail: cservice@eastcopro.com

41. ESP
37 John Glenn Dr.
Buffalo, NY 14228
(716) 691-7631
(716) 691-7732 fax
E-Mail: espinc@localnet.com
Website: www.esplcd.com

42. Europa Disc
75 Varick St.
New York, NY 10013
(212) 226-4401
(212) 966-0456 fax
E-Mail: ron@europadisc.com
Website: www.europadisc.com

43. Fleetwood Multi-Media
31 Monroe St.
Lynn, MA 01901
(781) 559-2400
(800) 353-1830 fax
Website: www.fltwoodl.com

44. Frequency CD Manufacturing
PMB 535
1122 E. Pike St.
Seattle, WA 98122
(206) 624-4880
(206) 624-4879 fax
Website: www.frequencycd.com

45. Healey Disc Manufacturing, Inc.
75 Sherbourne St.
Toronto, ON M5A 2P9
(800) 835-1362
(416) 364-2650
E-Mail: 75healeydisc.com

46. Imperial Tape Co.
1928 14th St.
Santa Monica, CA 90404
(800) 736-8273
(310) 396-8894 fax
E-Mail: info@nutunes.com
Website: www.nutunes.com

47. Implosion Publishing
1921 E. Colonial Dr.
Orlando, FL 32803
(888) 323-5431
(407) 898-7565 fax
E-Mail: printing@implosion-mag.com
Website: www.implosionpublishing.com

48. Joe's Production & Grille
4919 N. Broadway, #22
Boulder, CO 80304
(800) 688-4212 phone
Website: www.joesgrille.com

49. JVC Disc America, Inc.
9255 Sunset Blvd., Ste. 717
Los Angeles, CA 90069
(310) 274-2221
(310) 274-4392
Website: www.jvcdiscusa.com

50. Kyric Corp.
1131 E. Locust St.
Ontario, CA 91761
(800) 221-0503

(909) 923-8867 fax
E-Mail: sales@kyric.com
Website: www.kyric.com

17 Workshops & Conferences

1. Association for Independent Music (AFIM)
147 E. Main St.
Whitesburg, KY 41858
(606) 633-0946
(606) 633-1160 fax
E-Mail: info@afim.org
Website: www.afim.org

2. Billboard & BET On Jazz Conference
1515 Broadway
New York, NY 10036
(212) 536-5002
(212) 536-1400 fax
E-Mail: mquigley@billboard.com
Website: www.billboard.com

3. Billboard Dance Music Summit
1515 Broadway
New York, NY 10036
(212) 536-5002
(212) 536-1400 fax
E-Mail: mquigley@billboard.com
Website: www.billboard.com

4. Billboard International Latin Music Conference & Awards
1515 Broadway
New York, NY 10036
(212) 536-5002
(212) 536-1400 fax
E-Mail: mquigley@billboard.com
Website: www.billboard.com

5. Canadian Music Week
P.O. Box 91015
666 Burnhamthorpe Rd.
Etobicoke, Ont. M9C 2Z0
(416) 695-9236
(416) 695-9239 fax
E-Mail: CMW@ican.net
Website: www.cmw.net

6. CMJ Music Marathon, Music Fest & Film Fest
11 Middleneck Rd.
Great Neck, NY 11021
(516) 466-6000
(516) 466-7159 fax
E-Mail: marathon@CMJ.com
Website: www.CMJ.com

7. **Emerging Artists & Talent in Music (EAT'M)**
2341-A Renaissance Dr.
Las Vegas, NV 89119
(702) 312-5881
(702) 792-5748 fax
E-Mail: LTenner@aol.com
Website: www.eat-m.com

8. **Gavin Seminar**
140 Second St.
San Francisco, CA 94105
(415) 495-1990
(415) 495-2580 fax
E-Mail: Gavin1@mail.gavin.com
Website: www.gavin.com

9. **Louisiana Music New Orleans Pride (LMNOP)**
P.O. Box 3469
New Orleans, LA 70177
(504) 592-9800
(504) 592-9809 fax
E-Mail: LMNOPinfo@aol.com
Website: www.offbeat.com/LMNOP

10. **Midem**
125 Park Ave. South
New York, NY 10017
(212) 689-4220
(212) 689-4348 fax
E-Mail: midem@aol.com
Website: www.midem.com

11. **NEMO**
Zero Governors Ave.
Medford, MA 02155
(718) 306-0441
(718) 306-0442 fax
E-Mail: Cavery@ultranet.com
Website: www.NEMO99.com

12. **North by North East (NXNE)**
189 Church St.
Toronto, Ont. M4K 1NZ
(416) 863-NXNE
(416) 469-0576 fax
E-Mail: inquire@NXNE.com
Website: www.NXNE.com

13. **North by North West (NXNW)**
P.O. Box 4999
Austin, TX 8765
(512) 467-7979
(512) 451-0754 fax
E-Mail: nxnw@nxnw.com
Website: www.nxnw.com

14. **South By South West (SXSW)**
P.O. Box 4999
Austin, TX 8765
(512) 467-7979
(512) 451-0754 fax

E-Mail: sxsw@sxsw.com
Website: www.sxsw.com

15. **Winter Music Conference**
3450 NE 12th Terrace
Ft. Lauderdale, FL 33334
(954) 563-4444
(954) 563) 6889 fax
E-Mail: wmcconfab@aol.com
Website: www.wmcon.com

16. **Country Radio Seminar**
819 18th Ave. South
Nashville, TN 37203
(615) 327-4487
(615) 329-4492 fax
E-mail: Info@CRB.org

17. **New Music West**
1376 Seymour Street
Vancouver, Canada V6B3P3
(604) 684-9338
Website: www.newmusicwest.com

52 Associations

1. **Academy of Country Music**
6255 Sunset Blvd., Ste. 923
Hollywood, CA 9028
(323) 462-2351
(323) 462-3253 fax
E-Mail: acmoffice@value.net
Website: www.acmcountry.com

2. **AES (Audio Engineering Society)**
60 E. 42nd St., Ste. 2520
New York, NY 10165
(212) 661-8528
(212) 682-0477 fax
Website: www.aes.org

3. **AFIM (Association For Independent Music)**
P.O. Box 988
Whitesburg, KY 41858
(606) 633-0946
(606) 633-1160 fax
E-Mail: info@afim.org
Website: www.afim.org

4. **AFTRA (American Federation of TV and Radio Artists)**
5757 Wilshire Blvd., 9th Fl.
Los Angeles, CA 90036-3689
(323) 634-8100
(323) 634-8147 fax
E-Mail: swhite@aftra.com
Website: www.aftra.com

5. **American Composers Forum**
332 Minnesota St., #E-145
St. Paul, MN 55101
(651) 228-1407
(651) 291-3497 fax
E-Mail: mail@composersforum.org
Website: www.composersforum.org

6. **American Disc Jockey Association**
10882 Demarr Rd.
White Plains, MD 20695
(301) 705-5150
(301) 843-7284 fax
Website: www.adja.org

7. **American Federation of Jazz Societies**
2787 Del Monte St.
West Sacramento, CA 95691
(916) 372-5277
(916) 372-3479 fax

8. **American Federation of Musicians**
1501 Broadway, Ste. 600
New York, NY 10036
(212) 869-1330
(212) 764-6134 fax
E-Mail: info@afm.org
Website: www.afm.org

9. **American Music Conference**
5790 Armada Dr.
Carlsbad, CA 92008
(760) 431-9124
(760) 438-7327 fax
E-Mail: patp@namm.com
Website: www.amc-music.com

10. **ASCAP (American Society of Composers, Authors and Publishers)**
One Lincoln Plaza
New York, NY 10023
(212) 621-6000
(212) 724-9064 fax
E-Mail: info@ascap.com
Website: www.ascap.com

7920 W. Sunset Blvd., 3rd Fl.
Los Angeles, CA 90046
(323) 883-1000
9323) 883-1049 fax

844 Alton Rd., Ste. 1
Miami Beach, FL 33139
(305) 673-3446
(305) 673-2446 fax

2 Music Square W.
Nashville, TN 37203
(615) 742-5000
(615) 742-5020 fax

1608 West Belmont Ave., Ste. 200
Chicago, IL 60657
(773) 472-1157
(773) 472-1158 fax

541-400 10th St. NW
Atlanta, GA 30318
(404) 753-4679
(404) 755-4373 fax

11. **Black Rock Coalition**
P.O. Box 1054, Cooper Station
New York, NY 10276
(212) 713-5097
E-Mail: brcny@aol.com

P.O. Box 329
6201 Sunset Blvd.
Hollywood, CA 90028
(213) 960-7730 phone

12. **The Blues Foundation**
49 Union Ave.
Memphis, TN 38103
(901) 527-2583
(901) 529-4030 fax
Website: www.blues.org

13. **Blues Music Association**
Box 3122
Memphis, TN 38173
(901) 572-3843 phone
Website:
www.BluesMusicAssociation.org

14. **BMI (Broadcast Music Inc.)**
320 W. 57th St.
New York, NY 10019
(212) 586-2000
(212) 246-2163 fax
E-Mail: newyork@bmi.com
Website: www.bmi.com

8730 Sunset Blvd.
Los Angeles, CA 90069
(310) 659-9109
(310) 657-6947 fax
E-Mail: losangeles@bmi.com

10 Music Square East
Nashville, TN 37203
(615) 401-2000
(615) 401-2707 fax
E-Mail: nashville@bmi.com

5201 Blue Lagoon Dr., Ste. 310
Miami, FL 33126
(305) 266-2442 phone/fax

P.O. Box 19199
Atlanta, GA 31126
(404) 261-5151 phone

15. **The City Limits**
P.O. Box 7261
Olympia, WA 98507

(360) 786-0783 phone
E-Mail: previous@olywa.net
Website: www.olywa.net/previous/

16. **Country Music Association**
One Music Circle S
Nashville, TN 37203
(615) 244-2840
(615) 726-0314 fax
E-Mail: cmac@cmaworld.com
Website: www.cmaworld.com

17. **Gospel Music Association**
1205 Division St.
Nashville, TN 37203
(615) 242-0303
(615) 254-9755 fax
E-Mail: gma@gospelmusic.org
Website: www.gospelmusic.com
and   : www.doveawards.com

18. **House Ear Institute**
2100 W. Third St.
Los Angeles, CA 90057
(213) 483-4431
(213) 483-8789 fax
E-Mail: webmaster@HEI.org
Website: www.HEI.org

19. **IBMA (International Bluegrass Music Association)**
207 E. 2nd St.
Owensboro, KY 42303
(270) 684-9025
(270) 686-7863 fax
E-Mail: ibma@ibma.org
Website: www.ibma.org

20. **IMF (International Manager's Forum)**
P.O. Box 1067
Los Angeles, CA 90078-1067
(323) 850-7463 phone/fax
E-Mail: inf_usa@hotmail.com
Website: www.imf-us.org

21. **International Entertainment Buyers Association**
P.O. Box 128376
Nashville, TN 37212
(615) 244-0628
(615) 244-6228 fax
E-Mail: info@ieba.org
Website: www.ieba.org

22. **International Fan Club Organization**
P.O. Box 40328
Nashville, TN 37204
(615) 371-9596
(615) 371-9597 fax
E-Mail: ifco@ifco.org
Website: www.ifco.org

23. **International Festivals and Events Association**
P.O. Box 2950
Port Angeles, WA 98362
(360) 457-3141
(360) 452-4695 fax
Website: www.ifea.com

24. **LARAS (Latin Academy of Recording Arts & Sciences)**
311 Lincoln Rd., #301
Miami Beach, FL 33139
(305) 672-0047
(305) 672-6846 fax
E-Mail: laras@grammy.com
Website: www.grammy.com

25. **Lifebeat - The Music Industry Fights AIDS**
72 Spring St., Ste. 1103
New York, NY 10012
(212) 965-8900
(212) 966-3910 fax
E-Mail: lbeat@aol.com

26. **MPGA (Music Publishers Guild of the Americas)**
216 N. Lucerne Blvd.
Hollywood, CA 90004
(323) 462-8850
(323) 462-1677 fax

27. **NACA (National Association for Campus Activities)**
13 Harbisen Way
Columbia, SC 29212
(803) 732-NACA
(803) 749-1047 fax
Website: www.naca.org

28. **NAMM (National Association of Music Merchants)**
5790 Armada Dr.
Carlsbad, CA 92008
(760) 438-8001
(760) 438-7327 fax
E-Mail: namm@namm.com
Website: www.namm.com

29. **NARAS (National Academy of Recording Arts and Sciences)**
3402 Pico Blvd.
Santa Monica, CA 90405
(310) 392-3777
(310) 392-9262 fax
Website: www.grammy.com

157 W. 57th St., Ste. 902
New York, NY 10019
(212) 245-5440
(212) 489-0394 fax

1904 Wedgewood Ave.
Nashville, TN 37212
(615) 327-8030
(615) 321-3101 fax

999 Peachtree St. NE, # 110
Atlanta, GA 30309
(404) 249-8881
(404) 249-8882 fax

29. **NARAS (National Academy of Recording Arts and Sciences) (cont.)**
168 Beale St., 2nd Floor
Memphis, TN 38103
(901) 525-1340
(901) 521-6553 fax

1702 Union St.
San Francisco, CA 94123
(415) 749-0779
(415) 749-1780 fax

224 S. Michigan Ave., # 250
Chicago, IL 60605
(312) 786-1121
(312) 786-1934 fax

260 S Broad St., # 205
Philadelphia, PA 19102
(215) 985-5411
(215) 985-5427 fax

7447 Bee Cave Rd., # 208
Austin, TX 78746
(512) 328-7997
(512) 328-7998 fax

311 Lincoln Rd., #301
Miami Beach, FL 33139
(305) 672-4060
(305) 672-2076 fax

3417 Freemont Ave. N, #225
Seattle, WA 98103
(206) 633-7833
(206) 633-7836 fax

30. **National Songwriters Association Interational**
1701 West End Ave., Ste. 300
Nashville, TN 37203
(615) 256-3354
(615) 256-0034 fax
E-Mail:
NSAI@nashvillesongwriters.com
Website:
www.nashvillesongwriters.com

31. **National Academy of Popular Music**
330 W. 58th St.
New York, NY 10019
(212) 957-9230

(212) 957-9227 fax
E-Mail: 7375.1142@compu-serve.com
Website: ww.songwritershalloffame.org

32. **National Music Council**
425 Park St.
Upper Montclair, NJ 07043
(973) 655-7974
(973) 655-5432 fax
E-Mail: Sandersd@montclair.edu
Website: www.musiccouncil.org

33. **National Music Publishers Association**
711 Third Ave.
New York, NY 10017
(212) 370-5330
(212) 953-2384
Website: www.nmpa.org

34. **National Traditional Country Music Association**
P.O. Box 492
Anita, IA 50020
(712) 784-3001 phone/fax

35. **Noise Action Coalition**
514 9th St.
Brooklyn, NY 11215
(212) 592-3677 phone
E-Mail: nac@webcom.com

36. **Percussive Arts Society**
701 NW Ferris Ave.
Lawton, OK 73507
(580) 353-1455
(580) 353-1456 fax
E-Mail: percarts@pas.org
Website: www.pas.org

37. **The Red Hot Organization**
73 Spring St., Ste. 602
New York, NY 10012
(212) 343-0043
(212) 343-0042 fax
E-Mail: seth@redhot.org
Website: www.redhot.org

38. **Reggae Ambassadors Worldwide**
1057 S. Denver St.
Salt Lake City, UT 84111
(801) 335-1405 phone
E-Mail: pilgrim@xmission.com
Website: www.reggaeambassadors.com

39. **Rhythm and Blues Foundation**
1555 Connecticut Ave. NW, Ste. 401
Washington, DC 20036
(202) 588-5566
(202) 588-5549 fax
E-Mail: ranb@aol.com
Website: www.rhythm-n-blues.org

40. **RIAA (Recording Industry Association of America)**
1330 Connecticut Ave. NW, Ste. 300
Washington, DC 20036
(202) 775-0101
(202) 775-7253 fax
Website: www.riaa.com

41. **Rock for Choice**
8105 W. 3rd St.
Los Angeles, CA 90048
(323) 651-0495
(323) 653-2689 fax
E-Mail: rfc@aol.com
Website: www.feminist.org

42. **Rock the Vote**
10950 Washington Blvd., Ste. 240
Culver City, CA 90232
(310) 237-2000
(310) 237-2001 fax
E-Mail: field@rockthevote.org
Website: www.rockthevote.org

43. **SESAC**
55 Music Squar East
Nashville, TN 37203
(615) 320-0055
(615) 321-6290 fax
Website: www.sesac.com

421 W. 54th St.
New York, NY 10019
(212) 586-3450
(212) 489-5699 fax

44. **The Songwriters Guild of America**
1500 Harbor Blvd.
Weehawken, NJ 07087
(201) 867-7603
(201) 867-7353 fax
Website: www.songwriters.org

6430 Sunset Blvd., Ste. 705
Hollywood, CA 90028
(323) 462-1108
(323) 462-5430 fax
E-Mail: lasga@aol.com

1560 Broadway
New York, NY 10036
(212) 768-7902
(212) 768-9048 fax
E-Mail: songnews@aol.com

1222 16th Ave. S
Nashville, TN 37212
(615) 329-1782
(615) 329-2623 fax
E-Mail: runsga@aol.com
Website: www.songwriters.org

45. **Soundscan**
1 N. Lexington Ave., 14th Fl.
White Plains, NY 10601
(914) 328-9100
(914) 328-0234 fax
E-Mail: trudy@soundscan.com

46. **Street Arts Advocates**
P.O. Box 380570
Cambridge, MA 02238
(617) 522-3407 phone/fax
E-Mail: shbaird@world.std.com

47. **Sweet Relief Musicians Fund**
P.O. Box 39666
Los Angeles, CA 90039
(888) 955-7880
(323) 662-7067 fax
E-Mail: info@sweetrelief.org
Website: www.sweetrelief.org

48. **Victory Music**
P.O. Box 2254
Tacoma, WA 98401
(253) 428-0832 phone
E-Mail: victory@nwlink.com
Website: www.victorymusic.org

49. **Women In Music**
P.O. Box 441 - Radio City Station
New York, NY 10101
(212) 459-4580 phone
Website: www.womeninmusic.com

50. **World Studio Group**
216 N. Lucerne Blvd.
Los Angeles, CA 90004
(323) 465-7697
(323) 465-7793 fax
Website: www.worldstudio.com

51. **FIDOF**
4230 Stansbury Ave. #105
Sherman Oaks, CA 91423
(818) 789-7596
(818) 784-9141 fax

52. **National Association of Recording Merchanisers**
9 Eves Dr., Suite 120
Marlton, NJ 08053
(609) 596-2221
Website: www.narm.com

27 Festivals

1. **American Music Festival**
   Beach Events
   305 Lynnhaven Pkwy.
   Virginia Beach, VA 23452
   (757) 463-1940
   (757) 463-3769 fax
   Website: www.beacheventsfun.com

2. **Ben and Jerry's Newport Folk Festival**
   Festival Productions
   311 W. 74th St.
   New York, NY 10023
   (212) 496-9000
   (212) 847-3700 fax
   Website: www.newportfolk.com

3. **Coors Light Jazz Festival**
   1821 Summit Rd., Ste. 417
   Cincinnati, OH 45237
   (513) 761-4600
   (513) 761-0600 fax

4. **Jimmie Rodgers Festival**
   P.O. Box 2170
   Meridian, MS 39302
   (800) 396-5882 phone
   Website: www.jimmierodgers.com

5. **JVC Jazz Festival Newport**
   Festival Productions
   311 W. 74ht St.
   New York, NY 10023
   (212) 496-9000
   Website: www.festivalproductions.net

6. **JVC Jazz Festival New York**
   Festival Productions
   311 W. 74th St.
   New York, NY 10023
   (212) 496-9000
   Website: www.festivalproductions.net

7. **Kerrville Folk Festival**
   P.O. Nbox 291466
   Kerville, TX 78029
   (800) 435-8429
   Website: www.kerrville-music.com

8. **Mamou Cajun Music Festival**
   1895 James Ortego Ln.
   Mamou, LA 70554
   (318) 468-2258

9. **Michigan Womyn's Music Festival**
   P.O. Box 22
   Walhalla, MI 49458
   (616) 898-3707
   (616) 898-3708 fax
   Website: www.michfest.com

10. **Mississippi Delta Blues and Heritage Festival**
    119 S. Theobald St.
    Greenville, MS 38701
    (601) 335-3523
    (601) 334-2939
    E-Mail: mace@tecinfo.com
    Website: www.deltablues.org

11. **Monterey Bay Blues Festival**
    P.O. Box 1400
    Seaside, CA 93955
    (831) 649-6544
    (831) 649-4124 fax
    Website: www.montereyblues.com

12. **Monterey Jazz Festival**
    P.O. Box JAZZ
    Monterey, CA 93942
    (831) 373-3366
    (831) 373-0244 fax
    E-Mail: jazzinfo@montereyjazzfest.com
    Website: www.montereyjazzfestival.org

13. **Montreux Atlanta Music Festival**
    Artist Submissions
    675 Ponce de Leon Ave., 5th Fl.
    Atlanta, GA 30308
    (404) 817-6851 phone
    Website: www.atlantafestivals.com

14. **Music Midtown**
    Atlanta Concerts
    3110 Roswell Rd.
    Atlanta, GA 30305
    (404) 233-8889
    (404) 233-8884 fax
    Website: www.musicmidtown.com

15. **National Fiddle Competition**
    Ozark Folk Center
    Box 500
    Mountain View, AR 72560
    (870) 269-3851
    (870) 269-2909 fax
    E-Mail: ofcmusic@mvtel.net
    Website: www.ozarkfolkcenter.com

16. **New Orleans Jazz and Heritage Festival**
    Music Production
    336 Camp St., Ste. 250
    New Orleans, LA 70130
    (504) 410-4100
    (504) 410-4123 fax
    Website: www.nojazzfest.com

17. **Newark Beats Festival**
    Urban Beats Project of New Jersey
    148 Chancellor Ave., Ste. C2
    Newark, NJ 07112
    (973) 923-8900

(973) 923-6190 fax
E-Mail: ubpnj@cs.com

18. **One World Music Festival**
P.O. Box 96
Placerville, CO 81430
(970) 728-1726
(970) 728-3032 fax
Website: www.oneworldfestival.com

19. **Phoenix Folk Traditions Music Festival**
Encanto Park
2700 N. 15th Ave
Phoenix, AZ 85007
(602) 261-8993
(602) 495-5557 fax

20. **San Francisco Blues Festival**
575 Hill St.
San Francisco, CA 94114
(415) 826-6837 phone
E-Mail: sfblues@earthlink.net
Website: www.sfblues.com

21. **Scott Joplin Ragtime Festival**
321 South Ohio
Sedalia, MO 65301
(660) 826-2271
(660) 826-5054 fax
Website: www.scottjoplin.org

22. **Southwest Louisiana Zydeco Music Festival**
328 Congress St.
Opelaousas, LA 70570
(318) 942-2392
(318) 942-9201 fax
E-Mail: sdf-opelousas@worldnet.att.net
Website: www.zydeco.org

23. **Telluride Jazz Celebration**
P.O. Box 727
Telluride, CO 81435
(970) 728-7009 phone
E-Mail: paul@telluridejazz.com
Website: www.telluridejazz.com

24. **W.C. Handy Blues and Barbecue Festival**
2961 US 41 N
Henderson, KY 42420
(270) 826-3128
(270) 826-0234 fax
Website: www.handyblues.org

25. **Woody Guthrie Free Folk Arts Festival**
P.O. Box 661
Okemah, OK 74859
(918) 825-5156
(918) 825-8203 fax
E-Mail: woody@galstar.com
Website: www.woodyguthrie.com

26. **Montreux Jazz Festival**
Fondation Du Festival De Jazz De Montreux
Sentier de Collonge 3
Case Postale 126
CH-1820 MONTREUX-TERRITET
+41 21 966 44 46
Website: www.montreuxjazz.com

27. **Neewollah Celebration**
P.O. Box 386
Independence, KS 67301
(316) 331-1890

43 Schools

1. **The Halsey Institute**
P.O. Box 52129
Tulsa, OK 74152
(918) 295-8113
(918) 295-7751 fax
E-Mail: info@halseyinstitute.com
Website: www.halseyinstitute.com

2. **Full Sail**
3300 University Blvd.
Winter Park, FL 32792
(800) 226-7625
(407) 678-0070 fax
E-Mail: admissions@fullsail.com
Website: www.fullsail.com

3. **Art Institute of Pittsburgh**
420 Boulevard of the Allies
Pittsburgh, PA 15219
(800) 275 2470
(412) 263-6600
(412) 263-6667 fax

4. **Berklee College of Music**
1140 Boylston
Boston, MA 02215
(617) 266-1400
(617) 536-2632 fax
Website: www.berklee.edu

5. **Brigham Young School of Music**
C-550 HFAC
Provo, UT 84602
(801) 378-3083
(801) 378-5973 fax
E-Mail: music@byu.edu
Website: www.byu.edu/muisc

6. **California Institute of the Arts**
24700 McBean Pkwy.
Valencia, CA 91355-2340
(805) 253-7816
(805) 255-0938 fax
E-Mail: info@music.calarts.edu
Website: www.music.calarts.edu

7. **California Recording Institute**
1137 Howard St.
San Francisco, CA 94103
(650) 324-0464
(650) 321-4772 fax
E-Mail: mixr@hooked.net
Website: www.californiarecording.com

8. **Conservatory of Recording Arts & Sciences**
2300 E. Broadway Rd.
Tempe, AZ 85282
(800) 562-6383
(602) 829-1332 fax
E-Mail: cras@amug.org

9. **Harris Institute for the Arts**
118 Sherbourne St.
Toronto, ON M5A 2R2
(416) 367-0178
(416) 367-5534 fax
E-Mail: harrisi@interlog.com

10. **Harrison Music**
5077 Lankersheim Blvd.
N. Hollywood, CA 91601
E-Mail: school@harrisonmusic.com
Website: www.harrison.com

11. **Humber College, Jazz Studies**
3199 Lakeshore Blvd. W.
Toronto, ON M8V 1K8
(416) 675-6622 phone

12. **Integrated Electronic Arts at Rensselaer**
1108 St.
Troy, NY 12180
(518) 276-4778
(518) 276-4780 fax
Website: www.arts.rpi.edu

13. **International College of Broadcasting**
6 S. Smithville Rd.
Dayton, OH 45431
(937) 258-8251
(937) 258-8251 fax
Website: www.icbroadcasting.com

14. **Los Angeles Music Academy**
370 S. Fair Oaks
Pasedena, CA 91105
(626) 568-8850
(626) 568-8854 fax
E-Mail:
104216.1751@compuserve.com
Website: www.lamusicacademy.com

15. **Los Angeles Recording Workshop**
5278 Lankersheim Blvd.
N. Hollywood, CA 91601
(818) 763-7400

(818) 763-7447 fax
E-Mail: larw@idt.net

16. **Manhattan School of Music**
120 Claremont Ave.
New York, NY 10027
(212) 749-2802 phone
Website: www.msmnyc.edu

17. **Mannes Jazz & Contemporary Music Program at the New School**
55 W 13th, 5th Fl.
New York, NY 10010
(212) 229-5896 ext.305
E-Mail: howell1@newschool.edu
Website: www.newschool.edu

18. **Middle Tennessee State University**
Department of Music
P.O. Box 47
Murfreesboro, TN 37132
(615) 898-2469
(615) 898-5037 fax
E-Mail: music@mtsu.edu
Website: www.mtsu.edu/~music

Department of Recording Industry
P.O. Box 21
Murfreesboro, TN 37132
(615) 898-2578
(615) 898-5682 fax
E-Mail: record@frank.mtsu.edu
Website: www.mtsu.edu/~record

19. **The Music School**
P.O. Box 603038
2 S. Angel St.
Providence, RI 02906
(401) 272-9877 phone

20. **Muscians Institute**
1655 McCadden Place
Hollywood, CA 90028
(800) 255-PLAY
Website: www.mi.edu

21. **Music Tech**
304 N. Washington Ave.
Minneapolis, MN 55401
(612) 338-0175
(612) 338-0804 fax
Website: www.musictech.com

22. **Musicians Institute**
1655 N. McCadden Place
Hollywood, CA 90028
(213) 462-1384
(213) 462-6978 fax
E-Mail: musicinst@earthlink.net
Website: www.mi.edu

23. **New England Conservatory**
290 Huntington Ave.

Boston, MA 02115
(617) 536-2412 ext.430
(617) 369-5644 fax
Website:
www.newenglandconservatory.edu

24. **NewYork Institute of Technology**
Communication Arts Department
P.O. Box 8000
Old Westbury, NY 11568
(516) 686-7553
(516) 686-7921 fax

25. **Old Towne School of Folk Music**
4544 N. Lincoln Ave.
Chicago, IL 60625
(773) 728-6000
(773) 728-6999 fax
Website: www.oldtowneschool.org

26. **Omega Studios School of Applied Recording Arts & Sciences**
5609 Fishers Lane
Rockville, MD 20852
(301) 230-9100
(301) 230-9103 fax
E-Mail: pete@omegastudios.com
Website: www.omegastudios.com

27. **Ontario Institute of Audio Recording Technology**
502 Newbold St.
London, ON N6E 1K6
(519) 686-5010
(519) 686-0162 fax
E-Mail: inquiry@oiart.org
Website: www.oiart.org

28. **Peabody Institute of the Johns Hopkins University**
1 E Mt. Vernon Pl., Ste. 216
Baltimore, MD 21202
(410) 659-8136
(410) 547-7908 fax
Website:
www.peabody.jhu.edu/recordingarts

29. **Princeton University Department of Music**
Woolworth Center of Musical Studies
Princeton, NJ 08544
(609) 258-4241
(609) 258-6793 fax
Website: www.music.princeton.edu

30. **Recording Arts Canada**
P.O. Box 11025
981 Highway B
Stoney Creek, ON L8E 5P9
(905) 662-2666
(905) 543-7520 fax
E-Mail: admissions@recordingarts.com
Website: www.recordingarts.com

31. **Recording Institute of Detroit**
14611 E. Nine Mile Rd.
Eastpointe, MI 48021
(800) 683-1743
(810) 772-4320 fax
Website: www.recording-institute.com

32. **The Recording Workshop**
455 Massieville Rd.
Chillicothe, OH 45601
(800) 848-9900
(740) 663-2427 fax
E-Mail: info@recordingworkshop.com
Website: www.recordingworkshop.com

33. **Sound Master Recording Engineer School, Audio/Video Institute**
10747 Magnolia Blvd.
N. Hollywood, CA 91601
(213) 650-8000
(818) 506-8926 fax

34. **Skidmore Jazz Institution**
815 N. Broadway
Sarasota Springs, NY 12866
(518) 580-5320
(518) 580-5340 fax
E-Mail: mmccoll@skidmore.edu

35. **Trebas Institute Career College**
305-112 E. 3rd Ave.
Vancouver, BC V5T 1C8
(604) 872-2666
(604) 872-301 fax
Website: www.trebas.com

410 Dundas St. E.
Toronto, ON M5A 2A8
E-Mail: trebasto@total.net

451 Saint Jean St.
Montreal, QC H2Y 2R5
(514) 845-4141
(514) 845-2581 fax
E-Mail: trebasmtl@total.net

36. **University of the Arts**
320 S. Broad St.
Philadelphia, PA 19102
(800) 616-ARTS
(215) 875-5458 fax
Website: www.uarts.com

37. **University of California at Berkley**
Department of Music
104 Morrison Hall
Berkeley, CA 94720
(510) 642-2678
(510) 642-8480 fax
Website:
www.is.berkeley.edu/dept/music

38. **University of Miami**
School of Music
P.O. Box 248165
Coral Gables, FL 33124
(305) 284-2245
(305) 284-6475 fax
Website: www.music.miami.edu

39. **University of Texas at Austin**
School of Music
25 Dean Keeton Dr.
Austin, TX 78712
(512) 471-7764 ext. 5505
(512) 471-2333 fax
Website: www.utexas.edu/cofa/music/

40. **University of Texas at San Antonio**
Department of Music
6900 N. Loop, 1604 W.
San Antonio, TX 78249
(210) 458-4354
(210) 458-4381 fax
E-Mail: dallan@lonestar.utsa.edu

41. **University of Wisconsin at Stevents Point**
Department of Music
UWSP
Stevens Point, WI 54481
(715) 346-3107
(715) 346-3163 fax
E-Mail: rkase@uwsp.edu
Website: www.uwsp.edu

42. **Virgina Tech**
Department of Music
Blacksburg, VA 24061
(540) 231-4719
(540) 231-5034 fax

43. **Liverpool Institute for Performing Arts**
Mount Street, Liverpool, L1 9HF
United Kingdom
+44 (0) 151 330 3000
+44 (0) 151 330 3131 fax
E-mail: reception@lipa.ac.uk
Website: www.lipa.ac.uk

102 Record Companies

1. **40 Acres & A Mule**
8 Saint Felix St. First Floor
Brooklyn, NY 11217
(718) 624-2901
Website: www.40acres.com

2. 550 Music
550 Madison Ave.
New York, MY 10022-3211

(212) 833-7442
Website: www.music.sony.com

2100 Colorado Ave.
Santa Monica, CA 90404

3. **A&M Records**
1416 North La Brea Ave.
Los Angeles, CA 90018
(213) 469-2411
Website: www.amrecords.com

825 Eighth Ave. 27th Floor
New York, NY 10019
(212) 333-1328

4. **All American Music**
808 Wilshire Blvd.
Santa Monica, CA 90401-1810
(310) 289-3080
Website: www.allamermusic.com

5. **Almo Sounds**
360 N. La Cienega Blvd.
Los Angeles, CA 90048
(310) 289-3080
Website: www.geffen.com/almo

1904 Adelicia Ave.
Nashville, TN 37212
(615) 321-0820

110 Greene St. Suite 801
New York, NY 10012
(212) 226-1000

6. **American Gramaphone**
9130 Mormon Bridge Rd.
Omaha, NE 68152
(402) 457-4341
Website: www.amgram.com

7. **Angel/EMI/Virgin**
810 Seventh Ave.
New York, NY 10019
(212) 603-8700
Website: www.emiclassics.com

8. **Ardent Records**
2000 Madison Ave.
Memphis, TN 38104-2794
(901)725-0855
Website:
www.wspice.com/ardent/ardent.html

9. **Arista Records**
6 West 57th St.
New York, NY 10019
(212) 489-7400
Website: www.aristarec.com

9975 Santa Monica Blvd.
Santa Monica, CA 90212
(310) 789-3900

10. **Arista Records Nashville**
7 Music Circle North

Nashville, TN 37203
(615) 780-9100
Website:
www.bmg.com/labels/arista.html

11. **Asylum Records**
1906 Acklen Ave.
Nashville, TN 37212
(615) 292-7990
Website: www.elektra.com

12. **Atlantic Classics**
1290 Avenue of the Americas
New York, NY 10104
(212) 707-2000
wesite:
www.atlantic-records.com

13. **Atlantic Records**
1290 Avenue of the Americas
New York, NY 10104
(212) 707-2000
Website:
www.atlantic-records.com

9229 Sunset Blvd.
Los Angeles, CA 90069
(310) 205-7475

14. **Atlantic Nashville**
1812 Broadway
Nashville, TN 37203
(615) 327-9394
Website:
www.atlantic-records.com

15. **Bar/None Records**
P.O. Box 1704
Hobokken, NJ 07030
(201) 795-5048
Website: www.bluenote.com

16. **BMG Entertainment**
1540 Broadway
New York, NY 10036
(212) 833-8000
Website: www.columbiarec.com

2100 Colorado Ave.
Santa Monica, CA 90404
(310) 449-2100

17. **BNA Records**
1 Music Circle North
Nashville, TN 37203-4310
(615) 780-4400
Website: www.twangthis.com

18. **Capitol Records**
1750 North Vine St.
Los Angeles, CA 90028
(213) 462-6252
Website: www.hollywoodandvine.com

1290 Avenue of the Americas 35th
Floor

New York, NY 10104
(212) 492-5300

19. **Capitol Nashville**
3322 West End Ave. 11th Floor
Nashville, TN 37203-1000
(615) 269-2000
Website: www.capitol-nashville.com

20. **Capricorn Records**
1100 Spring St. Suite 103
Atlanta, GA 30308
(404) 873-3918
Website: www.capri.corn.com

450 14th St. N.W. Suite 201
Atlanta, GA 30308
(404) 873-3918

21. **Children's Group**
1400 Bayly St. Suite 7
Pickering, ONT L1W 3R2
Canada
(905) 831-1995

22. **CMC International Records**
106 West Horton St.
Zebulon, NC 27595
(919) 269-5508
Website: www.cmcinternational.com

23. **Columbia Records**
550 Madison Ave.
New York, NY 10022-3211

38 North Foothill Rd.
Beverly Hills, CA 90210
(310) 278-1181
Website: www.silence.net/virgin.htm

24. **Concord Records**
2888 Willow Pass Rd.
Concord, CA 94519
(510) 682-6770
Website: www.aent.com/concord

25. **Curb Records Inc.**
47 Music Square East
Nashville, TN 37203
(615) 321-5080
Website: www.curb.com

3907 W. Alameda Ave.
Burbank, CA 91505
(818) 843-2872

26. **Def Jam/RAL**
160 Varick St. 12th Floor
New York, NY 10013
(212) 229-5200
Website: www.defjam.com

27. **Delicious Vinyl**
6607 Sunset Blvd.
Los Angeles, CA 90028
(213) 465-2700
Website: www.dvinyl.com

28. **DreamWorks Records**
9268 W. 3re St.
Beverly Hills, CA 90210
(310) 234-7700
Website: www.geffenworld.com

1619 Broadway 9th Floor
New York, NY 10019
(212) 603-1893

29. **ECM Records**
1540 Broadway 40th Floor
New York, NY 10036
(212) 930-4996
Website: www.ecmrecords.com

30. **Elektra Records**
75 Rockefeller Plaza
New York, NY 10019-6907
(212) 833-7442
Website: www.elektra.com

345 N. Maple Dr. Suite 123
Beverly Hills, CA 90210
(310) 288-3800

31. **Epic Records**
550 Madison Ave.
New York, NY 10022-4051
(212) 833-7442
Website: www.epiccenter.com

2100 Colorado Ave.
Santa Monica, CA 90404
(310) 449-2100

32. **Fantasy Records**
Tenth & Parker
Berkely, CA 94710
(510) 549-2500
Website: www.fantasyjazz.com

33. **Geffen/DGC Records**
9130 Sunset Blvd.
Los Angeles, CA 90069-6197
(310) 278-9010
Website: www.geffen.com

1755 Broadway
New York, NY 10019
(212) 841-8600

34. **GRP Records**
555 West 57th St.
New York, NY 10019
(212) 424-1000
Website: www.grp.com

35. **Hollywood Records**
500 South Buena Vista St.
Burbank, CA 91521
(818) 560-5670
Website: www.hollywoodrec.com

170 5th Ave.
New York, NY 10010
(212) 645-2722

36. **Imago**
530 Broadway
New York, NY 10012
(212) 343-3400
Website: www.imagorec.com

37. **Interscope**
10900 Wilshire Blvd. Suite 1230
Los Angeles, CA 90024
(310) 208-6547
Website: www.interscoperecords.com

540 Madison Ave. 34th Floor
New York, NY 10019
(212)508-5900

38. **Island Records**
825 Eigth Ave. 24th Floor
New York, NY 10019
(212) 333-8000
Website: www.polygram-us.com

8920 Sunset Blvd. 2nd Floor
Los Angeles, CA 90069
(310) 276-4500

39. **Jive/Silvertone Records**
137-139 West 25th St. 11th Floor
New York, NY 10001
(212) 727-0016

9000 Sunset Blvd. Suite 300
Los Angeles, CA 90069
(310) 247-8300

700 North Green St. Suite 200
Chicago, IL 60622
(312) 942-9700

40. **JVC Music**
3800 Barham Blvd. Suite 305
Los Angeles, CA 90068
(213) 878-0101
Website: www.jvc music.com

41. **Knitting Factory**
74 Leonard St.
New York, NY 10013
(212) 219-3006
Website: www.knittingfactory.com

42. **LaFace**
3350 Peachtree Rd. Suite 1500
Atlanta, GA 30326
(404) 848-8050
Website: www.aristarec.com/laface/

43. **London Records**
825 8th Ave. 23rd Floor
New York, NY 10019
(212) 603-3999
Website: www.polygram-us.com

44. **Malaco Records**
3023 West Northside Dr.
Jackson, MS 39213
(601) 982-4522

Website: www.malaco.com

45. **Maverick**
8000 Beverly Blvd.
Los Angeles, CA 90048
(213) 852-1177
Website: www.wbr.com/maverick

1290 6th Ave. 9th Floor
New York, NY 10019
(212) 399-6973

46. **MCA Records**
70 Universal City Plaza
New York, NY 10019
(818) 777-4000
Website:
www.mca.com/mca-records

1755 Broadway
New York, NY 10019
(212) 841-8000

47. **MCA Nashville**
60 Music Square East
Nashville, TN 37203
(615) 320-0110
Website: www.mca-nashville.com

48. **Mercury Records**
Worldwide Plaza
825 Eighth Ave.
(212) 333-8000
Website: www.polygram.com

49. **Metal Blade Records**
2828 Cochran Suite 302
Simi Valley, CA 93065
(805) 522-9111
Website: www.iuma.com/metal blade

50. **Mojo Records**
1749 14th St. #201
Santa Monica, CA 90404 310) 260-3181
Website: www.mojorecords.com

51. **Motown Records**
825 Eighth Ave. 29th Floor
New York, NY 10019
(212) 333-8000
Website: www.motown.com

52. **N2K Encoded Music**
55 Broad St. 10th Floor
New York, NY 10004
(212) 378-6100
Website www.n2k.com

53. **Narada Records**
4650 N. Port Washington Rd.
Milwaukee, WI 53212
(414) 961-8350
Website: www.narada.com

54. **Nonesuch Records**
75 Rockefeller Plaza

New York, NY 10019
(212) 275-4910
Website:
www.atlantic-records.com

55. **Point Music**
c/o Polygram Classics & Jazz
825 Eighth Ave. 26th Floor
New York, NY 10019
(212) 603-6701
Website: www.pointmusic.com

56. **Priority Records**
6430 Sunset Blvd. Suite 900
Los Angeles, CA 90028
(213) 467-0151

57. **Profile Records**
740 Broadway 7th Floor
New York, NY 10003
(212) 529-2600

58. **Qwest Records**
3008 Barham Blvd.
Los Angeles, CA 90068
(213) 874-3028
Website: www.qwestrecords.com

59. **Radioactive Records**
8570 Hedges Place
Los Angeles, CA 90069
(310) 659-6598
Website: www.radioactive.net

60. **Rap-A-Lot Records**
P.O. Box 924190
Houston, TX 77292
(713) 680-8588
Website: www.virginrecords.com

61. **RCA Records**
1540 Broadway
New York, NY 10036
(212) 930-4000
Website: www.bmg.com/labels/rca.html

8750 Wilshire Blvd.
Beverly Hills, CA 90211
(310) 358-4000

62. **RCA Records Nashville**
1 Music Circle North
Nashville, TN 37203 (615) 664-1200
Website:
www.bmg.com/labels/rcana.html

63. **Red Ant**
9720 Wilshire Blvd. 4th Floor
Beverly Hills, CA 90210
(310) 247-1133
Website: www.red-ant.com

64. Relativity Records
79 Fifth Ave. 16th Floor
New York, NY 10003
(212) 337-5300
Website: www.relativityrecords.com

3420 Ocean Park Blvd. Suite 3050
Santa Monica, CA 90405
(310) 581-8270

65. Reprise Records
3300 Warner Blvd.
Burbank, CA 91505-4694
(818) 846-9090
Website: www.repriserec.com

75 Rockefeller Plaza
New York, NY 10019
(212) 275-4500

66. Restless Records
1616 Vista Del Mar Ave.
Los Angeles, CA 90028
(213) 957-4357
Website: www.restless.com

67. Rhino Records
10635 Santa Monica Blvd.
Los Angeles, CA 90025-4900
(310) 474-4778
Website: www.rhino.com

68. Rounder Records
One Camp St.
Cambridge, MA 02140
(617) 354-0700
Website: www.harp.rounder.com

89. Ruthless Records
8201 W. 3rd St.
Los Angeles, CA 90048
(213) 782-1888
Website: ruthlessrecords.com

70. Rykodisc
Shetland Park
27 Congress St.
Salem, MA 01970
(508) 744-7678
Website: www.rykodisc.com

71. Shanachie
13 Laight St. 6th Floor
New York, NY 10013
(212) 334-0284
Website: www.shanachie.com

72. Sire Records
2034 Broadway
Santa Monica, CA 90404
(310) 828-1033

73. Sony Classical
550 Madison Ave. 16th Floor
New York, NY 10022
(212) 833-4765

Website:
www.sony.com/music/classical/

74. Sony Discos
605 Lincoln Rd. 7th Floor
Miami, FL 33139
(305) 535-0800
Website:
www.sony.com/music/musicindex.html

11365 Ventura Blvd. Suite 155
Studio City, CA 91604
(818) 753-9696

75. Sony Music Entertainment
550 Madison Ave.
New York, NY 10022
(212) 8338000
Website:
www.sony.com/music/musicindex.htm

2100 Colorado Ave. L-225
Santa Monica, CA 90404-3504
(310) 449-2100

76. Sony Music Nashville
34 Music Square East
Nashville, TN 37203
(615) 742-4321
Website:
www.music.sony.com/music/nashville/

77. Sparrow Records
P.O. Box 5010
101 Winners Circle
Brentwood, TN 37024-5010
(615) 371-6800

78. SST Records
P.O. Box 1
Lawndale, CA 90260
(562) 590-8853

79. Tommy Boy Music
902 Broadway 13th Floor
New York, NY 10010
(212) 388-8300

80. Universal Music Group
70 Universal City Plaza
Universal City, CA 91608
(818) 777-4000
Website: www.mca.com/mca_records

1755 Broadway 7th Floor
New York, NY 10019
(212) 373-0600

81. Verve Records
Worldwide Plaza 825 Eighth Ave.
New York, NY 10019
(212) 333-8000
Website: www.verveinteractive.com

82. Virgin Records
3 York, NY 10036

(212) 930-4000
Website: www.bmg.de

83. **Virgin Records**
1790 Broadway 20th Floor
New York, NY 10019
(212) 586-7700

84. **Warner Alliance Records**
20 Music Square East
Nashville, TN 37203
(615) 214-1488
Website: www.wbr.com/alliance

85. **Warner Bros. Records**
3300 Warner Blvd.
Burbank, CA 91505
(818) 846-9090
Website: www.wbr.com

86. **Warner/Reprise Nashville**
20 Music Square East
Nashville, TN 37203
(615) 748-8000
Website: www.wbr.com

87. **Windham Hill Group**
BMG Entertainment
8750 Wilshire Blvd. 3rd Floor
Beverly Hills, CA 90211-2713
(310) 385-4800
Website: www.windham.com/

88. **Word Entertainment**
3319 West End Ave. Suite 200
Nashville, TN 37203
(615) 385-9673
Website:
www.worldrecords.com/index-j.html

89. **The WORK Group**
2100 Colorado Ave.
Santa Monica, CA 90404
(310) 449-2666
Website: www.sony.com/music/work

CANADA

90. **Alma Records**
260 Adelaide Street East, Suite 10
Toronto, Ont M5A 1N1
(416) 494-2562
(416) 494-2030 fax

91. **Anthem Entertainment Group**
189 Carlton St.
Toronto, Ont M5A 2K7
(416) 923-5855
(416) 923-1041 fax

92. **Aquairus Records/DKD Vibe**
1445 Lambert Closse, Suite 200
Montreal, Queb H3H 1Z5
(514) 939-3775
(514) 939-1691 fax

93. **Attic Music Group**
102 AtlanticAvenue
Toronto, Ont M6K 1X9
(416) 532-4487
(416) 532-9545 fax

94. **Borealis Recording Co.**
67 Mowat Ave, Suite 233
Toronto, Ont M6K 3E3
(416) 530-4288
(416) 530-0461 fax
E-Mail: brc@interlog.com

95. **Captain Records**
1057 Steeles Ave. W.
-or- P.O. Box 81584
Willowdale, Ont. M2R 3X1
(416) 633-6490
(416) 633-1372 fax
E-Mail: captainrecords@yahoo.com

96. **CBC Records**
P.O. Box 500, Station A
Toronto, Ont. M5W 1E6
(416) 205-6033
(416) 205-2376 fax

97. **Delinquent Records Music**
#5-920 Tobruch Ave.
North Vancouver B.C. V7P 1V8
(604) 984-3153
(604) 986-2421 fax

98. **Jazz Focus Records**
Suite 304, 1640 - 16th Ave. N.W.
Calgary, AB T2M 0L6
(403) 210-1440
(403) 210-1456 fax
E-Mail: jazz@canuck.com

99. **KLM Records**
5348, rue Jean-Talon Est,
Montreal, Quebec, H1S 1L5
(514) 374-8065
(514) 374-3749 fax
E-mail: mail@klmrecords.com

100. **Le Groupe BMG Quebec**
3485, Boul. Saint-Laurent, 3e etage
Montreal, Quebec, H2X 2T6
(514) 288-6118
(514) 288-6119

101. **Marquis Records**
30 Kenilworth Ave.
Toronto, Ont. M4L 3S3
(416) 748-7440
(416) 690-346
E-Mail:
marquis_classics@compuserve.com

100 Music Publishing Companies

1. **615 Music Productions, Inc.**
   1030 16th Avenue South
   Nashville, TN 37212
   (615) 244-6515
   (615) 242-2455 fax
   E-Mail: info@615music.com

2. **ABC Music - American Broadcasting Companies, Inc.**
   47 West 66th St.
   New York, NY 10023
   (212) 456-3233
   (212) 456-3084 fax

3. **Allour Records**
   1205 Farragut Str. N.W.
   Washington, DC 20011
   (202) 487-7373
   (202) 291-8742 fax

4. **Americana Masters**
   825 19th Avenue South
   Nashville, TN 37203
   (615) 327-9988
   (615) 327-3776 fax

5. **Amerocka**
   P.O. Box 1712, Grand Central Station
   New York, NY 10163-1712
   (718) 875-8530
   (718) 246-2665 fax
   E-Mail: info@amerocka.com

6. **AMRA (American Mechanical Rights Agency, Inc.)**
   1888 Century Park East, Suite 222
   Los Angeles, CA 90067
   (310) 785-2004
   (310) 785-1800 fax
   E-Mail: AMRACALIF@aol.com

7. **Antpen Music**
   110 W. 40th Street, Suite 703
   New York, NY 10018
   (212) 921-5031
   (212) 921-2782 fax

8. **Apollo Music Group**
   10061 Riverside Drive, Suite 810
   Toluca Lake, CA 91602
   (818) 842-2641
   (818) 842-1791 fax
   E-mail: apollomusic@loop.com

9. **A Train Management**
   PO Box 29242
   Oakland, CA 94604
   (510) 893-4705
   (510) 893-4807

10. **Avatar Records**
    1319 N. La Brea Avenue
    Los Angeles, CA 90028
    (323) 878-1100
    (323) 878-1114 fax

12. **Babylon Entertainment, Inc.**
    BABYLON RECORDS,
    244 W. 54th St., Suite 501
    New York, NY 10019
    (212) 258-2182
    (212) 307-7201 fax

13. **Balmur Entertainment**
    1105 17th Ave. S.
    Nashville, TN 37212
    (615) 329-0230
    (615) 321-0240 fax
    E-Mail: BalmurEnt@aol.com

14. **Barbara Orbison Productions / Orbison Records**
    1625 Broadway, 6th Floor
    Nashville, TN 37203
    (615) 242-4201
    (615) 242-4202 fax

15. **Bearsville Records / Fourth Floor Music**
    PO Box 135
    Bearsville, NY 12409
    (914) 679-7303
    (914) 679-5731 fax

16. **The Bicycle Music Company**
    8075 West Third Street, Suite 400
    Los Angeles, CA 90048-4318
    (323) 938-2266
    (323) 938-5357 fax
    E-Mail: all@bicyclemusic.com

17. **Blue Jackel Entertainment**
    P.O. Box 87
    Huntington, NY 11714
    (516) 423-7879
    (516) 423-7875 fax
    E-Mail: bluejackel@earthlink.net

18. **BMG Music Publishing - Worldwide**
    1540 Broadway
    New York, NY 10036
    (212) 930-4000
    (212) 930-4263 fax

19. **BOK Music**
    3435 Stoneridge Court
    Calabasas, CA 91302
    (818) 222-9969
    (818) 222-0853 fax
    E-Mail: boksongs@aol.com

20. **Brian Bennett Music**
    13011 Galewood St.
    Studio City, CA 91604

(818) 789-9100
(818) 789-5276 fax
E-Mail: composer@filmscores.com

21. **CAL IV Entertainment**
808 19th Avenue South
Nashville, TN 37203
(615) 242-4200
(615) 242-6989 fax
Website & E-Mail: www.cal4ent.com

22. **CMC Music**
151 West 76 St., Suite 3
New York, NY 10023
(212) 978-7970
(212) 343-9803 fax
E-Mail:cucmusicbod@compuserve.com

23. **Coco Music Publishing**
P.O. Box 61128
Staten Island, NY 10306
(718) 761-6552
(718) 494-1076 fax
E-Mail: cocomus@aol.com

24. **Cutting Records, Inc.**
481 8th Avenue, Suite 1518
New York, NY 10001
(212) 868-3154
(212) 868-1061 fax
E-Mail: cutting@cuttingnyc.com

25. **Dancefloor Distribution/Echo International**
77-99 W. Sheffield Ave.
Englewood, NJ 07631
(201) 568-0040
(201) 568-7821 fax
F-Mail: echorecords.com

26. **David Rose Publishing Co./Angela Rose White, Esq.**
13033 Ventura Blvd., Suite H
Studio City, CA 91604
(818) 789-9420
(818) 789-3705 fax

27. **Destiny Music**
3550 West 6th Street, Suite 320
Los Angeles, CA 90020
(213)385-0355
(213) 385-7094 fax

28. **The Diamond Music Companies**
8075 West Third Street, Suite 400
Los Angeles, CA 90048-4318
(323) 938-2266
(323) 938-5357 fax

29. **Diamond Time (US) Ltd.**
73 Spring Street, Suite 504
New York, NY 10012
(212) 274-1006
(212) 274-1938 fax

30, **Disk Eyes Productions**
10020 Main Street, Suite A233
Bellevue, WA 98004
(425) 454-5359
(425) 454-7902 fax
E-Mail: diskeyes@msn.com

31. **Diva Records LLC/Grzanna Jazz Productions LLC**
P.O. Box 511735
Milwaukee, WI 53203-0291
(414) 967-9067 phone
E-mail: grzannajazz@mixcom.com

32. **DMG Entertainment**
4470 Sunset Blvd., Suite 792
Los Angeles, CA 90027
(323) 953-6117
(323) 953-6164 fax

33. **Dreyfus Records Inc.**
c/o Alan S. Bergman & Associates
19 West 44th Street, Suite 1716
New York, NY 10036
(212) 944-1630
(212) 944-1631

34. **DRG Records Inc.**
130 West 57th Street
New York, NY 10019
(212) 582-3040
(212) 459-9437 fax
E-Mail: drgrecords@aol.com

35. **Eightball Records**
175 Fifth Ave, Suite 714
New York, NY 10010
(212) 253-6700
(212) 253-7833 fax

36. **EMI Music Publishing New York**
1290 Avenue of the Americas
New York, NY 10104
(212) 492-1200
(212) 492-1864 fax

37. **Fantasy, Inc.**
2600 Tenth Street
Berkely, CA 94710
(510) 549-2500
(510) 486-2015 fax
E-Mail: fantasyjazz.com

38. **FIDOF (International Federation of Festival Organizations)**
4230 Stansbury Avenue, Suite 105
Sherman Oaks, CA 91423
(818) 789-7596
(818) 784-9141 fax

39. **Fox Family Worldwide, Inc.**
10960 Wilshire Blvd., 3rd Floor
Los Angeles, CA 90035
(310) 235-5792
(310) 235-9583 fax

40. **Fox Music, Inc.**
10201 West Pico Blvd.,
Building 18/Room 107
Los Angeles, CA 90035
(310) 369-3341
(310) 369-1137 fax

41. **Full Scale Productions, Inc.**
4576 - 150th Ave. NE
Redmond, WA 98052
(425) 881-9322
(425) 881-3645
E-Mail: fsccorp@aol.com

42. **Future Fossil Music**
P.O. Box 6248
Hoboken, NJ 07030
(201) 659-3868
(201) 659-3868 fax

43. **Global Eyes Entertainment, Inc.**
P.O. Box 270033
Nashville, TN 37227
(615) 883-6334
(615) 883-8656 fax
E-Mail: globaleyes@mindspring.com

44. **GNP Crescendo Records**
8480-A Sunset Blvd.
West Hollywood, CA 90069
(323) 656-2614
(323) 656-0693 fax
E-Mail: gnp@pacificnet.com

45. **Gold Leaf Production, Inc.**
P.O. Box 12042
Charolette, NC 28220-2042
(704) 339-0775
(704) 339-2042 fax
E-Mail: goldleaf@mindspring.com

46. **Grand Cru Entertainment Group, Inc.**
825 19th Avenue South
Nashville, TN 37203
(615) 327-9988
(615) 327-3776 fax
E-mail: grndcruent@aol.com

47. **Green Linnet Records/Xenophile Records**
43 Beaver Brook Road
Danbury, CT 06810
(203) 730-0333
(203) 730-0345 fax

48. **Guidance Records, Inc.**
160 N. Halsted Street, 2nd Floor
Chicago, IL 60661

(312) 226-8387
(312) 226-1343 fax
E-Mail: 33rpm.com

49. **Hacate Entertainment Group, LLC**
250 W. 57th St., Suite 1517-140
New York, NY 10107
(212) 586-4229
(212) 586-4239 fax

50. **Hanalei Music Group, Inc.**
P.O. Box 160
Franklin, TN 37065-0160
(615) 791-0292
(615) 791-8241 fax

51. **Hardcorps Recordings**
1462 E. Republican St., Suite 122
Seattle, WA 98112
(206) 617-4077
(206) 322-6031 fax

52. **Heavy Harmony Music**
6433 Topango Canyon Blvd., Suite 445
Canoga Park, CA 91303
(818) 887-7073
(818) 887-4614
E-Mail: HeavHrmMsc@aol.com

53. **(HSRA) High School for Recording Arts 'Studio 4'**
550 Vandalia Street
St. Paul, MN 55114
(612) 917-6959
(612) 917-6961 fax

54. **Ingram - Le Brun Music, Inc.**
1201 16th Avenue South
Nashville, TN 37212
(615) 320-7707
(615) 329-2569 fax

55. **Inspire Productions, Inc./Joy Records**
302 E. Pettigrew St., Suite 101
Durham, NC 27701
(919) 688-8563
(919) 688-8565 fax

56. **Integrated Copyright Group, Inc.**
P.O. Box 24149
Nashville, TN 37202
(615) 329-3999
(615) 329-4070 fax
E-Mail: icgi@ix.netcom.com

57. **Interhit Records**
1438 N. Gower Street, Bldg 42, 14th Floor
Los Angeles, CA 90028
(323) 468-3434
(323) 468-3435 fax
E-Mail: interhit@earthlink.net

58. **James Stewart Muisc**
825 19th Avenue South
Nashville, TN 37203
(615) 385-1559
(615) 327-3776 fax

59. **Jane Peterer Music Corporation**
80 Pine Street, 33rd Floor
New York, NY 10005-1702
(212) 344-5588
(212) 344-5566 fax
E-Mail: music@jpmc.com

60. **Joey Boy Records**
3081 N.W. 24th St.
Miami, FL 33142
(305) 635-5588
(305) 633-7127 fax

61. **JRE Entertainment Group, Inc.**
52 Dianthus
Rancho Santa Margarita, CA 90048
(949) 766-7979
(949) 589-0655 fax

62. **Junior Entertainment Corp**
33 W. 81st St., Suite 4R
New York, NY 10024
(212) 712-9640
(212) 712-9641 fax

63. **Kazo Records**
5935 Stenenview
Memphis, TN 38161
(901) 363-2447
(301) 521-9965 fax

64. **Koch International L.P.**
2 Tri-Harbor Court
Port Washington, NY 11030-4817
(516) 484-1000
(516) 484-4746 fax

65. **Lieber & Stoller Music Publishing**
9000 Sunset Blvd., Suite 1107
Los Angeles, CA 90069
(310) 273-6401
(310) 273-1591 fax

66. **Marathon Music International**
21166 Cedar Falls Drive
Saugus, CA 91350
(805) 263-8677
(805) 263-1596 fax
E-Mail: mmiusa@email.com

67. **MCA Music Publishing - New York**
1755 Broadway, 8th Floor
New York, NY 10019
(212) 841-8209
(212) 841-8045 fax

68. **MCA Music Publishing - California**
2440 Sepulveda Boulevard, Suite 100
Los Angeles, CA 90064

(310) 235-4700
(310) 235-4901 fax

69. **MCA Music Publishing - Latin**
1425 Collins Ave
Miami Beach, FL 33139
(305) 604-1310
(305) 604-1319 fax

70. **Megatrax Production Music, Inc.**
11684 Ventura Blvd., Suite 978
Studio City, CA 91604
(818) 503-5240
(818) 503-5247 fax

71. **MGM Music**
2500 Broadway
Santa Monica, CA 90404
(310) 449-3000
(310) 449-8955 fax

72. **MIA Records**
315 Church Street
New York, NY 10013
(212) 966-9664
(212) 966-1287 fax

73. **Mick Lloyd Productions**
1018 17th Avenue So, Suite 11
Nashville, TN 37212
(615) 329-9093
(615) 329-9094 fax

74. **Modern World Music**
143 Avenue B
New York, NY 10019
(212) 529-5881
(212) 529-5882 fax

75. **Mojo Records**
1749 14th Street, Suite 201
Santa Monica, CA 90404
(310) 285-5370
(310) 285-5349 fax

76. **Moonshine Music**
8525 Santa Monica Blvd.
West Hollywood, CA 90069
(310) 652-8145
(310) 652-8146 fax

77. **Murram Rich Baierle Int'l.**
1605 17th Avenue South
-or- P.O. Box 128109
Nashville, TN 37212
(615) 386-0025
(615) 386-0026 fax

78. **Music Enterprises, Inc.**
5626 Brock St.
Houston, TX 77023
(713) 926-4438
(713) 926-8303 fax

79. **National League Music**
16161 Ventura Blvd., Suite 712
Encino, CA 91436
(818) 708-1222
(818) 708-1625 fax
E-Mail: nationleag@aol.com

80. **National Music Publishers**
Association and the Harry Fox
Agency, Inc.
711 Third Avenue
New York, NY 10017
(212) 922-3262
(212) 953-2471
Website: www.nmpa.org

81. **O'Neil Hagaman, PLLC**
1025 16th Avenue South, Suite 202
Nashville, TN 37212
(615) 320-5291
(615) 320-5651 fax
E-Mail: oneilhag@aol.com

82. **Online Music**
Company/licensemusic.com
301 Durant Ave
Mill Valley, CA 94941
(415) 381-9440
(415) 381-8789 fax
Website: www.licensemusic.com

83. **Overseas Music Services, Inc.**
P.O. Box 1285
Water Mills, NY 11976
(516) 726-7500
(516) 726-7510 fax

84. **Pacific Time Entertainment Co.**
4 East 12th Street
New York, NY 10003
(212) 741-2888
(212) 807-9501 fax
E-Mail: Pactimeco@aol.com

85. **Peermusic Ltd.**
810 Seventh Avenue
New York, NY 10019-5818
(212) 265-3910
(212) 489-2465 fax

86. **P. Family Records Inc.**
322 Cedar Avenue South
Minneapolis, MN 55454
(612) 664-0526
(612) 664-0528 fax

87. **Reach Music International, Inc.**
217 East 86th Street, Suite 117
New York, NY 10128
(212) 348-9506
(212) 348-4594
E-Mail: reachint@aol.com

88. **Real Records, Inc.**
P.O. Box 958

-or- 434 Avenue U
Bogalusa, LA 70427
(504) 732-2942
(504) 732-4963 fax
E-Mail: realrecords@hotmail.com

89. **Records/Records & Filmworks,**
Inc.
16528 Ventura Blvd., Suite 299
Tarzana, CA 91356
(818) 988-4420
(818) 787-3483 fax

90. **Rhythm Stick Productions**
51 MacDougal Street, Suite 368
New York, NY 10012
(212) 769-7150
(212) 262-6299 fax
E-Mail: Rhythmstick@hotmail.com

91. **Riostar Entertainment, Inc.**
1212 17th Avenue South
Nashville, TN 37212
(615) 322-1212
(615) 322-1230 fax
E-Mail: riostar@aol.com

92. **Robbins Entertainment**
30 West 21st Street, 11th Floor
New York, NY 10010
(212) 675-4321
(212) 675-4441 fax

93. **The Royalty Network, Inc.**
246 Fifth Avenue, Suite 300
New York, NY 10001
(212) 889-6500
(212) 889-1874 fax
E-Mail: mail@roynet.com
Website: www.roynet.com/

94. **RYKO Corp.**
Shetland Park
27 Congress Street
Salem, MA 01970
(978) 825-3200
(978) 741-4506 fax
E-Mail: info@rykodisc.com

95. **Rykodisc, Inc.**
The Times Building, Suite 300,
Suburban Square
Ardmore, PA 19003
(610) 649-7400
(610) 649-1122 fax
E-Mail: info@rykodisc.com

96. **Sanachie Entertainment**
13 Laight Street
New York, NY 10013-2119
(212) 334-0284
(212) 334-5207 fax

97. **Sigma Media Concepts**
212 N. 12th Street

Philadelphia, PA 19107
(215) 561-3660
(215) 496-9321

98. **Sirius Star Entertainment**
7223 Beverly Blvd., Suite 205
Los Angeles, CA 90036
(323) 938-7555
(323) 938-7556 fax
E-Mail: siriusstar@earthlink.net

99. **Skywriter Productions, Inc.**
4718 Saint Clair Ave.
North Hollywood, CA 91607
(818) 766-0877
(818) 766-1077 fax

100. **Tappedinto.com, Inc.**
P.O. Box 120876
Nashville, TN 37212
(615) 221-4006
(615) 320-5806/0889
Website: www.untapped.com/

200 Fairs & Expositions

ALABAMA

1. **National Peanut Festival and Fair**
1691 Ross Clark Cir.
Dothan, AL 36301-5438
(334) 793-4323
(334) 793-3247 fax

2. **Greater Gulf State Fair**
P.O. Box 8307
Mobile, AL 36689-0307
(334) 344-4573
(334) 344-0056 fax
E-Mail: fair@mobilefair.com
Website: www.alnationalfair.org

3. **Alabama National Fair & Agricultural Exposition**
P.O. Box 3304
Montgomery, AL 36109-0304
(334) 272-6831
(334) 272-6835 fax
Website: www.alnationalfair.org

4. **North Alabama State Fair**
P.O. Box 2736
Muscle Shoals, AL 35662-2736
(256) 383-3247
(256) 383-1817 fax
E-Mail: NASFAIR@aol.com

ALASKA

5. **Tanana Valley State Fair**
1800 College Rd.
Fairbanks, AK 99709-4190
(907) 452-3750
(907) 456-7971 fax

E-Mail: fair@mosquitonet.com
Website: www.tananavalleyfair.org

6. **Southeast Alaska State Fair**
P.O. Box 385
Haines, AK 99827-0385
(907) 766-2476
(907) 766-2478 fax
E-Mail: seakfair@seaknet.alaska.edu

7. **Kenai Peninsula State Fair**
P.O. Box 3110
Ninilchik, AK 99639-0210
(907) 567-3670
(907) 567-3670 fax

8. **Alaska State Fair**
2075 Glenn Hwy.
Palmer, AK 99645-6770
(907) 745-4827
(907) 746-2699 fax

ARIZONA

9. **Arizona State Fair**
P.O. Box 6728
Phoenix, AZ 85005-6728
(602) 252-6771
(602) 495-1302 fax
E-Mail & Website: www.azstatefair.com

10. **Maricopa County Fair**
1826 W. McDowell Rd.
Phoenix, AZ 85007-1612
(602) 252-0717
(602) 252-4279 fax
E-Mail: info@maricopacountyfair.com
Website: www.maricopacountyfair.com

11. **Pima County Fair**
11300 S. Houghton Rd.
Tucson, AZ 85747-9755
(520) 762-9100
(520) 762-5005 fax
E-Mail: office@swfair.com
Website: www.swfair.com

12. **Yuma County Fair**
2520 E. 32nd St.
Yuma, AZ 85365-3611
(520) 726-4420
(520) 344-3480 fax

ARKANSAS

13. **Arkansas-Oklahoma State Fair**
P.O. Box 4145
Fort Smith, AR 72914-4145
(501) 783-6176
(501) 782-9944 fax

14. **Craighead County Fair**
P.O. Box 2397
Jonesboro, AR 72402-2397
(870) 935-4331
(870) 931-0971 fax

15. **Arkansas State Fair & Livestock Show**
P.O. Box 166660
Little Rock, AR 72216-6660
(501) 372-8341
(501) 372-4197 fax
Website: www.ArkFairgrounds.com

16. **Four States Fair**
P.O. Box 1915
Texarkana, AR 75504-1915
(870) 773-2941
(870) 772-0713 fax
E-Mail: lisab@fourstatesfair.com
Website: www.fourstatefair.com

CALIFORNIA

17. **Orange County Fair & Exposition Center**
88 Fair Dr.
Costa Mesa, CA 92626-6521
(714) 708-3247
(714) 641-1738 fax
Website: www.ocfair.com

18. **Fresno Fair**
1121 S. Chance Ave.
Fresno, CA 93702-3707
(209) 650-3247
(209) 650-3226 fax
E-Mail: fairp@thesocket.com
Website: www.fresnofair.com

19. **Los Angeles County Fair**
P.O. Box 2250
Pomona, CA 91769-2250
(909) 623-3111
(909) 629-2067 fax
E-Mail: Robinson@fairplex.com
Website: www.fairplex.com

20. **California State Fair**
P.O. Box 15649
Sacramento, CA 95852-1649
(916) 263-FAIR
(916) 263-3304 fax
E-Mail: sallyckf@aol.com
Website: www.bigfun.org

COLORADO

21. **El Paso County Fair**
305 S. Unioun Blvd.
Colorado Springs, CO 80910-3123
(719) 575-8690
(719) 575-8692 fax
E-Mail:
Jim_Abendschan@co.el-paso.co.us
Website:
www.co.elaso.co.us/cntyfair/main/html

22. **National Western Stock Show & Rodeo**
4655 Humboldt St.

Denver, CO 80216-2818
(303) 297-1166
(303) 292-1708 fax
Website: www.nationalwestern.com

23. **Adams County Fair & Rodeo**
9755 Henderson Rd.
Brighton, CO 80601-8114
(303) 637-8000
(303) 637-8015 fax

24. **Boulder County Fair & Livestock Show**
9595 Nelson Rd.
Longmont, CO 80501-6359
(303) 772-7170
(303) 651-2305 fax
Website: bcn.boulder.co.us/bcfair

CONNECUTICUT

25. **Brooklyn Fair**
P.O. Box 410
Brooklyn, CT 06234-0410
(203) 779-0012
(203) 779-1822 fax

26. **Durham Agricultural Fair**
P.O. Box 225
Durham, CT 06422-0225
(860) 349-9495
(860) 349-3101 fax
Website:
ctguide.atlantic.com/vacguide/dfair

27. **Hebron Harvest Fair**
P.O. Box 145
Hebron, CT 06248-0145
(860) 228-0892
(860) 228-2617 fax

28. **Woodstock Fair**
P.O. Box 1
Woodstock, CT 06281-0001
(860) 928-3246
(860) 928-5429 fax

DELAWARE

29. **Delaware State Fair**
P.O. Box 28
Harrington, DE 19952-0028
(302) 398-3269
(302) 398-5429 fax
E-Mail: fair@dmv.com
Website: www.delawarestatefair.com

FLORIDA

30. **Dade County Fair & Exposition**
10901 S.W. 24th St.
Miami, FL 33165-2337
(305) 223-7060
(305) 554-6092 fax
Website: www.FairExpo.com

31. **Central Florida Fair**
4603 W. Colonial Dr.
Orlanda, FL 32808-8158
(407) 295-3247
(407) 295-2082 fax
E-Mail: cff@centralfloridafair.com
Website: www.centralfloridafair.com

32. **Florida Strawberry Festival and Fair**
P.O. Box 1869
Plant City, FL 33564-1869
(813) 752-9194
(813) 754-4297 fax
E-Mail:
berryinfo@flstrawberryfestival.com
Website: www.flstrawberryfestival.com

33. **Sarasota County Fair**
3000 Ringling Blvd.
Sarasota, FL 34237-5333
(941) 365-0818
(941) 364-8888 fax

34. **North Florida Fair**
441 Paul Russell Rd.
Tallahassee, FL 32301-6959
(850) 878-3247
(850) 942-6950 fax
E-Mail: ddowler@northfloridafair.com
Website: www.northfloridafair.com

35. **South Florida Fair & Palm Beach County Expositions, Inc.**
P.O. Box 15915
West Palm Beach, FL 33416-5915
(407) 793-0333
(407) 790-5210 fax
E-Mail: fairbuck@aol.com
Website: www.southfloridafair.org

GEORGIA

36. **Greater Columbus Fair**
P.O. Box 1340
Columbus, GA 31902-1340
(706) 653-4482
(706) 653-4481 fax

37. **Gwinnett County Livestock and Fair Association**
P.O. Box 1352
Lawrenceville, GA 30046-1352
(770) 963-6522
(770) 963-4644 fax

38. **North Georgia State Fair**
P.O. Box 777
Kennesaw, GA 30144-4105
(770) 423-1330
(770) 528-1170 fax

39. **Georgia National Fairgrounds & Agricenter**
P.O. Box 1367
Perry, GA 31069-1367
(912) 987-3247
(912) 987-7218 fax
E-Mail: mterptow@alltel.net
Website: www.gnfa.com

HAWAII

40. **Hawaii State Farm Fair**
2343 Rose St.
Honolulu, HI 96819-2438
(808) 848-2074
(808) 848-1921 fax

41. **Maui County Fair**
P.O. Box 95
Kahului, HI 96733-6595
(808) 242-6934 fax
E-Mail: abc@aloha.net

IDAHO

42. **Eastern Idaho State Fair**
P.O. Box 250
Blackfoot, ID 83221-0250
(208) 785-2480
(208) 785-2483 fax
E-Mail: thefair@ida.net
Website: fair.ida.net

43. **Western Idaho Fair**
5610 Glenwood St.
Boise, ID 83714-1338
(208) 376-3247
(208) 375-9972 fax
E-Mail: fgevansl@ac1.co.ada.id.us
Website: www.idahofair.com

44. **North Idaho Fair**
P.O. Box 2437
Coeur D'Alene, ID 83816-2437
(208) 765-4969
(208) 765-3168 fax

45. **Twin Falls County Fair**
P.O. Box 2587
Filer, ID 83328-0257
(208) 326-4396
(208) 326-3337 fax
E-Mail: TFCfair@cyberhighway.net
Website:
www.cyberhighway.net/~tfcfair/

ILLINOIS

46. **Boone County Fair**
118 Buchanan St.
Belvidere, IL 61008-3702
(815) 544-4066
(815) 544-6808 fax

47. **Du Quoin State Fair**
655 Executive Dr.
Du Quoin, IL 62832
(618) 542-9373
(618) 542-3871 fax

48. **Stephenson County Fair**
P. O. Box 630
Freeport, IL 61032-0630
(815) 235-2918
(815) 233-1644 fax

49. **Winnebago County Fair**
P.O. Box K
Pecatonica, IL 61063-0670
(815) 239-1641
(815) 239-1653 fax

50. **Heart of Illinois Fair**
P.O. Box 3334
Peoria, IL 61612-3334
(309) 691-6332
(309) 691-2372 fax

51. **DeKalb County Fair**
121 S. Main St.
Sandwich, IL 60548-2158
(815) 786-2389
(815) 786-6242 fax

52. **Illinois State Fair**
P.O. Box 19427
Springfield, IL 62794-9427
(217) 782-6661
(217) 782-9115 fax
Website: www.state.il.us/fair/

INDIANA

53. **Lake County Fair**
P.O. Box 327
Crown Point, IN 46307-0327
(219) 663-3617
(219) 663-0699 fax

54. **Elkhart County 4-H Fair**
17746 County Road 34
Goshen, IN 46528-9261
(219) 533-3247
(219) 534-3743 fax
E-Mail: info@4hfair.org
Website: www.4hfair.org

55. **Indiana State Fair**
1202 E. 38th St.
Indianapolis, IN 46205
(317) 927-7500
(317) 927-7695 fax
E-Mail: indstate@iquest.net
Website: www.indianastatefair.com

56. **St. Joseph County 4-H Fair**
5117 S. Ironwood Rd.
South Bend, IN 46614-9734
(219) 291-4870
(219) 291-7302 fax

IOWA

57. **Mississippi Valley Fair**
3815 W. Locust St.
Davenport, IA 52804-3343
(319) 326-5338
(319) 326-3111fax

58. **Iowa State Fair**
400 E. 14th St.
Des Moines, IA 50319-9001
(515) 262-3111
(515) 262-6906 fax
E-Mail: webmaster@iowastatefair.com
Website: www.iowastatefair.com

59. **Clay County Fair**
P.O. Box 527
Spencer, IA 51301-0527
(712) 262-4740
(712) 262-4741 fax
E-Mail: clayfair@rconnect.com
Website: www.claycountyfair.com

60. **National Cattle Congress**
P.O. Box 298
Waterloo, IA 50704-0298
(319) 234-7515
(319) 234-8865 fax

KANSAS

61. **Johnson County Fair Association**
P.O. Box 361
Gardner, KS 66030-0361
(913) 856-8860 phone

62. **Kansas State Fair**
2000 N. Poplar St.
Hutchinson, KS 67502
(316) 669-3640
(316) 669-3640 fax
E-Mail: ksfair@southwind.net
Website: www.ink.org/public/ksfair

63. **Wyandotte County Fair**
1405 N. 98th St.
Kansas City, KS 66111-1827
(913) 788-7898
(913) 788-3183 fax
E-Mail: wcfa@aol.com
Website: members.aol.com/wcfa

64. **Johnson County Old Settlers**
202 N. Chestnut St.
Olathe, KS 66061-3407
(913) 782-5252
(913) 764-8456 fax
E-Mail: jaylang@sound.net

KENTUCKY

65. **Grant County Fair and Horse Show**
300 Cull Ln.
Crittenden, KY 41035-8812

(606) 824-5943 phone

66. **Kentucky State Fair**
P.O. Box 37130
Louisville, KY 40233-7130
(502) 367-5000
(502) 367-5109 fax
Website:
www.kyfairexpo.org/kystfair.html

67. **North American International Livestock Exposition**
P.O. Box 36367
Louisville, KY 40233-6367
(502) 595-3166
(502) 367-5299 fax

68. **McCracken County Fair**
2414 Monroe St.
Paducah, KY 42001-3159
(502) 444-6413 phone

LOUISIANA

69. **Greater Baton Rouge State Fair**
P.O. Box 15010
Baton Rouge, LA 70895-5010
(504) 755-FAIR
(504) 273-0997 fax
E-Mail: gbrsf@tlxnet.net
Website: www.gbrsf.com

70. **Cajun Heartland State Fair**
444 Cajundome Blvd.
Lafayette, LA 70506-4286
(318) 265-2100
(318) 265-2311 fax

71. **State Fair of Louisiana**
P.O. Box 38327
Shreveport, LA 71133-8327
(318) 635-1361
(318) 631-4909 fax

MAINE

72. **Bangor State Fair**
100 Dutton St.
Bangor, ME 04401-6842
(207) 947-5555
(207) 947-5105 fax
E-Mail: basspar1@acadia.net

73. **Fryeburg Fair**
P.O. Box 78
Fryeburg, ME 04037-0078
(207) 935-3268
(207) 935-3662 fax
E-Mail: fryefair@nxl.com
Website: www.fryeburgfair.com

74. **Skowhegan State Fair**
P.O. Box 39
Skowhegan, ME 04976-0039
(207) 474-2947 phone and fax

MARYLAND

75. **Allegany County Fair**
110 LeFevre Rd.
Cumberland, MD 21502-2610
(301) 777-0911
(301) 729-7873 fax

76. **Montgomery County Agricultural Fair**
16 Chestnut St.
Gaithersburg, MD 20877-2403
(301) 926-3100
(301) 926-1532 fax
Website: www.mcagfair.com

77. **Maryland State Fair**
P.O. Box 188
Timonium, MD 21094-0188
(410) 252-0200
(410) 2561-5610 fax
E-Mail: msfair@msn.com
Website: www.bpcl.net/~mdstfair

MASSACHUSETTS

78. **Brockton-Middleboro Agricultural Fair**
P.O. Box 172
Brockton, MA 02767-0172
(508) 586-8000
(508) 822-4396 fax
E-Mail: maura@brockfair.com
Website: www.brockfair.com

79. **Barnstable County Fair**
1220 Nathan Ellis Hwy.
East Falmouth, MA 02536-4244
(508) 563-3200
(508) 563-5790 fax

80. **Marshfield Fair**
P.O. Box 4
Marshfield, MA 02050-0004
(781) 834-6629
(781) 837-3724 fax

81. **Topsfield Fair**
P.O. Box 134
Topsfield, MA 01983-0234
(978) 887-5000
(978) 887-3016 fax
E-Mail: essex@topsfieldfair.org
Website: www.topsfieldfair.org

82. **Eastern States Exposition**
1305 Memorial Ave.
West Springfield, MA 01089-3525
(413) 737-BIGE
(413) 787-0127 fax
E-Mail: mkt@thebige.com
Website: www.thebige.com

MICHIGAN

83. Allegan County Fair
P.O. Box 10
Allegan, MI 49010-0010
(616) 673-6501
(616) 673-2522 fax
E-Mail: acfair@net-link.net
Website: www.allegancountyfair.org

84. St. Joseph County Grange Fair
P.O. Box 578
Centreville, MI 49032-0578
(616) 467-8935
(616) 467-7036 fax

85. Michigan State Fair and Exposition Center
1120 W. State Fair Ave.
Detroit, MI 48203-1040
(313) 369-8250
(313) 369-8410 fax
Website: www.mda.state.mi.us/statefair

86. Ionia Free Fair
P.O. Box 96
Ionia, MI 48846-0096
(616) 527-1310
(616) 527-4388 fax
E-Mail: iff@iserv.net

87. Midland County Agricultural & Horticultural Fair
6905 Eastman Ave.
Midland, MI 48642-7898
(517) 835-7901
(517) 835-2336 fax

88. Genesee County Fair
731 E. Mount Morris St.
Mt. Morris, MI 48458
(810) 687-0953
(810) 687-0954 fax
Website: www.gcf.org

MINNESOTA

89. Mower County Fair
P.O. Box 426
Austin, MN 55912-0426
(507) 433-1868
(507) 433-9422 fax

90. Steele County Free Fair
P.O. Box 650
Owatonna, MN 55060-0650
(507) 451-5305
(507) 451-4154 fax
Website: www.ll.net/scff/index.htm

91. Minnesota State Fair
1265 Snelling Ave. N.
St. Paul, MN 55108-3099
(651) 642-2200
(651) 642-2440 fax

E-Mail: fairinfo@statefair.gen.mn.us
Website: www.statefair.gen.mn.us/

92. Carver County Fair
5325 County Road
Waconia, MN 55388-9336
(612) 442-2333
(612) 442-2996 fax

MISSISSIPPI

93. Mississippi Coast Fair & Exposition
2350 Beach Blvd.
Biloxi, MS 39531-4914
(228) 388-8010
(228) 385-2412 fax
E-Mail: coliseum@gulfcoast.org
Website: www.mscoastcoliseum.com

94. Mississippi State Fair
P.O. Box 892
Jackson, MS 39205-0892
(601) 961-4000
(601) 354-6545 fax
Website: www.mdac.state.ms.us

95. South Mississippi Fair
P.O. Box 2367
Laurel, MS 39442-2367
(601) 649-3535
(601) 649-7824 fax
E-Mail: ljccdc@c-gate.net

MISSOURI

96. Montgomery County Fair
P.O. Box 11
Montgomery City, MO 63361-0011
(573) 564-3526 phone
E-Mail: rrhopper@ktis.net
Website:
www.montgomerycountyfair.org

97. Missouri State Fair
2503 W. 16th St.
Sedalia, MO 65301-2569
(660) 530-5600
(660) 530-5609 fax
Website: www.mostatefair.com

98. Ozark Empire Fair
P.O. Box 630
Springfield, MO 65801-0630
(417) 833-2660
(417) 833-3769 fax

99. Washington Town and Country Fair
323 W. Main St.
Washington, MO 63090-2124
(314) 239-2715
(314) 239-1381 fax
E-mail: irmaw@washmo.org
Website: www.washmofair.com

MONTANA

100. Montana State Fair
P.O. Box 1888
Great Falls, MT 59403-1888
(406) 727-8900
(406) 452-8955 fax
E-Mail: expopark@city-of-great-falls.com
Website: www.city-of-great-falls.com

101. Northwest Montana Fair & Rodeo
265 N. Meridian Rd.
Kalispell, MT 59901-3849
(406) 758-5810
(406) 756-8936 fax

NEBRASKA

102. Platte County Fair
822 15 Street
Columbus, NE 68601
(402) 564-0133
(402) 564-0990 fax

103. Adams County Agricultural Society
947 S. Baltimore Ave.
Hastings, NE 68901-6718
(402) 462-3247
(402) 462-4731 fax

104. Nebraska State Fair
P.O. Box 81223
Lincoln, NE 68501-1223
(402) 474-5371
(402) 473-4114 fax
E-Mail: jskold@statefair.org
Website: www.statefair.org

105. Ak-Sar-Ben 4-H Livestock Exposition
6800 Mercy Rd., Ste 206
Omaha, NE 68106-2627
(402) 554-9602
(402) 554-9609 fax
E-Mail: knights@aksarben.org
Website: ww.aksarben.org

NEVADA

106. Clark County Fair
P.O. Box 143
Logandale, NV 89021-0143
(702) 398-3247
(702) 398-3747 fax
E-mail: ccfair@comnett.net

107. Nevada State Fair
1350 N. Wells Ave., #A
Reno, NV 89512-2447
(775) 688-5767
(775) 688-5763 fax
E-Mail: nvstatefair@inetworld.com
Website: www.nevadastatefair.org

NEW HAMPSHIRE

108. Hopkinton State Fair
P.O. Box 700
Contoocook, NH 03229-0700
(603) 746-4191
(603) 746-3037 fax
E-Mail: hsfair@conknet.com
Website: www.hsfair.org

109. Deerfield Fair
P.O. Box 156
Deerfield, NH 03037-0156
(603) 463-7421
(603) 463-7414 fax

110. Rochester Fair
72 Lafayette St.
Rochester, NH 03867-2624
(603) 332-6585
(603) 332-1896 fax

111. Stratham Fair
P.O. Box 595
Stratham, NH 03885-0595
(603) 433-GAME phone

NEW JERSEY

112. Sussex County Farm & Horse Show
38 Broad St.
Branchville, NJ 07826-5602
(973) 948-5500
(973) 948-0147 fax
E-Mail: thefair@ptd.net
Website: www.Sussex-County-Fair.org

113. Ocean County Fair
24 Germania Ct.
Toms River, NJ 08755-8039
(908) 914-9466
(908) 914-0591 fax

114. Flemington Agricultural Fair
P.O. Box 293
Flemington, NJ 08822-0293
(908) 782-2413
(908) 806-8432 fax

NEW MEXICO

115. New Mexico State Fair
P.O. Box 8546
Albuquerque, NM 87198-8546
(505) 265-1791
(505) 266-7784 fax
E-Mail: info@nmstatefair.com
Website: www.nmstatefair.com

116. San Juan County Fair
100 S. Oliver Dr., Ste. 100
Aztec, NM 87410-2400
(505) 325-5415
(505) 325-5525 fax
E-Mail: sjcmcgee@mn.net
Website: www.sjcmcgee.com

117. **Lea County Fair and Rodeo**
101 S. Commercial Ave.
Lovington, NM 88260-4093
1-800-658-9955
(505) 396-4554 fax

118. **Eastern New Mexico State Fair**
P.O. Box 824
Roswell, NM 88202-0824
(505) 623-9411
(505) 623-0688 fax

NEW YORK

119. **Altamont Fair**
P. O. Box 506
Altamont, NY 12009-0506
(518) 861-6671
(518) 861-7251 fax
E-Mail: altamontfair@yahoo.com
Website: www.crisny.org/not-for-
profit/altfair

120. **Saratoga County Fair**
162 Prospect St.
Ballston Spa, NY 12020-1354
E-Mail: thefair@global2000.net
Website: saratogacountyfair.org

121. **Brooklyn's County Fair**
275 Madison Ave., Ste. 1000
Brooklyn, NY 10016-1101
(212) 689-8600
(212) 686-0252 fax
E-Mail: MKF555@IDT.Net.mail.com
Website: members.aol.com/
graphking/brooklyn.html

122. **Washington County Fair**
P.O. Box 134, Rt. 29
Greenwich, NY 12834-0134
(518) 692-2464
(518) 692-1021 fax
Website:
www.washingtoncountyfair.com

123. **Erie County Fair and Exposition**
5600 McKinley Pkwy.
Hamburg, NY 14075-3933
(716) 649-3900
(716) 649-4687 fax
E-Mail: ecfair@ecfair.org
Website: www.ecfair.org

124. **Orange County Fair**
P.O. Box 3116
Middleton, NY 10940-0808
(914) 343-4826
(914) 343-8765 fax

125. **Dutchess County Fair**
P.O. Box 389
Rhinebeck, NY 12572-0389
(914) 876-4001

(914) 876-4003 fax
E-Mail: fair@vh.net
Website: www.duchessfair.com

126. **New York State Fair**
581 State Fair Blvd.
Syracuse, NY 13209-1551
(315) 487-7711
(315) 487-9260 fax
E-Mail: nysfair@dreamscape.com

127. **Greater Westchester County Fair
& Exposition**
500 Central Park Ave.
Yonkers, NY 10704-3055
(914) 968-4200
(914) 968-1121 fax

NORTH CAROLINA

128. Cabarrus County Agricultural Fair
P.O. Box 563
Concord, NC 28026-0563
(704) 786-7221 phone and fax

129. **North Carolina Mountain State
Fair**
1301 Fanning Bridge Rd.
Fletcher, NC 28732-9237
(704) 687-1414
(704) 687-9272 fax
E-Mail: bill-
edmondson@mail.agr.state.nc.us
Website:
www.agr.state.nc.us/markets/fairs98

130. **Wayne County Agricultural Fair**
P.O. Box 1100
Goldsboro, NC 27533-1100
(919) 735-7277
(919) 731-7669 fax

131. **Pitt County American Legion
Agricultural Fair**
P.O. Box 1293
Greenville, NC 27835-1293
(252) 758-6916 phone

132. **North Carolina State Fair**
1025 Blue Ridge Rd.
Raleigh, NC 27607-3902
(919) 821-7400
(919) 733-5079 fax
E-Mail:
wesley_wyatt@ncdamail.agr.state.nc.us
Website: www.ncstatefair.org

133. **Cleveland County Fair**
1751 E. Marion St.
Shelby, NC 28152-6260
(704) 487-0651
(704) 487-9192 fax

134. **Dixie Classic Fair**
P.O. Box 7525

Winston-Salem, NC 27109-7525
(336) 727-2236
(336) 727-2799 fax
E-Mal: feedback@dcfair.com
Website: www.dcfair.com

NORTH DAKOTA

135. **Stutsman County Fair**
P.O. Box 757
Jamestown, ND 58402-0757
(701) 252-2404
(701) 252-3490 fax

136. **North Dakota State Fair**
P.O. Box 1796
Minot, ND 58702-1796
(701) 857-7620
(701) 857-7622 fax
E-Mail: ndsf@minot.com
Website: minot.com/-ndsf

137. **North Dakota Winter Show**
P.O. Box 846
Valley City, ND 58072-0797
(701) 282-2000
(701) 282-6909 fax

OHIO

138. **Cuyahoga County Fair**
P.O. Box 135
Berea, OH 440178-0135
(440) 243-0090
(440) 243-0344 fax
Website: www.cuyfair.com

139. **Canfield Fair**
P.O. Box 250
Canfield, OH 44406-0250
(330) 533-4107
(330) 533-8331 fax

140. **Stark County Fair**
P.O. Box 80297
Canton, OH 44708-0279
(330) 452-0621
(330) 452-0787 fax

141. **Ohio State Fair**
717 E. 17th Ave.
Columbus, OH 43211-2489
(614) 644-4000
(614) 644-4031
Website: www.ohiostatefair.com

142. **Hartford Independent
Agricultural Society**
P.O. Box 317
Croton, OH 43013-0317
(740) 893-4881
(740) 893-4810 fax

143. **Delaware County Fair**
P.O. Box 1278
Delaware, OH 43015

(740) 362-3851
(740) 363-4132 fax
E-Mail: fair@delawarecountyfair.com
Website: www.delawarecountyfair.com

144. **The Great Darke County Fair**
P.O. Box 605
Greenville, OH 45331-0605
(937) 548-5044
(937) 548-8286 fax

OKLAHOMA

145. **State Fair of Oklahoma**
P.O. Box 74943
Oklahoma City, OK 73147-0943
(405) 948-6700
(405) 948-6828 fax
E-Mail: oklafair@oklafair.org
Website: www.oklafair.org

146. **Tulsa State Fair**
P.O. Box 4735
Tulsa, OK 74159-0735
(918) 744-1113
(918) 744-8725 fax
Website: www.exposquare.com

OREGON

147. **Clackamas County Fair**
694 N.E. 4th Ave.
Canby, OR 97013-2339
(503) 266-1136
(503) 266-2833 fax

148. **Jackson County Fair**
P.O. Box3635
Central Point, OR 97502-0025
(541) 776-7237
(541) 776-7270 fax
E-Mail: cphoro@mind.net
Website: www.jcfairgrounds.com

149. **Lane County Fair**
796 W. 13th Ave.
Eugene, OR 97402-4010
(541) 682-4292
(541) 682-3614 fax
E-mail:
Kathee.McDermott@co.lane.or.us
Website: www.atthefair.com

150. **Deschutes County Fair**
3800 S.W. Airport Way
Redmond, OR 97756
(541) 548-2711
(541) 923-1652 fax
E-mail: abrander@dcfe.com
Website: www.dcfe.com

151. **Oregon State Fair**
2330 17th St. N.E.
Salem, OR 97310-1306
(503) 378-3247
(503) 373-1788 fax
E-Mail: lin.murakami@fair.state.or.us
Website: www.fair.state.or.us

PENNSYLVANIA

152. **The Great Allentown Fair**
302 N. 17th St.
Allentown, PA 18104-5013
(610) 433-7541
(610) 433-4005 fax
E-Mail: allenfair@aol
Website: www.allentownfairpa.org

153. **Bloomsburg Fair**
P.O. Box 479
Bloomsburg, PA 17815-0479
(717) 784-4949
(717) 387-4140 fax
E-Mail: TheScoop@bloomsburgfair.com
Website: www.bloomsburgfair.com

154. **West End Fair**
P.O. Box 115
Gilbert, PA 18331-0115
(717) 992-4456
(610) 681-4313 fax
E-Mail: westendfair@pafairs.org
Website: www.pafairs.org/westendfair

155. **Pennsylvania Farm Show**
2301 N. Cameron St.
Harrisburg, PA 17110
(717) 787-5373
(717) 783-8710 fax
Website: www.pda.state.pa.us

RHODE ISLAND

156. **Washington County Fair**
78 Richmond Townhouse Rd.
Richmond, RI 02812-1036
(401) 539-7042
(401) 789-8246 fax

SOUTH CAROLINA

157. **Anderson County Fair**
P.O. Box 274
Anderson, SC 29622-0274
(864) 226-6114
(864) 226-8001 fax

158. **Coastal Carolina Fair**
P.O. Box 762
Charleston, SC 29456-0762
(803) 572-3161
(803) 572-3126 fax
E-Mail: ccfair@awod.com

159. **South Carolina State Fair**
P.O. Box 393
Columbia, SC 29202-0393
(803) 799-3387
(803) 799-1760 fax
E-Mail: geninfo@scstatefair.org
Website: www.scstatefair.org

160. **Upper South Carolina State Fair**
P.O. Box 5206
Greenville, SC 29606-5206
(864) 269-0852
(864) 288-3056 fax

161. **Piedmont Interstate Fair**
P.O. Box 4965
Spartanburg, SC 29305-4965
(864) 582-7042
(864) 583-2366 fax

SOUTH DAKOTA

162. **Brown County Fair & 4-H Show**
25 Market St.
Aberdeen, SD 57401-4227
(605) 626-7110
(605) 626-4010 fax

163. **Central States Fair**
800 San Francisco St.
Rapid City, SD 57701-3057
(605) 355-3861
(605) 355-3800 fax

164. **Sioux Empire Fair**
4000 W. 12th St.
Sioux Falls, SD 57107-0236
(605) 367-7178
(605) 355-3800 fax

TENNESSEE

165. **Appalachian Fair**
P.O. Box 8218
Gray, TN 37615-0218
(615) 477-3211
(615) 477-3853 fax
E-Mail: appfair@pretend.com
Website: www.appalachianfair.com

166. **Tennessee Valley Agricultural and Industrial Fair**
P.O. Box 6066
Knoxville, TN 37914-0066
(615) 637-5840
(615) 637-7914 fax
E-Mail: fair@korrnet.org
Website: www.korrnet.org/fair

167. **Wilson County Fair**
12110 Lebanon Rd.
Lebanon, TN 37122-2520
(615) 443-2626
(615) 443-2604 fax
E-Mail: karenatfg@aol.com

168. **Warren County Agriculture & Livestock Fair**
5822 Great Falls Rd.
Rock Island, TN 38581-4229
(931) 686-8379
(931) 686-8211 fax

169. **Mid-South Fair**
940 Early Maxwell Blvd.
Memphis, TN 38104-5931
(901) 274-8800
(901) 274-8804 fax
E-Mail: libland@bellsouth.net
Website: www.midsouthfair.com

TEXAS

170. **Brazoria County Fair**
P.O. Box 818
Angleton, TX 77516-0818
(409) 849-6416
(409) 849-6985 fax
E-Mail: bcfa@mastnet.net

171. **South Texas State Fair**
P.O. Box 3207
Beaumont, TX 77704-3207
(409) 832-9991
(409) 838-0402 fax

172. **State Fair of Texas**
P.O. Box 150009
Dallas, TX 75315-0009
(214) 565-9931
(214) 421-8710 fax
E-Mail: pr@greatstatefair.com
Website: www.texfair.com

173. **Southwestern Exposition & Livestock Show**
P.O. Box 150
Forth Worth, TX 76101-0150
(817) 877-2400
(817) 877-2499 fax
Website: www.fwstockshowrodeo.com

174. **Houston Livestock Show & Rodeo**
P.O. Box 20070
Houston, TX 77225-0070
(713) 791-9000
(713) 794-9528 fax
Website: www.hlsr.com

175. **Longview Jaycees Greeg County Fair & Exposition**
P.O. Box 1124
Longview, TX 75606-1124
(903) 753-4478
(903) 753-5452 fax
E-Mail: bgcsr8@aol.com

176. **Panhandle-South Plains Fair**
P.O. Box 208
Lubbock, TX 79408-0208

(806) 763-2833
(806) 744-5903 fax

177. **Fort Bend County Fair**
P.O. Box 428
Rosenberg, TX 77471-0428
(713) 342-6171
(713) 342-0808 fax
Website: www.fortbend.net

178. **San Antonio Livestock Exposition**
P.O. Box 200230
San Antonio, TX 78220-0230
(210) 225-5851
(210) 227-7934
E-Mail: saleadmin@sarodeo.com
Website: www.sarodeo.com

179. **East Texas State Fair**
2112 W. Front St.
Tyler, TX 75702-6828
(903) 597-2501
(903) 597-0692 fax
E-Mail: statefair@tyler.com
Website: www.statefair.com

UTAH

180. **Utah State Fair**
1000 W.
Salt Lake City, UT 84116-3307
(801) 538-8400
(801) 538-8455 fax
E-Mail: donnad@fiber.net
Website: www.utah-state-fair.com

VERMONT

181. **Champlain Valley Exposition**
P.O. Box 209
Essex Junction, VT 05453-0209
(802) 878-5545
(802) 879-5404 fax
E-Mail: cvfair@aol.com
Website: www.cvfair.com

VIRGINIA

182. **Rockingham County Fair**
4808 South Valley Pike
Harrisonburg, VA 22802
(540) 434-0005
(540) 432-6544 fax
Website: www.svta.org/fair/

183. **State Fair of Virginia**
P.O. Box 26805
Richmond, VA 23261-6805
(804) 228-3200
(804) 228-3252 fax
E-Mail: kth@statefair.com
Website: www.statefair.com

WASHINGTON

184. Kitsap County Fair
1200 Fairgrounds Rd. N.W.
Bremerton, WA 98311-8504
(360) 692-3655
(360) 337-4781 fax
E-Mail: lmeyerco.kitsap.wa.us

185. Southwest Washington Fair
2555 N. Main St.
Centralia-Chehalis, WA 98532-2404
(360) 736-6072
(360) 740-1478 fax
E-Mail: swwfair@localaccess.com

186. Grays Harbor County Fair
P.O. Box 1229
Elma, WA 98541
(360) 482-2651
(360) 482-3297 fax
E-Mail: ghfair@techline.com

187. King County Fair
P.O. Box 246
Enumclaw, WA 98022-1229
(360) 825-7777
(206) 296-8891 fax
E-Mail: mark.campbell@metrokc.gov
Website: www.metrokc.gov/parks/

188. Evergreen State Fair
P.O. Box 129
Monroe, WA 98272-0129
(360) 794-4344
(360) 794-8027 fax
E-Mail: info@evergreenfair.org
Website: www.evergreenfair.org

189. Western Washington Fair
P.O. Box 430
Puyallup, WA 98371-0162
(253) 845-1771
(253) 841-5390 fax
E-Mail: cowbnga@thefair.com
Website: www.thefair.com

190. Clark County Fair
17402 N. E. Delfel Rd.
Ridgefield, WA 98642-9473
(360) 397-6180
(360) 397-6185 fax
E-Mail: ccfair@clarkcofair.com

191. Central Washington State Fair
P.O. Box 1381
Yakima, WA 98907-1381
(509) 248-7160
(509) 248-8093 fax
E-Mail: cwsf@fairfun.com
Website: www.fairfun.com

WEST VIRGINIA

192. State Fair of West Virginia
P.O. Box 986
Lewisburg, WV 24901-0986
(304) 645-1090
(304) 645-6660 fax
E-Mail: wvstatefair@wvstatefair.com
Website: www.statefair.com

WISCONSIN

193. Walworth County Fair
P.O. Box 286
Elkhorn, WI 53121-0286
(414) 723-3228
(414) 723-3202 fax

194. Rock County 4-H Fair
P.O. Box 170
Janesville, 53547-0170
(608) 755-1470
(608) 755-0227 fax
E-Mail rcfair@inwave.com
Website: www.rockcounty4hfair.com

**195. Central Wisconsin State Fair
Association, Inc.**
P.O. Box 748
Marshfield, WI 54449-0748
(715) 387-1261
(715) 384-9745 fax

196. Wisconsin State Fair
P.O. Box 14990
Milwaukee, WI 53214-0990
(414) 266-7000
(414) 266-7007 fax
E-Mail: state.fair@wsfp.state.wi.us
Website: www.wsfp.state.wi.us

197. Sheboygan County Fair
P.O. Box 495
Plymouth, WI 53073-0495
(920) 893-5751
(920) 892-2399 fax
E-Mail: shebfair@excel.net
Website: www.shebcofair.org

198. Wisconsin Valley Fair
500 Forest St.
Wausau, WI 54403-5554
(715) 261-1539
(715) 848-3196

WYOMING

199. Central Wyoming Fair and Rodeo
1700 Fairgrounds Rd.
Casper, WY 82604-2919
(307) 235-5775
(307) 266-4224 fax

**200. Sweetwater County Events
Complex**
3320 Yellowstone Rd.

Rock Springs, WY 82901-2812
(307) 352-6789
(307) 352-6787 fax
E-Mail: llloyd@sweetwater.net
Website:
ww.swl.k12.wy.us/eventscomplex.htm

50 Clubs

ALABAMA

1. **Five Points South Music Hall**
   1016 20th S., S.
   Birmingham, AL 35205
   (205) 322-2207
   (205) 326-3750 fax

2. **Zydeco**
   2001 15th St., S.
   Birmingham, AL 35205
   (205) 942-6600
   (2050 930-0313 fax

ARIZONA

3. **The Celebrity Theatre**
   440 N. 32nd St.
   Phoenix, AZ 85008
   (602) 267-1600
   (602) 267-4882 fax
   E-mail:
   rcrockett@celebritytheatre.com
   Website: www.celebritytheatre.com

4. **Rhythm Room**
   1019 E. Indian School Rd.
   Phoenix, AZ 85004
   (602) 994-1234
   (602) 265-4842 fax
   Website: ww.rhythmroom.com

ARKANSAS

5. **LJ's**
   1220 N. College
   Fayettville, AR 72703
   (501) 442-8837
   (501) 443-2329 fax

6. **Vino's**
   923 W. 7th
   Little Rock, AR 72201
   (501) 375-8468
   (501) 375-3457 fax

CALIFORNIA

7. **House of Blues**
   8430 Sunset Blvd.
   Los Angeles, CA 90069
   (213) 848-5100

8. **Fillmore**
   1805 Geary
   San Francisco, CA 94142

(415) 281-9298
(415) 243-9603 fax
E-mail: michael-bailey@bgp.com

9. **The Viper Room**
   8852 Sunset Blvd.
   West Hollywood, CA 90069
   (310) 358-1881
   (310) 652-8471 fax
   E-mail: vr001@aol.com
   Website: www.viperroom.com

COLORADO

10. **Avalanche Productions, Inc.**
    P.O. Box 1265
    Aspen, CO 816+12
    (970) 925-1461
    (970) 920-4159 fax
    E-mail: dlaugh@csn.com

11. **The Grizzly Rose**
    5450 N. Valley Hwy.
    Denver, CO 80216
    (303) 295-1941
    (303) 297-0747 fax
    Website: www.grizzlyrose.com

CONNECTICUT

12. **Tuxedo Junction**
    2 Ives St.
    Danbury, CT 06810
    (203) 748-2561
    (203) 791-9897 fax
    Website: www.moonsite.com/tuxedo

13. **Toad's Place**
    300 York St.
    New Haven, CT 06511
    (203) 562-5694
    (203) 772-4089 fax
    E-mail: skmadsnet.net
    Website: www.toadsplace.com

DELAWARE

14. **Bottle and Cork**
    1807 Highway One
    Dewey Beach, DE 19971
    (302) 227-7272
    (302) 227-8585 fax

15. **Rusty Rudder at Ruddertowne**
    Dickenson St. On the Bay
    Dewey Beach, DE 19971
    (302) 2368-2001
    (302) 226-2402 fax
    E-mail: rrudder@dmv.com
    Website: dmv.com/~rrudder

DISTRICT OF COLUMBIA

16. **Capitol Ballroom**
    1015 Half St. S.E.
    Washington, D.C. 20003
    (202) 549-ROCK
    (202) 554-0922 fax
    E-mail: capball@erols.com
    Website: www.capitolballroom.com

17. **Nine Thirty Club**
    815 "V" St., N.W.
    Washington, D.C. 20001
    (202) 265-0930
    (202) 265-1397 fax
    E-mail: nclub930@aol.com
    Website: www.930.com

FLORIDA

18. **The Moon**
    1105 E. Lafayette St.
    Tallahassee, FL 32301
    (850) 878-6900
    (850) 656-6562
    E-mail: ssc@nettally.com
    Website: www.moon.talstar.com

19. **The Masquerade**
    1503 E. Seventh Ave.
    Tampa, FL 33605
    (813) 247-2518
    (813) 248-2620 fax
    E-mail: masq-tpa@mindspring.com
    Website: www.mbus.com

GEORGIA

20. **Roxy Theatre**
    3110 Roswell Rd.
    Atlanta, GA 30305
    (404) 233-1062
    (404) 233-1087 fax
    E-mail: consopro@mindspring.com
    Website: www.atlantaconcerts.com

HAWAII

21. **Rock Corp. AKA "The Cellar"**
    205 Lewers
    Honolulu, HI 96815
    (808) 923-9952
    (808) 942-8971 fax

IDAHO

22. **Blues Bouquet**
    1010 Main St.
    Boise, ID 83702
    (208) 345-6605

ILLINOIS

23. **Buddy Guy's Legends**
    754 S. Wabash
    Chicago, IL 60605
    (312) 427-1190
    (312) 427-1192 fax
    Website: www.buddyguy.com

INDIANA

24. **The Patio**
    6308 n. Guilford Ave.
    Indianapolis, IN 46220
    (317) 253-0799
    (317) 255-2828 fax
    E-mail: vogue@spitfire.net
    Website: www.thevogue.com

IOWA

25. **The Union Bar**
    121 E. College
    Iowa City, IA 52240
    (319) 339-7713
    (319) 339-7739 fax
    E-mail: union_bar@msn.com
    Website: www.unionbar.onplanet.com

KANSAS

26. **Cotillion Ballroom**
    11120 W. Kellogg
    Wichita, KS 67209
    (316) 722-4201
    (316) 722-4204 fax
    E-mail: ballroom@feist.com
    Website: www.thecotillion.com

KENTUCKY

27. **Phoenix Hill Tavern**
    644 Baxter Ave.
    Louisville, KY 40204
    (502) 589-4957
    (502) 589-0815 fax

LOUISIANA

28. **Varsity Theatre**
    353 Highland Rd.
    Baton Rouge, LA 70802
    (504) 383-7018
    (504) 346-0453 fax
    E-mail: mail@varsitytheatre.com
    Website: www.varsitytheatre.com

MASSACHUSETTS

29. **Mama Kin**
    36 Landsdowne St.
    Boston, MA 02215
    (617) 536-2100
    (617) 424-6995 fax
    Website: www.mamakin.com

MICHIGAN

30. **The Intersection**
    1520 Wealthy St.
    Eastown, MI 49516
    (616) 554-3102
    (616) 554-3107 fax
    E-mail: jnewman.com
    Website: www.section.com

MINNESOTA

31. **First Avenue/Seventh St. Entry**
    701 N. 1st St.
    Minneapolsi, MN 55403
    (6+12) 338-8388
    (612) 338-5416 fax
    E-mail: firstave@bitstream.nnet
    Webstie: www.first-avenue.net

MISSISSIPPI

32. **The Dock Of Mississippi**
    287 Dyke Rd.
    Ridgeland, MS 39157
    (601) 856-7765
    (601) 856-1618 fax
    Website: www.dockrocker.com

MISSOURI

33. **Grand Emporium**
    3832 Main St.
    Kansas City, MO 64111
    (816) 531-1504
    (816) 531-8946 fax
    Website: www.grandemporium.com

MONTANA

34. **Jay's Upstairs**
    119 W. Main
    Missoula, MT 59802
    (406) 728-9915
    (406) 543-0021 fax
    Website: www.montana.com/jays

NEVADA

35. **Billboard Live**
    5100 West Sahara
    Las Vegas, NV 89146
    (702) 248-0063
    (702) 248-0962 fax

NEW JERSEY

36. **MGM Grand Hotel & Casino**
    6595 Delilah Rd.
    Egg Harbor Towship, NJ 08234
    (609) 484-1300
    (609) 484-7675 fax

NEW MEXICO

37. **El Ray Theatre**
    622 Central SW
    Albuquerque, NM 87102
    (505) 265-7877
    (505) 345-2454 fax

NEW YORK

38. **C.B.G.B.**
    315 Bowery
    New York, NY 10003
    (212) 982-4052
    Website: www.cbgb.com

NORTH CAROLINA

39. **Tremont Music Hall & The Casbah**
    400 W. Tremont Ave.
    Charlotte, NC 28203
    (704) 343-9432
    (704) 343-9432 fax
    Website:
    www.creativeloafing.com/charlotte/hal/
    tremontmusi

NORTH DAKOTA

40. **Windbreak Lounge**
    3150 39th St. SW
    Fargo, ND 58104
    (701) 282-5507
    (701) 282-7529 fax

OHIO

41. **Ludlow's**
    485 S. Front St.
    Columbus, OH 43215
    (614) 224-3808
    (614) 241-2070 fax
    E-mail: bulldogpro@aol.com
    Website: www.ludlows.com

OKLAHOMA

42. **Cain's Ballroom**
    423 N. Main St.
    Tulsa, OK 74103
    (918) 584-2306
    (918) 583-8247 fax

OREGON

43. **Mount Tabor Pub**
    4811 SE Hawthorne
    Portland, OR 97215
    (503) 238-1646
    (503) 238-6515 fax

PENNSYLVANIA

44. **Metropol**
    1650 Smallman St.
    Pittsburgh, PA 15222
    (412) 261-4513
    (412) 471-5144 fax
    E-mail: mullen@sportsrock.com
    Website: www.sportsrock.com

SOUTH CAROLINA

45. **The Windjammer, Inc.**
    1008 Ocean Blvd.
    Isle of Palms, SC 29451
    (864) 886-8596
    (864) 886-8993 fax
    E-mail: bross@awod.com
    Webstie: www.the-windjammer.com

SOUTH DAKOTA

46. The Sioux Falls Brewing Co.
431 N. Phillips Ave
Sioux Falls, SD 57104
(605) 332-4847
(605) 332-4314 fax
E-mail: laurel@sfbrewco.com
Website: www.sfbrewco.com

TENNESSEE

47. Wildhorse Saloon
120 Second Ave.
Nashville, TN 37201
(615) 256-WILD
(615) 902-8218 fax
Website: www.country.com

TEXAS

48. Trees
2709 Elm St.
Dallas, TX 75226
(214) 342-1700
(214) 342-2265 fax

UTAH

49. The Westerner
3360 S. Redwood Rd.
West Valley City, UT 84119
(801) 974-5943
(801) 973-2509 fax
E-mail: greg@westerner.com
Website: www.westerner.com

VERMONT

50. Club Metronome
188 Main St.
Burlington, VT 05401
(802) 865-4563
(802) 865-4652 fax
E-mail: metro@together.net
Website: www.clubmetronome.com

50 Venues

ALABAMA

1. Mobile Civic Center
401 Civic Center Dr.
Mobile, AL 36602
(334) 208-7788
(334) 208-7551 fax

2. Montgomery Civic Center
300 Bibb St.
Montgomery, AL 36104
(334) 241-2100
(334) 241-2117 fax
E-mail:
haustin@civiccenter.ci.montgomery.al.us

Website:
www.civic-center.ci.montgomery.al.us

ALASKA

3. George M. Sullivan Sports Arena
1600 Gambell St.
Anchorage, AK 99501
(907) 279-0618
(907) 274-0676 fax

4. Carlson Center
2010 Second Ave.
Fairbanks, AK 99701
(907) 451-8258
(907) 451) 1195 fax

ARIZONA

5. Blockbuster Desert Sky Pavillion
2121 N. 83rd Ave.
Phoenix, AZ 85035
(602) 254-7200
(602) 849-6663 fax

6. Phoenix Civic Plaza Convention Center & Symphony Hall
Third St., Monroe to Jefferson
Phoenix, AZ 85004
(800) 282-4842
(602) 495-3642 fax
E-mail: cplaza@ci.phoenix.az.us
Website: www.ci.phoenix.az.us/civplaza

ARKANSAS

7. Robinson Center
400 W. Markham
Little Rock, AR 72201
(501) 376-4781
(501) 374-2255 fax
E-mail: eventplan@littlerock.com
Website: www.littlerock.com

8. Pine Bluff Convention Center
1 Convention Center Plz.
Pine Bluff, AR 71601
(870) 536-7600
(870) 535-4867 fax
E-mail: pbinfo@pinebluff.com
Website: www.pinebluff.com

CALIFORNIA

9. The Greek Theatre
2700 N. Vermont
Los Angeles, CA 90027
(323) 468-1710
(323) 468-1722 fax
E-mail: concerts@nederlander.com
Website:
www.nederlander.com/greek.html

10. The Henry Fonda Theatre
6126 Hollywood Blvd.
Los Angeles, CA 90028
(323) 468-1710

(323) 462-1722 fax
E-mail: concerts@nederlander.com
Website: www.nederlander.com

11. **Santa Monica Civic Auditorium**
1855 Main St.
Santa Monica, CA 90401
(310) 458-8551
(310) 394-3411 fax

COLORADO

12. **Red Rocks Ampitheatre**
Denver, CO 80204
(303) 640-7300
(303) 640-7330 fax

13. **Fox Theater**
1135 13th St.
Boulder, CO 80302
(303) 786-7030
(303) 440-6455 fax

CONNECTICUT

14. **Hartford Civic Center**
1 Civic Center Plz.
Hartford, CT 06103
(860) 249-6333
(860) 241-4226 fax

15. **Lincoln Theater**
200 Bloomfield Ave.
West Hartford, CT 06117
(860) 768-4536
(860) 768-4229 fax

DELAWARE

16. **Bob Carpenter Center**
University of Delaware-Newark
Newark, DE 19716
(302) 831-4016
(302) 831-4019 fax

17. **The Grand Opera House**
818 N. Market St.
Wilmington, DE 19801
(302) 658-7897
(320) 652-5346 fax
E-mail: grandopera@aol.com

DISTRICT OF COLUMBIA

18. **John F. Kennedy Center for the Performing Arts**
c/o Kennedy Center
Washington, D.C. 20566
(202) 416-8000
(202) 416-8205 fax

FLORIDA

19. **Miami Areana**
701 Arena Blvd.
Miami, FL 33136
(305) 530-4400
(305) 530-4429 fax

GEORGIA

20. **Coca-Cola Lakewood Amphitheatre**
2002 Lakewood Way
Atlanta, GA 30315
(404) 627-9704
(404) 627-1013 fax

HAWAII

21. **Maui Community Arts & Cultural Center**
Kahului Beach Rd.
Kahului, HI 96732-1137
(808) 242-2787
(808) 242-4665 fax

IDAHO

22. **Idaho State University**
550 Memorial Dr.
Boise, ID 83209
(208) 236-2831
(208) 236-4089 fax
Website: www.isu.edu/isutour/build-descrip/holt-arena.html

ILLINOIS

23. **Aragon Ballroom**
1106 W. Lawrence Ave.
Chicago, IL 60640
(773) 561-9500
(773) 561-9585 fax
Website: aragon.com

INDIANA

24. **Embassy Theatre**
125 W. Jefferson Blvd.
Fort Wayne, IN 46802
(219) 424-6287
(219) 424-4806
E-mail: embassy2@fortwayne.infi.net
Website: www.ft-wayne.in.us/arts/embassy

IOWA

25. **Civic Center of Greater Des Moines**
221 Walnut St.
Des Moines, IA 50309
(515) 243-0766
(515) 243-179 fax

KANSAS

26. **Sandstone Amphitheatre**
633 N.130th St.
Bonner Springs, KS 66012
(913) 721-3400
(913) 721-1404 fax

KENTUCKY

27. **Kentucky Center for the Arts**
5 Riverfront Plaza
Louisville, KY 40202
(502) 562-0100
(502) 562-0150 fax

LOUISIANA

28. **Heymann Performing Arts & Convention Center**
1373 S. College Rd.
Lafayette, LA 70503
(318) 291-5540
(318) 291-5580 fax
E-mail: hpacc@licknet.net

MAINE

29. **Augusta Civic Center**
Community Dr.
Augusta, ME 04330
(207) 626-2405
(207) 626-5968 fax

MARYLAND

30. **Joseph Meyerhoff Symphony Hall**
1212 Cathedral St.
Baltimore, MD 21201
(410) 783-8100
(410) 783-8004 fax
E-mail:
gpurviance@baltimoresymphony.org
Website: www.baltimoresymphony.org

MASSACHUSETTS

31. **Berklee Performance Center**
136 Massachusetts Ave.
Boston, MA 02115
(617) 747-2474
(617) 375-9228 fax

MICHIGAN

32. **Kellogg Arena**
1 McCamly Sq.
Battle Creek, MI 49017
(616) 963-4800
(616) 968-8840 fax
E-mail: jwalczak@battlecreek.net

MINNESOTA

33. **The Historic State Theatre**
805 Hennepin Ave.
Minneapolis, MN 55402
(612) 373-5600
(612) 339-4146 fax
E-mail: htg@orpheum.com

MISSISSIPPI

34. **Mississippi State Fairgrounds**
1207 Mississippi St.
Jackson, MS 39202
(601) 961-4000
(601) 354-6545 fax

MISSOURI

35. **Riverport Amphitheatre**
14141 Riverport Dr.
Maryland Heights, MO 63043
(314) 298-9944
(314) 291-4719 fax

MONTANA

36. **MetraPark**
308 Sixth Ave. N.
Billings, MT 59101
(406) 256-2400
(256-2479 fax
Website: www.metrapark.com

NEBRASKA

37. **Pershing Auditorium**
226 Centennial mall S.
Lincoln, NE 68508
(402) 441-8744
(402) 441-7913 fax
E-mail: pershing@ci.lincoln.ne.uw
Website: interlinc.ci.lincoln.ne.us

NEVADA

38. **MGM Grand Garden Arena**
3799 Las Vegas Blvd. S.
Las Vegas, NV 89019
(702) 891-7800
(702) 891-7831 fax
E-mail: prowsm@aol.com
Website: www.mgmgrand.com

NEW HAMPSHIRE

39. **John F. Kennedy Memorial Coliseum**
625 mammoth Rk.
Manchester, NH 03104
(603) 624-6567
(603) 624-6569 fax

NEW JERSEY

40. **Count Basie Theatre**
99 Monmouth St.
Redbank, NJ 07701
(732) 842-9000
(7632) 842-9323 fax

NEW MEXICO

41. **Red Rock State Park**
PO Box 328
Church Rock, NM 87311
(505) 722-3839
(505) 863-1297 fax

NEW YORK

42. **Carnegie Hall**
154 W. 57 St.
New York, NY 10019
(212) 903-9710
(212) 581-6539 fax

43. **Radio City Music Hall**
1260 Avenue of the Americas
New York, NY 10020
(212) 632-4000
(212) 632-3950 fax
Website: www.radiocity.com

OKLAHOMA

44. **Mabee Center**
8023 S. Lewis
Tulsa, OK 74136
(918) 495-6000
(918) 495-6478 fax
Website: www.mabeecenter.com

OREGON

45. **Portland Civic Stadium**
1844 SW Morrison
Portland, OR 97205
(503) 248-4345
(503) 221-3983 fax
E-mail: mariarojo@oregoncc.org

PENNSYLVANIA

46. **Coca-Cola Star Lake Amphitheatre**
Rte. 18 at Rte. 22
Burgettstown, PA 15021
(724) 947-7400
(724) 947-7414 fax

RHODE ISLAND

47. **Providence Civic Center**
One LaSalle Sq
Providence, RI 02903
(401) 331-0700
(401) 751-6792 fax
Website: www.provcc.com

SOUTH CAROLINA

48. **Myrtle Beach Convention Center**
2101 N. Oak St.
Myrtle Beach, SC 29577
(843) 918-1225
(843) 918-1243 fax
E-mail: smeadows@sccoast.net
Website:
www.myrtlebeachconvcntr.com

TENNESSEE

49. **Starwood Amphitheatre**
3839 Murfreesboro Rd.
Antioch, TN 37013
(615) 641-5888
(615) 641-7619 fax

TEXAS

50. **Coca-Cola Starplex**
1818 First Ave.
Dallas, TX 75210
(972) 421-1111
(972) 428-8365 fax

87 Artist Managers

1. **19 Management**
Unit 32 Ransomes Dock,
35-37 Parkgate Rd.
London, SW11 4NP ENG
(171) 738-1919
(171) 738-1819 fax

2. **Bruce Allen Talent**
406-68 Water St.
Vancouver, BC V6B 1A4 Canada
(604) 688-7274
(604) 688-7118 fax
E-mail: info@bruceallen.com

3. **Air Tight Management**
115 West Road -or- P.O. Box 113
Winchester Center, CT 06094
(860) 738-9139
(860) 738-9135 fax
E-Mail: airtight@snet.net

4. **Bellamy Brothers**
c/o Refugee Management International
209 10th Avenue South, Suite 300
Nashville, TN 37212
(615) 256-6615
(615) 256-6717 fax

5. **Big Management**
915 Broadway, Suite 1607
New York, NY 10010
(212) 475-2700
(212) 475-2907 fax

6. **Boo Management**
10675 Santa Monica Blvd.
Los Angeles, CA 90025
(310) 234-2611
(310) 234-2601 fax
E-mail: boomania@earthlink.net

7. **Borman Entertainment**
1208 17th Ave. South
Nashville, TN 37212
(615) 320-3000
(615) 320-3001 fax

8. **Burton Goldstein & Company**
156 E. 56th Street #1803
NYC, NY 10019
(212) 582-9700
(212) 582-8273 fax
E-mail: jefftunes@aol.com

9. **Buzz International Group**
449 Santa Fe Dr., Suite 260
Encintas, CA 92024
(760) 634-1232
(760) 634-1283 fax

10. **Fritz-Byers Entertainment**
451 N. Canon Dr. Suite 1
Beverly Hills, CA 90210
(310) 888-0039
(310) 271-3567 fax

11. **CCA3 Productions**
11225 Ruffner Avenue
Granada Hills, CA 91344
(818) 363-1521
(818) 363-1521 fax

12. **William N. Carter Management**
1028 B 18th Ave. South
Nashville, TN 37212
(615) 327-1270
(615) 321-0802 fax
E-mail: wncmgmt@aol.com

13. **Choice Management and Associates**
21601 Devonshire St., Suite 320
Chatsworth, CA 91311
(818) 780-7503
(818) 780-1027 fax

14. **Coleman Entertainment Group**
One Columbus Place, Suite S-7D
New York, NY 10019
(212) 845-6890
(212) 845-6898 fax

15. **Columbia Artist Management Inc.**
165 W. 57th St.
New York, NY 10019
(212) 841-9500
(212) 841-9552 fax

8383 Wilshire Blvd., Suite 932
Beverly Hills, CA 90211
(213) 653-4141
(213) 653-4040 fax

16. **Diggit Entertainment**
244 W. 54th St. #501
NY, NY 10019
(212) 399-6070
(212) 399-6112 fax
E-mail: billydig@aol.com

17. **Michael Dixon Management**
119 Pebblecreek Rd.
Franklin, TN 37064
(615) 791-7731
(615) 791-7732 fax
E-Mail: sodarock@aol.com

18. **Duboi Entertainment**
139 Ralph McGill Blvd.
Atlanta, GA 30308
(404) 522-6933
(404) 523-7671 fax
E-mail: duboi@bellsouth.net

19. **Marty Erlichman Productions**
5670 Wilshire Blvd. #2400
Los Angeles, CA 90046
(323) 653-1555
(323) 653-1593 fax

20. **O'Neil Hagaman, PLLC**
1025 16th Avenue South, Suite 202
Nashville, TN 37212
(615) 320-5291
(615) 320-5651 fax
E-Mail: oneilhag@aol.com

21. **Emerald Hill**
560 West 43rd St. #38E
NY, NY 10036
(212) 947-2595
(212) 967-6362 fax
E-mail: kingdomet@aol.com

22. **Endangered Species Artist Mgt.**
4 Berachah Ave.
South Nyack, NY 10960-4202
(914) 353-4001
(914) 353-4332 fax
E-Mail: Endangers@mjet.com

23. **Estefan Enterprises**
555 Jefferson Ave.
Miami, FL 33139
(305) 534-4330
(305) 534-5220 fax
E-mail:
janetdearmas@estefanenterprises.com

24. **The Firm**
9000 Sunset Blvd. #525
West Hollywood, CA 90069
(310) 246-9000
(310) 246-1999 fax
E-mail: pkatsis@firmentertainment.net

25. **The Fitzgerald Hartley Company**
1908 Wedgewood Ave.
Nashville, TN 37212
(615) 322-9493
(615) 322-9582 fax

26. **Great Northern Arts**
c/o Fuller Music Marketing
2692 Circle Drive
Newport Beach, CA 92663
(949) 650-5888
(949) 646-8193 fax

27. **Greg Spotts Entertainment Inc.**
1124 5th Street, Suite 304
Santa Monica, CA 90403
(310) 434-9227
(310) 434-9217 fax

28. **Headfirst Mangement**
P.O. Box 52
Syosset, NY 11791

(516) 433-1488
(516) 822-8442 fax

29. Hellfire Enterprises, LTD.
P.O. Box 75995
Oklahoma City, OK 73147
(405) 524-0094
(405) 524-1259 fax

30. Herbert Barrett Management Inc.
1776 Broadway, Suite 1610
New York, NY 10019
(212) 245-3530
(212) 397-5860 fax

31. I C M Artists Ltd.
40 W. 57th St.
New York, NY 10019
(212) 556-5600
(212) 556-5677 fax

32. I.M.S. (International Management Services)
818 19th Ave., South
Nashville, TN 37203
(615) 321-5025
(615) 327-0321 fax
E-mail: clinthygham@earthlink.net

33. Image Management Group
27 Music Sq. E.
Nashville, TN 37203
(615) 256-9850
(615) 256-0900 fax

34. Industrial Management
3450 3rd St. #2A, Ste. 300
San Francisco, CA 90036
(415) 285-7744
(415) 285-2374 fax

35. Jacobson Talent Management
12111 N. 56th St.
Tampa, FL 33617
(619) 757-2683
(619) 757-8176 fax
E-mail: jtm4097@aol.com
Website: www.jtmink.com

36. William Jones
26 Bernard Dr.
Newport News, VA 23602
(757) 988-0637
(757) 988-0564 fax

37. JRE Entertainment Group
17291 Irvine Blvd., Suite 200
Tustin, CA 92680
(714) 508-0794
(714) 508=-0793 fax

38. Kragen and Company
112 N. Shelbourne Dr.
Los Angeles, CA 90069
(213) 848-4400

39. Launch Production, Inc.
574 West End Avenue, Suite 4
New York, NY 10024-2725
(212) 580-7997
(212) 580-7992 fax

40. Left Bank Management
9255 Sunset Blvd., 2FL
West Hollywood, CA 90069
(310) 385-4700
(310) 385-4710 fax
E-mail: receptionist@lbank.com

41. Left Bank Organization
6255 Sunset Blvd., Ste. 1111
Los Angeles, CA 90028
(213) 466-6900
(213) 957-0121 fax

437 Madison Ave., 32nd Fl.
New York, NY 10022
(212) 415-2500
(212) 415-3555 fax

6609 Currywood Dr.
Nashville, TN 37205
(615) 352-1217
(615) 352-1864 fax

42. W.F. Leopold Management
4425 Riverside Rd., Ste. 102
Burbank, CA 91505
(818) 955-8511
(818) 955-9602 fax
E-mail: wfo@leopoldmanagement.com

43. Lewis Entertainment, Inc.
45 E. Putnam Ave., Suite 118
Greenwich, CT 06830
(203) 661-6262
(203) 661-2768 fax
Website: www.lewisentertainment.com

44. Peter Lopez, Esq.
2049 Century Park East #3180
Los Angeles, CA 90067
(310) 286-9696
(310) 286-6445 fax
E-mail: plopez@kllbc.com

45. The Lytle Management Group
P.O. Box 40263
Nashville, TN 37204
(615) 333-1992
(615) 832-0900 fax
E-mail: lmg33@juno.com

46. Mad Money Entertainment
6947 Tampa Ave. #302
Tarzana, CA 91356
(818) 344-0662
(818) 344-0459 fax

47. **Major Label Records**
15490 Ventura Blvd., Suite 220
Sherman Oaks, CA 91403
(818) 981-4400
(818) 981-4418
E-Mail: silvlite@aol.com

48. **Major Production**
5253 W. Adams Blvd.
Los Angeles, CA 90016
(800) 345-691
(213) 525-1916

49. **Maroon Entertainment**
170 West 73rd St. #8A
NY, NY 10023
(212) 737-1300
(212) 787-9473 fax
E-mail: tinabi9623@aol.com

50. **Metro Artist Management**
12440 Landale St.
Studio City, CA 91604
(818) 980-7871
(818) 980-0785 fax
E-mail: goodmanjoe@aol.com

51. **Mind Level Music Group Inc.**
136 E. 57th St.
New York, NY 10022
(212) 388-8088
(212) 980-4311 fax

52. **Monster Management**
150 5th Ave., Ste. 729
New York, NY 10011
(212) 620-0022
(212) 620-0024 fax

53. **MT Blues**
Via Irnerio 16
Bologna 40126 Italy
(39)(51) 251117
(39)(51) 251123

54. **Stan Moress Management**
1102 18th Ave. South
Nashville, TN 37212
(615) 329-9945
(615) 321-3457 fax

55. **OK Management**
275 S. Beverly Dr., Ste. 215
Beverly Hills, CA 90212
(310) 550-1341
(310) 550-1854 fax

56. **Overbook Entertainment**
100 Universal City Plaza, Bldg. 6111
Universal City, CA 91608
(818) 777-2224
(818) 866-6206 fax

57. **Overseas Entertainment**
P.O. Box 2203
Beverly Hills, CA 90213

(323) 462-2784
(310) 342-0306 fax

58. **Passionate Entertainment**
250 W. 49th St., Ste. 301
New York, NY 10019
(212) 765-7543
(212) 397-4019 fax

59. **PBS**
1320 Braddock Place
Alexandria, VA 22314
(703) 739-5166
(703) 739-5295 fax

60. **Pele Productions Intl.**
271 Netherwood Avenue
Plainfield, NJ 07062
(908) 769-8240
(908) 769-8240 fax
E-Mail: pelepro@hotmail.com

61. **The Powell Firm**
561 Broadway, Suite 10-C
New York, NY 10012-3918
(212) 941-8033
(212) 334-9144 fax

62. **R.E.M./Athens Ltd.**
P.O. Box8032
Athens, GA 30603
(706) 353-6689
(706) 546-6069 fax

63. **RRS Management**
221 W. 6th St., Suite 1560
Austin, TX 78701
(512) 472-8463
(512) 472-8464 fax
E-Mail: rrs@onr.com

64. **Raw Entertainment**
3435 Ocean Park Blvd., Ste. 112
Santa Monica, CA 90405
(310) 207-6438
(310) 207-8269 fax

65. **Real Entertainment**
11684 Ventura Blvd., Ste. 134
Studio City, CA 91604
(818) 286-9135
(818) 386-2862 fax

66. **Refugee International**
209 10th Ave., South #347
Nashville, TN 37203
(615) 256-6615
(615) 256-6717 fax
E-mail: jsrefugee@aol.com

67. **Refugee Management Inc.**
1025 16th Ave. S. Ste. 300
Nashville, TN 37212
(615) 256-6615
(615) 320-0387 fax

68. **Santana Management**
PO Box 10348
San Rafael, CA 94912-0348
(415) 458-8130
(415) 458-8145 fax

69. **Scott Management**
8033 Sunset Blvd., Ste. 1200
W. Hollywood, CA 90046
(310) 856-4826
(310) 462-1442 fax

70. **Mark Shimmel Management**
8889 Beverly Blvd., Ste. 100
Los Angeles, CA 90046
(310) 276-3766
(310) 276-3834 fax

71. **Paul Simon Music**
1619 Broadway, Ste. 500
New York, NY 10019
(212) 541-7571
(212) 582-7607 fax

72. **Andrew Slater Management**
9200 Sunset Blvd. #1000
Los Angeles, CA 90069
(310) 550-5258
(310) 550-5241 fax

73. **Sorkin Productions**
2717 Motor Ave.
Los Angeles, CA 90064
(310) 559-5580
(310) 559-5581 fax

74. **Sound Entertainment Management**
1008 16th Ave. S.
Nashville, TN 37212
(615) 254-4477
(615) 353-3886 fax

75. **Spring Hill Music & Media**
1835 38th Street, Suite SW
Boulder, CO 80301
(303) 938-1188
(303) 938-1191 fax

76. **Star Ray Management**
2080 Cobb Parkway
Smyrna, GA 30080
(415) 776-7724
(415) 776-7784 fax
E-mail: tim@stroke9.com

77. **Stiletto Entertainment**
5443 Beethoven St.
Los Angeles, CA 90066
(310) 306-4490
(310) 306-5350 fax

78. **Sunset Boulevard Entertainment**
740 N. La Brea Avenue, 1st Floor
Los Angeles, CA 90038

(323) 933-9977
(323) 933-0633 fax
E-Mail: sbe740@earthlink.net

79. **TKO Artist Management**
4219 Hillsboro Rd., #318
Nashville, TN 37215
(615) 383-5017
(615) 292-3328 fax
E-mail: tkomgt@aol.com

80. **Tilton Management**
7135 Hollywood Blvd., Ste. 601
Los Angeles, CA 90046
(213) 851-8552
(213) 850-1467 fax

81. **Titley-Spalding Management**
300 10th Ave. South
Nashville, TN 37203
(615) 255-1326
(615) 254-4267 fax

82. **Third Rock Entertainment**
50 Music Square West, #300
Nashville, TN 37203
(615) 320-1219
(615) 320-0558 fax
E-mail: mittatte@aol.com

83. **Truth Management Co.**
1310 Clinton St., Ste. 217
Nashville, TN 37203
(615) 327-4540
(615) 615) 322-5396 fax

84. **Turner Management Group**
9220 Sunset Blvd., #220
Los Angeles, CA 90069
(310) 550-5333
(310) 550-5335 fax
E-mail: turnergrp1@aol.com

85. **Weisberg & Associates**
4451 Canoga Dr.
Woodland Hills, CA 91364
(818) 592-6260
(818) 592-6261 fax

86. **Erv Woolsey Company**
1000 18th Ave, South
Nashville, TN 37212
(615) 329-2402
(615) 327-4917 fax

87. **The Wright Entertainment Group**
7648 Southland Blvd. #105
Orlando, FL 32809
(407) 826-9100
(407) 826-9107 fax
E-mail: dbrownweg@aol.com

62 Booking Agents

1. **A-1 Artist Agency**
   6960 Platt Ave
   West Hills, CA 91307
   (818) 888-1030
   (818) 888-3070 fax
   E-mail: bluesboy@a1music.com
   Website: www.a1music.com

2. **Advanced Booking & Management**
   PO Box 271056
   Nashville, TN 37227
   (615) 872-8974
   (615) 831-0991 fax

3. **AKON (All Kinds of Noise)**
   PO Box 1408
   Mill Valley, CA 94942-1408
   (415) 389-0654
   (415) 389-6723 fax
   E-mail: AKONsound@aol.com

4. **Alone Booking**
   926 1/2 S. Holt Ave.
   Los Angeles, CA 90035
   (310) 652-6759
   (310) 661-4344 fax

5. **American Talent Group**
   221 W. 57th Ave., 8th Fl.
   New York, NY 10019
   (212) 713-0050
   (212) 713-0062 fax

6. **The Berkley Agency**
   2608 Ninth St.
   Berkley, CA 94710
   (510) 843-4902
   (510) 843-7271 fax

7. **Bowen Agency/Admiral Talent**
   504 W. 168th St.
   New York, NY 10032
   (212) 927-0312
   (212) 923-7099 fax

8. **Box Office Inc.**
   1010 16th Ave. S.
   Nashville, TN 37212-2303
   (615) 256-5400
   (615) 256-5440 fax

9. **Creative Artists Agency**
   9830 Wilshire Blvd.
   Beverly Hills, VA 90212
   (310) 288-4545
   (310) 288-4800 fax

   3310 West End Ave., 5th Fl.
   Nashville, TN 37202
   (615) 383-8787

   (615) 383-4937 fax

10. **DMR Booking Agency**
    The Galleries of Syracuse, Ste. 250
    Syracuse, NY 13202
    (315)475-2500
    (315) 475-0752 fax

11. **East Coast Entertainment**
    67 Peachtree Park NE, Ste. 101
    Atlanta, GA 30309
    (404) 351-2263
    (404) 351-1558 fax

    PO Box 11283
    Richmond, VA 23230
    (804) 355-2178
    (804) 372-9436 fax

    512 East Blvd.
    Charlotte, NC 28203
    (704) 339-0100
    (704) 372-9436 fax

12. **Entertainment Artists**
    819 18th Ave. S.
    Nashville, TN 37203
    (615) 320-7041
    (615) 320-0856 fax

13. **Entourage Talent Asociates**
    25 W. 39th St., 10th Fl.
    New York, NY 10018
    (212) 997-1900
    (212) 997-0505 fax

14. **Famous Artists Agency**
    1700 Broadway, 5th Fl.
    New York, NY 10019
    (212) 245-3939
    (212) 459-9065 fax

15. **Flower Booking Agency**
    PO Box 477567
    Chicago, IL 60647
    (312) 486-6997
    (312) 486-6998 fax

16. **Free World**
    105 W. 28th St., 3rd Fl.
    New York, NY 10001
    (212) 563-1366
    (212) 563-3097 fax

17. **Frontier Booking International**
    2230 Maravilla Dr.
    Los Angeles, CA 90068
    (213) 850-5373
    (213) 850-5377 fax

    1560 Broadway, Ste. 1110
    New York, NY 10036
    (212) 221-1919 phone

18. **Jim Halsey Co.**
    PO Box 40703
    Nashville, TN 37204

(615) 244-7900
(615) 256-8028 fax

19. **Headline Talent Inc.**
1650 Broadway, Ste. 508
New York, NY 10019
(212) 581-6900
(212) 581-6906 fax

20. **Abby Hoffer Enterprises**
223 1/2 E. 48th St.
New York, NY 10017-1538
(212) 935-6350
(212) 758-4987 fax

21. **International Creative Management**
40 W. 57th St.
New York, NY 10019
(212) 556-5600
(212) 556-5665 fax

8492 Wilshire Blvd.
Beverly Hills, CA 90211
(310) 550-4000
(310) 550-4100 fax

22. **International Talent Group**
729 Seventh Ave., 16th Fl.
New York, NY 10019
(212) 221-7878
(212) 302) 0335

822 S. Robertson Blvd., Ste. 200
Los Angeles, CA 90035
(310) 289-2780
(310) 652-5591 fax

23. **Jazz Tree Artists Agency**
211 Thompson St. Ste., 1D
New York, NY 10012
(212) 475-0415
(212) 475-0502 fax

24. **Buddy Lee Attractions Inc.**
38 Music Square E., Ste. 300
Nashville, TN 37203
(615) 244-4336
(615) 726-0429 fax

25. **Long Distance Entertainment**
1938 Hollywood Blvd., 2nd Fl.
Hollywood, FL 33020
(305) 922-8400
(305) 922-8409 fax

26. **Major Production**
5253 W. Adams Blvd.
Los Angeles, CA 90016
(800) 345-6911
(213) 525-1916 fax

27. **McFadden Artists Copr.**
818 18th Ave. S.
Nashville, TN 37203
(615) 242-1500

(615) 255-7200 fax

28. **Menu Entertainment**
6113 Muholland Hwy.
Hollywood Hills, CA 90068
(213) 460-4069
(213) 460-5124 fax

29. **Mission Control**
14755 Ventura Blvd., Ste. 541
Sherman Oaks, CA 91403
(818) 905-6488
(818) 907-9839 fax

30. **Monterey Artists**
901 18th Ave. South
Nashville, TN 37212
(615) 321-4444
(615) 321-2446 fax

31. **Monterey Penninsula Artists**
509 Hartnell St.
Monterey, CA 93940
(312) 640-7500
(312) 375-2623 fax

32. **Phoenix Talent Agency, Inc.**
581 9th Ave., #3A
New York, NY 10036
(212) 564-4206
(212) 868-1017

33. **Pinnacle Entertainment**
83 Riverside Dr.
New York, NY 10024
(212) 580-1229
(212) 362-8326 fax
E-Mail: pinn_ent@aol.com

34. **Presence Productions**
602 3rd St., #1
San Francisco, CA 94107
(415) 546-7117
(415) 546-9127 fax
E-Mail: presenceprod@aol.com

35. **Producers, Inc.**
11806 N. 56th St.
Tampa, FL 33617
(813) 988-8333
(813) 985-3293
E-Mail: info@producersinc.com

36. **The Rosebud Agency**
PO Box 170429
San Francisco, CA 94117
(415) 386-3456
(415) 386-0599 fax
E-Mail: rosebudus@aol.com

37. **Showtime Agency Inc**
6301 Johnsdale Rd.
Raleigh, NC 27615
(919) 790-0490
(919) 872-1066 fax

38. **St. John Artists**
PO Box 619
Neenah, WI 54957
(920) 722-2222
(920) 725-2405 fax
Website: stjohn-artists.com

39. **Starleigh Entertainment**
205 E. Joppa Rd., #106
Baltimore, MD 21286
(410) 828-9400
(410) 823-6619 fax
Website: www.starleigh.com

40. **Third Coast Talent, LLC**
PO Box 334
Kingston Springs, TN 37082
(615) 952-3181
(615) 952-2736 fax
E-Mail: thirdcoast@iname.com

41. **TLC Booking Agency**
37311 N. Valley Rd.
Chattaroy, WA 99003
(509) 292-2201
(509) 292-2205 fax
E-Mail: tlcagent@ix.netcom.com

42. **Tough Guy Booking**
2217 Nicollet Ave. S.
Minneapolis, MN 55404
(612) 874-2445
(612) 874-2430 fax
E-Mail: tguy@t.net

43. **Universal Attractions**
225 W. 57th St.
New York, NY 10019
(212) 582-7575
(212) 333-4508 fax

44. **UNO Productions**
10122 Riverside Dr.
Toluca Lake, CA 91602
(818) 763-1501
(818) 763-0466 fax
E-Mail: unoprod@earthlink.net

45. **Vanguard Entertainment**
264 Mallory Stn Rd.
Franklin, TN 37067
(615) 771-6355
E-Mail: veat1234@aol.com

46. **Variety Artists International**
555 Chorro St.
San Lois Obispo, CA 93401
(805) 544-1444
(805) 544-2444 fax
E-Mail: Varietyary@aol.com

47. **Vision International**
PO Box 201
Highland, MD 20777

(301) 854-0888
(301) 854-0999
E-Mail: ajsvision@aol.com

48. **William Morris Agency**
1325 Avenue of the Americas
New York, NY 10019
(212) 903-110
(212) 246-3583 fax

151 El Camino Dr.
Beverly Hills, CA 90210
(310) 859-4000
(310) 859-4462 fax

2100 W. End Ave. Ste. 1000
Nashville, TN 37203
(615) 963-3000
(615) 963-3090 fax

49. **Works of Heart**
1012 Fair Oaks Ave., Ste. 195
South Pasadena, CA 91030
(818) 568-5995
(818) 403-9777 fax

50. **World Class Talent**
1522 Demonbreun St.
Nashville, TN 37203
(615) 244-1964
(615) 256-8772 fax

51. **A.B.C. (Associated Booking Corp.)**
1995 Broadway, #501
New York, NY 10023
(212) 874-2400
(212) 769-3649 fax

52. **Buddy Lee Attractions**
38 Music Square East, Ste. 300
Nashville, TN 37203
(615) 244-4336
(615) 726-0429 fax

53. **C.A.A. (Creative Artists Agency)**
9830 Wilshire Blvd.
Beverly Hills, CA 90212
(310) 288-4545
(310) 288-4800 fax

54. **Dale Morris & Assoc.**
818 19th Ave., South
Nashville, TN 37203
(615) 327-3400
(615) 327-0312 fax

55. **F.B.I.**
9000 Sunset Blvd. #515
West Hollywood, CA 90069
(310) 858-1859
(310) 858-3037 fax

56. **Famous Artists**
250 West 57th St. #821
New York, NY 10107

(212) 245-3939
(212) 459-9065 fax

57. I.C.M.
40 West 57th St.
New York, NY 10019
(212) 556-5600
(212) 556-5665 fax

58. Monterey Artists
901 18th Ave., South
Nashville, TN 37212
(615) 321-4444
(615) 321-2446 fax

59. Monterey Peninsula Artists
509 Hartnell St.
Monterey, CA 93940
(408) 375-4889
(408) 375-2623 fax

60. Pyramid Entertainment Group
89 Fifth Ave., 7th Floor
New York, NY 10003
(212) 242-7274
(212) 242-6932 fax

61. The Agency Group
1775 Broadway, #433
New York, NY 10019
(212) 581-3100
(212) 581-0015 fax

62. William Morris Agency
1325 Ave. of the Americas
New York, NY 10019
(212) 586-5100
(212) 246-3583 fax

151 El Camino Dr.
Beverly Hills, CA 90212
(310) 274-7451
(310) 859-4462 fax

56 Publicists and PR Companies

1. 360 Media
PO Box 725188
Atlanta, GA 31139
(404) 577-8686
(404) 577-8644 fax
E-Mail: tmurphy647@aol.com
Website: www.360media.net

2. Kathy Acquaviva Media
10646 Londelius St.
North Hills, CA 91343
(818) 893-8458
(818) 920-0044 fax
E-Mail: kathymedia@aol.com

3. Andranigian Media
PO Box 9996
Glendale, CA 91226
(818) 507-0221
(818) 507-7623 fax
E-Mail: rakelle11@aol.com

4. Aristomedia
1620 16th Ave. South
Nashville, TN 37212
(615) 269-7071
(615) 269-0131
E-Mail: cbann@aristomedia.com
Website: www.aristomedia.com

5. Autotonic
PO Box 41246
Memphis, TN 38174
(901) 276-2225
(901) 276-6554 fax
E-Mail: press@aotonic.com

6. Baker/Northrop Media Group
13351-D Riverside Dr.
Sherman Oaks, CA 91423
(818) 501-0056
E-Mail: mail@bakernorthrop.com

7. Jay Bernstein Public Relations
9360 Beverly Crest Drive
Beverly Hills, CA 90213
(310)858-1485
(310) 858-1607 fax

8. Nicole Blackman PR
121 E. 36th St.
New York, NY 10016
(212) 685-3001
E-Mail: blackmanpr@aol.com

9. Blue Moon Productions
1112 9th St.
New Orleans, LA 70115
(504) 895-0739
(504) 895-6070 fax
Website: www.bluesproject.com

10. Costa Communications
8265 Sunset Blvd. #101
Los Angeles, CA 90046
(323) 650-3588
(323) 654-5207 fax
E-Mail: rprfirm@aol.com
Website:
www.coastacommunications.com

11. Creative Network
PO Box 2818
Newport Beach, CA 92659
(949) 494-0181
(949) 494-0982 fax

12. **Def Press**
430 S. Niagra St., Ste. 210
Burbank, CA 91501
(818) 843-8026

13. **Draw the Line**
622 Broadway, Ste. 5A
New York, NY 10012
(212) 460-8687
(212) 460-5537 fax
E-Mail: dj@ftl.com
Website: www.dtl.com

14. **ESP Public Relations**
8117 W. Manchester Ave., Ste. 320
Playa del Ray, CA 90293
(310) 827-9727
(310) 827-9616 fax
E-Mail: esppr@aol.com

15. **Fanatic Promotion, Inc.**
1538 MacArthur Dr.
Boulder, CO 80303
(303) 245-0285
(303) 245-0286 fax
E-Mail: info@fanaticpromotion.com
Website: www.fanaticpromotion.com

16. **FORCE**
1505 16th Ave.South
Nashville, TN 37212
(615) 824-4646

17. **Formula PR Incorporated**
225 Lafayette St., Ste. 1006
New York, NY 10012
(212) 941-9701
(212) 941-9740 fax
E-Mail: formulapr@earthlink.net

18. **Girlie Action**
270 Lafayette St., Ste. 1302
New York, NY 10012
(212) 334-3200
(212) 334-4413 fax
E-Mail: info@girlie.com

19. **Grassroots Media**
1815 Division St., Ste. 202
Nashville, TN 37203
(615) 340-9596
(615) 340-9597 fax
E-Mail: groots@mindspring.com

20. **Green Galactic**
1680 N. Vine St.
Los Angeles, CA 90028
(323) 466-5141
(323) 466-5121 fax
Website: www.greengalatic.com

21. **Groove Addicts**
2048 Armacost Ave.
Los Angeles, CA 90025
(310) 442-1444

(310) 442-1448 fax
E-Mail: info@grooveadicts.com
Website: www.grooveadicts.com

22. **Cathy Gurley Publicity**
1609 Horton
Nashville, TN 37212
(615) 269-0474
(615) 385-2052 fax

23. **Hatchet Man Presents**
PO Box 54535
Atlanta, GA 30308
(404) 888-0188
(404) 874-5558 fax
E-Mail: mail@hatchetman.com
Website: www.hatchetman.com

24. **Jazzmyne Public Relations**
11800 Gager St.
LakeView Terrace, CA 91342-6115
(310) 288-6061
(818) 890-7428
E-Mail: Jazzmyne@artnet.net
Website: www.artnet.net/-jazzmyne

25. **Kathode Ray Music**
PO Box 121135
Nashville, TN 37212
(615) 460-9595
Website: www.katoderaymusic.com

26. **Kayos Productions**
16 W. 19th St., 5thFl.
New York, NY 10011
(212) 645-9178
(212) 727-8282 fax
E-Mail: kayospro@aol.com

27. **Ketchum PR**
292 Madison Ave.
New York, NY 10017
(212) 448-4359
(212) 448-4484 fax
E-Mail:
theano.apostolou@ketchum.com

28. **Levenson Public Relations**
600 N. Pearl St.
Dallas, TX 75201
(214) 880-0200
(214) 880-0601 fax

29. **Lewis Management**
1109 17th Ave. South
Nashville, TN 37212
(615) 329-9447

30. **LM Public Relations**
580 Broadway
New York, NY 10012
(212) 431-5227
(212) 431-68189 fax
E-Mail: jim_inc@pipeline.com

31. **Bobbi Marcus**
131 N. Bundy Dr.
Los Angeles, CA 90049
(310) 889-9800
(310) 889-0019 fax
E-Mail: Bmarcuspr@aol.com

32. **Mazur Public Relations**
PO Box 360
East Windsor, NJ 08520
(609) 426-1277
(609) 426-1217 fax
E-Mail: mazurpr@aol.com
Website: www.mazurpr.com

33. **McGuckin Entertainment Group**
609-A Wood St.
Austin, TX 78703
(512) 478-0578
(512) 477-8060 fax
E-Mail: megjill@aol.com

34. **McMullen & Co.**
9744 Wilshire Blvd. #301
Beverly Hills, CA 90212
(310) 276-5214
(310) 276-6133 fax

35. **Megavents Public Relations and Ent. Coordination**
15332 Antioch St., Ste. 187
Pacific Palisades, CA 90272
(310) 454-0487
(310) 454-7920 fax
E-Mail: megavents@earthlink.net

36. **Mixx-N Company**
1731 Howe Ave., Ste. 474
Sacramento, CA 95825
(916) ITS-MIXX
(916-489-FAXX
E-Mail: mixxula@aol.com

37. **Moon Public Relations**
41 Union Sq., Ste. 806
New York, NY 10003
(212) 989-7530
(212) 989-7532 fax
E-Mail: Nmoon@infohouse.com

38. **Motormouthmedia**
1680 N. Vine St., Ste. 508
Hollywood, CA 90028
(323) 856-9021
(323) 856-0541 fax
E-Mail: wigbox@aol.com

39. **Moxie Press**
3819 Effie St.
Los Angeles, CA 90026
(323) 882-6543
(323) 882-6516 fax
E-Mail: AmyBMoxi@4link.com

40. **MSO**
14724 Ventura Blvd., Ste. 410
Sherman Oaks, CA 91403
(818) 380-0400
(818) 380-0430 fax
Website: www.msopr.com

41. **Nicoletti Music**
PO Box 2818
Newport Beach, CA 92659
(949) 494-0181
(949) 494-0982 fax

42. **No Problem Productions**
260 Harrison Ave., Ste. 407
Jersey City, NJ 07304
(201) 433-3907
(201) 433-8635 fax
E-Mail: noprob@mindspring.com

43. **PLA Media**
1303 16th Ave. South
Nashville, TN 37212
(615) 327-0100
(615) 320-1061 fax
E-Mail: Plewis@edge.net
Website: www.PLAmedia.com

44. **Praxis PR**
97 Clinton St., Ste 3B
New York, NY 10002
(212) 677-4225
(212) 677-3582 fax
E-Mail: praxis@bway.net

45. **PRB Publicity**
80 Broadway, Ste. 1005
New York, NY 10012
(212) 966-7334
(212) 966-9573 fax
E-Mail: prbinfo@aol.com
Website: www.prbmedia.com

46. **The Press Network**
1305 16th Ave. South, 2nd Floor
Nashville, TN 37212
(615) 322-5445
(615) 322-1293 fax
E-Mail: Lisa@pressnetwork.com
Website: www.pressnetwork.com

47. **Presto Public Relations**
PO Box 89990
Tucson, AZ 85752
(520) 579-8064
(520) 579-3259 fax
E-Mail: prestols@aol.com

48. **ProSource**
PO Box 7328
Lakeland, FL 33807-7238
(941) 648-4222
(941) 648-1778 fax
E-Mail: wade@psanet.com
Website: www.psanet.com

49. **Pyramid Communications**
1000 Lenora St., Ste. 415
Seattle, WA 98121
(206) 625-6939
(206) 625-0652 fax
E-Mail: pyramid@pyramid.com

50. **Reach Media Relations, Inc.**
295 Greenwich St. #109
New York, NY 10007
(212) 226-1050
(718) 965-3841 fax
E-Mail: Dmflash@aol.com

51. **Red Rooster Publicity**
2028 Dracena Dr.
Los Angeles, CA 90027
(323) 660-0672
(323) 661-8074 fax
E-Mail: roosterpub@aol.com

52. **Rogers & Cowan Public relations**
1888 Century Park East Suite 500
Los angeles, CA 90069
(310) 201-8800
(310) 788-6600 fax

622 3rd Avenue, 14th Floor
New York, NY 10017
(646) 658-8300
(646) 658-8369 fax

53. **Stan Rosenfield Public Relations**
2029 Century Park East, Ste. 1240
Los Angeles,CA 90064
(310) 286-7474
(310) 286-2255 fax

54. **Sacks**
427 W. 14th St., 2nd Fl.
New York, NY 10014
(212) 741-1000
(212) 741-9777 fax
E-Mail: prestols@aol.com

55. **Serge Entertainment PR**
PO Box 672216
Marietta, GA 30006-0037
(770) 850-9560
(770) 850-9646 fax
E-Mail: SergeEnt@aol.com
Website: www.serge.org/sepr.htm

56. **Jill Siegel Communications**
305 E. 86th St., PH-D
New York, NY 10028
(212) 289-8533
(212) 410-0189 fax